19883A

LEADERSHIP

A. Dale Timpe
Editor

Facts On File Publications
New York, New York ● Oxford, England

Leadership
Volume 3 in Facts On File's series *The Art and Science of Business Management*

Copyright © 1987 by KEND Publishing, Inc.

Library of Congress Cataloging-in-Publication Data

Leadership.

  (The Art and science of business management)
  Bibliography: p.
  Includes index.
  1. Leadership. 2. Management. I. Timpe, A. Dale.
II. Series.
HD57.7.L43 1987   658.4'092   86-24167
ISBN 0-8160-1462-0

Interior design by Debbie Glasserman
Composition by Facts On File/Maxwell Photographics

Printed in the United States of America.

10 9 8 7 6 5 4 3 2 1

CONTENTS

PART III: LEADERSHIP STYLES

PART IV: MANAGER OR LEADER?

PREFACE

Leadership is not a synonym for *management*; it is a higher-order capability. Leaders determine where the business is going, with broad internal and external objectives, and align the assets and skills of the organization with the opportunities and risks presented by the environment. The leader is the strategist that establishes the organization's objectives; the manager focuses on how the organization will achieve them. Leadership research has not revealed a single trait possessed by all successful leaders, but rather, a number of characteristics common to many. Each leader has his or her own distinctive style; whether democratic, authoritarian, or benevolent. One distinguishing aspect of the leader, however, is the aura of authority. The manager possesses a level of power commensurate with his or her position and responsibility. The leader's power, however, is often derived from opinion, respect, and esteem as well as from the power to dominate and command.

Social change, technological innovation, and increased competition pose difficult challenges for today's business leaders. In this demanding environment, a company's leadership talent can give it an important competitive edge. Moreover, the organization must also have the foresight to train its next generation of leaders.

This compendium provides access to a broad spectrum of practical knowledge, research, and theory relating to leadership ability and how to develop it. The diversity of insights, experience and theoretical concepts presented here offers many useful solutions for human resource planning. The sources represent a wide range of professional publications, including a number not readily available to most executives. For those wanting a more detailed discussion on a particular aspect, the bibliography provides a valuable resource tool.

A. Dale Timpe
Series Editor

ACKNOWLEDGMENTS

The articles presented in this volume are reprinted with the permission of the respective copyright holders and all rights are reserved.

Bennis, Warren. "Leadership Transforms Vision into Action" from *Industry Week* by permission of Penton Publishing Co., © 1982.

Benson, Gary. "Mind Games" from *Management World* by permission of the Administrative Management Society, © 1984.

Bisesi, Michael. "Strategies for Successful Leadership in Changing Times" from *Sloan Management Review* by permission of the Sloan Management Review Association, © 1983.

Bolt, James F. "Management Resource Planning: Keys To Success" from *Human Resource Planning* by permission of the Human Resource Planning Society, © 1982.

Braham, James. "Hazards at the Top" from *Industry Week* by permission from Penton Publishing Inc., © 1985.

Cerami, Charles A. "This Test Spots Leaders" from *Nation's Business* by permission from U. S. Chamber of Commerce, © 1964.

Collons, Rodger D. "Spotlight on Leadership Traits" from *Best's Review*, Life/Health Edition, by permission from A. M. Best Company, © 1980.

Day, Charles R., Jr. "What It Takes to Be a CEO" from *Industry Week* by permission from Penton Publishing Inc., © 1979.

Drake, Rodman L. "Leadership: It's a Rare Blend of Traits" from *Management Review* by permission from American Management Association, © 1985.

Elsasser, Paul. "I Have Met the Enemy" from *Supervision* by permission from the National Research Bureau, Inc., © 1985.

Fram, Eugene H. and DuBrin, Andrew J. "Time-Span Orientation: A Key Factor of Contingency Management" by permission of *Personnel Journal*, © 1981.

Garfield, Charles A. "The Right Stuff" from *Management World* by permission from Charles A. Garfield, © 1984.

Glassman, Edward. "Your Leadership Style" from *Executive Female* by permission of Edward Glassman, © 1983.

Hines, Gary K. "Management Leadership Style" from *Supervision* by permission from the National Research Bureau, © 1980.

Hosmer, LaRue Tone. "The Importance of Strategic Leadership" from *Journal of Business Strategy* by permission from Warren, Gorhan & Lamont, Inc., © 1982.

Howard, Ann and Wilson, James A. "Leadership in a Declining Work Ethic" from *California Management Review* by permission from the Regents of the University of California, © 1982.

Hutchinson, Charles T. "Prospectus for Corporate Leadership" from *Business Horizons* by permission from the Foundation for the School of Business at Indiana University, © 1983.

Kennedy, Dennis L. "Understanding Personal Power" from *Supervisory Management* by permission from American Management Association, © 1984.

Kleiner, Brian H. "Tracing the Evolution of Leadership Styles" from *Management World* by permission from the Administrative Management Society, © 1981.

Kovach, Jeffrey L. "10 Reasons Why Executives Fail" from *Industry Week* by permission from Penton Publishing Inc., © 1985.

Lester, Richard I. "Leadership: Some Principles and Concepts" by permission from *Personnel Journal*, © 1981.

Litzinger, William and Schaefer, Thomas. "Leadership Through Followership" from *Business Horizons* by permission from the Foundation for the School of Business at Indiana University, © 1982.

Martin, William B. "Are You a Manager or a Leader?" from *Industry Week* by permission from Penton Publishing Inc., © 1985.

McMaster, Irvin. "A New Look at Leadership" from *Supervision* by permission from The National Research Bureau, © 1981.

McMurray, Robert N. "How Your Company Can Avoid Weak Leadership" from *Nation's Business* by permission from the U. S. Chamber of Commerce, © 1982.

Mendell, Jay S. and Gerjuoy, Herbert G. "Anticipatory Management or Visionary Leadership: A Debate" from *Managerial Planning* by permission from the Planning Executives Institute, © 1984.

Miles, Mary. "The Case of the Missing Boss" from *Computer Decisions* by permission from the Hayden Publishing Co., © 1985.

Miles, Mary. "The Effective Manager: Semi-Tough" from *Computer Decisions* by permission from the Hayden Publishing Co., © 1984.

Nation's Business. "A Checklist of Qualities That Make a Good Boss" from *Nation's Business* by permission from the U. S. Chamber of Commerce, © 1984.

Nation's Business. "Traits That Will Take You to the Top" from *Nation's Business* by permission from the U. S. Chamber of Commerce, © 1972.

Nelson, Harry. " Reality Supervision" from the *Journal of Business Strategy* by permission from Warren, Gorham & Lamont, Inc., © 1984.

Owens, James. "A Reappraisal of Leadership Theory and Training" from *Personnel Administrator* by permission from The American Society for Personnel Administration, © 1981.

Peters, Thomas J. "Excellence at the Top: A Leadership Style That Works" from *The Cornell Hotel and Restaurant Administration Quarterly* by permission from the Cornell University School of Hotel Administration, © 1980.

Plachy, Roger J. "Leading vs Managing: A Guide to Some Crucial Distinctions" from *Management Review* by permission from American Management Association, © 1981.

Post, Charles T. "Profile of Power—So You Think You're a Superleader?" from *Iron Age* by permission from Chilton Publishing Co., © 1982.

Scanlan, Burt K. "Managerial Leadership in Perspective: Getting Back to Basics" by permission from *Personnel Journal,* © 1979.

Scanlan, Burt K. and Atherton, Roger M., Jr. "Participation and the Effective Use of Authority" by permission from *Personnel Journal,* © 1981.

Scholl, Richard W. and Brownell, Winifred W. "Let Management Development Score for Your Organization" by permission from *Personnel Journal,* © 1983.

Schrader, Alert W. "How Companies Use University-Based Executive Development Programs" from *Business Horizons* by permission from the Foundation for the School of Business at Indiana University, © 1985.

Schriesheim, Chester A., Tolliver, James M. and Behling, Orlando C. "Leadership Theory: Some Implications for Managers" by permission from *Business Topics,* Mississippi State University, © 1978.

Sinetar, Marsha. "Developing Leadership Potential" by permission from *Personnel Journal,* © 1981.

Smith, Harold T. "20 Critical Competencies for Managers" from *Management World* by permission from The Administrative Management Society, © 1978.

Steger, Joseph A., Manners, George E., Jr. and Zimmerer, Thomas W. "Following the Leader: How to Link Management Style to Subordinate Personalities" from *Management Review* by permission from American Management Association, © 1982.

Taylor, Hugh R. "Power at Work" by permission from *Personnel Journal,* © 1986.

Tichy, Noel M. and Ulrich, David O. "The Leadership Challenge—A Call for the Transformational Leader" from *Sloan Management Review* by permission from Sloan Management Review Association, © 1984.

Watson, Craig M. "Leadership, Management, and the Seven Keys" from *Business Horizons* by permission from the Foundation for the School of Business at Indiana University, © 1983.

Yukl, Gary and Taber, Tom. "The Effective Use of Managerial Power" from *Personnel* by permission from American Management Association, © 1983.

Part I
LEADERSHIP:
THE EFFECTIVE
TRAITS

1.
LEADERSHIP:
IT'S A RARE BLEND OF TRAITS

Rodman L. Drake

Successful corporate leaders in today's demanding environment tend to
share at least eight personal characteristics.

"Major corporation seeks president and chief executive officer. Must be able
to direct the activities of a large multidivisional corporation with installations
worldwide. Reports to board of directors. An opportunity for a senior manager
with proven credentials for this prestigious position. Leadership ability a
must."

Leadership ability may be the last item—the "kicker"—in this fictitious ad,
but at any company, large or small, it unquestionably belongs at the top of the
list of the traits one seeks in a chief executive officer. No single factor provides
a greater benefit to an organization than effective leadership, especially when
the economic outlook is less than bright; when wrenching changes occur in a
company, its industry and markets, or an entire society. But how do you actually define leadership? More importantly, how do you determine if an executive
is a leader? In its most basic sense, leadership simply means going out in front of
others; using your body, your forward motion, your communications skills to
direct others to the route they should take. The word "leadership" may bring to
mind images of a military officer marching at the head of his troops toward a
strategic objective, or a seasoned mountain guide in the vanguard of a group of
climbers along a treacherous path. Both roles involve significant risks—an important measure of leadership potential. A true leader must always be alert to
risks and ready to react swiftly.

In a corporate setting, the chief executive officer's principal role is to provide
leadership; to set objectives and to allocate the organization's
resources—financial and human—to meet these goals. The CEO must remain
constantly on guard for any trouble that could stand in the way of this mission.
A CEO in today's environment must deal with more complex problems and

make decisions faster than CEOs of fifteen to twenty years ago. Finally, and most importantly, decisions made by the CEO of a large corporation may have far-reaching consequences for the company, its employees, and society at large for many years in the future.

EIGHT TRAITS

Successful corporate leaders in today's demanding environment tend to share at least eight personal characteristics. Obviously, some of these characteristics are more pronounced, and others less so, in any one individual. Nevertheless, the accomplished organizational leader should ideally possess some combination of most of the following:

The ability to focus attention. The CEO who can capture the attention of everyone in the organization has one of the most important ingredients of leadership. Such a person conveys a high degree of single-mindedness and dedication to a vision—an agenda or blueprint for the future. Having this vision is what distinguishes the effective leader from less-gifted ones. CEOs with vision never lose sight of the long-term objectives as they deal with short-term opportunities or setbacks in an ever-changing environment.

Think about it. When are you most effective in your working or personal life? Usually it is when you have a firm idea of what you want. When do you feel the least effective? More often than not, it's when your expectations are foggy and your goals are unclear.

Walter Wriston and Roger Smith are two CEOs with exemplary vision. Wriston, the recently retired head of Citicorp, saw an urgent need to place Citibank, the organization's primary subsidiary, in the lead of bank technology. He realized he had to make Citibank an aggressive competitor in the changing, deregulated financial services sector, particularly in its retail banking portion. Smith, the CEO of General Motors, foresaw the need to transform GM—the world's largest industrial enterprise—into a far more flexible and innovative firm than it has been. He knew the company should be better prepared for the continuing face-off with Japanese automakers.

Both Wriston and Smith perceived the need for change. They had a clear vision of the direction their companies should go, communicated the vision, created a commitment throughout the organization, and effected the necessary change. Wriston left a permanent stamp on Citicorp, positioning it as a formidable competitor in the financial services marketplace; Smith continues to oversee the significant changes that are transforming GM.

An emphasis on simple values. The corporate leader who articulates a set of basic values, and continually stresses them in speeches, written material, and meetings with employees, fosters unity within the organization. These values also can provide a framework that can assist managers in making decisions. If, for example, customer service is high among the company's priorities—as it has been at IBM since the days of Thomas Watson—it then becomes a criterion in the decision-making process.

Basic values give everyone in the organization a means of comprehending events; the values provide a guiding spirit. They encapsulate in terse, understandable terms the organization's culture. At Deluxe Check Printers, Inc., founder W.R. Hotchkiss created an atmosphere in which people had significant value—both customers and employees. His efforts helped promulgate the simple value that everyone in the organization played a role in its overall success. Hotchkiss firmly believed that if a company provided exceptional service, it would prosper. He was also committed to the idea that all of Deluxe's employees were partners with the firm's customers. These values helped make possible an enviable record of thirty-two consecutive years of increased earnings.

Staying in touch with people. Effective leaders are rarely thought of as aloof and remote. Like W. R. Hotchkiss, who translated his values into tangible successes, the CEO who gives employees a basic, understandable message helps to mold the attitudes of the staff. Staying in touch with people outside the organization is as important as staying in touch internally. The effective CEO usually has a carefully assembled network of external contacts among key customers, peers (CEOs in one's own and other industries, particularly the financial community), and government, scientific, and academic leaders. Reliable, credible outside contacts can counterbalance the CEO's internal sources. By listening to them with an open mind, the CEO may garner valuable "second opinions" to weigh against the filtered information that flows to the top of most large organizations.

Avoiding pseudoprofessionalism. Over the last two decades, the tools of management—particularly information systems that instantaneously retrieve and analyze huge amounts of data—have grown tremendously. New management concepts concerning formulation of strategic planning also have proliferated.

Many senior corporate managers employ these tools and concepts effectively. Others do not. A large number of this latter group can be classified as "pseudoprofessionals," often rushing into the latest approach regardless of its cost or potential results.

Given today's pace of change, companies need to undertake the type of solid planning that forces management to examine medium- and long-term objectives, as well as the steps needed to reach them. The CEO most likely to leave a mark on an enterprise has an aversion to pseudoprofessionalism. The true leader knows where the organization should be going and avoids unproductive exercises.

Managing change. This trait complements vision. Besides having a vision of the company's future, the CEO must be skilled at instituting change. An accomplished leader should "make it happen."

Allied Corporation's acquisition of Bendix, for example, reflects a step in CEO Edward L. Hennessy's thoughtfully formulated strategy to alter the direction of his company, to change it over time from a chemical and energy company to a broadly diversified enterprise with a concentration in the automotive and aerospace industries. Hennessy involved Bendix executives in the business of integrating the companies and retained key Bendix managers.

Implementing change involves building organizational support and consensus, as well as the ability to deal with risk. The CEO must be able to sequence decisions appropriately and should have a well-developed sense of timing.

Selecting people. Every effective CEO is adept at identifying and retaining talented subordinates: promoting them from within the organization, hiring them from competing firms, or even recruiting them from companies in other industries.

"My job when I came in as president," James Evans, currently the chairman of Union Pacific, was quoted as saying, "was to hire all the right people for the jobs that had to be done." In today's environment of rapid change, the right people frequently represent different cultural values. For example, some of the key executives who have made Citibank a powerhouse in the consumer banking industry came from marketing-oriented organizations like General Foods and Proctor & Gamble. It takes guts to know when to break step and recognize the need for a new breed of executive with different values.

Of course, not all chief executives are adept at selecting qualified subordinates who can contribute substantially to the company's success. But the effective CEO who lacks this ability will recognize this and seek the counsel of managers skilled in selecting the best candidates for key positions.

Avoiding "do-it-allism." The chief executive of a large organization who attempts to "do it all" is heading for potential disaster. Successful leaders know they are not omniscient; as humans, they can only know and do so much. No matter how dedicated a CEO may be, each individual's time and energies are finite.

Successful corporate leaders tend to direct their attention to a relatively limited number of performance indicators. These indicators disclose how the company is doing currently, as well as the performance expected for the short-, mid-, and long-terms. Sophisticated systems are available to measure and monitor the organization's performance in just about every sphere of activity; so are skilled staff members with responsibility for closely tracking potential problems, before they become liabilities, and potential opportunities, so the company can seize them before competitors do. The successful CEO will effectively monitor the environment, spot potential problems early, select key executives whose views and values represent the future instead of the past, and allocate resources boldly in accordance with a firmly held vision of the future.

Facing up to failure. Finally, another trait of a successful leader is the ability to deal with failure. It is not uncommon for a well-regarded corporate leader who has been buoyed by a string of successes to suddenly be sunk by a few failures that cause a major reversal of his or her—and the company's—fortunes. The truly superior leader, however, will not hesitate to face up to setbacks and, where appropriate, take the blame for failure. More importantly, such a leader will learn from mistakes and will keep moving on.

One area that separates the average leader from the truly great leader is the knack of knowing when to get out of marginal businesses. Too many CEOs become emotionally committed to lines of business or product lines. They keep hoping that changing circumstances will eventually lead to a stronger bottom line. Reducing or ending a division's accustomed levels of financial resources (or, at an extreme, divesting the unit) means confronting colleagues in the executive suite with bad news; a message that can have serious ramifications for their future prospects. Strong leaders do not need to wait for the Bass brothers or Sir James Goldsmith to recognize the need to restructure or redeploy assets.

Like a perpetual motion machine, corporations should be able to continue functioning effectively forever. But a true perpetual motion machine has eluded inventors, and few companies are capable of immortality. The greatest challenge CEOs face is to assure the survival and well-being of the organization; it is a challenge that can involve suppressing short-term operating gains in order to achieve success over the long-term; developing capable subordinates; and putting unrelenting stress on merit— both their own and that of everyone in the organization.

Rodman L. Drake is managing director of Cresap, McCormick, and Paget, a New York-based international management consulting firm.

2.
WHAT IT TAKES TO
BE A CEO

Charles R. Day, Jr.

This most demanding of all managerial positions almost defies a pat description. Generally, a corporation's immediate needs serve as the "job specs." There are, however, some common traits that every CEO—and would-be CEO—needs to develop.

Rays of morning sunshine sliced through gray autumn skies, barely arresting the attention of the intent, properly attired gentleman secluded high in a corner office. He had arrived much earlier, in a darkness that matched his mood. He scanned his schedule. The gathering of the finance committee promised to be long, and bitter—quarterly earnings and the company's stock price were dropping sharply. He also was due in Washington, for another command performance before a Congressional hearing. Politics. His distaste for it grew daily. Surveying the morning, he strolled to an inviting Colonial chair, a favorite place in which to relax and reflect. Regular visitors made it a point not to sit there. On a table rested a glass of club soda, spiced with lime; far better refreshment than coffee, he mused, taking a sip. Then he sat back, and allowed his eyes to close . . .

Somewhere within the fabric of industry there may be a chief executive officer who cuts that profile. Among workers, it remains a popular stereotype: the hard-driving, twenty-four-hours-a-day whirlwind who shoves aside a personal life without bothering to see who languishes in the rubble—all for the sake of a better, brighter bottom line. A recent survey among chief executive officers, executive officers—or CEOs—partially confirms that portrait: profits are their No. 1 concern.

And yet, many argue, there is no stereotype. Indeed, some believe the "workaholic" to be a dying breed. There actually is no "average" corporation, anyway, others submit; hence, there can be no average CEO, either. There is general agreement, however, that a person aspiring to the top would do well to identify and refine certain traits.

8

Common Thread. Many of these qualities and disciplines can collectively be defined in one word: leadership. The latter is described in various terms: strength, dedication, "corporate quarterbacks," just to name a few. One chairman and CEO likens the job to that of a concert orchestra leader, then notes that the leadership required is such that it "can operate in an ustructured environment, as opposed to something . . . like law or accounting."

"The CEO has to be the problem-solver. He has to be able to crack open problems, as I call it, then call on others for expertise, reduce the problem to manageable pieces," and then develop "a framework for judgement," considers E. M. (Ted) Lee, president and CEO, Information Handling Services (IHS), Englewood, Colo. (a unit of Indian Head Inc., New York), which gathers, prepares, classifies, and packages a variety of industrial and technical data.

The CEO can call on a vast reservoir of self-confidence that, in turn, inspires confidence in those around him. "It's often a quiet confidence as well," thinks Wilhemus B. Bryan III, senior vice president, William H. Clark Associates Inc., a New York executive recruiter. It's not a "rah-rah," cheerleader variety that may be spectacularly effective for short bursts of time but lacks the consistency that is vital. A corporate leader must be able to discern his firm's strengths and weaknesses fairly quickly, accentuate the former, and deemphasize or liquidate the latter. And finally, he must be able to rally the troops to an overriding, easily identifiable cause.

The job he seeks and maintains is not one that just any manager can handle. Ambition and resolution alone don't fashion a Harold Geneen from the likes of a Dagwood Bumstead.

There is certain "responsibility of power" required of a CEO, observes Aldo DeFrancesco, Narco Scientific Inc., Ft. Washington, Pa. As president and chief operating officer, he analyzes the No. 1 job from the second rung on the ladder. "You must have honesty, fairness, and sincerity in the way you operate, especially in cases where you are not dealing with a union." Tyrannical CEO's may be respected in a peculiar sort of way, and succeed in spite of their style, "but that's so rare."

Desire essential. If there is a responsibility for power, there may well be a thirst for it as well. For some CEO's, like John H. Connor, president, Varlen Corp., a Rolling Meadows, Ill. metal-working firm, the appetite for the job is better described as "an all-consuming passion. There is no question about it, and I think the same is true for many chief executives." Without that drive, he submits, a CEO will not succeed over the long haul. The rigorous demands of the job almost require that sort of devotion. Some add that a similar desire is needed just to position oneself to be even considered for corporate high command.

Accomplishment can be the fuel that ignites such desire, believes Robert Lamalie, president, Lamalie & Associates Inc., a Tampa, Fla.-based executive search firm. "He has to want the job badly, no doubt about it. If he possibly was trapped, and never really sought it, he'll be trapped by the pressures.

"Most of the candidates I have run across have set out to be CEOs," Mr. Lamalie continues, expressing a sentiment which many endorse. Successful aspirants kept that goal in sight all the way to the top, proving to themselves—and others—that they could handle the job. "Even if such desire isn't openly stated, it's there just the same," adds Clark Associates' Mr. Bryan. "It remains high in their minds that they are shooting high."

Moreover, a man has to be equally determined to hold onto his lofty rank, remarks Steve Loidl, vice president-finance, Leeds & Northrup Co. (L&N), North Wales, Pa. Mr. Loidl also sheds light on a second popular contention: that at some point in a manager's career there comes the moment to decide whether or not to aim for the pinnacle. "Anyone who achieves officer status in a significantly sized firm" does so, he maintains. "I know I did." (In his case, he decided against it. Becoming a CEO "would have killed me, and my family." He also concluded that his desire lacked the necessary intensity. So he set his sights on becoming a chief financial officer, which he is today.)

Taking aim. This burning desire is latent in every potential CEO in any corporation with sales exceeding $20 million. If not, the candidate will be found wanting, contends Charles Boren, industrial sales manager-distribution, Gates Rubber Co., Denver. He believes the decision is made at a major turning point early in a person's career, or during "a life crisis. We all make major decisions that knowingly will affect us the rest of our lives. The one to seek the CEO role is one," he explains.

"You get opportunities given to you which prompt those decisions," notes Kevin O'Connor, director of merchandising, case goods and bedding for Ethan Allen Inc., a Danbury, Conn., furniture manufacturer. Those opportunities reveal a fairly clear path through the future.

Having been provided some glimpses of the path down which a CEO must journey, both Mr. Boren and Mr. O'Connor express reservations about joining the parade. To be sure, they've made no irrevocable decisions. Perspectives change with the years, they quickly acknowledge. Still, "one has to ask himself if it's worth it," comments Mr. Boren, 34, whose family is still young enough to require and deserve far more attention than it will in, say, ten years. Family pressures "have got to be severe" at the CEO level, he reasons. "The job has to come first or the man probably isn't going to make it. There has to be a sacrifice."

Mr. Boren feels he's reached a point where he has to evaluate his career, and where it may lead. His home and family are important factors to consider. A man's home is not only his castle, "but also his oasis," he submits, where one "can refuel, kick off his shoes, and prepare for the next battle."

"I don't think I'd want to look back at fifty-five or sixty and have to say that I was CEO at Ethan Allen, but I didn't know my kids," reflects Mr. O'Connor, who has seen others crumble in pursuit of an all-consuming job. "Raising a family is important to me. Naturally, as it grows, it will become less dependent.

Now, however, I have three pre-schoolers and a wife who need ME." Most younger managers can identify with that attitude, he adds.

Reluctance aside, Mr. O'Connor acknowledges a certain desire—a small desire—to run a corporation, "if it were the right opportunity for me and my family, and if I could see that I could conduct my life the way I wanted to and still do a job." Yet, in sorting his options, he allows he might also be satisfied with a lesser position, "knowing that I could have done better, but chose not to."

Exhausting. There is ample testimony as to the time and dedication demanded of a CEO. "Sixty to seventy hours a week have got to be the norm," contends Mr. Connor of Varlen with conviction. "The welfare of the corporation and the interests of the shareholders have simply got to be the most paramount motivation in a CEO's life, bar none." Pausing for emphasis, he adds, "I don't think you'll find very many chief executives who are dissatisfied with the circumstances, provided they really enjoy the job—as I do." The true CEO, he submits, thrives on pressure. "People ask me about that, and I tell them what I'll tell you: I love it."

Circumstances can reach the point where they do "begin to encroach on one's private life," concedes one CEO—to the point where they all but obliterate a life away from the executive suite.

Not everyone agrees with this tension-filled profile. A minority vigorously contends that an equally realistic portrait can be painted with a different brush on a far softer canvas. A man does NOT have to begin a passionate pursuit of high command at age twenty-one, this view asserts. Nor must he abdicate his role of husband and father. "I would speculate—and it's only that—that in many of the major corporations, say the *Fortune 1000,* a majority DID NOT start eyeing the top immediately, but rather, began working up the ladder," offers Ralph W. Rogers, president, Rogers, Hill & Slade Inc., a Greenwich, Conn., executive recruiter.

"Until I was interviewed for the presidency of this company, I had no idea it would happen," pointedly says H. Robert Sharbaugh, chairman, Sun Co., Radnor, Pa. (Mr. Sharbaugh, who was named president in 1970 and chairman in 1975, is leaving the company following a brouhaha which most observers feel resulted more from differences with the controlling family's interests than from his performance as Sun's chief executive.) He did, he concedes, aspire "to rise in the organization," yet that hope did not distract him from the task then at hand. Anyone who handles his current job in a mediocre fashion and instead connives to get the next promotion "is engaging in a fruitless venture," he believes.

"I have a great desire to contribute leadership in a business role. But I am not a workaholic," maintains Mr. Lee of IHS politely but firmly. He is resolved to being "damn good" in what he does, yet "passion," he adds, would constitute an inappropriate definition. "One earns the right to become a CEO," he feels strongly.

Disclaimer. Both Mr. Lee and Mr. Sharbaugh insist that a CEO can have an enjoyable and rewarding private life and still be successful (one of Mr. Lee's hobbies is climbing 14,000-feet peaks in the Colorado Rockies!). "That doesn't mean you don't work hard, or long hours. You do," Mr. Lee cautions, "where you need to." But there are occasions when he will ensure that his schedule allows him time to watch his son play baseball, "because that is important, too."

Mr. Sharbaugh challenges the widely held notion that a CEO's time frame differs radically from that of other managers. Yes, situations can arise in an instant, demanding an immediate reply. Yet every level of management has responsibilities that require that sort of attention, just as they did during his days as a refinery supervisor. "The nature and timing of those duties were different," he says, "but the total impact wasn't all that much different."

The respective performances of Sun and IHS attest to the quality of the men at the top.

Sun's revenues exceeded $6.4 billion in 1977; net income was some $362 million. Both figures sparkle when compared with most previous years.

IHS, over a three-year period, had lost $1 million and was a prospect for the commercial graveyard. After his predecessor—of necessity—had successfully trimmed the company, it was left to Mr. Lee to fashion a rebirth. He led the firm to an operating profit of nearly $1 million in 1971, his first year at the helm. Record sales and profits have followed, and now "we're a $40 million company headed for $100 million," he beams.

Such companies reflect an openness, as if to say that success does not have to be accented by cold austerity and dark woodwork bordering drab, stuffy offices.

On a limb. There is little arguing about another point, however. CEOs not only enjoy pressures and risks, they must also be conditioned to them, almost as a way of life. "You go out on a limb once in a while." observes Varlen's Mr. Connor. "Obviously you want to gather all the information you can in evaluating risk. And you don't want to make any snap decisions."

But if one continually plays everything close to the vest, he'll fail. Indeed, that sort of manager is an unlikely CEO candidate in the first place. Competitors who do roll the dice and win sixty percent of the time "will run you over." A high-risk orientation is virtually a CEO prerequisite. "That's the only way you make quantum jumps," says L&N's Mr. Loidl.

But when does risk-taking become tantamount to suicide? It varies with each firm, like the number of mistakes a CEO can commit before his hold on the job becomes tenuous at best. As executive recruiter Mr. Rogers notes, some boards have an aversion to "bet the farm issues"—those that can make or break a company.

Other firms, naturally, seek a river-boat gambler type. Here, the key is not so much knowing that big bets are common, but rather knowing when to put the bundle on the table. Smart CEOs will seldom tackle crucial encounters early in their reign. It's far better to first determine which way the cards are going.

IHS's Mr. Lee considers risk this way: First, avoid catastrophe; second, meet or beat the current plan; finally, plan for growth. Do so "in this order," he advises. "Most important, downside risk must always be considered before you look at upside potential. You do want to seize opportunity . . . but there is nothing wrong with understanding how deep a hole you may be digging for yourself."

A CEO who's always armed with a "Plan B" can make a multitude of mistakes without arousing concern, he adds. Another axiom: A CEO must be willing to admit his errors. If he isn't, all the Plan Bs in the world won't help him.

Being in good health also helps in shouldering risks and the accompanying pressures. Hobbies or recreation—golf or tennis, for instance—help one cope with the rigors of the job, most CEOs agree. But not all, and therein lies part of the difficulty of precisely measuring a CEO.

Shopping list. Plucking individual sets of "CEO specs" reaps an overwhelming harvest of proficiencies, experiences, and managerial tools. Were one obliged to possess all of them in abundant amounts, just squeezing through the door of the building would be challenge enough. The premier suggestion is that a CEO have some solid experience in running a profit center—be it a large division of a major firm, a group of divisions, or even another enterprise. Some firms prefer previous CEO experience; a few insist on it. Many also desire a man from within their own industry, or at least a related one. In any event mere potential is no substitute for a proven track record.

Recruiter Mr. Rogers lists the following "qualifications," based on clients' requests. A *consistency of style*, not just occasional bursts of charisma. *Relentless persistence*, a personal discipline that precludes periodic coasting: a CEO *leads*, he doesn't point, and there is a difference. *Respect* for others as human beings. Superb, continuous *organization*. *Commitment* to the business and the company, and, finally, a *sense of humor*.

Stun's Mr. Sharbaugh identifies three "principal resource management problems" which are likely to come to the attention of a corporation's highest levels; human, financial, "plus one that's hard to define. It is a combination of public affairs, policy and image, and constituency interface management." Each, he says, is critical. A fourth, facilities resource management, "usually falls in line if the other three are being managed satisfactorily. It is less likely to be an issue" at the top levels.

It matters little, he feels, where "responsible work in each of these areas" has been gained, unless one finds oneself atop a single-line kind of business where technical knowledge is critical to the decision-making process.

Other needed talents and abilities are submitted at random, and blanket the executive waterfront. Financial expertise is almost universally cited—and most put it near or at the top of the list. A need for international experience is growing in importance, as we spin toward an interdependent world economy, suggests one source. Several recommend marketing experience. "In our business, a thorough understanding of the consumer is a must, and will continue to be," offers Ethan Allen's Mr. O'Connor.

L&N's Mr. Loidl likes to see "a little bit of the dreamer" in CEOs, a kind of quality that asks not why, but why not? It also indicates an executive's propensity for driving himself harder than anyone else— another desirable quality. (Mr. Loidl has served three CEOs at his company, and led the search for the electronics firm's current leader, David T. Kimball).

How valuable is an M.B.A. degree? Today it remains an extra; tomorrow it could be a prerequisite. "More and more executives coming into industry have them, so I suspect it will become essential", thinks recruiter Mr. Lamalie. Most important, no one regards the graduate degree as anything more than a tool. A law degree is seen in the same light, and several advise a few years in business before undertaking graduate study.

No but . . . Age should not be a factor, all agree, "but one probably has to cross a certain threshold to gain experience," considers Pat McFadden, manager, Denver operations, Gates Rubber. For many firms, the threshold appears to be around "forty-five or fifty"—to the point where some younger managers complain of an unwritten code which all but eliminates the young CEO. Too often, one charges, a standard pattern of advancement governs promotions. "Most senior managers spent a great deal of time working up the ladder. They struggled, and they expect others to do the same. That's totally wrong and a misuse of talent," bristles one source.

In truth, it's more likely the lack of a proven track record, not age, that excludes most young "whiz kids" from the top command. If there is an "unwritten law," it may soon be repealed anyway, some suggest, citing the growing need for CEOs.

Varlen's Mr. Connor contributes a valuable thought: "To judge maturity by . . . age alone is in itself an immature thought! That pearl of wisdom was reportedly uttered by a fifteen-year-old scholar seeking admission to Princeton. He got in."

Long-term service doesn't necessarily mean experience, either, adds Mr. Connor. It's possible for a manager to have "one year's experience twenty times."

A CEO need not have a very specific personality, either, it is agreed, though some equate personality with leadership potential. A CEO may become more deliberate, and is likely to become somewhat molded by the job, but "there is really no limit at all," reflects Mr. DeFrancesco of Narco. The value of "outside interest" and activities elicits a variety of opinions. Some applaud them, regarding them as evidence of social conscience. Mr. Loidl of L&N, for example, takes great stock in a proper amount of athletic prowess—"so as not to make Jack a dull boy is the best way to explain it." Community activities, plus service as an outside director, rank high in the minds of many executives, but they warn that a CEO dare not let these pursuits encroach on his No. 1 task.

Many insist that that task is so demanding that it all but prohibits expending any energy elsewhere. Of course, countless chief executives have their names associated with causes and organizations. "I suspect, however, that many are front men, while the actual work is handled by others," says one source wryly. "The interest may be there," notes Varlen's Mr. Connor, "but the time seldom is."

People prowess. If the job *is* paramount, many stress that a CEO's ability to recognize managerial talent ranks only below leadership and desire in importance. Gates' Mr. Boren says it is this ability that separates the outstanding CEO from the run-of-the-mill.

Inherent in the ability to judge talent, however, is also a responsibility to periodically appraise it. Some CEOs either neglect or abdicate this responsibility altogether, it is charged; occasionally, that can turn out to be their undoing. For others, talent appraisal constitutes an immense pressure that weighs on them heavily—"because it is so subjective," explains recruiter Mr. Rogers, recalling a CEO who took great satisfaction in working with numbers "because they were so tangible."

However, when the time comes to dismiss a top executive who doesn't measure up, a CEO may find himself wondering whether the eventual replacement will be even more deficient! The CEO must also put up with executives who seek better titles, or more responsibility—or those who regard themselves as "indispensable." The shades of gray that accompany these problems are endless. Often, the CEO alone must render the verdict. Talking to a subordinate is inappropriate. And the odds of being able to confide in a board member are often slim.

"In some cases, you wind up with a CEO struggling over such decisions with his wife! And what does she know!" quips a source.

More headaches. People pressures aren't the only "special" ones to confront a CEO. A host of others are cited. Decisions that must be made in solitude can be most perplexing. "The loneliness of high command can be real at times," maintains Mr. Rogers. On other occasions, a CEO may reach a conclusion that's diametrically opposite to that of his staff. So does he follow its recommendation? Or go with his own?

The pressure to outpace the last quarter's earnings can be tremendous, confides Mr. De Francesco of Narco. Others agree, quickly. "Some day it's going to come to an end," comments one, pleading anonymity. "So I am prepared to fail, in that regard. I don't know if the board is, but I am!"

Managing growth where the prospects are dazzling can squeeze a CEO in a special way as well, offers IHS's Mr. Lee. It's a matter of knowing how fast to move, not when. He also remains concerned about keeping pace with technical developments that continually impact his business. "I don't care to know EVERYTHING about them—just enough to be able to weigh options."

External pressure can turn a CEO's hair gray—or help to contribute to its shortage. Legal matters, particularly, annoy Mr. De Francesco because they actually are beyond his control: he has no choice but to put his complete faith and trust in counsel. "And the CEO also faces his firm's toughest critics," adds L&N's Mr. Loidl, "the financial analysts. He must be able to handle every question that arises. If not, he'll look sick." To a lesser degree, the same can be said for dealings with shareholders.

In addition, a CEO may have to tolerate a "fishbowl" existence. The man's every move is monitored. Company personnel take their cue from their CEO, which is why "consistency" becomes so important a virtue. Those who dislike being "shadowed" and constantly watched had better explore other career opportunities.

Sharing? Apart from this last one, other "special" pressures are to be shared, thinks Mr. O'Connor of Ethan Allen. Technically and legally, yes, the responsibility for an enterprise does rest on the CEO's shoulders. "But if you have the right relationship with your management and operating people, those pressures should be felt by them as well. Quite often I think they are too."

Only an "idiot will try to go it alone," assesses Varlen's Mr. Connor. If the headquarters of a $71 million corporation is any indication, he practices what he preaches. The headquarters staff consists of eight persons, five executives and three assistants. "We're here to offer help where needed," and not meddle in affairs that can be managed by others, he says sharply.

Failure to delegate leads another laundry list of practices that can render a CEO ineffective. These practices vary from the expected—illness, liquor, sex—to the not-so-expected: lack of attention to the business, which in turn leads to chaos; or outright boredom with the job, which can happen, assures L&N's Mr. Loidl.

The regal trappings and splendor of the job alone can quickly disarm a CEO, alerts Mr. Connor. He has little regard for those who squander a career over such trivial indulgences. Improper use of time is another "effectiveness robber," as in isolation. "Think about what screening means," advises IHS' Mr. Lee. "You always screen something *out*. You never screen in." He has only contempt for those who surround themselves with an entourage of aides who stifle communications.

Sun's Mr. Sharbaugh uses but one word to explain the root cause of ineffectiveness: "Timidness."

Standout. What, then, signals the exemplary CEO? Most say, simply, results, the bottom line. "It's also the way those results are achieved," responds Mr. Loidl. They can be attained, he reasons, without "destruction and bloodshed," even when a new man arrives on the scene. At L&N, Mr. Kimball could have cleaned house in a roughshod manner, Mr. Loidl explains. He didn't. Instead, he blended new and old talents to achieve sparkling results.

Mr. Sharbaugh, too, faults those who would simply say "results." To him the more pressing forces which encompass an enterprise are those which exert their greatest impact "five or ten years after their presence can be sensed." The mark of an outstanding CEO, then, lies in the ability to build the strength and flexibility to cope with those forces rather than to merely focus on near term results.

Regardless of how they're measured, on a scale of one to ten, most CEOs would rank near the top, believes Mr. Bryan of Clark Associates, dispelling any notion of a "bell curve." If the majority were bunched lower, they wouldn't be good enough. And a ranking of middle is insufficient in the CEO league.

One factor which can assist an executive's entry into that league hasn't been addressed: Luck. Whether Dame Fortune grins just slightly or smiles broadly on emerging CEOs is—as one might expect—a matter of opinion, some of it lively.

Luck can account for up to thirty percent of the forces and factors that shape a man's career, contends Varlen's Mr. Connor. Marco's Mr. De Francesco is among those endorsing the opposite end of the spectrum that luck per se need not be a factor at all. A company, he believes, "should understand what it's looking for and go get him. For a CEO, you certainly ought to have the personnel and psychological skills to know what you are viewing." When a firm lets luck gain a role in the selection, he implies, it has added a totally un-necessary variable.

"I prefer to call it fate," offers Mr. Boren of Gates, asserting that it taps everyone's shoulder at some time or another, either delicately or with the force of a falling building. Further, says Mr. Boren, fate seems to care not a whit about career plans. He relates how another firm once paraded an alluring offer before his eyes. A haphazard chain of events, including a thunderstorm, delayed his decision—until Gates presented an even better opportunity.

"There are always circumstances which bring a man into the spotlight, to attention," says Mr. Connor. "What do you call that? I'd call it luck."

Far too many managers leave far too much of their careers to luck, asserts recruiter Mr. Rogers. Ability alone is not enough, he stresses, because "to get to the top, you have to be *selected*. Good successful CEOs also have solid personal reputations." Selection doesn't come by accident. For those who have their heart, mind, and soul set on becoming a CEO, Mr. Rogers suggests "personal PR, to help spread their names, and a determined effort to meet key people in their companies and industries.

"Every person is really the CEO of his own career, yet too few realize it," he says firmly. Personal planning is a must—just as a detailed plan is essential to corporate well-being.

If executives leave too much to chance, so do too many companies, laments Mr. Loidl of L&N. Too often he says, a firm is content to appoint as CEO an insider who happens to be at the right place at the right time, instead of diligently seeking the best possible candidate.

The insider always has a leg up in the dash for the brass ring. He's in a position to do some "campaigning" and if he happens to be the favorite of the retiring CEO, his lead can be all but insurmountable. Recruiters acknowledge that they often comb the landscape just to discover a man who will serve as the leading insider's competition. "We would prefer not to work this way, but often that turns out to be the case," says recruiter Mr. Bryan.

Yet, the fair-haired boy can be vulnerable, too, he adds, merely because he IS the fair-haired boy. People like success stories, apparently, yet many are prone to hang the hero when he closes in on the treasure.

Changing role. For those who do get the crown, the job may be even more demanding in the not-too-distant future; 81% of the CEOs polled in a survey felt that their job would change, and an overwhelming number saw the need to become aware of external factors as the No. 1 reason for the change. Hordes of critics challenge corporations today, as private enterprise becomes increasingly public. As the leading corporate spokesman, the CEO is going to have to be able to respond and relate to these varied publics. If nothing else, Congress and regulatory bodies will have a tremendous impact on CEOs in the next ten years.

CEOs, therefore, need to become far more knowledgeable about how government works—even if some of the lessons are a bit frightening. That aspect of CEOs' collective performance "is still comparatively poor," assesses recruiter Mr. Rogers.

"So many CEOs are elevated without any government experience, and all of a sudden they become the top spokesman."

Analyzing the anticipated demands and the levels of concentration required, several suggest that the job will change hands faster in the future, that a CEO with ten years' experience in the same office will be a rare breed indeed. At that point, effectiveness begins to wane anyway, some submit.

One of the most appealing "perks" of the CEO position has been its independence, thinks recruiter Mr. Lamalie, but now that is diminishing because of government influence and the other factors cited.

"In a sense," he says, "some of the fun of the job is vanishing." There is evidence that a more open, externally oriented CEO is already at hand. The CEOs interviewed for this article warmly gave ample time for discussion. Many other CEOs, heads of giant organizations, regularly take time from pressing agendas to meet with the media and outside publics.

In a $1 billion-plus firm, naturally there may be some differences and pressures that the head of a smaller firm would not be aware of, concedes Mr. Lee. "Yet I would hope that my style and feelings about the job wouldn't change ever."

His goal is to build a "21st century company," where all employees realize "they can make a difference," and will delight in responding to managerial motivation.

One factor will remain: a CEO's opportunity to offer leadership and spirit to his organization. The rewards for those who put forth the effort, assures Mr. Lee, "are going to be super."

3.
MANAGERIAL LEADERSHIP IN PERSPECTIVE: GETTING BACK TO BASICS

Burt K. Scanlan

> We have lost sight of some of the basic ingredients of results-oriented leadership and need to return to fundamentals. In addition, to some extent at least, we have created a sort of hesistancy about leadership.

Over the past several years, a number of frameworks have been developed for examining the leadership function. Emphasis has ranged from those which identify alternative styles of management, with either a direct or indirect suggestion that there is one best style, to those which are clearly contingency theories maintaining that the appropriate style is dependent on any number of variables. All of the various frameworks serve several valuable purposes: 1) they stimulate a degree of serious thought among managers about the dynamics of this important function, 2) they help mangers to gain insight into what their own style of management is, 3) they help managers understand why they get the reaction they do either in general or in a given situation, and 4) they suggest alternative styles of leadership.

Unfortunately, while training and developing managers in accordance with these various theories, we have lost sight of some of the basic ingredients of results-oriented leadership and need to return to fundamentals. In addition, to some extent at least, we have created a sort of hesitancy about leadership which can work to the disadvantage of the organization, the individual manager and the employees.

With the above thoughts in mind, let's look at several key elements of effective leadership which have either gotten lost in the shuffle or become obscured. They are not magical, nor do they represent brilliant new theories, but to the veteran manager, these ideas will probably make good common sense. For the newer supervisor, they may help clear away some of the obscurity surrounding leadership.

LET PEOPLE KNOW WHAT IS EXPECTED

A coach will tell us that every player must know what is expected on a particular play—not just what is expected in terms of blocking the defensive end, but the results to be achieved, e.g., knocking the opponent down or holding him to the outside for a minimum of two seconds. People must know what is expected not only from the standpoint of the typical job description which describes physical responsibilities, but in terms of results to be achieved from those activities. The superior and subordinate must reach mutual agreement in five basic areas, including:

- The work that an employee does or the major activities for which he or she is responsible
- Where the job fits into the total picture and why it is important
- The factors upon which performance will be judged, such as quality, quantity, cost, innovation, estimation of accuracy, self-development and service to other people or departments
- How performance will be measured. It may be through quantitative measures or a series of statements describing the conditions which will exist when that area of the job has been adequately performed
- Specific minimum results or standards of performance which should be met in each of the above areas of accountability as they apply to the job.

Once these are clearly established and understood, subordinates must know that they will be held accountable for the results achieved.

ESTABLISH AND MAINTAIN HIGH PERFORMANCE EXPECTATION

By and large and within reason, managers get the type and level of job performance they expect or informally accept over a period of time. Low expectations breed low performance and apathy, while high expectations lead to high performance and a more demanding performance tone. Regarding low expectations, it is important to remember that standards can be set by default if one is not careful. Failure to confront lower than desired levels of performance is tantamount to acknowledging them as acceptable. High expectations means setting challenging but achievable goals. It means pinpointing exactly what you want, communicating it, and holding people accountable. It does not mean playing such games as: "If I as manager say I want this, I am pretty sure I can get that, and if I don't, it won't be too bad." Nor does it mean the subordinate giving all kinds of reasons for a low level of performance and the manager pretty well buying into the conversation, thus getting the subordinate off the hook, so to speak. The focus of high expectations is not only on results as such, but on results which are challenging, motivating and attainable, results which provide people with a sense of accomplishment. Again, given some matters yet to be discussed, employees will generally perform at the level expected of them, and when performance levels are not what you would like, the reason is often that people are doing what they know will be accepted.

LET PEOPLE KNOW WHERE THEY STAND

There are several dimensions to this aspect of results-oriented leadership. First, people must know where they stand with respect to the performance goals established, so that if those goals are not being met, they know precisely where they are falling short. This serves to reinforce attention to the achievement nature of the work climate. Also, it provides a vehicle for the superior and subordinate to discuss and reaffirm the goals and what needs to be done to achieve them, whether by the subordinate, the supervisor or both.

Just as important is letting people know when a job is being done well. So often in organizations we forget to "accentuate the positive" and can't understand why people are not more enthused. The answer may be that they feel nobody really cares anyway. In a situation like this, over a period of time the motivation to succeed will dwindle, and a concern for one's own interests will prevail. Recognition cannot amount to superficial "pats on the back," and it is the results accomplished which should receive emphasis. Recognition, like other leadership techniques, is another way of fostering mental and emotional involvement in a job, and can contribute significantly to the process by which organizational goals are internalized by employees. In other words, a strong sense of personal identification with organizational goals takes place because it is directly related to benefits for the individual. In this case psychological reward is the form of recognition.

EMPLOY BROAD-BASED COMMUNICATION

Effective leadership requires a broad-based program of communication that is both organizationwide and manager-centered. An approach to communication which goes beyond basic job information can accomplish several things. It promotes a sense of identification, a feeling of being a more important part of a broader whole. This in turn fosters the interest, commitment and closeness which are so important to the process of internalization mentioned previously. Broad-based communication can foster a "team" atmosphere by promoting cooperation through better understanding on the part of everyone. It can get people thinking and talking about "their" organization instead of falling back on the discouraged comment, "I just do my job. That's what I'm paid for." In short, increased supervisor-employee communication creates a feeling of importance, of being in on things.

CREATE A SUPPORTIVE CLIMATE

This is a common element of just about every framework for studying leadership that has been developed. In spite of this emphasis, "supportive climate" is very often misinterpreted, misapplied or inadequately defined. Among other things, a supportive climate would include the following behavior on the part of the manager:

- Exhibiting confidence and trust by allowing subordinates to pursue goals without undue reporting, constant checking and other exaggerated forms of control
- Taking positive actions to contribute to employees' growth and development
- Discussing possible causes of and solutions to specific problems which are making an employee's job difficult
- Training and helping the subordinate to find better ways of doing the work
- Giving help and assistance in solving problems as opposed to always giving the answer
- Making available to the best of one's ability the physical resources required to do the job
- Seeking out and using employees' ideas on how to do the job rather than always projecting the "my way is the best way" image
- Being totally approachable so as to build something beyond a formal superior-subordinate relationship.

LEARN HOW TO DELEGATE

Regarding managerial delegation, all of the following observations are significant:

- Failure to delegate, according to most subordinates, is a common managerial error
- Sound delegation is a key determinant of the long-term growth and development of subordinates
- The true nature of delegation is not always clearly understood
- In addition to contributing to people's growth and development, delegation is a way of maximizing the use of a person's skill and ability, triggering motivation, and freeing the manager to manage, as opposed to becoming overly involved in details
- Delegation is a means by which we develop active, independent and responsible subordinates.

There are many credible reasons why, given certain circumstances, managers do not always delegate and why subordinates may not accept delegation. The bottom-line issue, however, is that properly paced and managed delegation is a hallmark of consistently effective leadership.

Note that delegation is not dumping activities on people to perform, it is not imposing what are perceived as arbitrary standards on people and then applying pressure to have them met, it is not abdication or avoidance of decisions, and it does not mean that the manager loses control.

Delegation does mean knowing how to handle and distribute responsibility, authority and accountability.

Assigning Responsibility: The assigning of responsibility is the phase of delegation which over the years has received the greatest emphasis. Most managers give their people a clear indication of the duties or tasks they are to perform. Similarly, most employees could give a quite adequate description of their job in terms of "operations." In assigning responsibility, however, the manager must go beyond the typical job description and specify what results are expected from the work. It is this latter area that management has most often been remiss.

In defining results expected, one must consider the following questions: For what do we pay people? Do we pay them for working some number of hours during which time they are expected to perform certain tasks, or are we trying to achieve certain specified results through the performance of these tasks? The latter is much more logical. Accordingly, Hank Jones's job amounts to more than running a drill press or assembling component parts; instead, he is responsible for producing a given quantity of parts, for meeting certain quality requirements, for informing the supervisor when materials are in low supply, and so on. Similarly, the job of the production control manager goes beyond the design and day-to-day administration of a production-control program. The stated responsibility should also include minimizing lost time due to parts shortages, establishing the most economical work flow and equipment utilization, scheduling so that manufacturing occurs in the most economic lot sizes, and working with line managers on a continual basis to identify and overcome material flow problems. Delegation of responsibility requires a clear understanding and agreement between a manager and subordinates as to:

- The activities or tasks they are responsible for performing
- The areas of the job in which they are responsible or accountable for achieving results
- The specific results for which they are accountable in each area
- The way performance will be measured in each area of responsibility.

Granting Authority: A manager cannot grant authority without incurring some personal managerial and leadership obligations at the same time. The process of granting authority can be divided into two phases: preliminary planning and continuing support. Assuming understanding and agreement have been reached concerning the results expected, the planning phase of granting authority involves the following:

- Having the subordinates present their ideas and plans as to how the desired results can best be achieved
- Raising questions, suggesting possible alternatives, and opening discussion in order to help them explore all aspects of the situation
- Helping subordinates identify potential problems that might arise and develop solutions to overcome them
- Reaching mutual agreement on the proposed course of action to be followed.

The continuing support phase of granting authority was summarized by Drucker:

> The manager has responsibility downward, to his subordinate managers. He has first to make sure they know and understand what is demanded of them. He has to help them set their own objectives. Then he has to help them reach these objectives. He is, therefore, responsible for their getting the tools, the staff, the information they need. He has to help them to do better.[1]

The granting of authority is a blending of two factors: a subordinate's skills, abilities, knowledge and potential to contribute, and a manager's guidance, counsel and help. According to Nathaniel Cantor:

> The manager is responsible for helping the assistant to discover how he can perform his own objectives more effectively and how to make the best use of his potentialities to carry out his, the subordinate's assigned responsibilities.[2]

Creating Accountability: Accountability on the part of the subordinate is the end production of delegation, and without this accountability, there is no true delegation. If a manager has been careful in assigning responsibility and granting authority, then the recipients must be held accountable for the results (good or bad) of their activities.

Performance Appraisal: Two of the main purposes of a coaching and development program should be to lay the groundwork for future improvement and to stimulate employees' desire for such improvement. The chances are good that these objectives will not be accomplished if performance appraisal dwells too heavily on the negative. People have a maximum tolerance level for the amount of criticism they can accept, whether it is aimed at several areas of performance or just one or two. Once this level is reached, further criticism merely makes employees defensive to the point of rejecting the manager's viewpoint.

Managers undertaking a performance review must especially guard against the tendency to overemphasize the negative aspects of performance in a particular area where they would like to see improvement. Instead, once it has been agreed that the area in question is an important one, the emphasis should be on developing plans for improvement. A second caution: avoid trying to accomplish too much, too soon. If there are several areas of concern, then the one or two most important issues should receive attention first and the rest be left for another time. Finally, remember that the negative effects produced by too much criticism cannot be offset by sandwiching in a few complimentary remarks here and there.

In addition, it should be remembered that like the rest of the management function, performance appraisal works best—i.e., eventually results in improved performance—when specific goals and plans for achieving them are established.[3]

Lastly, intentionally or not, many appraisal systems end up focusing on possible wage/salary action, rather than on improvement of future performance. Certainly, rewarding people on the basis of performance is important and should not be underemphasized. However, as soon as the wage/salary issue comes into play, planning for improvement tends to take a back seat. This would suggest that salary and performance reviews should be separated. Not only is such separation desirable, but the review for improving performance should be held first, thus ensuring that definite plans for improvement will be made, which in turn lays the groundwork for the wage/salary decision itself.

Coaching Programs: Effective coaching is a day-to-day, not a once-a-year activity. The more time that managers spend in a supportive role with subordinates, rather than doing the work or telling them how to do it, the better the results will be. Their function should be one of discussing problems, getting agreement on objectives, and helping facilitate accomplishment of results by subordinates. Therefore, the process of coaching is a continuous and informal one which takes place as the need arises. This is not to suggest that a once-a-year formal review is not desirable. Indeed, this type of review has its advantages. Too often, however, it becomes a substitute for the day-to-day interaction between managers and their people.

Another weakness in many coaching systems is that the subordinate's role is a passive rather than a participative one. A successful program requires involvement and commitment on the part of the employee, so that the latter will be truly motivated to improve his or her performance. In this, as in any other area of work, the manager should tell employees what is expected of them; provide assistance and support when needed, as well as feedback on their performance; and reward them on the basis of results.

LEADERSHIP CHECK LIST

1. Have I made it clear what is expected in terms of results? Do I discuss these results with employees?
2. Have I let the employees know where they stand?
3. Do the employees know how to do the work?
4. Have I done a good job of training and development?
5. Do I give employees all the support I can?
6. What have I done or not done to cultivate positive personal relationships?
7. Do the employees know why their jobs are important, how they fit into the overall company structure, and the ramifications of poor performance?
8. Are employees kept informed on what is going on in the department and the company? Not just "need to know" items, but "nice to know"?
9. Do employees have adequate freedom in which to work?
10. Are employees too often put in a defensive position regarding performance?
11. What have I done to get employees mentally and emotionally involved in their jobs?
12. Have employees been allowed to participate in setting goals and deciding means of achieving them?
13. Have good aspects of performance received adequate and periodic recognition?
14. Do I accentuate the positive instead of the negative?
15. Have I shown adequate concern for employees as individuals? For their personal goals?
16. Am I flexible about listening to employees and giving them a chance to implement ideas and suggestions?
17. Have I ever consciously assessed employees' strengths and weaknesses with the idea of structuring the work to capitalize on the former?
18. Are employees adequately and reasonably challenged?

REFERENCES

1. Peter Drucker, *The Practice of Management* (New York: Harper Brothers, 1954), p. 143.
2. Nathaniel Cantor, *The Learning Process for Managers* (New York: Harper Brothers, 1958).
3. Herbert H. Meyer, Emanuel Key, J.R.P. French, Jr., "Split Roles in Performance Appraisal," *Harvard Business Review*, Vol. 43, No. 1, 1965.

Burt K. Scanlan is Professor of Management, College of Business Administration, University of Oklahoma, Norman, Oklahoma.

4.
THE EFFECTIVE MANAGER: SEMI-TOUGH

Mary Miles

> Leadership isn't simple. The constructive use of authority entails the
> ability to formulate clear goals and to determine what steps are necessary
> to achieve them, including getting people to do what you want. The
> requirements are hard work, self-confidence, good communication skills,
> and a secure sense of your own strengths.

"Leadership is a very simple proposition" wrote *Boston Globe* reporter David
Nyham in a recent column on the presidential candidates. "The test for
leadership is basic: *How well can you impose your will on others?*"

Clear, strong leadership is essential to achieve objectives and realize
corporate goals. How to go about imposing your will on your subordinates, in
order to reach those goals, is a different story. Those who wear the mantle of
authority easily seem to be in the minority. These fortunate few don't agonize
over how their style is perceived by subordinates; what people think of them is
less important than getting the job done. How do they do it? Are they incurring
respect and loyalty—or fear and discontent—on the part of their subordinates?

If you are new to your management position, you may be uncomfortable in
this role. You know you want to be on the fast track, but are you a leader? A
man recently put in charge of a large MIS department says, "I know the job: I
know what I want done and how it should be done; and I know who should do
it. But it's difficult for me to tell people what to do. I want to be a tough boss,
but I don't want to be feared. Can I have it both ways?"

Instead of focusing on work goals, this manager is wasting valuable time and
energy competing in a popularity contest, forgetting that a subordinate is an
employee *beneath* the boss in rank, power, and importance.

Trying to maintain a "nice-guy" attitude while cracking the whip can drive
you crazy. Constantly worrying about your image is very stressful. But the most
troublesome aspect of assuming power usually stems from anxieties about what
others think. You may be one of those people who has a difficult time reconcil-

ing the use of power with being a likeable person. If you have mixed emotions about how tough you should be, you're probably in trouble. It may be time to dispense with that eternal winning smile long enough to ponder ways of becoming an effective leader.

More easily said than done, true. It's a task that requires scrupulous self-examination. To get some pointers on developing a management style that allows you to do your job effectively without losing self-respect and the respect of others, *Computer Decisions* asked Madeline Klein, a consultant (M. I. Klein, Scarsdale, N.Y.) and seminar developer/leader for the American Management Associations (AMA), the following questions.

Question: Is it possible to be a strong boss and a popular, well-liked person?

Answer: Yes. People respond to you in terms of what you do and how you do it. If you set up clear goals and involve subordinates in these goals, they will become committed because they "own" part of the goals. They will follow you not because they like you or don't like you, but because they understand you and what you're doing.

Question: Aren't there times when you must be especially tough, when you have to fire someone, chew someone out, or tell a team its efforts have not paid off?

Answer: If by "tough" you mean making decisions that may be unpopular, certainly. That's what leadership is about. No matter how deeply a boss believes in bringing people into the decision-making process, in reality only the boss can make the final decision. But it's the *way* the decision's made that counts. For example, firing someone: If you've established a discipline process that ensures that subordinates are aware of the consequences of certain behavior, and someone chooses not to follow these rules, then it's up to *you* to endorse and enforce your rules. When you set up a consistent system, subordinates know what to expect and can respect you for your actions.

Naturally, during times of pressure (when the business is not going well, for example), it's tougher to be responsive to employees. That's when you're really tested as a leader.

Question: Is it possible to learn how to be a tougher, more decisive boss?

Answer: Yes, but it can't be done just by taking courses. You learn how to use power effectively and positively by building your own self-esteem. If you have a strong self-image, you can combat the rejection or disapproval you may get as a result of your actions.

Question: Are there some managers who are just too "nice" to be effective bosses?

Answer: Being a "nice" boss doesn't have anything to do with being an effective boss. Being *secure* has a lot to do with it. You can be a strong, decisive leader who makes unpopular decisions and be a likeable person, or you can be indecisive and weak and be a nasty person.

Question: What about maintaining the proper "distance" between the boss and subordinates?

Answer: The transition from co-worker to boss is extremely difficult. You want to be open and sensitive, but you are no longer a peer. It can be dangerous to continually emphasize that you are now on a higher level.

That's sort of playing your trump card. At the same time, you must maintain a degree of objectivity and professionalism. This means that while you're establishing the goals and standards of performance for your subordinates, you must do a lot of careful listening.

Question: Are there any specific measures you can take to find out how you are performing as a boss?

Answer: Absolutely. Give your people the opportunity to do a regular performance appraisal of you. Such evaluations must be anonymous and totally nonthreatening to employees' job security. You don't want to put them on the spot, because then they'll only tell you what they think you want to hear.

Question: You have to be strong to benefit from that kind of feedback, don't you?

Answer: Yes. Unfortunately, there's a sort of Catch-22 here. The secure managers who don't need such devices are polishing up their acts. Those who really need to hear the truth, the insecure managers, may never be able to accept it.

Leadership isn't simple. The constructive use of authority entails the ability to formulate clear goals and to determine what steps are necessary to achieve them, including getting people to do what you want. The requirements are hard work, self-confidence, good communication skills, and a secure sense of you own strengths. You also need respect for others and a willingness to listen, evaluate, and take appropriate action. The payoff can be very gratifying—to your organization, your subordinates, and, most of all, to you.

5.
SPOTLIGHT ON LEADERSHIP TRAITS

Rodger D. Collons

> Leadership research has not revealed a single trait that is possessed by all
> successful leaders, but a number of characteristics have been identified
> that are common to many of them.

For many years leadership researchers have attempted to identify a set of
traits that could be used to predict leadership success. Tall stature appeared to
be a good predictor, as evident in Charles DeGaulle. However, the diminutive
stature of his countryman, Napoleon, destroyed that assumption. Similarly,
the slenderness of Abraham Lincoln was placed in question by the rotund
Winston Churchill. In fact, contrary evidence has been found for all leadership
characteristics identified to date. Therefore, the wise manager should be extremely cautious in rejecting an otherwise promising candidate for a leadership
position merely because of the absence of a particular trait the manager feels is
essential.

Although leadership research has not revealed a single trait that is possessed
by all successful leaders, a number of characteristics have been identified that
are common to many of them. These include verbal fluency, problem-solving
ability, insights into group problems, flexibility, intelligence, acceptance of
responsibility, social skills, and awareness of self and surroundings.

Verbal Fluency—Verbal fluency is more than the possession of an extensive
vocabulary; it is the ability to communicate in the language of the led. Jimmy
Hoffa and Winston Churchill communicated differently, however, they both
had complete command of their audiences.

Ability to Solve Problems—The ability to solve the problems of the led, or
to contribute to their problem solving, is another characteristic of many effective leaders. Some leaders even contribute to problem solving by "not doing"

rather than by "doing." Einstein's boss, for example, contributed to the implementation of the theory of relativity by not inhibiting Einstein and by preventing others from inhibiting him.

Awareness of Needs—The effective leader understands the stated and unstated needs of the led and know how to satisfy those needs. For example, union members need a leader whom they can trust to communicate their needs for job security and job satisfaction. Likewise, a congregation needs a minister who understands and can articulate their spiritual needs.

Flexibility—A flexible leader is able to adapt the organization to meet changed needs with minimal unsettlement to the led. There is nothing more distressing or more destructive to creative problem solving than having a great idea summarily rejected because "That's not the way we do it here."

Intelligence—An effective leader need not be a genius. However, the members of the group should feel that the leader has the ability to help them fulfill their personal needs. A word of caution: there is a growing body of research which shows that the leader who is much more intelligent than the group will not be as effective as the leader who is perceived as just a bit more intelligent than the led.

Acceptance of Responsibility—The willingness to accept responsibility is another characteristic of many successful leaders. A group likes to know that the leader is getting the job done. Leaders must deliver unless the group is willing to "protect" the leader by taking on those leadership tasks which the leader fails to carry through.

Social Skills—Members of a group should not be put down in the eyes of their colleagues. A leader with tact, diplomacy, and the ability to relate to the group is valued by group members and therefore contributes to better performance.

Awareness of Self and Surroundings—Self-insight, sympathetic understanding, and keen awareness of the surrounding environment have all been found to be associated with effective leadership. Self-insight is a rare quality which is often mistaken for weakness. In fact, it is the rarest and probably the most important of all leadership qualities. If we are shaped by our experiences, yet do not understand how these experiences shaped our thinking, then we cannot understand the basis for our decisions.

RECOMMENDATIONS FOR MANAGEMENT

It is important to emphasize that when looking closely at people, one should realize that each person has a host of individual human characteristics. Different people have different human characteristics in varying degrees. These different characteristics make up the entire person or personality, and it is the entire person who is selected for a leadership position. It is extremely rare, if not impossible, for a person to possess all the leadership characteristics identified in this article; have them fully developed to the peak of perfection; and, in addition, have the technical background, education, training, and experience necessary to master a particular job.

The characteristics outlined in this article are desirable leadership characteristics which managers should keep in mind when selecting and developing leaders. However, they are no panacea and should be used only for the insights they provide, not as predictors in the complex responsibility of matching a leader to a particular leadership position.

Leadership effectiveness depends upon the personal characteristics of the individual, the character of the task assigned, and the place of the individual in the organizational hierarchy.

The challenge of managing is to select people with character who have genuine interest in managing and who also have the potential for developing those positive characteristics which have not fully matured. Management bears the responsibility of positive leadership skills. This is accomplished by assigning increased management responsibility, by consistently and regularly reinforcing positive leadership skills, and by quickly and quietly nipping negative techniques before they become habits.

Rodger D. Collons is the James S. Bingay Professor of Creative Leadership, The American College.

6.
20 CRITICAL COMPETENCIES FOR MANAGERS

Harold T. Smith

> To be effective, a manager should concentrate attention on developing the twenty competencies presented here. These areas will yield the greatest results.

One good way to increase your effectiveness as an administrative manager and as a person is to become familiar with the Pareto Principle and apply it to all aspects of your life. The Pareto Principle is the old 80-20 rule. In any given group of items, most of the items (say 80%) are relatively insignificant; whereas a small proportion (perhaps 20%) are extremely vital or critical and yield the most return.

For example, in reading professional journals, you may find that you gain only a few significant ideas from an article. However, those one or two ideas may be vital to you in successfully implementing a new system or in counseling a problem employee.

Two years ago, in thinking about the Pareto Principle, I wondered what activities are critical to the administrative management position. I decided that one way to find out would be to study Certified Administrative Managers to determine what abilities or competencies they consider to lie within that twenty percent critical area. C.A.M.'s are an elite group of administrative managers who have demonstrated their ability to achieve results. To be effective then, any manager could benefit by concentrating his or her attention on this list of critical abilities or competencies.

To set up the study, selected members of the Administrative Management Society were first interviewed to determine important abilities for administrative managers. From this list, a questionnaire containing seventeen general and seventy-three specific competencies was developed. A panel of twelve C.A.M.'s located across the country selected twenty of these specific competencies as critical. Then, a questionnaire containing the twenty abilities was mailed to four hundred fifty-seven members of the Academy of Certified

Administrative Managers who were asked to rate the items by categories of importance. About sixty-two percent or two hundred eighty-two members of the Academy responded.

Table 1 shows the list of twenty competencies that were judged to be critical for administrative managers. Each competency is ranked, with 1 being the most important and twenty the least important, and is classified by the degree of importance (super critical, highly critical, and critical).

Four observations about the twenty competencies are important. First, competencies related to communicating and working with people tend to be considered more important by the C.A.M.'s than technical abilities. The four top-ranked, super critical abilities were: (1) listen actively, (2) give clear, effective instructions, (3) accept your share of responsibility for problems, and (4) identify real problems. Even accountants and systems managers place less importance on expertise in their fields than on skills of working with people.

Second, most of the twenty abilities and all of the four rated as "Super Critical" are general types of skills that result from experience and general programs of education. Training which zeroes in on these specific competencies could prove to be beneficial.

Third, the single most important competency for a manager to develop is to learn to listen actively to his/her people. Active listening shows the person who is talking that you care and that you consider him/her to be important.

Finally, professional development activities, i.e., participating in professional activities such as seminars and reading professional periodicals and books, appear to be of marginal significance to C.A.M.'s since this item is ranked number twenty. This finding is somewhat alarming. If administrative managers hope to attain a position of influence as we move toward the office of the future, they are going to have to remain alert to dynamic changes that are even now occuring at a rapid pace.

Applying the Pareto Principle further, I decided to look more closely at the C.A.M.'s who have been most successful. By studying how managers who are on a fast promotional track view these competencies, I hoped to gain insight into managerial abilities needed for success. The criteria for determining which C.A.M.'s should be included in this fast track group for further study were (1) salaries in excess of $30,000, (2) age less than 50 (and less than 40), and (3) management level.

Four subgroups, set up in accordance with these criteria, were analyzed. In general, managers in these subgroups tended to place a different level of importance on certain competencies as compared with the total group. For sake of simplicity, only the finding for the subgroup of C.A.M.'s who earned in excess of $30,000, were less than forty years of age, and were members of top management will be presented. This group will be identified as young, top managers.

These young, top managers identified the following four competencies as "super critical" and ranked all four of them as tied for the first position of importance:

1. Identify the real problem
2. Manage time
3. Shift priorities
4. Explain work

In other words, this group of young top managers places a premium on managing time, which also means shifting priorities as necessary, working on real problems rather than symptoms; and explaining to their subordinates what is expected so that the subordinates can move on their own initiative. To be effective, a manager should concentrate attention on developing the twenty competencies presented in Table 1. Applying the 80-20 rule, particular attention should be give to the twenty percent or top four or five of these abilities as identified by the fast track managers. These areas will yield the greatest results.

The top four abilities identified by the fast track managers will be discussed below to point out how you might implement these.

Identify the real problem. Think about the symptoms and causes of the problem and gather preliminary information to help you identify the real problem. Then discuss the problem situation with those persons who are closest to it. Also talk with outside persons who can give you an objective perspective. Finally, write out your key findings and tentative statement of the problem.

Table 1.
20 Critical Managerial Competencies

Importance Rating	Survey Rank & Competency
Super Critical	1. Listen Actively 2. Give Clear, Effective Instructions 3. Accept Your Share of Responsibility for Problems 4. Identify Real Problem
Highly Critical	5. Manage Time; Set Priorities 6. Give Recognition for Excellent Performance 7. Communicate Decisions to Employees 8. Communicate Effectively (Orally) 9. Shift Priorities If Necessary 10. Explain Work 11. Obtain and Provide Feedback in Two-Way Communication Sessions

Critical

12. Write Effectively
13. Prepare Action Plan
14. Define Job Qualifications
15. Effectively Implement Organizational Change
16. Explain and Use Cost Reduction Methods
17. Prepare and Operate Within a Budget
18. Develop Written Goals
19. Justify New Personnel and Capital Equipment
20. Participate in Seminars and Read

Managing time effectively and shift priorities as necessary. Apply the 80-20 rule to your time, assigning priorities to those activities which will return the greatest benefit to you. Write down the tasks you should do each day and assign a priority designation (A, B, or C) for each item according to its importance. Do "A" priority items first each day. Delegate or procrastinate those items which are least important.

In addition, develop a daily time scheduling and management plan that is workable for you. Spend at least fifteen minutes per day in planning your day. A good idea is to keep a time log to periodically review how you are spending your time. Finally, eliminate unnecessary interruptions and distractions.

You should also set up a list of long-range goals which are readily available. Then develop intermediate and short-range objectives which will help you attain your goals. Consider your long-term goals when assigning priorities to your daily or weekly objectives and shift priorities to keep them meaningful and relevant.

Explain work. Explain specifically and in detail what you expect of your subordinates. Keep in mind expected results, delegated authority, reporting relationships, and progress reviews. So you and your employees have a clear idea of their functions, compare written statements of objectives prepared by you and your subordinates and resolve any differences.

Point out what criteria you will use for measurement of their performance. As employees become ready to assume more responsibility, allow them to move on their own. Conduct periodic reviews to keep informed of progress and problems.

Listen actively. Develop genuine interest in your employees and in their activities. Ask yourself, what is this person really trying to say? Check your understanding by restating in your own words what you think you understand. It also helps to pay attention to verbal and non-verbal cues. As well, use pauses, non-verbal cues, and neutral comments to express your desire to hear more from the person. Try to avoid giving advice and allow the person to develop his/her own solutions.

These are a few specific actions you can take with regard to the critical competencies we have been discussing. No doubt you can add to this list. The key point is that the application of the Pareto Principle to your life through concentrating on critical competencies can help you to become more effective as an administrative manager.

Dr. Harold T. Smith, C.A.M., is an associate professor of business education at Brigham Young University, Provo, Utah. Dr. Smith is also a consultant and has co-authored a textbook, The Administrative Manager.

7.
THIS TEST SPOTS LEADERS

Charles A. Cerami

Clues to a manager's potential can be found in the way he or she is handling the job now. This questionnaire can help you to narrow the search.

One of the most rewarding accomplishments in business is identifying the men who really make an operation go.

Whenever a promotion or replacement has to be made or an expansion program forces you to pick men who will have more responsibility, you may discover that no one is quite sure which executives have been the driving forces and which have merely moved along on the momentum of the others. Both types are needed, but the few real pushers and risk-takers are the heart of any business.

It is hard enough to find men who have the knowledge, experience and judgement to run things—the ability to manage; it is much harder to spot those few who have the will to manage. Usually, it is only after a spectacular success or a resounding failure that a company recognizes who really likes the feel of the helm.

This questionnaire can help you to narrow the search.

It will not spot the real managers unerringly. Nothing will do that. But it will serve as a check list to prevent oversights and call your attention to areas that usually make the difference between the men who can take charge and those who may make fine crew members, but who shrink from lone decisions.

Whenever one of your subordinates is being considered for a job that will require more independent action, ask yourself these questions about him:

1. Think back to the last several times something went wrong in his department. Did others get the impression that this man was:

( ) a. largely responsible for the mistakes?
( ) b. only slightly involved?
( ) c. entirely free from blame?

2. When he has complaints, does he discuss them mainly with:

( ) a. men at his own level or below?
( ) b. his superior?

3. Recalling the last few times that this man came up with suggestions, did they tend to be about:

( ) a. objectives?
( ) b. methods for achieving objectives?

4. With his colleagues and subordinates, is he:

( ) a. completely and consistently friendly?
( ) b. slightly aloof on some subjects?

5. When he talks about important company decisions, does he refer to them as something that:

( ) a. we did?
( ) b. they did?

6. In his work has more than half of his time been spent handling:

( ) a. recurring subjects that vary mainly in detail?
( ) b. subjects to which entirely new answers have to be devised repeatedly?

7. After he has expressed a definite point of view on a decision that is hanging fire, does he:

( ) a. keep pushing hard to make it go his way?
( ) b. quickly defer to the majority if the tide is against him?

8. Since he took up his present responsibilities, do you have the feeling that:

( ) a. he has fitted in with the way his department operates?
( ) b. some of his colleagues have changed their ways to suit him?

9. Whenever he has been unhappy about something, have his complaints
    centered on:

    ( ) a. a specific person or action?
    ( ) b. the way things are going in general?

10. If an idea is presented to him and he disapproves, does he:

    ( ) a. point out flaws?
    ( ) b. suggest another course?

11. Whenever he has a dispute with a colleague, does it tend:

    ( ) a. to persist strongly?
    ( ) b. to smolder?
    ( ) c. to flare up and then end?

12. When he has to go ahead with a course of action that some of his
    subordinates oppose, does he seem:

    ( ) a. to be cheerfully oblivious of the opposition?
    ( ) b. to be genuinely troubled at having to force his way?
    ( ) c. to be reluctantly determined to go ahead anyway?

Consult the test answers to see how the profile of this man, as outlined by
your answers, compares with the type who stands up best under the strain of
leadership.

TEST ANSWERS

1. Either a. or b. is the answer to hope for, depending on what level of
responsibility this man now has in his department. A certain number of
mistakes is going to be made in every operation. The man who is judged to be
responsible for these is also likely to be the chief cause of the triumphs—although credit for success is often harder to trace.

2. b. is preferred. The man who goes to his superior with a complaint
means to get something done. The one who chews it over with everyone else is
seldom the real managerial type.

3. a. has the edge. Suggesting methods for achieving objectives is all to the
good. But when you find the rare individual who thinks along with top
management about where the company ought to be going, you have probably
spotted a man who can handle bigger problems.

4. b. is preferable. A man who is raised above others, given a greater

responsibility, must inevitably do things that tread on toes. The size and politeness of modern business practice often obscures this for long periods of time. But that only sharpens the distinction when the boss has to criticize one man, promote another, transfer a third, and perhaps even fire a person who had come to think of him as a friend. A manager who can't help becoming personally involved with the men around him will hurt himself and his subordinates much more when those difficult moments come.

5.   a. is obviously the answer to hope for on this one. But it is surprising how few executives really think of themselves as part of management. At a recent conference where several groups of experienced businessmen debated the responsibilities of management, it was noted that very few of the statements reflected a feeling that the speaker was part of the managerial circle. One man after another stressed the need for changes in management, but most of them seemed startled when reminded that they were actually calling for changes in themselves. So if your answer reveals that the man mentally includes himself in the praise and blame for what the company is doing, you have spotted an important trait.

6.   b. is the response wanted here, and again it is a readily apparent one. Note in this case, however, that the less favorable answer does not necessarily reflect against the man's will to take responsibility. It may mean only that he has not yet been given the chance. But it is still a warning that even though his present work may be very important in its own way, a change to duties requiring creative decision-making will be a very new departure for the individual. As a group of British business experts— Management Selection, Ltd.—recently pointed out, more and more executives today work on programmed subjects that are routine or capable of delegation. But it is still the nonprogrammed areas that separate the managers from the managed.

7.   The man who earns an a. answer on this question will make things run, although he may often seem a nuisance to those around him. To understand why, imagine a whole management team made up of agreeable fellows who are quick to understand and adjust to a majority view. This need not mean yes men, for there is not even one dominant figure on hand to whom they must nod. They are just a fine group of entirely reasonable men. Will the company ever move, grow, adjust to new situations? Certainly not.

8.   b. is the best in this case. Managing involves give and take, it is true. So it is not suggested that you look for a man who must dominate in every situation. That, in fact, is often a sign of insecurity. But a compliant individual who quickly senses the accepted pattern of behavior in a new environment and brings nothing of his own to it is like an empty vessel that can only take in and cannot give out. Most men who will ultimately make good managers are apt to win some concessions from others in the way things are done.

9.   It may be a surprise that the preferred answer is a. The other choice—complaining about things in general—is not at all a sign of broad-guage thinking. It is the mark of either a malcontent or a fuzzy thinker who knows that something is wrong, but doesn't focus on just what it is.

Picking out the specific person or action that is at the core of his complaint is a sign that this man is at least trying to think through the problem on his own.

10. Here the answer b. is the mark of the better manager. Many men of good judgement play an important role as staff members by calling attention to dangers in a suggested plan. But only a few among them are equally anxious to take the next step and propose how the approach can be improved.

11. c. is the response to hope for. It means that the person has a knack for confronting others with a strong difference of opinion and yet not leaving a permanent scar. A man who doggedly continues to feud with a colleague or who lets bad feelings simmer destructively below the surface is either incapable of making his point convincingly or too lacking in confidence to accept a defeat.

12. c. is again the first choice. Anyone who seems to care nothing for the approval of other men may be putting on an act; if not, he is dangerously self-willed. At the other extreme, the sensitive man who suffers from the knowledge that what he is doing seems wrong to some of the persons around him will probably end up with serious physical symptoms if he has to face such a task often. The manager who is likely to weather this recurring discomfort best is the one who notes the disapproval, weighs it carefully, then reluctantly goes ahead without too long a period of anguish.

THE UNIQUE QUALITY

If you find that the man you are looking at merited the preferred answer in eight or nine of these situations, he probably can stand solo responsibility.

Perhaps you noticed that half of these questions were related to conflicts, differences of opinion, or times when things go wrong. That is not because half of an executive's life is necessarily involved with trouble. It is because trying times are the test of a forceful manager. Many men sparkle when things are going well. They are of great importance in rounding out all the skills that make a company whole and consistent. But they may have only enough drive to keep things rolling after someone else has given the big push. The men who can keep their operations moving when the climb gets steep, or who can get them started again after they have sputtered and stopped, have a unique gift for which there is no substitute.

8.
TRAITS THAT WILL
TAKE YOU TO THE TOP

Nation's Business

> Do you hope to be the successor to a successful executive? Here is the way
> some of them describe the qualities they want to see—or not to see—in
> people moving up through the ranks.

Leader or non-leader? What do top company officers look for in picking
successors, or candidates for major promotion in their firms? What traits turn
them off?

A *Nation's Business* survey compiles a long list of positive factors that such
executives think a successor should have. Intelligence, drive, willingness to
work hard and leadership capabilities are some of the traits most frequently
mentioned.

On the negative side, many say the "poor personality" syndrome— defined
by one savings and loan association president as "arrogance, know-it-all
attitude and lack of patience"—doom an otherwise capable subordinate from
moving higher in corporate ranks. Stupidity, impulsiveness, poor judgement
and lack of integrity are also widely viewed as the kiss of death.

T. Vincent Learson, chairman of International Business Machines Corp.,
Armonk, N.Y., looks for "an intelligent person, who is people- and results-
oriented and has the capacity to lead others." On the negative side, Mr.
Learson thinks "indecisiveness, business immaturity and a person who lacks
the courage of his or her convictions" are things to watch out
for.

"Judgement, leadership, intelligence, rationality and technical
competence" rate high as vital qualities for Franklin A. Cole, president of
Walter E. Heller International Corp., Chicago, Ill. "Less-than-broad integrity, rashness and unwillingness to accept responsibility" stand out on the
minus side, he thinks.

An aspiring executive "should have a good track record of managerial and
supervisory effectiveness," comments Joseph L. Gray, president of Gray

Manufacturing Co., Inc., St. Joseph, Mo. Also, Mr. Gray says, he should be "hungry, ambitious, stable, hard-nosed" and should have an "understanding of people and of economic principles."

A serious health or family problem, and lack of integrity, perspective or sense of direction are traits he wouldn't want in a candidate for a major promotion.

"A broad, general knowledge of the industry, ability to manage people and the sense of need for social and community involvement" are three top positive criteria in the mind of Louis W. Menk, chairman of Burlington Northern Inc., St. Paul, Minn. He adds that "a difficult personal life, inability to delegate authority and being a specialist never involved in general management" would count against an aspirant.

"The most important attribute," remarks Rodney C. Gott, chairman of AMF, Inc. White Plains, N.Y., "is a very general one and also the hardest to find. That is that intangible quality of leadership. It involves intellectual energy, curiosity, consideration of others and a sense of humor. Too many times, men reach the top and wear the epaulets, but there is no true leadership underneath."

High on the list of Winston V. Morrow Jr., president and chairman of Avis, Inc., Garden City, N.Y., is "the ability to make fast decisions only after complete reviews of the facts." He also rates "innovation (a strong requisite in a service industry) and the ability to motivate subordinates" as highly desirable traits. "Indecisiveness, resistance to new concepts and inaccessibility" can hurt the chances of a man in line for a promotion, he says.

"BULLDOGS, NOT POMERANIANS"

F.T. Blake Jr., president and treasurer of Geo. F. Blake, Inc., Worcester, Mass., prefers candidates with "a lot of drive" who are "self-starters." He says: "I want bulldogs, not Pomeranians." He adds: "I want no 'yes' men. I want constructive idea men. I want leaders, not drivers, I want loyal, honest trustworthy believers in the free enterprise system."

Walter E. Hoadley, executive vice president of the Bank of America, San Francisco, Calif., makes this statement: "The major attributes for executive leadership in the years ahead will be optimism, a sense of balance between profitable and social performance, a broad understanding of both economic and social forces in the world as well as the national economy, ability to lead while reacting quickly to changing conditions, and an acute sensitivity to changing human values and personal needs of customers and employees."

Anyone considered for a major promotion, Mr. Hoadley says, "should not be inflexible in his opinions, too authoritative in dealing with subordinates, destructively critical or without principled convictions."

Like many executives responding to the survey, F. Ritter Shumway, honorary chairman of Sybron Corp., Rochester, N.Y., thinks a prime qualification is the ability "to get along with and handle people." Being "technically skilled, sincere, credible and factual also are important," he says. Chief drawbacks, in his mind, are "arrogance, being impressed with status symbols, and impetuosity."

John W. Eckman, president of Rorer-Amchem, Inc., Port Washington, Pa., thinks a good managerial prospect will be adept at handling problems. "He should have the ability to perceive the fundamentals and to reach a creative solution," Mr. Eckman says, "and the far-sightedness to anticipate the problem." An inability to get along with people and "inflexibility" are basic deficiencies for the up-and-coming executive, he says.

One positive attribute would be "a total commitment to the interests of our stockholders," comments M.A. Ellsworth, president of Fluor Corp., Los Angeles, Calif. "Another would be the ability to understand the rapidly changing economic-social environment in which the company operates. We would not want a person too preoccupied with very short-run, apparent results when they might conflict with the long-run best interests of the corporation."

O.E. Scherer, president of Associated Baby Services, Inc., New York, City, seems to come as close as any one executive in summing up what businessmen look for in subordinates. "Drive, a progressive attitude, demonstrated sound analytical judgement, and demonstrated ability to motivate others constructively" are his positive factors. Characteristics to avoid are "poor judgement, lack of confidence in self, company or peers, and lack of understanding of others' needs."

Arnold C. Greenberg, executive vice president of Coleco Industries, Inc., Hartford, Conn., says his company looks for "intensely hard-working" managers who have "entrepreneurial instincts, aggressiveness, loyalty." Traits that are not desirable include "a low golf handicap and a desire to leave work at five or five-thirty P.M."

"Leadership capabilities" rate high with John H. Lumpkin, chairman of South Carolina National Bank, Columbia, S.C. He says: "Obviously, such an individual must have a good solid intellect, but he doesn't have to be brilliant; I much prefer common sense."

"NO BOOZE"

"Smart, experienced, a 'people-related' man," fills the bill for C.M. Hoover, chairman and president of Roper Corp., Kankakee, Ill. He emphasizes: "No booze and no 'big spender' image."

"High character and integrity" is a quality J. Henry Smith, president of the Equitable Life Assurance Society of the United States, New York City, looks for. Also important are the ability "to adapt to new situations, quickly grasp essentials of new problems and deal with people."

On the negative side, Mr. Smith thinks lack of the above qualities would hold an aspiring executive back.

Franklin Briese, chairman of the Minnesota Mutual Life Insurance Co., St. Paul, Minn., rates "the necessary courage (guts) to make vital decisions for the good of the company" as one of the most important attributes in a successful manager.

Some answering the survey reduce the requirements to short phrases: The head of a Midwestern manufacturing concern says a successor should have a "sales personality and humility." A Connecticut banker calls his ideal candidate a "progressive conservative."

In listing traits that turn them off, many top officers rule out managers who strike them as too complacent, lazy, timid, careless or "soft-minded." But at the other end of the personality spectrum, an equally large number say the overly aggressive, abrasive, self-centered egotist whose personal ambition exceeds his loyalty to the company is not their cup of tea either. Business is basically a team effort, they seem to be saying.

There are some humorous notes in the survey.

The head of a contracting firm has a quick, efficient way of weeding out possible successors. "No long hair," he says. And one company president comments, without listing anything he looks for in a successor: "The son of the chairman will succeed me as president."

9.
LEADERSHIP THEORY: SOME IMPLICATIONS FOR MANAGERS

Chester A. Schriesheim
James M. Tolliver
Orlando C. Behling

> While studying and emphasizing leadership certainly has its merits, it could be argued that there is much to be gained by treating leadership effectiveness as but one component of managerial effectiveness.

In the past seventy years more than 3,000 leadership studies have been conducted and dozens of leadership models and theories have been proposed.[1] Yet, a practicing manager who reads this literature seeking solutions to supervisory problems will rapidly become disenchanted. Although we have access to an overwhelming volume of leadership theory and research, few guidelines exist which are of use to a practitioner. Nevertheless, interest in leadership—and in those qualities which separate a successful leader from an unsuccessful one—remains unabated. In almost any book dealing with management one will find some discussion of leadership. In any company library there are numerous volumes entitled "Increasing Leadership Effectiveness," "Successful Leadership," or "How to Lead." Typical management development programs conducted within work organizations and universities usually deal with some aspect of leadership. This intensity and duration of writing on the subject and the sums spent annually on leadership training indicate that practicing managers and academicians consider good leadership essential to organizational success.

What is meant by leadership, let alone *good* leadership? Many definitions have been proposed, and it seems that most are careful to separate management from leadership. This distinction sometimes becomes blurred in everyday conversations. The first term, *management*, includes those processes both mental and physical, which result in other people executing prescribed formal duties for organizational goal attainment. It deals mainly with planning, organizing, and controlling the work of other people to achieve organizational goals.[2] This definition usually includes those aspects of managers' jobs, such as monitoring and controlling resources, which are sometimes ignored in current conceptualizations of leadership. *Leadership*, on the other hand, is a more restricted type of managerial activity, focusing on the interpersonal interactions between a leader and one or more subordinates, with the purpose of increasing organizational effectiveness.[3] In this view, leadership is a social influence process in which the leader seeks the voluntary participation of subordinates in an effort to reach organizational objectives. The key idea highlighted by a number of authors is that the subordinate's participation is voluntary.[4] This implies that the leader has brought about some change in the way subordinates want to behave. Leadership, consequently, is not only a specific process (more so than management), but also is undoubtedly political in nature. The political aspect of leadership has been discussed elsewhere, so at this point it suffices to note that a major implication of leadership's political nature is that such attempts at wielding influence will not necessarily succeed.[5] In fact, other types of managerial tasks may have a stronger influence on organizational effectiveness than those interpersonal tasks usually labeled leadership.[6]

Despite this shortcoming, the examination of leadership as it relates to interpersonal interactions is still worthwhile simply because managers may, in many cases, have more control over how they and their subordinates behave than over nonhuman aspects of their jobs (such as the amount and types of resources they are given). In addition, some information does exist concerning which leadership tactics are of use under various conditions. For this information to be of greatest use, however, practicing managers should have some concept of the direction leadership research has taken. Thus, before attempting to provide guidelines for practitioners, we shall briefly review major approaches to the subject of leadership and point out their weaknesses and limitations.

BASIC APPROACHES TO LEADERSHIP

Thinking concerning leadership has moved through three distinct periods or phases.

The trait phase. Early approaches to leadership, from the pre-Christian era to the late 1940s, emphasized the examination of leader characteristics (such as age and degree of gregariousness) in an attempt to identify a set of universal characteristics which would allow a leader to be effective in all situations. At first a few traits seemed to be universally important for successful leaders, but subsequent research yielded inconsistent results concerning these traits; in addition, research investigating a large number of other traits (about one hundred) was generally discouraging. As a result of this accumulation of negative findings and of reviews of this evidence, such as that conducted by R. M. Stogdill, the tide of opinion about the importance of traits for leadership effectiveness began to change.[7] In the late 1940s, leadership researchers began to move away from trait research. Contemporary opinion holds the trait approach in considerable disrepute and views the likelihood of uncovering a set of universal leadership effectiveness traits as essentially impossible.

The behavioral phase. With the fall of the trait approach, researchers considered alternative concepts, eventually settling on the examination of relationships between leader behaviors and subordinate satisfaction and performance.[8] During the height of the behavioral phase, dating roughly from the late 1940s to the early 1960s, several large research programs were conducted, including the Ohio State University leadership studies, a program of research which has received considerable publicity over the years.

The Ohio State studies started shortly after World War II and initially concentrated on leadership in military organizations. In one of these studies, a lengthy questionnaire was administered to B-52 bomber crews, and their answers were statistically analyzed to identify the common dimensions underlying the answers.[9] This analysis discovered two dimensions which seemed most important in summarizing the nature of the crews' perceptions about their airplane commanders' behavior toward them. Consideration was the stronger of the two factors, and it involved leader behaviors indicative of friendship, mutual trust, respect, and warmth.

The second factor was Initiation of Structure, a concept involving leader behaviors indicating that the leader organizes and designs the relationship between self and subordinates.[10]

In subsequent studies using modified versions of the original questionnaire, Consideration and Structure were found to be prime dimensions of leader behavior in situations ranging from combat flights over Korea to assembly line work.[11] In addition, studies were undertaken at Ohio State and elsewhere to compare the effects of these leader behaviors on subordinates' performance and satisfaction. A high Consideration-high Structure leadership style was, in many cases, found to lead to high performance and satisfaction. However, in a number of studies dysfunctional consequences, such as high turnover and absenteeism, accompanied these positive outcomes. In yet other situations, different combinations of Consideration and Structure (for example, low Consideration-high Structure) were found to be more effective.[12]

Similar behaviors were identified and similar results obtained in a large number of studies, such as those conducted at the University of Michigan.[13] Although the display of highly Considerate-highly Structuring behavior was sometimes found to result in positive organizational outcomes, this was not true in all of the cases or even in most of them.[14] The research, therefore, clearly indicated that no single leadership style was universally effective, as the relationship of supervisory behavior to organizational performance and employee satisfaction changed from situation to situation. By the early 1960s this had become apparent to even the most ardent supporters of the behavioral approach, and the orientation of leadership researchers began to change toward a situational treatment.

The situational phase. Current leadership research is almost entirely situational. This approach examines the interrelationships among leader and subordinate behaviors or characteristics and the situations in which the parties find themselves. This can clearly be seen in the work of researchers such as F. E. Fiedler, who outlined one of the first situational models.[15]

Fiedler claims that leaders are motivated primarily by satisfactions derived from interpersonal relations and task-goal accomplishment. Relationship-motivated leaders display task-oriented behaviors (such as Initiating Structure) in situations which are favorable for them to exert influence over their work group, and they display relationship-oriented behaviors (such as Consideration) in situations which are either moderately favorable or unfavorable. Task-motivated leaders display relationship-oriented behaviors in favorable situations and task-oriented behaviors in both moderately favorable and unfavorable situations. Fiedler's model specifies that relationship-motivated leaders will be more effective in situations which are moderately favorable for the leader to exert influence, and that they will be less effective in favorable or unfavorable situations; the exact opposite is the case for task-motivated leaders. (They are most effective in favorable or unfavorable situations and least effective in moderately favorable ones.) According to Fiedler, the favorableness of the situation for the leader to exert influence over the work group is determined by (1) the quality of leader-group member relations (the warmer and friendlier, the more favorable the situation); (2) the structure of the tasks performed by the leader's subordinates (the more structured, the more favorable); and (3) the power of the leader (the more power, the more favorable the situation).[16]

A number of other authors propose similar types of interactions among leader, the led, and the situation. We will not review all these other models, but the situational model of Victor Vroom and Phillip Yetton deserves mention.[17] Their model suggests the condition under which the leader should share decision-making power. Five basic leadership styles are recommended. These range from unilateral decisions by the leader to situations in which the leader gives a great deal of decision power to subordinates and serves as a discussion coordinator who does not attempt to influence the group. Which style is recommended depends upon the leader's "yes" or "no" response to seven quality and acceptability questions which are asked sequentially. In those cases where more than a single style is suggested, the leader is expected to choose between recommendations on the basis of the amount of time to be invested. While this model, as in the case with most of the situational models, has not been fully tested, the literature supports the basic notion that a situational view is necessary to portray accurately the complexities of leadership processes.

ORGANIZATIONAL IMPLICATIONS

What does this discussion of leadership theory and research have to do with the practice of management?

Selection does not seem to be the primary answer to the organization's need to increase the pool of effective leaders. The results of the numerous traits studies summarized by Stogdill and others indicate that the search for universal personality characteristics of effective leaders is doomed.[18] This statement requires qualification, however. It should be recognized that the assertion concerns leadership effectiveness, which is only one aspect of managerial effectiveness. A manager may contribute to organizational effectiveness in many ways other than by being an effective leader. The role of selection in picking effective managers, as distinguished from effective leaders, consequently may be much greater. Furthermore, present disappointment with attempts at leader selection is derived from research which has sought to identify universal characteristics of effective leaders in all situations. Summaries such as Stogdill's demonstrate that leadership effectiveness is highly dependent upon the relationship between leader characteristics and the demands of particular situations, and thus universal approaches will not work. Exploration of leader traits as they relate to performance in particular may reveal that careful selection has some potential. Unfortunately, given the many situational factors which appear to influence leadership effectiveness, it seems unlikely that selection procedures will be able to follow typical actuarial (statistical) selection procedures.[19] (It appears almost impossible to gather enough individuals in identical jobs to do this.) However, this does not preclude the use of clinical (judgemental) techniques for selection of leaders.

A further limitation on selection procedures as ways of increasing the pool of effective managers and/or leaders within organizations is the dynamic nature of managerial jobs and managers' careers. If, as research seems to indicate, leadership success is situation-specific, then the continual and inevitable shifts in the nature of a manager's assignment and his or her movement from one assignment to another may make the initial selection invalid.

Another implication is that existing forms of leadership training appear to be inappropriate, based on the evidence outlined here. There are two reasons for this. First, the majority of such training programs are based upon the assumption that there exists one best way to manage. Great emphasis usually is placed on an employee-centered (Considerate) approach or one which combines a concern for employees with a concern for high output (Initiating Structure). For example, the Managerial Grid and its associated Grid Organizational Development Program are popular approaches to management and organizational development.[20] Both are based on the premise that a managerial style which shows high concern for people and high concern for production is the soundest way to achieve excellence, and both attempt to develop this style of behavior on the part of all managers.[21] Rensis Likert's "System-Four" approach to managerial and organizational development, although different from the Grid approach, also assumes that one best way to manage exists (employee-centered leadership).[22] Clearly, these ideas are in conflict with the evidence and with contemporary opinion.

The other limitation of leadership training is that it seems ineffective in changing the behavior of participants. Leadership training aimed not directly at leadership behavior itself, but at providing diagnostic skills for the identification of the nature of the situation and the behaviors appropriate to it, appears to offer considerable potential for the improvement of leadership effectiveness. Obviously, however, additional research is needed to identify the dimensions of situations crucial to leadership performance and the styles effective under various circumstances.

Fiedler's suggestion that organizations engineer the job to fit the manager also has potential[23]. However, the idea is impractical, if not utopian. Application of this approach is limited because we have not identified the crucial dimensions of situations which affect leadership performance. Also, while the overall approach may offer theoretical advantages when leadership is treated in isolation, it ignores dysfunctional effects on other aspects of the organization's operations. Leadership effectiveness cannot be the only concern of administrators as they make decisions about job assignments. They must consider other aspects of the organization's operations which may conflict with their attempts to make good use of leadership talent. Some characteristics of job, task, or organization simply may not be subject to change, at least in the short run. Thus, engineering the job to fit the manager may increase leadership effectiveness, but this approach seems risky, at least for the forseeable future.

It should also be noted that it is not unusual for work organizations to use traits and trait descriptions in their evaluations of both leadership and managerial performance. A quick glance at a typical performance rating form usually reveals the presence of terms such as *personality* and *attitude* as factors for individual evaluation. Clearly, these terms represent a modern-day version of the traits investigated thirty years ago, and they may or may not be related to actual job performance, depending upon the specific of the situation involved. Thus, some explicit rationale and, it is hoped, evidence that such traits do affect managerial performance should be provided before they are included in performance evaluations. Just feeling that they are important is not sufficient justification.

INDIVIDUAL IMPLICATIONS

The implications of our discussion of leadership theory and research for individual managers are intertwined with those for the total organization. The fact that leadership effectiveness does not depend on a single set of personal characteristics with which an individual is born or which the individual acquires at an early age should provide a sense of relief to many managers and potential managers. Success in leadership is not limited to an elite, but can be attained by almost any individual, assuming that the situation is proper and that the manager can adjust his or her behavior to fit the situation. The process leading to effective leadership, in the words, is not so much one of changing the characteristics of the individual as it is one of assuming that he or she is placed in an appropriate situation or of teaching the individual how to act to fit the situation.

Thus, a manager's effectiveness can be improved through the development of skills in analyzing the nature of organizational situations—both task and political demands. Although it is difficult to provide guidelines, some recent research points to tentative prescriptions.[24]

Generally speaking, a high Consideration-high Structure style often works best. However, this approach cannot be used in all instances because dysfunctional consequences can result from such behaviors. For example, upper management sometimes gives highly considerate managers poor performance ratings, while in other instances high Structure has been related to employee dissatisfaction, grievances, and turnover. It sometimes will be necessary for a manager to choose between high Consideration and high Structure, and in these cases an individual's diagnostic ability becomes important.

If the diagnostician (manager) has little information, it is probably safe to exhibit high Consideration. Although it does not guarantee subordinate performance, its positive effects on frustration-instigated behavior—such as aggression—are probably enough to warrant its recommendation as a general style. However, in some situations Structure probably should be emphasized, although it may mean a decrease in subordinate perceptions of Consideration. Although the following is not an exhaustive list of these exceptions, it does include those which are known and appear important. The individual manager, for a careful analysis of the situation, must add any additional factors than can be identified.

Emergencies or high-pressure situations. When the work involves physical danger, when time is limited, or when little tolerance for error exists, emphasis on Initiating Structure seems desirable. Research has demonstrated that subordinates often expect and prefer high Structure in such instances.

Situations in which the manager is the only source of information. When the leader is the only person knowledgeable about the task, subordinates often expect him or her to make specific job assignments, set deadlines, and generally engage in structuring their behavior. This does not mean that the leader cannot be considerate if this is appropriate.

Subordinate preferences. There is limited evidence that some subordinates prefer high Structure and expect it, while others expect low Consideration and are suspicious of leaders who display high Consideration.

Other preference patterns undoubtedly exist, and managers should attempt to tailor their behavior to each individual employee, as the situation dictates.

Preferences of higher management. In some instances, higher management has definite preferences for certain leadership styles. Higher management sometimes prefers and expects high Structure and low Consideration, and rewards managers for displaying this behavioral style.

The manager should be sensitive to the desires of superiors, in addition to those of subordinates. While it is not possible to specify how these expectations may be reconciled if they diverge, compromise or direct persuasion might be useful.[25] Once again, the success of these methods probably will depend both upon the situation and the manager's skill. This leads to the last point—adaptability.

Leader ability to adjust. Some managers will be able to adjust their behavior to fit the situation. For others, attempts to modify behavior may look false and manipulative to subordinates. In these instances, the manager probably would be better off keeping the style with which he or she is most comfortable.

LIMITATIONS AND CONCLUSION

The situational approach avoids the major shortcomings of both the trait and behavioral approaches to leadership. However, the implicit assumption that hierarchical leadership is always important has recently come into question. Steven Kerr, for example, points out that many factors may limit the ability of a hierarchical superior to act as a leader for subordinates.[26] Factors such as technology (for example, the assembly line), training, clear job descriptions, and the like, may provide subordinates with enough guidance so that supervisor Structure may be unnecessary to ensure task performance. Also, jobs which are intrinsically satisfying may negate the need for supervisor Consideration, since Consideration is not needed to offset job dullness.

Another problem with the situational approach, and with leadership as a major emphasis in general, is that effective leadership may account for only ten to fifteen percent of the variability in unit performance.[27] While this percentage is certainly not trivial, it is clear that much of what affects performance in organizations is not accounted for by leadership.

While studying and emphasizing leadership certainly has its merits, it could be argued that there is much to be gained by treating leadership effectiveness as but one component of managerial effectiveness. As an earlier publication emphasized:

> It is necessary to note that leadership is only one way in which the manager contributes to organizational effectiveness. The manager also performs duties which are *externally oriented* so far as his unit is concerned. For example, he may spend part of his time coordinating the work of his unit with other units. Similarly, not all of the manager's *internally oriented* activities can be labeled leadership acts. Some of them concern the physical and organizational conditions under which the work unit operates. For example, the manager spends part of his time obtaining resources (materials, equipment, manpower, and so on) necessary for unit operations. This is an essential internally oriented activity but hardly constitutes leadership. Clearly, the manager must perform a mix of internal and external activities if his unit is to perform well. Leadership is only one of the internal activities performed by managers.[28]

Thus, the manager should not overemphasize the importance of leadership activities, especially if this causes other functions to be neglected.

For managers to be effective as leaders, they must attempt to be politically astute and to tailor their behaviors, taking into account differences in subordinates, superiors, and situations. Leadership should be kept in perspective. Clearly, it is important, but it cannot be treated in isolation; the importance of leadership depends upon the situation, and the practicing manager must take this into account.

REFERENCES

1. R. M. Stogdill, *Handbook of Leadership* (New York: The Free Press, 1974).
2. A. C. Filley, R. J. House, and Steven Kerr, *Managerial Process and Organizational Behavior*, 2nd ed. (Glenview, Ill.: Scott, Foresman 1976). See also R. C. Davis, *Industrial Organization and Management* (New York: Harper, 1957).
3. C. A. Gibb, "Leadership," in Gardner Lindzey and Elliot Aronson, eds., *The Handbook of Social Psychology* (Reading, Mass.: Addison-Wesley. 1969), vol. 4.

4. See, for example, R. H. Hall, *Organizations: Structure and Process* (Englewood Cliffs, N.J.: Prentice-Hall, 1972).
5. C. A. Schriesheim, J. M. Tolliver, and L. D. Dodge, "The Political Nature of the Leadership Process," unpublished paper, 1978.
6. For examples of other types of managerial tasks which may have more of an impact on organizations, see J. P. Campbell, M. D. Dunnette, E. E. Lawler, and K. E. Weick, *Managerial Behavior, Performance, and Effectiveness* (New York: McGraw-HIll, 1970).
7. R. M. Stogdill, "Personal Factors Associated with Leadership: A Survey of the Literature," *Journal of Psychology* 25 (January 1948): 35-71.
8. T. O. Jacobs, *Leadership and Exchange in Formal Organizations* (Alexandria, Va.: Human Resources Research Organization, 1970).
9. A. W. Halpin and B. J. Winer, "A Factorial Study of the Leader Behavior Descriptions," in R. M. Stogdill and A. E. Coons, eds., *Leader Behavior: Its Description and Measurement* (Columbus: Bureau of Business Research, The Ohio State University, 1957).
10. *Ibid.*, p. 42.
12. Steven Kerr, C. A. Schriesheim, C. J. Murphy, and R. M. Stogdill, "Toward a Contingency Theory of Leadership Based upon the Consideration and Initiating Structure Literature," *Organizational Behavior and Human Performance* 12 (August 1974): 62-82.
13. See, for example, Daniel Katz, Nathan Maccoby, and Nancy Morse, *Productivity, Supervision and Morale in an Office Situation* (Ann Arbor: Survey Research Center, University of Michigan, 1951).
14. Kerr et al., "Contingency Theory."
15. See F. E. Fiedler, "Engineer the Job to Fit the Manager," *Harvard Business Review* 43 (September-October 1965): 115-22.
16. F. E. Fiedler, *A Theory of Leadership Effectiveness* (New York: McGraw-Hill, 1967).
17. V. H. Vroom and P. W. Yetton, *Leadership and Decision-Making* (Pittsburgh, Pa.: University of Pittsburgh Press, 1973).
18. R. M. Stogdill, "Personal Factors."
19. Kerr et al., "Contingency Theory."
20. R. R. Blake and J. S. Mouton, *The Managerial Grid* (Houston, Texas: Gulf, 1964), and *Building a Dynamic Corporation Through Grid Organizational Development* (Reading, Mass.: Addison-Wesely, 1969).
21. *Ibid.*, p. 63.
22. Rensis Likert, *New Patterns of Management* (New York: McGraw-Hill, 1961), and *The Human Organization: Its Management and Value* (New York: McGraw-Hill, 1967).
23. Fiedler, "Engineer the Job."
24. Kerr et al., "Contingency Theory."
25. See Filley, House, and Kerr, *Managerial Process*, especially pp. 162-80; and George Strauss, "Tactics of Lateral Relations," in H. J. Leavitt and L. R.

Pondy, eds., *Reading in Managerial Psychology*, 1st ed. (Chicago: University of Chicago Press, 1964), pp. 226-48.

26. Steven Kerr, "Substitutes for Leadership: Their Definition and Measurement," unpublished paper, 1978.

27. O. C. Behling and C. A. Schriesheim, *Organizational Behavior: Theory, Research and Application* (Boston: Allyn and Bacon, 1976).

28. *Ibid.*, p. 294.

Chester A. Schriesheim is a faculty member in the Graduate School of Business, University of Southern California; James M. Tolliver is a faculty member in the Graduate School of Business Administration, Michigan State University; Orlando C. Behling is a faculty member at The Ohio State University.

Part II
PERCEPTIONS OF POWER AND AUTHORITY

10.
THE EFFECTIVE USE
OF MANAGERIAL POWER

Gary Yukl
Tom Taber

The skill with which leaders or managers exercise various types of power
determines their effectiveness in influencing subordinates. The authors
give guidelines on the effective use of five common types of leadership
power.

Influence over the attitudes and behavior of subordinates is the essence of
competent leadership. It is impossible to be an effective manager without influencing subordinates. Despite its obvious importance, however, the way in
which managers exert their power has not been subjected to much research.
There have been only a small number of studies on the relationship between
leader power and effectiveness. In most of these studies, power was classified in
terms of the taxonomy developed by J. R. P. French Jr. and B. Raven in 1959.
This taxonomy identifies five distinct types of power:

- *Authority* (legitimate power): the legitimate right of the leader to make
  certain kinds of requests.
- *Reward power*: the leader's control over rewards valued by subordinates.
- *Coercive power*: the leader's control over punishments.
- *Expert power*: the leader's task-relevant knowledge and competence as
  perceived by subordinates.
- *Referent power*: subordinate loyalty to the leader and desire to please him or
  her.

The research revealed that effective leaders rely most on expert and referent
power to influence subordinates. The use of expert and referent power was
positive correlated with subordinate performance or satisfaction in most of the
studies. Use of legitimate and coercive power tended to be negatively
correlated with effectiveness, or to be uncorrelated with it. Results for reward

power were mixed, with no clear trend across studies. The results from this research seem plausible, even though the correlations were not strong or consistent.

THE USE OF POWER AND SUBORDINATE REACTION

To understand how a leader's use of power can affect subordinate performance, it is necessary to consider such intervening processes as subordinate motivation and effort. The motivational outcome of an influence attempt by the leader can be classified according to whether it produces commitment, compliance, or resistance in the subordinate.

When subordinates are committed, they are enthusiastic about carrying out the leader's requests and make maximum effort to do so. Committed employees accept the leader's goals and exert maximum effort to accomplish them. Simple compliance, on the other hand, is only a partially successful outcome of leader influence. Subordinates go along with the leader's requests without necessarily accepting the leader's goals. They are not enthusiastic and may make only the minimal acceptable effort in carrying out such requests. Resistance, as most managers know, is a clearly unsuccessful outcome. Subordinates reject the leader's goals and may pretend to comply, but, instead, intentionally delay or sabotage the task. Unfortunately, only a few studies have considered subordinate motivation as an intervening variable. From the limited evidence available, we can piece together a picture of the likely causal relationships between leader power bases and subordinate motivation.

Figure 1.

Outcomes that Result from Different Types of Power

Power Source	Commitment	Compliance	Resistance
Authority	Possible	LIKELY	Possible
Reward Power	Possible	LIKELY	Possible
Coercive Power	Unlikely	Possible	LIKELY
Expert Power	LIKELY	Possible	Possible
Referent Power	LIKELY	Possible	Possible

As Figure 1 illustrates, expert and referent power tend to result in subordinate commitment, authority and reward power tend to result in compliance, and coercion tends to result in resistance. Because group performance is usually better when subordinates are highly motivated to do the task, the use of expert and referent power usually leads to a higher level of performance.

The problem with most of the power research is that it overlooks the leader's skill in exercising power. The outcome of a particular attempt to influence subordinates will depend as much on the leader's skill as on the type of power used. It is quite possible that expert and referent power could result merely in compliance or even in resistance if not used skillfully. By the same token, authority and reward power could result in subordinate commitment when used in an appropriate situation by a very skilled leader. Coercion does not necessarily have to result in resistance; it may result in subordinate compliance if used skillfully.

Thus the power studies yield somewhat misleading findings. One gets the false impression that an effective leader uses only expert and referent power—with no need at all to use authority, rewards or coercion. However, this impression is at odds with findings from motivation research that indicates that rewards can be very effective in increasing subordinate effort and performance in some situations. Motivation research also provides evidence that punishment is sometimes effective in getting subordinates to comply with rules and regulations. And various kinds of evidence indicate that exercising authority with a legitimate request is the most common approach used for influencing subordinates, and one that is quite important in the day-to-day operations of a work unit. Thus it is likely that effective leaders use all five types of power at one time or another. Leader effectivenss stems from knowing the appropriate type of power to use in each situation and how to exercise this power skillfully to maximize subordinate commitment.

Figure 2.

THE LEADERSHIP MODEL

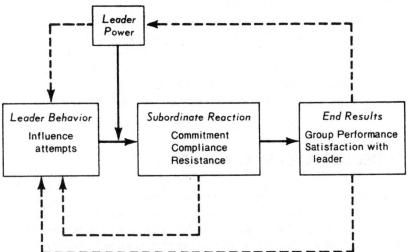

Figure 2 shows a model that depicts relationships between power and leader effectiveness. The model differs in some important respects from traditional thinking about leader power. First, the model holds that mere possession of power by itself has no consistent effects on subordinate motivation; power merely acts as a moderator variable to condition the effects of a leader's influence attempts. Second, the model clearly distinguishes between having power and using it. The successful use of power requires the leader to have relevant skill and a desire to exercise power, as well as the power resources themselves. Finally, the feedback loops in the model, indicated by dashed lines, recognize that power relationships are reciprocal and historical. A leader's behavior over time can increase or diminish his or her power, and the leader's behavior is itself influenced by subordinate behavior and performance.

In the process of accumulating power and exercising it, leaders are confronted with an interesting paradox. Any increase in power gives a leader greater potential for influencing subordinates, but a power differential also increases the propensity for resistance. The existence of a power differential is generally disturbing to the person who has lower power and status. Subordinates are aware that a powerful leader has the potential to cause them great harm or inconvenience. For this reason, even a benevolent leader's subordinates tend to be very sensitive to the leader's behavior, including subtle indications of approval or disapproval. Involuntary dependence on the whims of a powerful authority figure can cause resentment as well as anxiety, particularly for subordinates with strong needs for esteem and independence. A leader who treats subordinates as somehow inferior—who acts arrogant, bossy, and manipulative—will quickly elicit resistance to requests and commands.

Thus successful use of power requires influence attempts that do not threaten the subordinates' self-esteem. A number of other factors contribute to the success of an influence attempt, such as clarity of communication, timing and appropriateness of requests as well as the leader's ability to relate requests to subordinates' needs and concerns. Previous leadership research does not tell us much about the way to exercise power successfully. However, some useful insights are provided by studies of motivation, attitude change, counseling, and conflict resolution. From this research, we have learned enough to offer some tentative guidelines on how to use and maintain each of the five types of power.

GUIDELINES FOR USING AUTHORITY

Subordinates generally accept their boss's right to make requests and tell them what work to do. However, they do not like to be given orders in a way that implies the are not as good as the leader—people don't want to be treated like slaves. Thus effective leaders exercise authority by making polite requests, not by making arrogant demands.

Legitimate requests should be made in clear, simple language, and the leader should check to make sure subordinates understand what is required, especially if there is any indication that subordinates are confused. Whenever appropriate, the reason for the request should be explained so that subordinates understand why it is necessary. If anyone is likely to raise a question about the legitimacy of the leader's request, subordinates must be made to understand that it is indeed within the scope of the leader's formal authority to make such a request. Finally, the leader should follow up to verify that subordinates have complied with such requests. Subordinates who are reluctant to do something requested by the leader may wait to see if he or she is serious enough to insist on compliance. If the leader doesn't, subordinates may assume it is safe just to forget about it.

GUIDELINES FOR USING REWARDS

A common use of reward power is to offer specific incentives for doing what the leader wants. Incentive plans are usually very mechanical; subordinates automatically earn a bonus or commission for each item they make or sell. This type of mechanical incentive may be appropriate when there is a repetitious, tedious task with an objective output measure. But for more complex jobs, mechanical incentives are not the best way to exercise reward power. One danger in emphasizing explicit incentives is that subordinates quickly define their relationship to the leader in purely economic terms, and they come to expect special rewards every time the leader wants them to do something new or unusual. A much better relationship between leader and subordinate is one based on mutual loyalty and teamwork rather than an impersonal exchange of benefits.

There are other dangers in offering specific incentives. One is that they tend to make the leader appear manipulative—something subordinates may resent. Another limitation of incentives is that they are unlikely to result in commitment, even under the best of conditions. The typical response to specific incentives is to do only what is needed to earn the reward and no more. Subordinates may be tempted to neglect the less visible aspects of the task so they can complete it quickly.

Thus, in most situations, it is better to use rewards not as a bribe for doing what the leader wants, but rather to reinforce desirable behavior after it has already occurred. Tangible rewards can be used in conjunction with praise and recognition to communicate the message that the leader appreciates subordinates who are competent and committed. The size of the reward should be based on an evaluation of the subordinate's total performance, rather than on just some narrow aspect of it, as tends to be the case with incentives. The reward need not be limited to money. An effective leader will discover what other things subordinates value and use these as rewards also. It may be more time off, a better work schedule, or more desirable work assignments—but regardless of what type of reward is used, it is imperative to avoid the appearance of manipulation.

GUIDELINES FOR USING COERCION

Effective leaders generally avoid the use of coercive power except when absolutely necessary, because coercion is likely to create resentment and undermine their referent power. Coercion is most appropriately used to deter behavior that is very detrimental to the organization, such as violation of safety rules, reckless behavior endangering lives or valuable assets, and direct disobedience of legitimate requests. Skillfully used, coercion stands a reasonably good chance of getting subordinates to comply with rules, regulations, and orders.

Before criticizing or disciplining a subordinate, the leader should try to find out whether the subordinate is really at fault. A hasty reprimand that turns out to be unjustified can prove very embarrassing and seriously impair relations with subordinates. If a warning or punishment is needed, the leader should impose discipline promptly and consistently without showing any favoritism. Warnings should be stated in a way that avoids the appearance of personal hostility toward the subordinate. The leader should remain calm and convey a sincere desire to help the subordinate comply with rules and requirements to avoid the necessity for punishment. The subordinate should be invited to share in assuming responsibility for correcting disciplinary problems, including the setting of improvement goals and development of improvement plans. For all but the most serious of infractions, one or more warnings should be given before punishment is meted out. However, to protect the credibility of their coercive power, leaders should avoid issuing idle or exaggerated warnings that they are not prepared to carry out. Finally, when it is necessary to use punishment, the magnitude of the punishment should fit the seriousness of the infraction.

GUIDELINES FOR USING EXPERT POWER

Expert power depends on the subordinates' perception that the leader knows the best course of action in a given situation. A leader's expert power increases when he or she suggests a course of action that turns out to be highly successful. Expert power is decreased when the leader shows faulty judgement or makes decisions that lead to failure by the group. Thus, to accumulate expert power, a leader should foster an image of experience and competence. It is essential to preserve credibility by avoiding careless statements and rash decisions. The leader should keep informed about technical matters and outside developments that affect the group's work. In a crisis, it is essential to remain calm and act confident and decisive. A leader who appears confused, who vacillates or, even worse, is obviously panicked, will quickly lose expert power.

Like authority, expert power involves a risk of highlighting status differences between leader and subordinates. Leaders who act arrogant and talk down to subordinates encounter resistance to their directions. Comments that threaten subordinates' self-esteem are strictly taboo. Even leaders who are more knowledgeable than subordinates in a particular matter should show respect for subordinates' ideas and suggestions and try to incorporate these into plans whenever feasible. If subordinates have serious concerns about the leader's planned course of action, the leader should recognize these concerns and try to deal with them instead of simply dismissing then with such comments as, "Don't be ridiculous, you have nothing to worry about." The leader should carefully explain why the proposed plan of action is the best one possible and what steps will be taken to minimize any risk to subordinates.

GUIDELINES FOR USING REFERENT POWER

Referent power, like expert power, increases or decreases over the course of successive interactions between leader and subordinates. Referent power is increased by being considerate toward subordinates, showing concern for their needs and feelings, treating them fairly, and defending their interests when dealing with superiors and outsiders. Referent power is diminished when a leader expresses hostility, distrust, rejection, or indifference toward subordinates, or when the leader fails to defend subordinates' interests with superiors. Over time, actions speak louder than words, and a leader who tries to appear friendly but who takes advantage of subordinates or fails to stick up for them will eventually find that his or her referent power has eroded away.

One effective way to use referent power is to make a personal appeal that evokes subordinate feelings of loyalty. The leader should indicate that the request is personally very important and that he or she is counting on subordinates for their support and cooperation. The leader should be careful not to use personal appeals too often or to ask for more than is reasonable, given the nature of the relationship. There are limits to what can be asked in the name of loyalty and friendliness. If the request appears unreasonable to subordinates, the leader can end up with reduced referent power as well as resistance to the request.

A more indirect way to use referent power is through role modeling. Here the leader sets an example by behaving the way subordinates should behave. Subordinates will tend to imitate a leader whom they admire, because they want to please him or her and because they want to be more like him or her. Thus a leader with considerable referent power can influence subordinates in a positive way without even making explicit requests.

A CALL FOR FURTHER RESEARCH

These guidelines for using each type of power are tentative, most require further confirmation and elaboration. Much basic research remains to be done on how leaders use or should use power effectively. Past research has not explored the subject deeply enough to reveal many of the subtle nuances and nonverbal behaviors involved in influencing subordinates. Nor has previous research examined the complex interaction among the various forms of influence. In addition to taking the usual questionnaire approach, more observational studies are needed.

Researchers should also examine a broader range of influence behavior. It is now evident that the French and Raven Taxonomy fails to include some forms of influence that can be very important to leaders or managers, such as inspirational appeals, informational control, situational engineering (including job design), and use of participation. Finally, as mentioned earlier, the dynamic nature of influence processes requires more longitudinal research to examine the evolution of influence relationships between leader and followers over time. Research on how to use power effectively offers tremendous benefits to practicing managers, and it is time now to start taking this kind of research more seriously.

Gary Yukl is a professor of management at the State University of New York at Albany. He received his Ph.D. in industrial/organizational psychology from the University of California at Berkley. Dr. Yukl is the author of a book, Leadership in Organizations, *and was a coauthor of two earlier books. Tom Taber is an associate professor of management at the State University of New York at Albany. He received his Ph.D. in industrial/organizational psychology from the University of Illinois. His research interests include leadership and work design and he has written numerous articles on these subjects.*

11.
PARTICIPATION AND THE EFFECTIVE USE OF AUTHORITY

Burt K. Scanlan
Roger M. Atherton, Jr.

Participative management encourages employee involvement and commitment. Now take a look at authority and how to use it positively to draw out the full potential of employees.

The concept of participative management may create any number of negative reactions on the part of practicing managers. Included among these are time consuming meetings in a climate in which time is at a premium; decisions by consensus which may not reflect impartial objective analysis; involvement in decisions on the part of people who do not share organizational goals or put personal goals above those of the organization; the expectation on the part of people that they should be able to participate in all decisions whether or not they are directly or indirectly affected by them; erosion of managerial authority and ability to give needed emphasis to the total effort; the potential for increased degrees of interpersonal conflict and in-fighting; and compromise decisions which, although they may placate most people temporarily, have the potential for longer term negative effects on the operation.

All of these can function as very real potential disadvantages of using participation. However, disadvantages can many times be attributed to either mismanagement of the participative process or a misconception of what participation involves in the first place. The overall purpose of this article is to clarify what participation involves from a conceptual standpoint as well as to discuss the implementation of participation through the more effective use of authority.

THE MANAGER'S ROLE

Management has traditionally been defined as getting things done by, with and through people. This definition is often subject to criticism on the basis that it is oversimplistic and lacks a definitive description of exactly what it is that a manager does. Although, to a degree, this criticism may be valid, the definition cannot be dismissed lightly because it stresses the human element, which is one of the most basic and primary considerations in managing. Managers do not get things done by themselves and, when they try to do so, accomplishment will often be limited to the talents and energies of one individual.

The importance of the manager's role in getting results through others is highlighted by research which tells us that many times high achievers do not make the best managers.[1] Accordingly, the best salesman may not be the best sales manager, the most technically qualified engineer the best technical administrator, or the most accomplished academician a good dean or department head.

As McClelland found in his research on achievement motivation, there is a difference between achieving personally and inspiring other people to achieve. Inspiring others to achieve takes a different set of skills, abilities, talents and values. Among other things it requires someone who can draw personal satisfaction from the accomplishments of others instead of from just what they alone can accomplish. Whether it be a business, service organization, church or government, much of the essence of management involves gaining maximum productivity from our human resources. This means gaining their commitment via mental and emotional involvement in the goals at hand.

CASE STUDY EXAMPLE

Consider the following true life scenario which one of the authors encountered while in a consulting role:

Two engineers in a large organization with essentially the same educational backgrounds, experiences and tenure were placed in management positions almost simultaneously. At the end of the first six months Manager A was experiencing considerable success while Manager B was experiencing complete frustration. For the latter, problems were being encountered in meeting schedules, there was unrest among the engineers in his department, the work being completed was of marginal quality, and top management was expressing serious concern about the deteriorating situation.

Manager B was confused by his new role. When he realized he was no longer expected to do actual engineering work he became unsure of himself. Time had to be spent some way, so he began checking in detail everything every engineer did before it left the department. When an error was found he quickly called it to the attention of the person responsible but made the corrections himself. After finding a few such cases he concluded that more checking was needed and it almost became a challenge to find something wrong. He spent more and more time watching over people's shoulders to make sure things were done right.

There were certain high-priority projects Manager B felt demanded his personal attention and he worked on them himself, very often until late at night and on weekends. Meanwhile other things did not get done. Progress reports on other projects were not filed on time, cost data on projects were not available when needed, employees became passive and progressively assumed less responsibility, and one of the more experienced engineers resigned while two others filed transfer requests. Eventually, B failed as a manager of others.

Manager A, on the other hand, perceived and handled his new job differently. Initially he inventoried the department to determine both the work that had to be accomplished and the personnel available to do it. He concerned himself not only with the number of people available but their individual skills, abilities, strengths, weaknesses, personal growth, and development needs and desires. Using this as a base, priorities and schedules for various projects were formulated.

Through individual and department meetings Manager A communicated the role and importance of the department as a whole in the total organization, as well as the purpose and objectives of various projects in which they were involved. He shared and discussed with his subordinates his perception of problems inhibiting better departmental performance and obtained their suggestions for improving things. He took an active interest in each person individually and worked with them in a coaching capacity to set goals, improve performance, gain increased levels of job satisfaction and personal achievement.

The above example highlights several dimensions of managing people to achieve results, but most importantly for present purposes it illustrates the idea of getting things done by, with and through people. Whether the problems encountered by Manager B lie in bad selection or inadequate training to be manager is not our concern here. Rather, the point is that success as a manager is highly correlated with providing a climate that brings out the maximum potential of employees.

RIGHT CLIMATE IS CRUCIAL

Two final points deserve emphasis as they relate to the manager's role in motivation and productivity from a human resource perspective. First, people can be trained in achievement motivation, or put differently, the achievement motive can be developed. Second, the climate for achievement is more important than the achievement motive itself. Both of these observations are a result of McClelland's extensive research in the area.[2]

Regardless of how achievement oriented a person is, if the the job climate does not allow achievement or inhibits it, that person will not achieve, at least not to the limits they otherwise would. They will either quit or over time will direct a good portion of their energies to other pursuits. Conversely, if a person with an average or low level of achievement motivation is put in the right kind of climate they will become more achievement oriented. Some of the characteristics of such a climate include one in which 1) goals are explicit, challenging and achievable; 2) accountability is emphasized; 3) high performance expectations prevail; 4) performance feedback and positive reinforcement is a reality; 5) rewards of all types (including recognition, opportunities for growth and development, new experiences on the job, increased responsibility, wage and salary increases and promotion) are based on and consistent with achievement as perceived by the employee; 6) support is received in the form of needed communications, policies and procedures which facilitate accomplishment, physical resources, or sensitivity to job-related problems being encountered; and 7) people have an opportunity to participate.

It is the latter climate element, participation through the more effective use of authority, with which this article is concerned. Managers of high achieving employees tend to use higher degrees of participation than do managers of low and average achieving employees. This is true to the extent that participation is a major characteristic of achievement-oriented management.[3]

MANAGERIAL AUTHORITY IN PERSPECTIVE

There are about as many definitions of authority as there are writers who have dealt with the subject. Two of the common ingredients of almost all definitions is that authority encompasses the right to issue orders and or instructions which others are expected to follow and involves the process of exercising influence. Regardless of the definition used, we are referring to formal authority or that which is conferred by the organization, attaches to a position, belongs to whomever occupies that position, and is backed by the right and ability to apply sanctions or administer rewards.

It is commonly recognized that from a practical operating standpoint this view of authority is extremely limited because it fails to acknowledge that to be effective authority must be legitimate, which means that to some degree it must be accepted by the people subject to the authority. When considering authority, it is effectiveness rather than authority in and of itself that is the key issue. Regardless of how much authority a person has on paper, it is useless if it fails to elicit the desired responses on the part of subordinates. The old saying, "he has delusions of power," reflects the person with a lot of on-paper authority but whose followers for the most part march to their own music.

THE EFFECTIVENESS OF AUTHORITY

Douglas McGregor views the effectiveness of authority as a function of how dependent subordinates are on one job, with one organization and in one department of that organization. Dependency could range all the way from being completely dependent, to partially dependent, to relative independence.

The more dependent a person is the more effective formal authority is. As people experience varying degrees of independence, for whatever reasons, the effectiveness of authority goes downhill quite rapidly. McGregor maintains that most people are only partially dependent on one employment alternative and therefore formal authority is only partially effective in getting the job done. We would maintain that even if a person is completely dependent, relying on authority alone leads to antagonistic cooperation and minimal commitment. People will do only what they have to do and no more.

LIKERT'S ALTERNATIVE

The limited effectiveness of formal authority can also be viewed using Likert's alternative systems of management. The four systems he identifies are as follows: System 1: exploitive authoritative; System 2: benevolent authoritative; System 3: consultative or democratic; System 4: participative.

The managerial characteristic of each of the systems are implied by their respective labels. The key dimension of behavior differentiating the styles is the amount of participation the superior allows the subordinates. System 1 represents virtually no participation, while System 4 represents the maximum amount of participation. Three variables which are representative of Likert's participative system include 1) high performance goals, 2) use of supportive relationships, and 3) use of subordinate input into various phases of the decision process.

Likert also makes a distinction between what he calls causal, intervening and end-result variables. The causal variables refer to the four management systems. The contention is that the kind of management system that exists causes a certain type of reaction on the part of the people in the organization. The end-result variables refer to such tangible items as quality, quantity, costs and similar measures of effectiveness. Of key importance are the intervening variables. These include such things as loyalty, degree of conflict vs. cooperation, willingness to assist and help peers, attitudes, morale, the level of motivation and similar factors related to the human assets of the organization.

Likert maintains that an authoritative approach may initially achieve improvements in the end-result variables, but at the same time the intervening variables will begin to disintegrate. Eventually, as the situation with the human assets deteriorates, the end-result variables themselves will also show marked decline. On the other hand, it is maintained that a participative approach will lead to an upgrading of the human assets and as that occurs long-run permanent gains in end results.[4]

According to Likert then, participation is one of the very important ingredients in gaining employee commitment on an overall basis. This commitment can lead to less need for the use of formal authority, power, discipline, threat and pressure as a means for obtaining job performance.

Participation can become an effective substitute for pure authority. Yet, as indicated by the problems described earlier, participative management can lead to frustration, conflict, poor decisions, wasted time and poor performance. These are only some of the reasons why the use of participative management is not widespread.[5] It is our belief that much of the literature has not adequately considered the power needs of most managers and the increasing need for the use of power in most organizational situations. The purpose of the next section will be to point out when and why the use of power is necessary and to make suggestions about how the use of power and participation can be combined for higher performance than either can provide alone.

POWER VERSUS PARTICIPATION

Tannenbaum and Schmidt describe a continuum of leadership behavior from boss-centered to subordinate-centered, i.e., participative. It is clear that they believe the use of power versus participation is a matter of degree that should vary depending on the manager, the subordinates and the situation. The range of leadership behaviors they formulated is depicted in Figure 1.[6]

Figure 1.

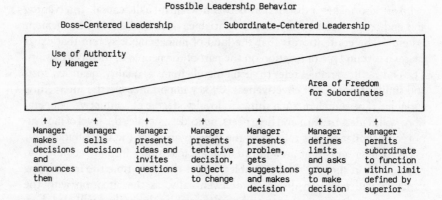

Possible Leadership Behavior

Boss-Centered Leadership   Subordinate-Centered Leadership

Use of Authority
by Manager

Area of Freedom
for Subordinates

| Manager makes decisions and announces them | Manager sells decision | Manager presents ideas and invites questions | Manager presents tentative decision, subject to change | Manager presents problem, gets suggestions and makes decision | Manager defines limits and asks group to make decision | Manager permits subordinate to function within limit defined by superior |

Clearly the use of power and participation were alternatives to one another, with the successful manager being one who accurately and flexibly adjusted leadership behaviors to the various situational constraints.

Vroom and Yetton have further elaborated on these ideas by considering the distinctions between the sharing of decisions with individual subordinates and with the subordinate group as a whole.[7] The criteria for choosing the proper style included the importance of decision quality, the importance of acceptance of a decision by subordinates, and the criteria of time and cost minimization. Other factors which they considered were who had the best information related to the decision, whether or not the problem is a structured one, the degree of subordinate motivation to achieve organization goals, and the amount of subordinate conflict. The astute manager would be able to analyze the relevant factors and decide what degree of decision-sharing would be most appropriate. In certain situations decreases in the use of power and authority are traded off for increases in participation and employee involvement. This type of trade-off becomes necessary when the manager does not have sufficient information to make a quality decision on his or her own, when the problem is not a clear-cut structured one, and when it is not likely that a unilaterally made decision will be accepted. More specifically, because of various dependencies on others that the manager is confronted with, it is necessary to adjust how we use our authority.

MANAGERIAL DEPENDENCY

The fact that managers are dependent on superiors, peers and subordinates to accomplish job-related objectives is a reality of managerial life. These are the vulnerable areas of the job, areas where lack of cooperation from others can negate achievement. Managerial dependencies, whether they are in the form of the need for interdepartmental cooperation, information that others have which the manager does not possess, or numerous other forms of needed support, result in a situation where managers must be able to positively influence those on whom they are dependent. Dependencies tend to increase at higher levels in the organization hierarchy and also with the number of people who report directly or indirectly to the manager. Dependencies also vary considerably as a function of organization size, environment, goals, technology, formal structure and the rewards system.[8] The greater the number and extent of dependencies the more managerial time and energy that must be put into authority and power-oriented behavior that facilitates rather than hinders the accomplishment of objectives. As a result, effective managers, even when they must use less participative and more authoritative approaches, typically avoid being coercive, arbitrary and self-serving because of the short and long-range negative impact of these actions.

The issue at hand is not whether the use of power and authority is necessary to perform the managerial job but rather how it is used, or more specifically, using it in a way that will have overall favorable effects. The successful use of power requires 1) sensitivity to what people perceive as legitimate behavior in acquiring and using power; 2) a good understanding of the various types of power and authority and methods of influencing others; 3) the development of the skill needed to use various types of power and authority; 4) the use of influencing methods that are in tune with the situation; 5) tempering the use of power with maturity and self-control; and 6) the recognition that the use of power and authority is legitimate and necessary.

POWER, AUTHORITY AND PARTICIPATION

The key to the successful use of both power and participation is knowing when and how to use them effectively. Similarly, the opposite of the use of personal power, which McClelland depicts as the desire to dominate people and use them as pawns, and which is exercised for the individual's own self-aggrandizement, may be socialized power. A manager who uses socialized power shows a concern for group goals, finds goals that will move people because they can relate to them, helps the group formulate goals as opposed to dictating them, and gives people a feeling of confidence and strength that they can accomplish the goals.[9]

Participation ranges from boss-centered, nonparticipative, nonshared decision-making, to employee-centered, participative and shared decision-making. Higher degrees of participation involve the following: 1) more two-way communication; 2) more opportunity for subordinates to have an influence on decision-making; 3) managers and supervisors take a less aggressive posture; and 4) a higher degree of recognition of the potential for employees to make positive and meaningful contributions.

Participation will usually yield more favorable long-term results for two reasons. First, it contributes to the process of authority being legitimatized or gaining the consent of the people subject to authority. Second, for the reasons cited above it serves to unleash the potential of people to make positive contributions. Since this is more likely to result in mental and emotional involvement, both motivation and commitment are heightened. *The important point to note is that by changing our approach to using authority we can begin to employ more participation and gain the advantages associated with participation.* Not the least of those advantages is participation motivation.

At different times and in different circumstances it is necessary to use alternative approaches to authority in order to accomplish the objectives at hand. As a generalization, nonparticipation may be effective in the short run but in the long run it may achieve less than a full measure of success. The earlier discussion concerning the effectiveness of purely formal authority helps explain why this is true.

A very important word of caution is in order. We do not mean to imply that nonparticipation is "off limits" and should be avoided. This is far from the case. Situations will arise in which nonparticipation is a feasible alternative and the most appropriate course of action available. The important point is that just as the degree and form of participation used must fit the situation, it must also fit the employees involved and the manager's own personality. The way in which authority is exercised must also be flexible to insure maximum results. The key is having a knowledge of the alternatives available, developing skill in using the various approaches, and being able to assess when they are most appropriate.

A BROADER VIEW OF PARTICIPATION

Participation can be defined as getting things done by, with and through people by creating a situation where they are *mentally* and *emotionally* involved in a situation that encourages positive contribution to objectives. The key thought in this definition is mental and emotional involvement. Any act on the part of the manager that generates mental and emotional involvement qualifies under the definition. Accordingly, the manager who communicates not just what employees have to know to do their jobs but also the kinds and types of information that they want to know, gives employees a greater sense of identity with the work unit or total organization. This manager is using the precepts of a participative approach.

The manager who recognizes and operates according to the principle that performance improves most when specific goals are set, and that participation in goal-setting improves subsequent performance, is using participation. The manager who works at letting employees know where they fit, that their job is important, and that they mean something individually will earn the benefits of mental and emotional involvement. Similarly, providing performance feedback and positive reinforcement as well as professionally managed delegation involves participation.

Although purists may argue against this broader view of participation, it opens up new vistas for the practicing manager and the organization that are interested in moving toward a more participatory climate. An appropriate place to start is by taking a look at authority and how we can use it positively to draw on the full potential of employees.

REFERENCES

1. David C. McClelland, "The Two Faces of Power," *Journal of International Affairs* Vol. 24, no. 1 (1970), pp. 24-47.

2. David C. McClelland and David H. Burnham, "Power is the Great Motivator," *Harvard Business Review* (March-April 1976), pp. 100-110.
3. Jay Hall, "To Achieve or Not: The Manager's Choice," *California Management Review* (Summer 1976), pp. 5-17.
4. Rensis Likert, *The Human Organization* (McGraw-Hill, 1967).
5. Donald P. Crane, "The Case for Participative Management," *Harvard Business Horizons* (April 1976), pp. 15-21.
6. Robert Tannenbaum and Warren H. Schmidt, "How to Choose a Leadership Pattern," *Harvard Business Review* (May-June 1972).
7. Victor H. Vroom, "A New Look at Managerial Decision Making," *Organizational Dynamics* Vol. 1, no. 4 (Spring 1973), p. 67.
8. John P. Kotter, "Power, Success, and Organizational Effectiveness," *Organizational Dynamics* (Winter 1978), pp. 26-40.
9. David C. McClelland, "The Two Faces of Power," *Journal of International Affairs* Vol. 24, no. 1 (1970), pp. 29-47.

Burt K. Scanlan is professor of management, College of Business Administration, University of Oklahoma, Norman, and earned his doctorate in management from the University of Nebraska. Dr. Scanlan is also president of Results Management in Action, a training and consulting firm. Roger M. Atherton, Jr., is a professor of management, College of Business Administration, University of Oklahoma, Norman. Dr. Atherton earned his doctorate in management at the University of Michigan.

12.
UNDERSTANDING PERSONAL POWER

Dennis L. Kennedy

To be a successful leader, you must provide adequate structure so that your followers know what to do and how to do it. Initiating structure is not, however, sufficient to ensure success in leadership.

Your personal power, also known as charisma, reflects your ability to interact with others. It's not determined by your authority to reward or punish as defined on some organization chart. Personal power comes from creating and sustaining positive interpersonal relationships.

A PICTURE IS WORTH . . .

You can graphically show your level of personal power. Think of that "very special person" (VSP) who would do almost anything for you. Draw a solar system in which you are the "star," and this individual is an orbiting satellite. Next, think of that "singularly obstinate being" (SOB) who would, at best, do nothing pleasant for you. Draw him or her in orbit also but at the far reaches of space.

With a little effort, you can fill in the rest of your "interpersonal solar system" (IS system). Think about the other people with whom you interact. The more willing they are to do things for you, the closer their orbits will be (see illustration).

Because personal power is defined as the ability to get others to do what you want *voluntarily*, your IS system graphically depicts your personal power. For example, if your IS system has numerous people in close orbits, you have a great deal of personal power. Conversely, if most people in your IS system are in distant orbits, you have little personal power.

To understand the importance of personal power, let's consider two applications.

Interpersonal Solar System

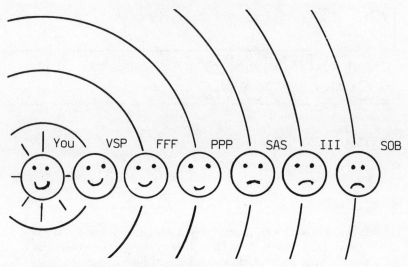

VSP: Very Special person (people).
FFF: Friends, family, and fans.
PPP: Persistently pleasant peers.
SAS: Superiors and subordinates.
III: Irritating and inconsiderate individuals.
SOB: Singularly obstinate beings(s).

Networking entails the development of career through the utilization of personal contacts. If you have high personal power, networking is easy, even automatic, because you have an abundance of interpersonal contacts who will be eager to assist you. But if you have low personal power, there will be only a few individuals in your IS system and they, in general, will be unwilling to help you.

Leadership provides another example of applied personal power.

Leadership is composed of two factors—initiating structure and consideration—according to Edwin Fleishman and David Peters, writing in *Personal Psychology* in 1962. Initiating structure is the extent to which an individual defines or structures his or her own behavior and the behavior of others. Consideration is the extent to which an individual achieves a high rapport or positive two-way communication with others. Consideration in essence is personal power.

A supervisor who bases his or her leadership on personal power (or consideration), in effect, creates an IS system in which employees are in relatively close orbits. Workers under such a leader tend to do the best they can because of the strong positive feelings they have toward him or her.

Unfortunately, many supervisors, instead, rely on positional power (their authority and the related ability to reward or punish) to get their subordinates to do what they want them to do. While such leaders may get compliance, it is forced. Their followers do what they are told but little more. They have very little positive feeling toward their leader and may even harbor feelings of resentment.

Given that personal power (or consideration) is desirable, how do you acquire it?

When people are asked to describe high-consideration leaders and/or people who have a great deal of personal power, they refer to the following traits: trustworthiness, concern for others, honesty, understanding, openness, caring attitude, empathetic behavior, and kindness. Low-consideration leaders and/ or people with little personal power, on the other hand, are considered to be untrusting, unconcerned, disrespectful, dishonest, intolerant, unaffectionate (cold), insensitive, and unkind—in other words, the exact opposite of those with a great deal of personal power.

It would seem, therefore, that to acquire or enhance personal power you must increase the number of individuals in your IS system who view you positively. This may be done by either bringing new people into your system or getting those already in your system who have a negative view to adopt a more positive perception.

You can improve the perceptions that others have of you, or create positive impressions in new contacts, by doing two things. First, you must unilaterally increase the level of trust, concern, respect, honesty, and the like that you extend to others. The goal is to get people to respond in kind. Second, you must persist in this until your goal is achieved even if the process takes a considerable amount of time.

Implementation of this strategy is by no means easy. When you extend consideration, you become vulnerable. Your trust may be violated or your kindness may be abused. However, very few people will fail to respond positively when consideration is extended to them over time. Even if on rare occasions you encounter someone who is incapable of returning the consideration extended, it would be foolish to allow this to deter you since it would entail a potential loss of personal power.

Much of your success in life is gained through the support and assistance of others. Personal power creates an interpersonal environment that is rich in both. To be a successful leader, you must provide adequate structure so that your followers know what to do and how to do it. Initiating structure is not, however, sufficient to ensure success in leadership. The truly successful leader instills in followers a desire to do what is needed through consideration, building personal power in the process.

Dennis L. Kennedy, Ph.D., is an associate professor, Human Resource Management, California State University, Sacramento.

13.
POWER AT WORK

Hugh R. Taylor

> Develop the power of your people selectively and wisely lest your failure
> be at the bank rather than with your organization. In short, power is
> neither an evil nor mystical concept.

Ever since Machiavelli wrote *The Prince* and Lord Acton made his rather
ridiculous comment, "Power corrupts and absolute power corrupts absolutely,"
people have been terrified of power and reluctant to discuss it.

The result is that we have failed to recognize and use one of the most interesting and valuable of human characteristics and assets.

That failure is apparent in countless everyday situations.

When you, as a manager, promote one of your people to a position of increased responsibility only to discover later that he or she is having problems
functioning at that level, you probably throw up your hands in despair.

The damage probably isn't irreparable, however, and just because you made
such a move doesn't mark you as an incurable incompetent.

All that has happened is that you and your employee have become the
victims of a common organizational phenomenon, the power failure.

Just as with an equipment failure, a human power failure can be corrected. In
both cases, you, the manager, must understand the reason for the failure and
accept at least some of the responsibility for its creation.

Does this mean that there is no such thing as a lazy, incompetent, or
dishonest employee? No. Just as some equipment doesn't work as advertised,
some people turn out to be less motivated, less willing or able to learn, and less
adaptable than others.

A productive, capable, effective worker who, after being promoted, is
overcome by his or her new job, is probably the victim of a power failure.

It will take an infusion of new power to restore that employee's effectiveness,
revitalize his or her performance and make the promotion a success.

This analogy is best understood through two examples of typical power
failures, one mechanical and one human, and ways in which they are normally
handled:

Suppose your company is in the business of cutting wiffles and, to increase your productivity, you buy a new, state-of-the-art wiffle-cutter.

The first thing you, as supervisor of the wiffle cutting line, do, of course, is sit down and read the operations manual for your new wiffle-cutter.

In doing so, you note that your new piece of equipment is designed to cut two-inch thick wiffles. Your company deals in the new, high-tech three-inch wiffles, but, since one wiffle is pretty much like another, you decide to go ahead and use the machine.

For a while the wiffle-cutter does a good job on the three-inch thick wiffles you're feeding to it, but as time passes, it begins to slow down and, eventually, it blows a fuse, heaves a sigh, rolls over, and dies.

Immediately, you and your wiffle-cutter troubleshooter examine the machine in an attempt to discover the cause of the problem. Naturally, you discover you've overloaded the machine and it has experienced a power failure.

After making necessary repairs, you decide you have two options available to you: You can either a) cut down on the thickness of the wiffles you feed to the machine; or b) beef up the wiffle-cutter so it can handle the three-inch wiffles you normally produce.

There is nothing amazing about this process; it happens all the time. You experienced a power failure with a piece of equipment and you took care of it.

Now, let's take a look at a human power failure and see how it's handled: Tom Miller is a journeymen air conditioning installer. He is not only the best worker on his crew, he is well-liked by his co-workers and management thinks he has outstanding ability in all phases of his job.

One day, Harvey Jones, Tom's supervisor, walks into the owner's office and announces that he's been offered a management position with another company.

As much as the owner of the small company for which Tom and Harvey work would like to keep Jones, he can't match the offer, so he wishes Harvey well and asks him whom he would recommend to take over his position.

Without hesitation, Harvey names Tom and the owner of the company heartily agrees.

Suddenly, Tom finds himself thrust into a supervisor's job. He is happy with the promotion, of course, and promises to do his best to justify his boss's faith.

Tom's former co-workers are also overjoyed with their new supervisor and pledge to support him.

For a short time, everything goes well; Tom continues to work hard and his people are happy. But, before long, there are signs that all is not well.

First there are a few petty grumblings. Gradually, the griping gets more intense and productivity begins to drop. Even Tom's performance begins to slide.

The owner's investigation reveals that Tom is having a hard time letting loose of his old job. When a problem comes up, he has a tendency to shove his crew aside and attempts to handle it himself.

This constant focus on the technical aspects of the job takes its toll in Tom's paperwork. His reports are always late and, occasionally, he's even slow getting his crew's time cards turned in and their paychecks are delayed.

He also seems to be responding to problems by throwing people and overtime at them, rather than thinking them through.

As the situation worsens, Tom begins to feel that his people no longer trust or respect him. He's right—they don't.

He even begins to feel that his boss is badgering him and constantly looking over his shoulder. Again, he's right—he is.

Tom's problems with his new job begin affecting his personal life. He often stops on the way home from work and tries to salve his wounded ego at the corner pub.

He has started becoming difficult at home and takes his work frustrations out on his wife and children.

Finally, after noting the increased overtime, lost productivity, and dissatisfaction in Tom's crew, the owner decides that Tom has, to paraphrase the Peter Principle, "reached his level of incompetence."

He doesn't feel it would be productive to demote Tom and put him back on a crew, so, taking the normal course of action for such a situation, he fires Tom and hires another supervisor.

Tom has to live with failure and the company has lost a good man. The crew must adjust to another change in supervision and it will probably be months before things are back to normal.

Two power failures—one mechanical and one human. In the case of the mechanical failure, management dived in and did everything possible to discover the source of the problem and fix it.

In the case of the human failure, however, the offending employee was tossed out and another person was brought in to take up the slack.

Why the difference? Why do we treat machines with such care, but so cavalierly give people the heave-ho?

The difference is that we understand mechanical and electrical power and know how to deal with them. But, unfortunately, few people understand human personal power and many are even afraid to try to deal with it.

ALL POWER COMES FROM EIGHT SOURCES

All personal power, whether possessed and used by individuals, groups, organizations, businesses, or nations, comes from the same eight sources. They are:

1. Positional power. Positional power is the power to approve or disapprove; to hire or fire; to make decisions; and to exercise authority.

It is derived from one's job or the position one holds in a relationship. It may include certain perks, but it also carries responsibilities.

2. Expertise power. Power that comes from the knowledge, skills, background, education, wisdom, or information held by a person, group or

organization, and the ability to use that knowledge effectively, is known as expertise power.

3. Charismatic power. Charismatic power is derived from the personality, charm, aura of confidence, or leadership characteristics (innate or acquired) of the person or group holding it.

Charismatic power is the ability to get people to do what one wants without having to resort to positional power or some form of reward and punishment.

4. Influential power. Power is also derived from a person's ability to do favors for others, lend power to them, give rewards, or fulfill the needs of those in one's relationship.

If expertise power consists of what one knows and what one studies in school, influential power is where one studies and with whom one went to school.

Money, incidentally, is an instrument of influential power.

5. Implied coercive power. If a favor, reward, or other benefit can be given, it can also be withheld.

Implied coercive power is established when a person lets others know that what he or she can give, he or she can also withhold or take back.

Implied coercive power is also derived from the tacit knowledge that one has the power to use actual coercion unless the desired behavior is exhibited.

6. Actual coercive power. There is a very fine line separating implied coercive power from its actual counterpart.

The difference lies in an individual's demonstrated willingness to actually withhold favors, rewards, or benefits in order to attain his or her desired ends.

Actual coercive power is often exhibited by revoking privileges and rewards as a means of altering behavior.

7. The power of applied pressure. If coercion does not work, it is sometimes necessary to apply sanctions, impose non-violent punishments shun, block, or otherwise chastise wrongdoers. The ability to do this is derived from the measure of one's power of applied pressure.

This form of power often entails borrowing power from others in order to strengthen its base.

8. The power of raw force. When all else fails, people resort to force. Parents spank, individuals fight, bosses fire, companies engage in economic warfare, and nations drop bombs.

Force is the final and ultimate source of power. If the user has more raw force than his or her opponent, he or she will win. If he or she has less than imagined, disaster can result.

THE EIGHT SOURCES OF POWER FORM CONCENTRIC CIRCLES

Now visualize, if you will, a target made up of eight concentric circles. Each of these circles represents one of the eight sources of power. See Figure 1.

The innermost circle, or the bull's-eye, is always positional power. The size of that center circle is determined by the amount of power inherent in the position held.

The positional power circle of the president of the United States, for example, is huge beyond comprehension. The positional power circle of a manager of an organizational department is fairly large, but a great deal smaller than that of the company president.

Figure 1

The Eight Circles of Power

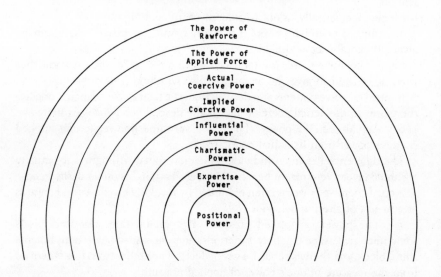

A worker on a production line has a very small circle of positional power since he or she is pretty much limited in decision making and other forms of authority.

The next circle is that of expertise power. Its size depends on the sum total of the background, education, knowledge, skill, and know-how a person brings to a job, a relationship, an organization, or whatever.

The circle of expertise power must be larger than the circle of positional power it surrounds. If it is not, the positional power will not have sufficient room to operate and expand.

No one has enough expertise power to handle the tremendous circle of positional power that goes with the job of president of the United States or of a large organization, such as General Motors, so the individuals in such positions surround themselves with staffs, assistants, and aides from whom they buy or borrow expertise power.

The greater the difference between the circle of expertise power and the positional power circle it surrounds, the greater the growth potential of the person in that position.

The next circle is charismatic power. The difference between this circle and the expertise power circle it surrounds is the person's ability to project his or her knowledge, act as a leader, and to sway people with his or her personality.

A narrow circle of charismatic power means that one's expertise and human relations skills are being directed inward, toward the position. Such a person is considered a weak leader, a bookworm, or simply anti-social.

The next circle is the influential circle and its measure is how well the leader is able to interpret the needs of others, provide favors, give rewards, or extend benefits.

Many people with potentially large circles of influential power lack the supporting charismatic power to use it effectively and, therefore, are seen as pushy.

The more influential power is allowed to grow, the more potential there is for effective use of the charismatic power it supports.

The circles continue outward through the other power sources, each supported by the circles closest on the interior and supporting the next one until the last circle, the power of raw force.

It follows, then, that people with a huge circle of the power of raw force, unsupported by the inward circles, might be exceedingly strong, but they would be perceived as bullies and thugs.

Physical strength, then, is one thing, but real, broad-base power is quite another.

The size of each circle is determined by the amount of power the person, organization, nation, or whatever has in that particular area. The amount of any power that can be exercised is dependent on the power available in that area.

The structure of this power model is such that as long as a person has sufficient power to make a given circle effective, that circle will protect the circle, or circles, inward from it. If any circle is too narrow to be effective, those circles inward from it will suffer.

The outer four circles tend to obtain short-term results and are escalatory in nature. This is, they are effective only so long as they are applied, get results only so long as the user's circle in that area is greater than the person on the receiving end of the power, and the use of one often prompts the recipient to attempt retaliation from the next circle outward.

For instance, if you, as a manager, attempt to use implied coercive power against an employee, that person may retaliate by attempting to use actual coercive power against you.

If you can't match the actual coercive power you are faced with, you might find yourself moving out to the circle of applied pressure to attempt to bring that person back into line. The employee, sensing the use of applied pressure and unable to match it, may respond with raw force.

However, you might be able to show sufficient applied pressure to force the employee back into line before that final escalation. Then again, you might not.

Obviously, the outer four circles are not the most effective in most managerial, interpersonal, intergroup or international situations.

If you want to be effective as a manager, a spouse, or a friend, you will find it advantageous to operate within the inner four circles where results are long-term and more likely to be accepted by law and tradition.

In your relationships with others, the closer to the center of the circles you operate the more likely you are to obtain lasting, effective results.

MOST POWER FAILURES BEGIN WITH A COLLAPSE AT THE CENTER

The most common power failure happens when there is a sudden expansion of the center circle of positional power that cannot be absorbed by the expertise power surrounding it.

This type of power failure causes managers the most grief and costs the greatest in human loss and personnel replacement expense. Such was the situation in the case of Tom's failure as a supervisor.

If Tom's boss had known more about power, he would have been able to discover that his new supervisor didn't have sufficient expertise power to handle the job, and could have taken steps to correct the situation.

As a manager or supervisor, you can learn from Tom's story if you take a good, hard, long look at the people you are considering for promotion and determine if they have the expertise power to handle the job.

If you find that they don't have that power, you must quickly find a way to increase that power. But, should you find some of them incapable of absorbing the necessary expertise power, you will either have to find a way to loan it to them (from yourself or others), or find others to promote.

Quite simply, if the expertise power isn't there in advance, if it can't be learned, and if it can't be loaned from someone else, a power failure will result.

In every job, no matter what the level, there are three requisite types of skills:

- Technical skills
- Interpersonal skills
- Conceptual skills

At each level in an organization, the nature of these types of skills and the emphasis placed on them change dramatically.

The degree to which this combination is present comprises the expertise power necessary for promotion.

When a person moves from a non-supervisory position into one calling for administrative, supervisory, or managerial expertise, the requisite skills are reorganized and reemphasized.

The technical skills for which the person was probably hired in the first place, such as manual dexterity, knowledge of certain pieces of equipment and procedures, and the ability to perform particular functions, become secondary.

Instead, the new supervisor is expected to know and perform managerial technical skills, such as advanced math functions, recordkeeping, the use of computers or calculators, and so on.

As a non-supervisor, the worker uses interpersonal skills that are generally based on one-to-one relationships. In a managerial position, however, the interpersonal skills required call for communication and interaction on a one-to-group and group-to-group basis.

In addition, instead of just being responsible for him- or herself, the new supervisor is accountable for a group, a change that requires a working knowledge of such esoteric subjects as delegation, time management, motivation, leadership styles, career planning, counseling, interpersonal power, and so forth.

Finally, there is a dramatic shift in conceptual skill requirements. Rather than thinking about his or her job in terms of those immediately related to it, the new supervisor must think about the entire corporate process and how his or her group's function relates to the whole.

The same considerations must also be applied to the issue of charismatic power. A worker on a line only needs the ability to get along reasonably well with coworkers—to fit in.

Any additional charismatic power, properly focused, is merely a plus. The worker with a great deal of charismatic power is normally a peacemaker, an informal group leader, the father or mother confessor for the group, their spokesperson, and so forth.

As a manager, however, he or she must lead the group, be able to induce them to follow his or her example, and to work for the organizational goals.

This quality can be learned, but unless it exists in some small, even latent, degree beforehand, developing it is difficult.

Almost no influential power is required of the non-supervisory worker. It is, therefore, one of the most difficult to identify in advance.

A manager, however, must be able to "read" the value systems and motivators of his or her group. He or she must offer rewards that others want and must put them within reach.

Without those hard-to-spot abilities, the manager cannot exercise workable influential power and will never be able to have effective implied or actual coercive power.

The true test of the powers of applied pressure and raw force is not whether the manager has them, but his or her sensitivity and reluctance to use them.

Modern managers are not measured so much by how much power they have in these areas, but by how seldom they have to resort to them.

MANAGERS MUST DIRECT THE USE OF POWER

Effective managers, those who understand power and how to use it, can help avoid conflict within an organization. They can detect misreadings of power and act to defuse the conflict before it becomes destructive.

To do this, you, as a manager, should remember three basic facts about power:

First, no one is powerless. You have power and the people working for you also have power. Some people are more powerful than others, but no one is without power.

Second, power is not "zero-based." For one person to gain power, it is not necessary for another to lose it. A power gain for one person in a group can result in a power gain for the entire group.

Third, just as you must never underestimate or overestimate your own power, never under- or overestimate the power of others.

Just when you think you hold all the cards and can call the shots, you will find that some other person, or persons, has control of something you need and can withhold it.

If that should happen in the outer four circles, an escalating conflict can rapidly develop.

Power failures at all levels can be avoided if you, the manager, take the time to examine the circuitry of the people you plan to plug into new outlets. This is really not as difficult as you might think. Use these techniques: *Examine the power requirements of the new job and weigh them against the current power levels of the prospective promotee.*

Begin at the circle of expertise power and work you way outward through the other circles. Does the person you want to put into the new position have a broad conceptual view of the organization?

Does he or she have the ability to communicate on multiple levels as well as one-to-one? Does the prospective promotee have a working knowledge of people, what makes them tick, how to get the most out of them, and how to effectively lead a group?

Is he or she willing to "let go" and allow others to do the job while remaining in a supervisory capacity? Is the person capable of providing an example for others and able to motivate them through the strength of his or her personality?

Does he or she know how to establish meaningful goals and reward systems? Does he or she know when to establish limits, when to push and when to give slack, when to punish and when to change goals in order to avoid conflict?

If the required powers are not present, determine if the prospective promotee has the capacity to acquire them.

You can teach an old dog new tricks, but you can't teach any tricks to a dog that cannot and will not learn.

The sorry fact is, some people, no matter how pleasant or hardworking they may be, just don't have the capacity to learn new skills and concepts.

If you can determine this in advance, and admit it, you will save yourself a great deal of time, money and grief later on.

If the necessary skills are missing, but can be learned, determine if the resources are available to teach them.

The best time to have the power necessary to manage and the worst time to try to acquire it is when it is needed.

Too many organizations are locked into what might be called the Great American Absurdity: they try to train people for the positions they already hold.

Supervisors often receive supervisory development after they have been promoted to supervisory positions, managers are put through management development after they have been made managers, and executives are introduced to executive development after they have moved up to the executive suite.

Outstanding line workers should be exposed to supervisory development *before* they are placed on the hot spot of having to practice supervisory skills.

Outstanding supervisors should begin receiving management development while they are practicing supervisors, not after they have been promoted to a management position.

If your organization is not investing in the training and development of future supervisors and managers, it might be setting up power failures as a matter of policy. Look into this possibility carefully.

If your organization is too small to have supervisory and management development programs, look for outside resources that can help—consultants, area workshops and seminars, college or other school programs, and so forth.

Consider a monitoring program if you have the people available who can provide that function.

Internal succession programs are the best way to ensure a continuation of organizational standards and of creating high personnel morale. But don't wait until you have a power failure on your hands before getting the wiring ready for an internal succession effort.

Before promoting, consider the possibility of wasted power.

Wasted power can be just as damaging as a power failure. A person capable of doing more than the job for which he or she has been picked will be wasted in a job that presents no challenge. Therefore, don't under promote.

People work best when challenged. When they are not fully tapped they can rapidly become counter-productive. When assessing the power of your people, make the maximum use of all the power you find.

If it ain't broke, don't fix it.

Don't take this advice as an admonition to start looking for power failures that don't exist. If your manager and supervisors are doing their jobs effectively and if your people are happy, productive, and working to their fullest capacities, don't buy a program you don't need.

Giving people unnecessary training is not only expensive, it can be destruct-ive.

Develop the power of your people selectively and wisely lest your power failure be at the bank rather than with your organization. In short, power is neither an evil nor mystical concept. It is real, it is useful, and it is essential for every organization. Properly used, it can be the button that turns on your brightest performers. Ignored, it can become a demotivator. Abused it can become destructive.

You can prevent power failure. You can develop powerful people and, in turn, become more powerful yourself.

Hugh R. Taylor is a management and organizational development consultant.

14.
LEADERSHIP TRANSFORMS
VISION INTO ACTION

Warren Bennis

> In today's society, leadership requires the ability to harness diffused
> power—and to empower others to translate a vision into reality. The
> vision must leave room for creativity.

Just what is it that enables some organizations to translate an idea into reality and sustain it?

The answer: transformative power—the essence of what it originally meant to be a leader.

The idea of a relatively small group of "movers and shakers" who get things done is obsolete. Increasing numbers of citizens and stakeholders (and even those who are only indirectly involved) are taking an interest in an issue's outcome—and when the decision goes the "wrong way," very noisily so.

The bigger the problem to be tackled, the more power is diffused and the more people have to be involved. Thus, decisions become more and more complex and ill-defined, and affect more and more different (sometimes conflicting) constituencies.

Inevitably, there will be frustration. Followers will ask, "Who's in charge here?" as more and more people or groups have to be consulted. Leaders will ask, "How do you get everybody into the act and still get some action?"

Leaders have to lead under uncertain, risky conditions where it's virtually impossible to get ready for something when you have to get ready for anything. Just as effective leaders are becoming more competent in coping with the politicization of our institutions—working more closely with legislative bodies at both state and federal levels and other key constituencies—they are also learning more about an enlarged concept of the "management team."

Some important clues about the nature of effective leadership have come out of my recently completed study of eighty chief executive officers plus ten in-depth interviews conducted over the last few months with ten successful, "innovative" leaders. These studies provide a basis for making some generalizations about those leaders who have achieved mastery over the noisy, incessant environment—rather than simply reacting, throwing up their hands, and living in a perpetual state of "present shock."

Leaders, not managers. Leadership is the first component of transformative power. We shall see later on, however, that leadership must be held within a context of other interacting factors.

What all these effective CEOs share and embody is directly related to how they construe the role of the CEO/chairman. To use a popular distinction, they view themselves as leaders, not managers; which is to say that they are concerned with an organization's basic purposes, why it exists, its general direction. They do not spend their time on the "How to"—the proverbial "nuts and bolts"—but are concerned with purpose, with paradigms of action. In short, they are concerned not with "doing things right" (the overriding concern of managers) but with "doing the right thing."

What common set of characteristics, if any, is possessed by leaders who are capable of translating intention into reality? In varying degrees, it seemed that all of the CEOs studied possess the following competencies:

1. *Vision*: the capacity to create and communicate a compelling vision of a desired state of affairs.
2. *Communication and alignment*: the capacity to communicate their vision in order to gain the support of their multiple constituencies.
3. *Persistence, consistency, focus*: the capacity to maintain the organization's direction, especially when the going gets rough.
4. *Empowerment*: the capacity to create environments—the appropriate social architecture—that can harness the energies and abilities necessary to bring about the desired results.
5. *Organizational learnings*: the capacity to find ways and means through which the organization can: monitor its own performance; compare the results with established objectives; have access to a continuously evolving data base on which to review past actions and base future ones; and determine how, if necessary, the organizational structure and key personnel must be abandoned or rearranged when faced with new conditions.

In short, nothing serves an organization better—especially during these times of agonizing doubts and paralyzing ambiguities—than leadership which knows what it wants, communicates those intentions successfully, empowers others, and know when and how to stay on course and when to change.

The intention. The second element of transformative power refers to the "compelling vision" mentioned earlier, or "the intention." The expression of an intention "takes" an organization to a place it has never been before, the unknown. The characteristics of the intentions that successful leaders employ include:

1. *Simplicity.* The intention is easily understood.
2. *Completeness.* All the available facts are included. In most organizations the bulk of the major tasks that have to be accomplished are readily incorporated within almost any kind of organizational structure. It is those few remaining tasks that test or prove the adequacy of the organization. Not only should the organization be capable of incorporating tasks that need to be performed at the time it is set up; it should also be capable of adjusting to and assimilating new tasks as they arise.
3. *Communicability.* The intentions of these leaders are communicable in two respects. The more obvious one relates to the ease with which an intention is understood by the organization. The robustness of the organization depends to a large extent on the degree to which the context is clear and understood. The other could be called "alignment"—not alignment of organizational members, but alignment with the particular organization's other intentions. In other words, to understand organizational structure and its significance, it is important to keep in mind that its effectiveness depends on the mutual relatedness of its various intentions.

The organization. Transformative power implies a transaction between the leader and the led, between the leadership and some sort of participative response. If the leadership has the characteristics noted earlier and if the intentions are effectively expressed, the organization becomes a blending of each individual's uniqueness into collective action.

Such an organization is similar to an individual with a healthy identity. We can assume that an organization possesses a healthy identity when it has a clear sense of who it is and what it is to do—which is a way of defining "organizational integrity."

Achieving organizational integrity is easier said than done. Part of the problem is the difficulty in understanding the various substructures that all organizations, no matter how small, contain. One block to our understanding is perpetuated by the myth of "organization-as-monolith," a myth reinforced almost daily by the media and the temptation of simplicity. The myth is not only grossly inaccurate, but dangerous as well. When the newspaper, for example, announces that the Defense Dept. or the University of California or IBM will pursue this or that course of action, the action is typically attributed to a single, composite body—management.

This body, whose parts seem to vibrate in harmony because we are denied a look at the human drama that leads up to its actions, takes on an air of superhuman detachment. Actually, into every step taken goes a complicated pattern of meetings, disagreements, conversations, personalities, emotions, and missed connections. This very human process is bureaucratic politics.

Our perceptions of organizational decision-making, based on such reports and other stimuli, tend to emphasize the *product* of decision-making—never (or rarely) the *process.* Those elements of chance, ignorance, stupidity, reck-

lessness, and amiable confusion are simply not reckoned with. They are selectively ignored, it seems. Thus, the public rarely sees the hundreds of small
tableaux, the little dramas, that result in a policy statement or a bit of strategy.
It sees only the move or hears only the statement, and it not unreasonably
assumes that such an action is the result of a dispassionate, almost mechanical
process in which problems are perceived, alternative solutions weighed, and
rational decisions made.

Four identities. In order for an organization to have integrity, it must have
an identity—that is, a sense of who it is and what it is to do. Perhaps an analogy
taken from personality theory will illustrate the point. Every person is a
summation of various "selves." If those units of the person are not in
communication, then that person cannot maintain valid communications
with others. The problem of integrity in organizations may be examined by
understanding the various "organizational selves," or structures, that exist.

Every organization incorporates four concepts of organization which are
often at odds with each other or exist in some strained cohesion. They include:
1.   the *manifest* organization that is seen on the organization chart and which
     is formally displayed.
2.   the *assumed* organization that individuals perceive and would depict were
     they asked to draw their view of the way things work.
3.   the *extant* organization—or the situation as revealed through systematic
     investigation, say, by an outside consultant.
4.   the *requisite* organization—or the situation as it would be if it were in
     accord with the reality of the environment within which it exists.

The ideal, but never totally realized, situation is that in which the manifest,
the assumed, the extant, and the requisite are aligned as closely as possible with
each other.

Another useful mental health analogy is that of health being based on the
degree to which the individual brings into harmony the various "selves" that
make up his or her personality. The healthy person will be much the same
person as he or she is perceived by others. Virtually the same criterion can be
used to evaluate organizational integrity; that is, the degree to which the
organization maintains harmony among and knowledge about the manifest,
assumed, extant, and requisite concepts.

It is not necessary that all four concepts be identical. Rather, all four should
be recognized and allowance made for the tensions created by imbalances. It is
doubtful that an organization can (or even should) achieve total congruence.
The important factor is recognition of the confusions and contradictions.

To achieve integrity in our organizations, each individual within the
organization—particularly the leader—must strive to be open. From its
embodiment in the individual, openness moves to the group level through
interaction and infuses the organizational culture which, in turn, sustains the

characteristics of openness. The process is as slow as the building of a pyramid, and far more complex.

Symbols. The degree to which leadership is truly effective depends on the extent to which individuals place symbolic value on the leaders' intentions and their expression. It's the relationship of the governed to the active centers of the social order that determines a leader's transformative power.

Such centers have nothing to do with geometry or geography. They are the points in a society where its leading ideas come together with its leading institutions to create an arena in which the events that most vitally affect members' lives take place. What's important is that the organization and its members are essentially concentrated on what appear to be serious acts. Involvement, even oppositional involvement, with such arenas and with the momentous events that occur in them translates intention into reality and sustains it. It is a sign of being near the heart of things.

It is not standing outside the social order in some excited state of self-regard that gives a leader that quality. It is an intimate involvement near or at the heart of things that motivates and empowers.

Effective leaders use a set of symbolic forms—ceremonies, insignia—to show that they are, in fact, leading. These crowns and coronations, limousines and conferences mark the center and give what goes on there its aura of being not merely important but, in some fashion, connected with the way the world is built.

Creative space. Where the intention is aesthetically and compellingly presented, the space within the vision can be ambiguous. The leader's intention is a playground, an arena surrounding an idea. It is Ed Land's vision of instant photography; it's Reaganomics; it's Robert Redford painting a verbal picture of the way he wanted the opening scene of "Ordinary People" to look. Mr. Redford did not say, "Use an f/8 opening with 600 ASA film and shoot from this angle." Within his rough, but clear tapestry of intentions, the camera crew had all the freedom in the world to make decisions, be creative, and play.

People knock themselves out in that kind of setting. In the cases of really successful leaders whom I have studied, they did create and express an overall set of intentions which was attractive enough to both involve people and empower them. The space generated by such visions makes transformative leadership genuinely participative and noncoercive.

When I began to realize that the expression of the intention is clear and simple while the space within is ambiguous and roomy, I then began to see that this is the art form of leadership.

Dr. Warren Bennis is professor of research at the University of Southern California's School of Business Administration. He is the author of twenty books and is completing one based on his studies of leadership.

15.
PROFILE OF POWER—
SO YOU THINK YOU'RE
A SUPERLEADER?

Charles T. Post

Today's oustanding leaders have a real desire for power. They are also extremely goal-oriented.

"Unlimited power is apt to corrupt the minds of those who possess it," warned William Pitt, British statesman and friend of the American colonies, more than two centuries ago.

"Power tends to corrupt; absolute power corrupts absolutely," reiterated Lord Acton, British historian, a century later.

"Not true," contends Warren Bennis, professor of management at the University of Southern California Graduate School of Business Administration. "I found that the wielders of power whom I sought out were no more immoral than anybody else.

"I think that powerlessness corrupts more than power does. You can see plenty of examples of people who feel desperate because they lack power and are helpless."

Dr. Bennis is qualified to speak. He is in the final stages of a four-year study of how leaders effectively use power within businesses and organizations.

He believes that universities are turning out M.B.A.s who have been taught to be administrators, but who have not been taught to use the power that goes with administration.

For the past four years, Dr. Bennis has been seeking out successful leaders and studying the qualities which have contributed to their success.

"I believe that power is desirable, that an understanding of its sources and a better understanding of how it is used should be passed along to the leaders of our organization," he asserts.

The foundation of his studies has been in-depth interviews with ninety successful leaders, sixty of them from the business community. The profile of the chief executives comes close to that sketched by the Conference Board: median age, fifty-six years; years in the job, nine; median salary, about $300,000. Almost all of them have a bachelor's degree, about twenty-five percent have an advanced degree. Of those with an advanced degree, about one-quarter received it in business administration.

The leaders in the public sector have diverse qualifications. Two were orchestra conductors, two city managers, two school superintendents, foundation presidents, a museum director, heads of large government agencies, three elected officials—a U.S. Senator, a mayor of a large city and a councilman—a basketball coach and a football coach. Dr. Bennis makes no pretense that this sample is representative, but believes that it is large enough and sufficiently diverse to be valid for his study.

The interviews were thorough. In two cases, he practically moved in with his subjects, spending ten days with each of them. In ten other cases he spent considerable time talking to all of the executives who reported to the CEO being studied and to members of the board of directors.

This is a study of people who are successful, powerful and possibly prominent. Certainly, they are dominant, not merely because of their positions, but by virtue of their ability to empower others and to create a work force that is motivated.

Dr. Bennis makes a sharp distinction between leaders and managers.

"Leaders do the right thing, but managers do things right. You can have people doing things right, but not doing the right things. I am looking for people who create, who haven't just mastered the basic routine but go beyond it. You find corporations and organizations, too, that are smugly doing things right, but doing totally the wrong things."

He acknowledges a popular conception that power in politics goes hand-in-hand with corruption.

"I don't want to say that politicians are impeccable people, but I saw no signs of their being any more or less corrupt than anybody else."

Questions in the interviews were wide-ranging. After establishing a leader's personal background, the train of questioning turned to formative experiences.

"I wanted to find out about the person's career—why he or she decided to take this job rather than that job, why he left a job when he did. I would go over their entire career trajectory. I was curious as to what shaped them as leaders or managers. Then I would ask them what they thought were the problems of innovation in this country. I would chat a little bit about their own leadership. I would ask them to tell me about a success and a failure that they had had in leadership, giving concrete cases.

"I would solicit any advice they might give to graduating M.B.A.s as to kinds of experiences they ought to have, what they should do to become successful as leaders.

"I wanted to know how they sized up a situation, how they made sense out of it. How did they evaluate and how did they form their impressions about reality?

"Is it common for leaders to start out desiring power? Or, did they just fall into it?

"On this point they divided," Dr. Bennis reports. Most of them talk about luck or fate, but I don't agree with that. I think they all have a real desire for power, for achievement. They are goal oriented.

"I was struck more by their diversity than by any common factor. They defied every categorization that you could think of. None of them, for example, had any particular management philosophy. None of the current theoretical 'patent medicine' or 'buzz words' seem to hold up."

Dr. Bennis isolated five traits common to all the leaders. However, he cautions that these possibly account for only fifteen percent of the total variable found in the group.

One of the five is self-regard, a sense of one's worth.

"These are people who know their strengths. They identify their strong points early in life and nurture them. They are very good in figuring out the fit between what they can do best and the needs of the institution they work for. If the fit isn't there, they know when to leave.

"They are very comfortable about themselves. They don't feel that they have to make a case. One of them said, 'I neither want to make a million dollars nor do I have to prove anything.'

"That may sound bloated, but it isn't. This individual really has a fairly good idea of what he can do and he capitalizes on it.

"Real leaders don't deal with failure the way a lot of ordinary mortals seem to; nor, do they get themselves so totally involved. They maintain some separation between themselves and the task. If they fail, take a misstep, or make a mistake, they just keep at it. They don't regard a mistake as failure.

"One of the leaders said, 'I keep making as many mistakes as I can as quickly as possible and get them over with.'"

"Another explained, 'A mistake is just a way of doing things.'"

"Most leaders are not introverted. They are not particularly self-conscious. They are not narcissistic. But they do have a healthy ego."

As a corollary, they spend very little time working on their weaknesses. In their leadership styles, they spend little time trying to domesticate dissent, or trying to win over people who aren't on their side. They work with people who want to work with them.

They don't spend much time worrying about sickness and pathology.

"These leaders really do have a positive outlook about their lives. They know they are going to discover what is out there. I don't know what they do with their doubts—it isn't as if they don't doubt. Doubt just doesn't dominate their thinking."

A second common denominator of great organizational leaders, along with self-regard, is the ability to translate intention into reality and sustain it.

Dr. Bennis points out that before an intention can be translated into reality, it must be expressed convincingly enough to attract and motivate participants. It must be a compelling vision "strong enough to take an organization or a business to a place it has never been before, and secondly, have the capacity to permeate through all levels."

He defines a compelling vision as "a set of symbolic forms expressing a tapestry of intentions."

"The intentions and its expression—crowns and coronations, limousines and conferences—gives what goes on in organizations its aura of being not merely important but, in some odd fashion, connected with the way the world is built."

In addition to symbolism, the studies point to the importance of serious purpose, and of being near the heat of things, in drawing together the leaders and members of the group.

One of the chief executives made the routine observation that it was the people who worked in his organization who made the difference. Then he explained, "The people were willing to take a chance because they felt a part of something magic. They wanted to work that extra hour or make that extra call or stay on that extra Saturday. Perhaps if we had had a different management group that did everything the same, except to instill that magic, we would not have made it."

The capacity to communicate their vision in order to gain the support of their constituencies is a third universal characteristic of the leaders studied.

The leaders all have the ability and capacity to empower others. This is a fourth common factor. Energies and abilities necessary to bring about the desired results are harnessed through the capacity of the leaders to create environments.

Persistency, consistency, and focus together provide a fifth quality common to powerful leaders. They have the ability to maintain the direction of the organization when the going gets rough.

"Leaders have a capacity to find ways and means through which the organization can monitor its own performance. It can compare results with established objectives and have access to a continually evolving data base on which to review past actions and base future ones," Dr. Bennis observes. "Even, if necessary, they possess the ability to rearrange or abandon the organizational structure and/or key personnel when faced with new conditions."

The biggest challenge to leadership, Dr. Bennis feels, does not come from within the organization, but externally.

A constant threat is the distortion of information by over-eager aides who tailor it to satisfy what they consider to be the leader's prejudices.

Dr. Bennis worries that, in too many organizations, a very few people are filtering the facts. Reality implicitly is skewed. Information is selected that provides an inaccurate picture on which a decision may be based.

"The leader cannot rely exclusively on his palace guards for information. Hard as it is to do, he must have multiple information sources and must remain accessible—despite the fact that, in modern times, accessibility seems one of the most underrated political virtues."

Part III
LEADERSHIP STYLES

16.
MANAGEMENT
LEADERSHIP STYLES

Gary K. Hines

> The dynamic and effective leadership shown by a company's management
> is the dominating element in determining the eventual success of a
> company.

When should I be democratic? Autocratic? When should decisions be made
alone; when should this responsibility be shared? How can a supervisor be
flexible enough to meet changing situations and still provide consistent
leadership?

Bill Woods, manager of the finishing department of the Chambers
Manufacturing Company, thought about these questions as he walked from the
main office building to his department. Bill and the other department
managers had just received a paternalistic, yet strongly worded, lecture by Mr.
Chambers on the need to run a "tight ship." Production was down; costs were
escalating; labor turnover high.

Opening the office door, Bill saw Alice Johnson typing. "Have you finished
typing the report I gave you this morning?"

"No sir," responded the clerk-typist. "I still have a few pages left."

"Well hurry up, Chambers wants it," replied Bill as he walked into his office
and shut the door. The three shift supervisors stopped talking and looked at
Bill. Their morning meeting was starting late.

Bill Woods sat down, pushed his white hard hat further back on his head and
spoke. "The company is having difficulties, some departments more so than
others. Mr. Chambers mentioned these things at our meeting. The major
problem is . . ."

"Now that you know about the difficulties, what can the four of us do to
improve our department?" As Bill finished speaking the phone rang.

After completing a brief phone conversation, Bill announced, "That was
the quality control director. Several of the QC people have been working in-

dependently on our parts rejection problem. They don't have an answer yet, but there are some promising leads."

"Now let's go back to the problems that Mr. Chambers mentioned. Do some thinking about possible improvements, and let's get together again on Thursday. I need some good inputs to give Chambers," said Bill as the department meeting concluded.

LEADERSHIP STYLES

Three separate leadership styles—autocratic, democratic and laissez-faire—were evident as Bill Woods talked with employees of Chambers Manufacturing.

Autocratic—The autocratic leader makes decisions alone as power is centralized in one person. Full authority and responsibility are assumed.

Supervision is tight, direct and precise. Decisions are enforced using rewards and the fear of punishment. Subordinates do as they are told. When provided, communication tends to be primarily downward. If the authority of the autocratic leader becomes oppressive, subordinates may become insecure and afraid.

The autocratic leader may become a benevolent autocrat. Subordinates are dealt with effectively and may achieve security and satisfaction. A benevolent autocrat may simply give orders, may use praise and demand loyalty and may make subordinates feel they are actually participating in decisions even though they are doing what the boss wants.

Democratic—The democratic (participative) leader consults the group on questions of interest to them and to which they can contribute. Communications flow freely; suggestions are made in both directions. Praise and criticism are both used. Some decision-making responsibilities still belong with the leader.

Subordinates participate in goal setting and problem solving. This participation encourages member commitment to the final decision. The democratic leader creates situations by which individuals can learn, enables people to check their own performance, allows subordinates to set challenging goals, provides opportunities for improved work methods and job growth and recognizes achievements and helps employees learn from errors.

Laissez-faire—The laissez-faire (free-rein) leader gives power to subordinates. The group can develop its own goals and solve its own problems.

Little or no direction is provided. This style is generally not useful but can be effective in highly motivated, professional groups.

Analyzing the discussions, Mr. Chambers appears to be a benevolent autocrat. The phone call would tend to suggest that the quality control director is using a laissez-faire leadership style; at least with some of the people. Bill Woods is autocratic with Alice Johnson, his clerk-typist, but democratic with the three shift supervisors. Bill is a leader in one group and a follower in the other because of the position he occupies relative to other group members.

There is a difference between leadership and management. Leadership is the activity of trying to successfully influence people to strive to attain the goals of the business. The supervisor's position in the organization gives authority which is enhanced by the respect and trust that subordinates have in the supervisor. This enables the leader to accomplish the plans, purposes and goals of the organization by working with people.

Management is the function of running the business. Common functions include plan, organize, staff, direct, control, coordinate, budget, innovate and represent. The manager gets things done through other people by using appropriate leadership.

The ideal leadership style utilizes all leadership styles to the best advantage. This means that the situation probably will determine the style used.

The effective leader should be concerned for both people and production. Attempt to create situations in which people work together to obtain quality results. Try to have people recognize that there is a strong relationship between job satisfaction and work achievement. The effective leader:

1. is flexible, chooses actions from a range of leader behavior;
2. is aware of himself or herself, the group and the situation. All are considered before selecting a leadership style;
3. lets subordinates know the influence they will have on each issue and how the leader's authority will be used;
4. uses general supervision; subordinates work out the daily details of the job and make many decisions concerning how to do the job within prescribed limits;
5. remembers both the immediate problem and the long term individual or group effectiveness before acting;
6. makes certain that appropriate and timely decisions are made—by the group, if feasible, or individually if the situation requires it;
7. is easy to find when subordinates have a problem to discuss, shows an interest in their ideas;
8. makes good on promises given to subordinates, quickly takes care of complaints and gives sincere answers with no runaround;
9. provides adequate instruction on job methods, safety improvements and how to avoid errors, keeping in mind the level of the worker's experience; reasons why are given.

The title of supervisor or manager does not automatically make one an effective leader. This comes slowly and often with difficulty, depending on you, the subordinates and the situation. However, effective leadership will certainly help a department to increase production, reduce accidents, lower turnover and decrease absenteeism.

As Douglas MacGregor challengingly put it, the manager must arrange things "such that the members of the organization can achieve their own goals best by directing their efforts toward the success of the enterprise." If this can be accomplished, even if only part of the time, your department objectives will be more easily reached.

LEADERSHIP BEHAVIOR

The effective leader uses many means, both complex and subtle, to exert influence and lead an individual or a group to be creative and productive. Leader behavior can be considered to be a continuous range from highly leader-centered (autocratic), to mutual inputs (democratic), to highly group-centered (laissez-faire). Other descriptive words for leadership behavior are: tell, persuade, consult, join and give.

Tell—The leader determines the problem, investigates, evaluates and interprets facts, considers alternative solutions and selects one solution.

Then the subordinates are told exactly what to do. The leader may or may not consider what he or she thinks group members believe or feel. Coercion may or may not be implied or used.

Persuade—As in telling, the leader makes the decision completely independent of the group. However, instead of announcing the decision, the manager tries to persuade group members to accept it. This is done by describing how the decision benefits the interests of both the business and the group.

Consult—At the beginning, group members are given the problem and appropriate background information. The leader asks members for ideas on how to solve the problem; a tentative solution may be given for their reaction. After considering the additional alternative solutions, the leader selects the most promising solution.

Join—The leader agrees in advance to carry out whatever decision the group makes. The leader is involved in the discussion as just another member.

However, limits placed on the leader by superiors are made known to the group.

Give—The leader defines the problem and any limits within which it must be solved. The problem is then completely turned over to the group to work out a solution satisfactory to them. The leader supports the solution, provided it fits into the established boundaries.

ESTABLISHING LEADERSHIP

Supervisor who is an effective leader will use many methods in order to implement objectives. These methods will vary depending upon the relationship with the people.

With subordinates—A very effective way to convey leadership is to clearly define objectives so subordinates understand production requirements. Make people feel like a team by informing them of their relationship with other parts of the organization. Always have the time to talk with subordinates in the office or on the job. Standards and rules must be clearly communicated and understood, then consistently and reasonably enforced in order to bring about corrective action as needed.

As a supervisor, the majority of your work is dealing with people. Your job is to mobilize the mental and social forces of individuals so they will be motivated to work together, with understanding and assurance, toward the common goal of productivity. High output results when you spend time coordinating and organizing group activities and keeping the work going. Do not do the same work as subordinates or output will suffer.

Follow these six leadership principles and you will hear complimentary comments from subordinates:

1. **Set goals and objectives with group members.** "Our boss frequently asks for our opinions and discusses changes with us before final decisions are made."
2. **Help subordinates reach group goals.** "My supervisor sees that we have good equipment and materials on hand when we need them."
3. **Coordinate work activities.** "We have a good boss. He gives all of us a chance at the good jobs—no favorites."
4. **Help members fit into the group.** "On our shift the boss sees that the right people work together. New employees are made to feel comfortable."
5. **Have an interest in the group, not a self-interest.** "Our leader usually pulls for us and will stick out her neck for us with those in the main office."

6. **Show human interest.** "My manager is easy to see and talk with. When I do a good job, appreciation is shown."

With higher management—When appropriate, support subordinate requests you present to superiors. If an error or complaint is made, take the responsibility for it instead of finding a scapegoat. When management makes an unpopular policy, present it to subordinates as if it were your own.

With other departments—Be totally aware of the relationship of your area with other departments. When difficulties arise that will affect others, inform them immediately. Cooperate with other departments in order to mutually achieve company goals.

With unions—Completely understand the labor contract, its provisions and its implementation. Recognize that the contract is a legal, signed operating agreement between the company management and employees who are represented by the union. Administer the contract fairly. Cooperate with union leaders so that a certain level of trust develops. At a later date, this mutual trust can be very important.

USING STYLES

The saying, "Leaders are born, not made," is only partially true. Leaders are made by understanding their potentials and limitations and then developing the latent leadership talents within them. A leader's effectiveness is determined by many factors.

Effective leaders may gain cooperation through their competence, personality and management approach in handling people. Leaders may come on strong in terms of getting the task done or in terms of relationships with people. Essentially effectiveness depends on a variety of styles in any situation and the degree of leadership exerted.

One's leadership effectiveness may depend upon the relationship of the manager to the subordinate, the job being done and the perceived power of the manager. Also the appropriateness of the leader's behavior may determine leadership effectiveness. Identical behavior by a boss may be very appropriate in the eyes of one subordinate but inappropriate as viewed by another subordinate.

The nature of the work, size of the group and the type of people involved are important. For a large work group, the supervisor needs to be an effective planner, organizer, coordinator and delegator. For a small work group, a supervisor who is located close to employees needs to be aware of and deal with individual considerations and needs of workers.

When managing people who are inclined to do the job because they want to, like to and enjoy it, the easy-going leadership styles (democratic, consult, join) will work best. But when supervising individuals who don't enjoy work, don't want to get ahead and see a job only as a means to make money to satisfy their own personal desires, the harder leadership styles (autocratic, tell, persuade) often are necessary if the job is to be correctly accomplished.

Communication is critical to effective supervisory leadership. Essential requirements are an ability to communicate well, to keep communication lines open at all times and to communicate in such a manner that workers' human-relations needs are satisfied.

Your effectiveness as a supervisor also is directly influenced by your attitudes which are shown or heard by others. Your attitude toward yourself, subordinates, other supervisors, higher management and company policies and objectives influence results obtained.

The skill of leadership largely lies in knowing when to use which style. Your problem as a supervisor is to vary the styles, and the degree, to fit the changing conditions under which each unique individual in your group is working.

17.
TRACING THE EVOLUTION
OF LEADERSHIP STYLES

Brian H. Kleiner

> To determine which leadership style is appropriate, it is necesary to
> determine the "task maturity" of the group members.

Leadership, the process of influencing the activities of others towards goal achievement, has long been recognized as a vital aspect of management. Accordingly, a tremendous array of studies has been conducted in this important area.

The current theory of leadership has evolved from fifty years of studies on this subject. It is derived from the best features of the earlier theories of leadership. First, though, it is important to examine the historical "roots" of this theory in order to bring us up to present-day thinking. Specifically, leadership will be viewed from five perspectives which illustrate the development of the current model: the leader; the leader and group; the leader, the group, and the situation; the leader's two primary concerns—production and people; and, finally, the contingency approach.

At one time, it was believed that leadership was a right that one inherited from birth. This went out of fashion with the realization that people born into leadership roles often are not leaders.

The first major formal approach to the study of leadership, known as the "trait approach," was the primary theory in leadership study between 1900 and 1940. In effect, researchers of that period started to ask: "How do leaders differ from followers in terms of personal traits?"

When the results of all the research efforts were studied collectively, there were some traits that leaders seemed to have in common. These traits included originality, popularity, sociability, aggressiveness, desire to excel, humor, cooperativeness, liveliness, and athletic ability. However, researchers slowly began to realize that this approach to the study of leadership was not entirely valid, as the results varied from one occupational group to another.

Researchers then began to ask: "What *styles of behavior* did leaders exhibit in their specific groups?" and a new perspective began to emerge.

THE LEADER AND THE GROUP

Two important studies were conducted by researchers that addressed the leader/group perspective. In one study, D. Cartwright and A. Zander developed the *functional* approach to leadership. They saw leadership behavior as a result of the performance of two functions: task (or goal achievement) functions and relationship (or maintenance) functions.

Task functions consist of facilitating and coordinating group effort in the selection, definition, and solution of a common problem. The leader will initiate ideas, seek and give information or opinions, clarify the ideas of others, elaborate upon the ideas of others, summarize the ideas shared by the group so far, and test to see if the group has a consensus on the issue under discussion.

Relationship functions involve developing the way in which members of the group work together, emphasizing loyalty to one another and to the group as a whole. The leader must be friendly, warm and responsive to others, express feelings sensed in the group, and harmonize and facilitate the participation of others.

In the other study, K. Lewin, R. Lippitt, and R. White identified three basic styles of leadership: Authoritarian (where the leader has all the power and influence in decision-making); democratic (where the leader shares power and influence in decision-making with his group); and laissez-faire (where all the power and influence in decision-making is given to the group members).

According to their research, the best leadership style in terms of productivity and group satisfaction was the democratic style. The study emphasized the democratic leadership style over the authoritarian leadership style, which was once widely believed to be the most effective style of leadership.

THE LEADER, THE GROUP AND THE SITUATION

The new emphasis put on the democratic style encouraged managers to reexamine their style of leadership. As a result, many changed their styles from authoritarian to democratic and obtained substantially better results.

However, a large number of managers still remained unconvinced that the democratic style was always better than the authoritarian style with every group in every situation.

During the late 1930's R. Tannenbaum and W. Schmidt plotted leadership styles along a continuum, based on the degree that power and influence in decision-making was retained by the boss or shared with subordinates. They identified four basic styles of leadership along this continuum—"tells," "sells," "consults," and "joins." "Tells" is the authoritarian style of leadership, and "joins" is the democratic style of leadership. Democratic leadership has many different shades of meaning based upon the relative degree that power and influence in decision-making is shared between the boss and his or her subordinates.

More importantly, however, they dispelled the notion that the democratic style is the best approach to leadership with all groups in all situations. Rather, they suggested a mix of all styles of leadership—ranging from "tells" to "sells" to "consults" to "joins"—may well be the best. To determine which would be the most effective at any point in time, it is necessary to consider three sets of forces—those within the leader, those within the group he or she leads, and those within the overall situation.

For instance, if the leader's natural style inclination was to keep the bulk of the power and influence in decision-making to him or herself, and his or her group did not have a great deal of ability or motivation to deal with the problem, and there was a fairly large amount of time pressure in the situation, then the "tells" or "sells" leadership style would probably be best. Conversely, if the leader's natural style inclination was to give a lot of power and influence in decision-making to his or her subordinates, and the group had a fairly large amount of motivation and ability to deal with the problem, and there was not much time pressure in the situation, then the "consults" or "joins" leadership style would probably be best.

The effective leader, then, is the one who has the sensitivity to determine the nature of the three sets of forces, the ability to decide which leadership style was most appropriate, and the behavioral flexibility to adopt the appropriate leadership style in actual work situations.

THE LEADER'S TWO PRIMARY CONCERNS: PRODUCTION AND PEOPLE

While the Tannenbaum and Schmidt leadership continuum model did much to extend current thinking at that time, the model can be criticized as being too cumbersome to understand in its entirety, in terms of the various styles of leadership as well as the wide array of forces within the leader, his group, and the situation. Furthermore, even if a manager could remember all the gradations of leadership styles and all the forces, there is no means of measuring the forces or indicating what style of leadership is appropriate with what combination of forces.

In the 1960's, a highly useful theory of leadership was developed by R. Blake and J. Mouton. Through their model called the "managerial grid," leadership was defined by two fundamental leadership concerns—concern for production and concern for people. Bearing these areas in mind, there are five basic styles of leadership, which are as follows:

- If a person showed a *high* concern for production but a *low* concern for people he or she was considered to lead in a *task* (or authority obedience) management style.
- If a person showed a *high* concern for people but a *low* concern for production, he or she was considered to lead in a *country club* management style.
- If a person showed a *low* concern for *both* production and people, he or she was considered to lead in an *impoverished* management style.
- If a person showed a *moderate* concern for *both* production and people, he or she was considered to lead in a *middle-of-the-road* (or "organization man") management style.
- If a person showed a *high* concern for *both* production and people, he or she was considered to lead in a *team* management style, considered to be the best leadership style.

The major drawback of this model is that it views the team management leadership style, which is essentially the same as the democratic style, as the best leadership style for all people in all situations. It also suggests that concern for production and concern for people should always be equal. In actual day-to-day management experiences, there are too many instances where this is not practical.

THE CONTINGENCY APPROACH

The best integration of ideas concerning leadership into one comprehensive and yet relatively understandable model, drawn up by P. Hersey and K. Blanchard, suggest that there are two sets of behaviors necessary to effective leadership: task behavior and relationship behavior. Given these two sets of behavior, four leadership styles are possible. They are:

- Telling—high task, low relationship behavior
- Selling—high task, high relationship behavior
- Participating—high relationship, low task behavior
- Delegating—low relationship, low task behavior

Like Tannenbaum and Schmidt, Hersey and Blanchard suggest that each of these leadership styles may yield highly effective results. To determine which style would be most appropriate, it is necessary to determine the "task maturity" of the members in one's group. Task maturity is defined as the degree of willingness and ability to assume responsibility.

- With subordinates of *low* task maturity, the *telling* approach is likely to be most effective.
- With subordinates with *moderately low* task maturity, the *selling* approach is likely to be most effective.

- • With subordinates with *moderately high* task maturity, the *participating* approach is likely to be most effective.
- With subordinates of *high* task maturity, the *delegating* approach is likely to be most effective.

This model illustrates the nature of effective leadership and capitalizes on the strong features of the earlier theories while avoiding their shortcomings. Thus, it currently is perhaps the single most impressive model for selecting the most effective leadership style for any work situation.

Brian H. Kleiner, Ph.D., is assistant professor of management with the School of Business Administration and Economics at California State University at Fullerton.

18.
YOUR LEADERSHIP STYLE

Edward Glassman

How to capitalize on subordinates' perceptions of you. To determine your real leadership style requires you to find out how you affect your subordinates and how they perceive you as a leader.

Your leadership style is the collection of characteristics you use to influence your subordinates in order to accomplish organizational goals.

Your real style is not always what you think it is, but is what your subordinates perceive it to be.

To determine your real style requires you to find out how you affect your subordinates and how they perceive you as a leader. To do this, make enough copies of the questionnaire for you and your subordinates. Ask each of your subordinates to fill them out honestly. (Even if you decide to be the only one who takes the survey, it will still provide helpful information, although the feedback from subordinates is best). Their answers should be anonymous, to encourage frankness, and arranged in such a way that potentially embarrassing information does not remain a part of the culture of the organization or is not deposited in its files. One way to do this is to give each subordinate a stamped envelope addressed to an outside consultant or friend, who will keep all responses confidential and reveal them only to you. This person will compile and deliver the answers to you in such a way that you do not associate any comments with a specific subordinate. In addition, your consultant can help you plan your response to your subordinates' feedback.

Fill out this survey as though you were one of your subordinates viewing yourself and save it to compare with the perceptions of your subordinates.

Determining Your Supervisor's Real Leadership Style

A Leadership interaction characteristics	B How often does your superior do this?	C How well does your superior do this?	D How often is this appropriate to your • willingness to do the task • ability to do the task • performance level
	Rarely — Very often	Needs much improvement — Very well	Rarely — Very often
I			
Decides and tells subordinates what to do.	1 2 3 4 5	1 2 3 4 5	1 2 3 4 5
Decides and tells subordinates how they are to do each task.	1 2 3 4 5	1 2 3 4 5	1 2 3 4 5
Decides and tells subordinates when to do each task.	1 2 3 4 5	1 2 3 4 5	1 2 3 4 5
Models and demonstrates how each task is to be done.	1 2 3 4 5	1 2 3 4 5	1 2 3 4 5
Decides solutions to disagreements alone.	1 2 3 4 5	1 2 3 4 5	1 2 3 4 5
Total Points			
II			
Solicits and listens to subordinates' ideas.	1 2 3 4 5	1 2 3 4 5	1 2 3 4 5
Coaches subordinates in their work when needed.	1 2 3 4 5	1 2 3 4 5	1 2 3 4 5
Gives frequent, informal feedback on performance.	1 2 3 4 5	1 2 3 4 5	1 2 3 4 5
Allows the person to participate more and more in planning and making decisions.	1 2 3 4 5	1 2 3 4 5	1 2 3 4 5
Negotiates disagreements by solving problems mutually.	1 2 3 4 5	1 2 3 4 5	1 2 3 4 5
Total Points			

III

Encourages independence.	1 2 3 4 5	1 2 3 4 5	1 2 3 4 5
Allows subordinates to make decisions and solve problems associated with their specific tasks.	1 2 3 4 5	1 2 3 4 5	1 2 3 4 5
Consults with subordinates on their assignments mainly to provide support and encouragement.	1 2 3 4 5	1 2 3 4 5	1 2 3 4 5
Listens and responds nonevaluatively.	1 2 3 4 5	1 2 3 4 5	1 2 3 4 5
Resolves disagreements between others in a catalytic, nonevaluative way.	1 2 3 4 5	1 2 3 4 5	1 2 3 4 5

Total Points

IV

Interaction of the task is mainly factual.	1 2 3 4 5	1 2 3 4 5	1 2 3 4 5
Delegates task and allows subordinates to work and make decisions on their own.	1 2 3 4 5	1 2 3 4 5	1 2 3 4 5
Allows subordinates to set their own pace and to determine ways to accomplish the tasks.	1 2 3 4 5	1 2 3 4 5	1 2 3 4 5
There is little or no day-to-day interaction on the task.	1 2 3 4 5	1 2 3 4 5	1 2 3 4 5
Allows subordinates to exercise talents and attain their own standards of performance.	1 2 3 4 5	1 2 3 4 5	1 2 3 4 5

Total Points

Messages To Your Superior At Work

Please list what you like about your superior's leadership style:

Please list what you want improved in your superior's leadership style:

Please list things your superior does that help increase your effectiveness at work:

SCORING

Add separately the numbers circled in columns B, C and D and record the total in the indicated space.

Column B: A score of 20 or above indicates you use this style a great deal. A score of 12 or less indicates you may want to use this style more often. The leadership style with the most points in column B is a rough indication of your leadership style. Most people have one strong style with a secondary style as backup.

Column C: A score of 20 or above indicates you probably are very skillful at this style. A score of 12 or below indicates you may want to develop your skill at this style. Characteristics marked 1 or 2 in column C indicate a need for change or more training. Only you can decide if this is true.

Column D: A score of 20 or above indicates you use this style appropriately to meet your subordinates' work-related needs, with respect to their willingness (motivation), ability and performance of specific tasks. A score of 12 or less indicates you may want to develop greater awareness and sensitivity to your subordinates' needs. Characteristics marked 1 or 2 in column D are red flags that can make subordinates resentful and lower motivation and productivity.

YOUR LEADERSHIP STYLE

Research has shown that most leadership characteristics at work fall into two basic types: *task behaviors*, which are directive, one-way communications explaining what each person is to do and when, where and how it is to be done, and *relationship behaviors*, which are supportive, two-way communications involving listening nonevaluatively and other types of encouragement. The relative frequency with which you combine and use these two types constitutes your leadership style.

Various combinations of task and relationship behaviors can be combined, resulting in four useful leadership styles (these styles correspond to those marked by Roman numerals). The are:

I. Directive style: Your predominant characteristics are telling, asserting and modeling.

II. Participative style: Your predominant characteristics are coaching, negotiating and collaborating.

III. Catalytic style: Your predominant characteristics are encouraging, facilitating and consulting.

IV. Nondirective style: Your predominant characteristic is delegating.

One factor in choosing which leadership characteristic to use is the ability of your subordinates to work independently of you. That is, they are *willing and motivated* to do the task, they have the *ability* to do the task and they have a *high performance level* with respect to the task.

A directive style is called for when subordinates are not very independent. Otherwise, exert less control.

RESPONSES TO YOUR SUBORDINATES

Respond to the feedback from your subordinates on your leadership style in a way that 1) increases their trust in you; 2) improves the overall productivity of your unit; 3) raises their motivation to do better, and 4) will improve your leadership style and effectiveness. For example, one way to do this is to call a meeting of your subordinates to thank them for their cooperation and to reveal what you learned. Then, as a team, plan ways to improve their motivation, raise productivity, and improve the quality of the unit's interactions.

CHANGING YOUR LEADERSHIP STYLES

Experience indicates leadership styles are often hard to change. Yet in the process of helping your subordinates to be more productive, you need the skills of all four leadership styles. How can you do this? One way is to become more effective in the leadership style you normally use, and then *add on* enough of the other skills, one at a time, so you can respond flexibly to your subordinates, treating each according to ability and motivation. To become a more flexible leader, you might decide to obtain training in how to *assert* for a more effectively directive style; how to *listen and respond nonevaluatively* for a more effective catalytic style; how to *delegate* for a more effective nondirective style; and how to *negotiate* disagreements using mutual problem-solving techniques for a more effective participative style.

Edward Glassman, Ph.D., is head of the Program for Team Effectiveness and a professor in the School of Medicine of the University of North Carolina at Chapel Hill.

19.
EXCELLENCE AT THE TOP:
A LEADERSHIP STYLE THAT WORKS

Thomas J. Peters

> Forget what you've read about Theory X and Theory Y, the managerial
> grid, and participatory versus authoritarian styles. An analysis of those
> who hold the reins at our top-performing companies produces a fascinat-
> ing profile of effective managers.

Can a control-minded chief executive successfully lead his company
through an era of aggressive expansion?

Is participative leadership effective in an industrial environment where cost-
competition is the name of the game?

Can a gifted marketing specialist give the right kind of leadership to a high-
technology business?

Why is it that brilliant entrepreneurs so often begin to flounder as their
companies push past the $50-million sales mark?

Such questions are familiar and fertile subjects among members of the business community, and in no industry are they more provocative than in the
hospitality field, where an increasingly less hospitable business environment
now mandates new approaches to management. As the days of explosive
growth and failure-proof management recede into memory, the managers of
hotel and restaurant firms must shift gears to hold the line against increasing
competition, turning their attention from expansion to such concerns as image
enhancement.

Recently, in quest of data relevant to the questions above, my colleagues and
I systematically reviewed the experiences of a score of companies that have
executed major shifts of direction with notable skill and efficiency. The results
suggested, surprisingly, that the similarities that mark effective leadership
styles may be a lot more important than the differences. Repeatedly and con-
spicuously, the chief executive officers of these companies exhibited a common
pattern of behavior: namely, obsessive attention to a myriad of small ways of
shifting the organization's attention to the desired new theme. The value of

brute persistence may be vastly more important than the scanty references to it in management literature would suggest.

Moreover, it appears to be accompanied, almost unfailingly, by a common set of supporting attributes:

- Consistency in support of the theme, usually over a period of years;
- Orchestration of all management systems, formal and informal, to achieve noticeable *shifts in organizational attention*;
- Conscious use of *symbolic behavior*, often regarded by outsiders as transparent hokum;
- Everyday execution-oriented activity characterized by positive reinforcement of small successes and the strong *encouragement of experimentation*;
- Extensive *contact with down-the-line managers*, often circumventing the official chain of command and usually involving an extraordinary amount of time in the field:
- Efforts to increase motivation through surprisingly large *grants of autonomy* far down the line: and
- A dominant theme or message concerned with building or enhancing just *one or two basic organizational skills.*

"MANAGEMENT BY WALKING ABOUT"

Before exploring these attributes, consider a few examples. None is more to the point than the transformation of United Airlines—from a paper-choked bureaucracy to a profitable, service-oriented business—achieved by Ed Carlson, whose skills in cultivating a service orientation were presumably honed during his tenure in UAL's hotel division. Immediately after taking over as chairman in 1970, Carlson hit the road and insisted that his colleagues do so as well. For nearly two years, they spent sixty-five percent of their time spreading the gospel of customer service at all levels. Carlson gave his 1,700 station managers added autonomy as a means of inducing innovative, service-oriented ideas. His deadly efficient, personally managed follow-up routines brought action within days after he returned from the field with lengthy "to-do" lists. He installed the same ethos—labeled as "visible management"—among his middle managers. (They called it "management by walking about.") By sheer brute persistence, time on the road, and tireless attention to the care, feeding, and autonomy of his key field troops, Carlson transformed UAL in just five years' time.

Against stiff odds: Take another case with implications for hospitality executives. Ren McPherson turned sleepy Dana Corporation into a $3 billion star performer over the last decade by incessantly preaching cost reduction and productivity improvement—again, to the people far down the line. Against stiff odds (for example, most members of the firm's work force are UAW members), Dana doubled its productivity in seven years—several times faster than the U.S. average. McPherson and his colleagues broke all the rules for a basic manufacturing business. He began by throwing out all the policy manuals and most of the detailed systems, replacing them with a one-page statement about achieving "productivity through people." Like Carlson, he and his colleagues spent an extraordinary amount of time in the field. And they stressed down-the-line autonomy as well, turning their plants as far as possible into independent entrepreneurial business units by establishing what they called the "store manager" concept. Notable among the numerous devices employed to stimulate exchanges of productivity ideas and programs within and among units is "Dana University," where thousands of managers meet with senior executives each year. Dana's uniform business philosophy is largely shaped in Dana University's classrooms. It took McPherson ten years of consistent plugging to accomplish his miracle.

Hammering it home: A final instance is the Bank of America, which over the past decade has surpassed its New York competition not only in size but also in profits. The dominant reason, in the view of the press and of industry observers, is Tom Clausen's decade-long emphasis on profit rather than volume—previously an anomaly in the banking business. "Ask an officer, 'How's business,' and you'd immediately hear how many loans he'd made," recalls Clausen. "I tried to leave my stamp by making everyone aware of profit." He accomplished it mainly through consistent, persistent questioning, hammering home his dominant concern with profits.

The men behind these three dramatic shifts of corporate direction run the gamut from introvert to extrovert. None of them is notably charismatic, and at least one of them has been described as colorless. Yet each, through five to ten years of determined effort, has somehow changed the "mind-set" of thousands upon thousands of managers.

Every cranny of the organization: The same pattern emerged from a recent study of a score of companies that have performed superbly over a period of years—Caterpillar Tractor, Hewlett Packard (HP), Johnson & Johnson, and 3M. Each of these companies still gives obsessive attention to the theme that historically drove it to a high level of excellence. Both 3M and HP, for instance, pride themselves on their ability to innovate: they manage to replace very nearly their entire product line every four to five years. In these companies the new-product theme dominates management systems, annual reviews, club meetings, even lunch-table chat. A senior accountant in one of these companies said to me, "Everyone here gets into the act, and I mean everyone. A week after I started in accounting, a division sales manager took me out on a customer call. I've been part of the market-customer team from the beginning. They showed me what the company stands for in our products, and how I could directly contribute in shaping and reacting to proposals." Similarly, the customer-service theme at IBM still intrudes, as it has done since the early days, into every cranny of the organization. Said a sales vice president, "Tom Watson Senior sure is alive and well—he's right here with us in this room."

But let us examine each of the basic elements of this common pattern of leadership, using examples from our sample of excellent companies.

BE CONSISTENT

Managers in the service industries may find some food for thought in a discussion I recently had with the chief executive of a service business. He complained that his best efforts to raise what he viewed as the unacceptable low level of quality delivered by his organization had had hardly any impact. He argued that he had always been four square behind quality. But the issue, of course, is *consistency*. Did he consistently stress quality over the dozens of competing themes in his communications with the organization? His colleagues claimed that he didn't: "Of course he's for quality. But he's for everything else too. It's a 'theme of the month' drill around here."

The executive found a partial solution in noticeably shifting much of his time and attention to quality-related issues. He undertook, for instance, a monthly three-day "quality review" in the field. For the first several months, the view from below was that "this too shall pass." It took him almost a year of doggedly beating the "quality" drum to convert skepticism to belief, and finally to commitment.

The tools of consistency are simple things like visits, calendar shifts, even informal memos. A division manager was trying to make his managers think longer and harder about competition. He developed the habit of going back to the office, after each presentation he saw, to dictate a half-dozen notes relating some key point he had heard about the competitor-analysis issue. By the end of a year, he had sent almost eight hundred notes, over seven hundred of them focused directly on issues of competitor analysis. Most were sent directly to junior staff and line managers.

A final form of consistency is consistency among media. In HP and 3M, all systems, reviews, and even social gatherings resound to the same tune. The annual reviews focus on new products. So does the starting job for the newly hired M.B.A. So does the extraordinary amount of budgeting devoted to getting R&D management out into the field with the customers.

A major mining company had long been handicapped competitively by poor exploration results. A consultant searching for the reason found no obvious differences between successful and unsuccessful mining companies. Both types budgeted comparable amounts for exploration: both types hired geologists from the same schools. But somehow it seemed to him that exploration was "in the air" at the successful companies. An analysis of top-management meetings and their minutes confirmed the impression. The winners talked endlessly about exploration, while the losers were preoccupied with a vast miscellany of issues. Top management in the problem company was accordingly persuaded to start revising its meeting agendas to stress the exploration theme. Over a three-year period these managers upped the exploration content of their meetings from fifteen to sixty percent. With the theme alive at the top-management level, the overriding concern with exploration began to gain credence throughout the organization—and, over time, the results did begin to improve.

SHIFT ATTENTION

There is no want of instances in which a senior executive has successfully seized hold of the channels of corporate communication—formal and informal—to force a *shift of attention* to a new theme or issue. The effects cannot be accurately modeled; the location and frequency of the response are, in fact, almost impossible to predict. But given time and repetition, the tactic works almost unfailingly.

USE SYMBOLIC ACTIVITIES

Tupperware produces about two-thirds of the $2.5-billion Dart Industries' earnings. Every week, each of Tupperware's 250 distributorships holds an assembly at which its "dealers" (Tupperware has 80,000 part-time salespeople) are individually welcomed to the stage in the order of their sales during the preceding week. Almost all of the distributorships have their own theme songs, and it's hard for a dealer to get through a year without accumulating a box full of medals.

This kind of hoopla is by no means limited to Tupperware and Avon; similar use of *symbolic activities* marks other, more staid institutions. A Bank of America executive notes, "Seldom does a week pass that we don't pat our branch managers on the back." At Texas Instruments (TI), a number of the company's hundreds of factory-floor productivity teams are regularly chosen to report to the full TI board on their successes. Similar devices are in use at Dana, IBM, HP, and 3M, among others.

Outsiders often call this sort of thing "Mickey Mouse." Insiders know it can't be cost-justified, but also know that it can be a priceless source of motivation, often for tens of thousands of employees. In most of the top-performing companies, one finds extraordinary zeal and dedication far down the line. The strength of IBM's sales and service people, Frito-Lay's sales force, and Dana's foremen and plan teams comes in large measure from the time and attention—largely symbolic—lavished on them by senior management.

ENCOURAGE EXPERIMENTATION

A Digital Equipment Corporation (DEC) executive told me, "When we've got a problem, we don't go by the books. We get the right people together, lock them in a room for a few days, and fix it." As president of Bell & Howell, Peter G. Peterson deplored the underutilization of the quick-and-dirty experiment: "Before we let an idea get emasculated, and before we let any thoroughly rational appraisal of the idea convince us that it will not work, we ask ourselves if there is any way we can experiment with it at low cost. The experiment is a powerful tool for getting innovation into action and is probably not as widely used as it should be. . . . If we can get the concept of the experiment built into our thinking and thereby get evidence on a lot of these 'can'ts,' 'won'ts,' and 'shouldn'ts,' good ideas will be translated into action."

The leaders of superb performers tend to live by the dicta "Try something," "Fix it," "Don't analyze it to death." The test-observe-retest loop is notably absent in a host of companies where the execution frame of mind has been eroded by a paralysis of analysis or other forms of death by delay.

We've come to label the *successful experimenting process* as the "small win" approach. Successful strategic-change managers—especially in their frequent visits to the field and contacts with down-the-line players—ceaselessly and opportunistically seek out small examples of desired behavior. Then, often with fanfare, they note it, reward it, and try to speed the diffusion of the successful new activity throughout the system.

"One of the problems in American corporations," said Ed Carlson in a recent *Organizational Dynamics* interview,[1] "is the reluctance of the chief executive officer to get out and travel, to listen to criticism. . . . Practicing visible management and talking to people, you will take a lot of heat, because employees will argue with you. But you've got to accept that, because those people have the same objective that you do. They want to be associated with success. Sometimes they're right and sometimes they're wrong, but by and large, people in management, office employees, and people in various other jobs have a better idea of what's good for the company than someone sitting at corporate headquarters. In short, it pays to listen."

The chief executives of our top-performing companies seem in almost every case to have taken that verity to heart. It is said that ex-chairman Patrick Haggerty of TI made a practice of stopping by a development lab on the way home each night when he was in town to chat with a few of TI's young engineers. Gene Milner of little Lanier Corporation, successfully competing in the word-processing business with such giants as IBM, insists that each of his twenty senior executives make field sales calls every month. Not surprisingly, Lanier is known for its exceptional customer orientation. And J. Willard Marriott, Sr., in his mid-eighties, still regularly visits hotel sites to instill in person his dogmatic approach to quality, returning home with long follow-up lists.

In all these cases, we see senior people actively keeping in touch with the customer and the technology. Perhaps more important, they are testing the credibility of the message at the grass roots. Is the sales rep actually calling on the newly identified customers? Does the customer recognize the new focus on service? Are the foremen actually coming up with new ways of stimulating productivity-related ideas from the factory floor?

LOOK DOWN THE LINE AND GRANT AUTONOMY

The power of a *down-the-line focus* was strikingly demonstrated in Toyota's recent cost-improvement effort. Top management decided to revitalize the mundane suggestion box. Through an intensive three-year campaign it increased the annual flow of suggestions from a few tens of thousands to well over a million—taking, in the process, fully a quarter of a billion dollars out of the company's cost base.

Effective CEOs and division chiefs know they cannot tap this power by communicating to the troops through channels. Deliberately and with tireless persistence, they take their message personally, regularly, and directly to the field.

When business units are given *substantial grants of autonomy*—even though there may be some duplication, internal competition, or loss of scale economies—a certain magical element appears. Fletcher Byrom, chairman of Koppers Corporation, recently increased the number of the firm's business units by a factor of six—not, as he made plain, in response to market pressures, but rather to give his thirty best young executives the chance to run their own shows.

Alfred Sloan once noted that one of GM's last hundred or so promotions into general management had come from the company's giant Chevrolet Division; all were from smaller business units. His explanation: Those in the smaller units learned more quickly to be good, well-rounded business people.

At 3M, an institution where "the eleventh commandment is never to kill a new product idea," attention is lavished on the "product champion," normally a volunteer. ("Our failure rate is dreadful whenever we force someone to be a champion," an executive notes.) The "champion" can go to a variety of sources for funds, and his bosses are graded on the number of new-product projects, especially from outside their own businesses, that they have taken on in the course of the year. The 3M new-product teams are staffed with full-timers, who stay together during the whole development-to-launch cycle and are rewarded as a group.

Or take TI's IDEA (Identify, Define, Expose, Act) program. It was explicitly designed to counter the idea-killing that marked formal review, and to promote the flow of new-product experiments by junior engineers. The process is designed to minimize hurdles: a young engineer can readily get twenty or thirty thousand dollars to test a new notion after convincing any one of a large number of specially designated senior technical-staff members. At any given time, several hundred projects are going on throughout the company. One notable recent success was TI's popular "Speak 'n' Spell" machine.

Envious competitors have called IBM "the biggest small business in the world." The point is of a piece with the rest of this argument. Somehow, despite the size of their organizations, the chief executives of the best-performing companies have managed—through brute persistence and attention to mundane but significant detail—to keep autonomy, idea flow, and entrepreneurial spirit alive all the way down to the shop floor, the sales branch, or the service desk. None of them has fallen prey to the notion that they or their teams ought to manage by remote control, through formal systems and staff-driven decision presentations.

FOCUS ON ONE OR TWO CONCERNS

So far, we have ignored the substance of the themes that these leaders so persistently strive to instill in their organizations. I believe, however, that even in a quick overview we ignore the issue of substance at our peril, because the nature of the themes themselves is remarkably consistent across our sample of top performers. A small handful of themes keep recurring—*a focus on just one or two basic organizational skills.*

Most common is a simple effort to turn the company's attention from internal (usually bureaucratic) to external concerns. At 3M, HP, and Johnson & Johnson, this effort takes the form of an overriding focus on new products. At DEC, IBM, Caterpillar, Frito-Lay, and Marriott the external emphasis takes the form of intensive concern with customer service and reliability. The other most common theme is productivity. It is gospel at Dana, Emerson Electric, TI, IBM, and P&G, among others. The virtues preached—new products, service, reliability, productivity—are simple and pervasive. They are subtly yet clearly linked to the "hands-on" style we have repeatedly noted.

The linkage is nicely captured by Alistair Mant, an ex-IBM executive, in his book, *The Rise and Fall of the British Manager.*[2] "I remember as a fairly lowly IBM employee, deploring the way the Management Review Committee—the holy of holies—concerned itself with detail out in the boondocks. Surely, I thought, they ought to stick to strategic matters. I see it better now; they were keeping their feet in the mud, and it made them better strategists. . . . My assumption is that a factory has a special character and personality when senior management understand its detailed working in their bones, and their hands; the system as a whole has a sense of integration in a way that split-off management can never achieve. A top Swedish engineering manager put it succinctly to me: 'If I go down on the line, it is because I want to see if the fix on yesterday's production worked; an Englishman probably goes down because they told him in a course that the workers like it. They can tell the difference!'"

APPLY OBSESSIVE, BRUTE PERSISTENCE

The similarities of style among the leaders of our top-performing companies have little to do with entrepreneurial versus bureaucratic behavior, or Theory X versus Theory Y ideology. Rather, they center on a common pattern of obsessive, brute persistence in pursuit of a few basic themes. All this may not be news to some. But it cannot be known to most, for companies exhibiting the contrary pattern are legion. We observe a constant shifting about of management attention; themes that center on trappings rather than fundamentals; inconsistency of management emphasis over time; programs that penetrate only three layers down in the organization; failure to instill the concept of work-group responsibility at the shop-floor or sales-branch levels; and, above all, a fickleness of focus that is the very antithesis of obsessive, brute persistence.

The adjectives "obsessive" and "brute" have been used deliberately. The phenomenon they describe is by no means confined to business. A recent study of Nobel prizewinners in science concluded that what really distinguishes the winners from their peers is remarkable persistence; they are more aptly described as good finishers than as creative marvels. There is no better example than Thomas A. Edison, a workaholic who, for instance, in a single twenty-two night stretch in April 1872 invented no fewer than twenty-three new devices to permit simultaneous two-way transmission on a single line. The last one worked.

Or take sports. An analysis of exceptionally successful baseball pitchers relative to lesser performers suggests that they succeed—that is, get more wins—by pitching more innings, especially against poor performers. They don't miss a turn against the Seattle Mariners or the Toronto Blue Jays. On being elected to the Hall of Fame, pitcher Robin Roberts remarked, "I had a lot of opportunities. [Fellow Hall-of-Fame member Warren Spahn] and I had the same secret; for twelve or thirteen years, we just didn't miss many starting turns."

So whether we are considering seven hundred memos about competitor analysis, the care and feeding of seventeen hundred station managers, a million cost-cutting suggestions, twenty-two all-nighters by Mr. Edison, or a dozen years of missing few starts on the mound, the message is the same. It seems that the absence of easy solutions and the presence of brute persistence are reliable common denominators of successful leadership styles. Managerial gimmickry rarely makes or saves the day; nor will getting the Theory X-ers and the Theory

Y-ers sorted out and assigned to the right slots assure successful corporate performance. There are, it appears, few if any short-cuts to sustained excellence or lasting strategic change.

REFERENCES

1. W. Dowling, "Conversation with Edward Carlson," *Organizational Dynamics*, Spring 1979, pp. 49-62.
2. Alistair Mant, *The Rise and Fall of the British Manager* (New York: Holmes and Meier, 1978).

Thomas J. Peters is a principal with McKinsey & Company, Inc., in San Francisco and serves as co-leader of the company's organizational effectiveness practice.

20.
THE CASE OF THE MISSING BOSS

Mary Miles

> Showmanship—all that running around with fantastic plans—may make
> an impression on superiors or peers outside the department, but
> subordinates won't be impressed with glamour—they need leadership to
> get the job done.

A boss is supposed to be dependable and strong; a leader who oversees
projects and intercepts disaster. But there's another kind of boss—the absentee
boss—whose neglect and indecisiveness is an albatross, weighing down
productivity and creating interoffice chaos.

There are two types of missing managers. The "hyperactive," fleet-footed
boss is a blur of movement, zipping to meeting to luncheon to meeting, in an
effort to sidestep work. The other type of boss is "there but not there." This
"passive" manager stays in the office but finds subtle ways to shed his or her
responsibilities.

The reasons why different executives become "missing managers" and the
ways they accomplish this vary tremendously. But all absentee executives share
one characteristic: the ability to shirk their commitments and responsibilities.
Many go to extraordinary lengths to do so.

Some hyperactive managers have what psychologists call "the dramatic
personality." They are usually aggressive, flamboyant, egocentric, impulsive,
adventuresome, uninhibited, and creative. Typically, they are so intent on
proving how busy and brilliant they are that their subordinates rarely see them.
These managers are rarely in the office—they're always busy organizing a new
task force, presenting hot ideas to upper management, fulfilling yet another
speaking engagement, winging off to London to start a branch location,
attending conferences . . .

When Dick Virunurm, an Atlanta based education and government consultant for the Burroughs Corp., Detroit, describes the absentee boss, he speaks
from experience. "In my line of work I see many 'hyperactive' absentee

managers," he says. "This syndrome is particularly common among smart young fast-trackers. Exceptionally bright whiz kids can either successfully use their brilliance or kill their careers with it. It's so easy to lose your perspective. The showmanship—all that running around with fantastic plans—may make an impression on superiors or peers outside the department, but subordinates won't be impressed with glamour—they need leadership to get the job done."

It's not uncommon for hyperactive bosses to be totally unaware that they're neglecting their responsibilities, says Virunurm. But there are warning signs for managers who suspect they have similar tendencies. "First you begin to notice that you're not hitting the deadlines like you used to," says Virunurm. "Then you find that your subordinates don't come to you with their problems anymore. A most ominous sign is when you realize your superiors are bypassing you to go directly to your subordinates for decisions and action."

What happens when a hyperactive manager is away on a jaunt? Most likely, his or her subordinates take over the neglected duties. If no one assumes leadership, chaos may result. If subordinates vie for power, infighting can occur. Then there's added confusion when the lines of authority become muddled each time the hyperactive boss reappears to regain command. The returning manager will barge through the office, changing procedures and interrupting the work that has progressed in his or her absence. Because these bosses are away so often, they have lost sight of long-term objectives and tend to concentrate on trivialities. They often nitpick endlessly until they become distracted or get the urge to travel once again.

Another characteristic of the hyperactive boss is an inability to successfully delegate responsibilities. These managers are so tied up in ego, ideas, and motion—that they have little time or energy to devote to mentorship. "Most hyper bosses are very insecure," says Virunurm. "When managers are frequently absent, it becomes difficult for them to define work goals or recognize problems. Productivity and morale suffer as the manager's problems spiral throughout the department. Ultimately, these problems can affect the entire organization."

Passive bosses also have trouble delegating and assigning tasks. Although they tend to stick close the the office, their doors remain closed as they agonize over charts, lists, and trivia. And if their doors are open, it's probably because they're away from their desks socializing or involved in an insignificant task. Because of this absorption with minutiae, they seldom accomplish any substantial projects. And when it's time for decisions to be made, they're nowhere to be found. Passive bosses are so reluctant to commit to any form of action that eventually their authority and credibility wither away.

To compensate for this lack of leadership, other employees may take over for the passive boss. Even when these replacements are not the most logical candidates to pinch-hit, most passive managers are pleased to be relieved of tough decisions; they'd rather be seen as good guys—or not seen at all.

Cheryl Lieberman, senior project director at Goodmeasure Inc., a

Cambridge, MA, consultancy, says "Unlike hyperactive managers, who run around and are highly visible but don't accomplish much, passive bosses are stationary. They may chit-chat around the water cooler or they may be reclusive and distant. But one thing that passive bosses have in common is that they've ceased to believe in their abilities. They've lost control over their own destinies—they're almost 'retired on the job.' They have very little opportunity and very little power—they're stuck."

Some managers are so busy just holding their department together that they have little opportunity to keep informed on organizational changes and new technologies. Both Lieberman and Virunurm believe the corporate structure is responsible for this dilemma. "In MIS/dp, in particular, many talented managers get left behind," says Virunurm. "The organization doesn't press them to keep informed on general information because they are so vital to daily dp operations. They become the high priest of the black box. Before long, they become antiquated and resistant to change. They're experts one day and dinosaurs the next."

These specialists are rewarded by being promoted up and out of the mainstream into jobs that are either dead ends or don't truly suit their interests and abilities. Or they may be promoted into jobs demanding skills and responsibilities that they're unprepared for, says Lieberman. If you detect a bit of yourself in the description of either the hyperactive or the passive boss, it's not too late to break bad habits. If your job itself is causing avoidance behavior, Lieberman suggests that you "think hard about how your job is designed. Does your organization have career paths that let you keep growing by moving laterally or upward? Is there a suitable position that will offer you challenges, learning opportunities, and responsibilities within your capabilities?" You may have to seek the help of a career counselor or mentor, look for a more fulfilling position within the organization, or leave the organization entirely.

If the solution seems to be leaving the organization, hyperactive and passive bosses should seek out corporations that offer clear-cut career objectives that will help them stay on the right track. "Absentee managers develop a survivalist mentality that leads to confusion about goals and priorities," says Lieberman. Without a strong organizational structure, managers can easily lose themselves to superactivity or immobility—or anything else that will help them avoid their duties.

Is there any hope for those who are hit hardest by the missing manager: the subordinates? Although Virunurm is doubtful about whether a subordinate can turn a missing boss into a productive one, he does offer a suggestion: "The worst strategy is to proceed willy-nilly without consulting your boss. The entire department should meet to list the problems the boss's absence is causing. But be diplomatic—avoid making accusations."

To be a strong and supportive manager, you need critical organizational support and the ability to chart your own career. As Cheryl Lieberman says, "When managers are in jobs in which they have confidence, opportunity, and the power to accomplish their goals, the results are amazing."

21.
FOLLOWING THE LEADER: HOW TO LINK MANAGEMENT STYLE TO SUBORDINATE PERSONALITIES

Joseph A. Steger
George E. Manners, Jr.
Thomas W. Zimmerer

Two objectives of every employee—self-enhancement and self-protection—determine what kind of follower he or she is. The most effective leaders link their leadership strategies to subordinates' followership styles.

The successful manager has always led his or her subordinates, to a great extent, by examining and responding appropriately to their behaviors. This observation opens the possibility of developing a theory of "followership"—the other side of the leadership equation.

A followership theory would classify typical subordinate reactions to leaders into recognizable behavior patterns, just as there are identifiable leadership styles. This would help the leader develop appropriate behaviors of his own for interacting with subordinates. And, since we are all followers in some way, a followership theory can tell us more about ourselves.

THE ENHANCEMENT/PROTECTION CONFLICT

In managing others, the role of the leader is to convince followers that if they raise their incremental performances, they will receive some sort of identifiable reward, or increase security. Correspondingly the basic dimensions of followership are the desire for job enhancement and recognition, and the desire to be protected from failure.

Both tendencies affect the follower's willingness to take risks. Unfortunately, they are difficult to measure because they are always in conflict; desire for enhancement increases one's willingness to take risks, and failure avoidance decreases it.

Enhancement of Self. The follower's desire for enhancement of self implies a wish to participate more in the organization's formal system of status and explicit rewards. Thus a follower would seek enhancement by assuming more responsibility and taking greater risk. Therefore, every follower has some desire to "solo"—to be a star. This, however, is tempered in varying degrees by desire for:

Protection of Self. Fear of failure—and desire to protect oneself from it—is one of the most pervasive explanatory motives in organizational behavior literature. (Moreover, individuals frequently fear social consequences of failure as much as they fear failure itself.)

Fear of failure, organizational researchers tell us, manifests itself in such worker tendencies as apathy, defensiveness, and aggression. Regardless of a followers's desire for enhancement, the protection-from-failure motive can be so strong as to cancel the enhancement motive altogether. When this happens, it is natural for the leader to ask: Who is responsible? The organization, via its track record in reacting to employee's failure? Or the leader may question whether he, himself, is at fault. Or is the protection-from-failure motive innate to the follower and therefore uncontrollable?

FOLLOWERSHIP DYNAMICS

We must next examine how the relative strengths of these two variables mold systematic *behaviors* of followers. Willingness to take risks, after all, is only one tendency; the actual nature of followership, and its implications for the leader, is far more dynamic.

Figure 1. classifies individual followership behaviors into nine categories (each will be examined below) characterized by low, medium, and high levels of enhancement desire and failure avoidance. (These behaviors may also be seen as representative of entire occupational roles or entire organizations.) They may be learned behaviors—acquired by followers prior to joining an organization—and so ingrained that the organization may not modify them but only deal with their implications. Or the behaviors may have been acquired since joining the organization (as a function of the system of rewards and punishments) and/or maturation. (Motives for enhancement and protection must be somewhat correlated with age, social history, and so on, regardless of leaders' actions.)

Figure 1.

Followership Types
Derived From the Enhancement/Failure Avoidance Conflict
Protection of self and/or extended self*

	High	Medium	Low
High	The Game Player	The Achiever	The Kamikaze
	Substitutes status for performance. Focuses on political cues. Defensive. Uses power relations to resist change.	Productive. Persistent goal setter. Needs feedback. Definite movement for change.	High energy level. Productive. Organization change stressed. Occasional folly. Could be costly for the organization.
Medium	The Bureaucrat	The Super Follower	The Artist
	Productive. Enjoys status symbols but recognizes personal limits. Very low risk. Maintains status quo.	Productive. Average achiever. Some movement for change. The ultimate follower.	Productive. Positive attitude toward change. Must watch risk levels. Many times works for self-satisfaction but enjoys recognition.
Low	The Apathetic	The Donkey	The Deviant
	Nonproductive. Defensive. Withdrawn. Apathy actually represents fear.	Low level of productivity. Has no interest in formal system of status and rewards. No movement unless pushed.	Impossible to motivate. Could-not-care-less attitudes. High turnover rate. Can be destructive.

(Left vertical axis label: Enhancement of Self and/or Extended Self)

*Extended self would apply primarily to one's family but, under some conditions, might also apply to one's work group.

What implications do these categories have for leadership behavior? And, indeed, what implications do they have for followers, in understanding their impact on leaders and other members of the organization? In analyzing each followership style, emphasis will be placed on the manager's role and methods used to influence followers' behavior. Most followers can be effectively led if the leader is aware of what the followers want and what they fear.

The Game Player

One might assume that intense desire for enhancement in terms of formal status symbols and rewards and great desire for protection from failure would be incompatible. However, such is not always the case: The Game Player simply does not recognize the dissonance. This individual wants all the trappings of status and power but none of the risks. The Game Player actually substitutes, intellectually, symbols of performance for performance per se.

Game Players are sensitive to organizational politics and, if they acquire staying power, can be valuable to the leader. However, this individual is invariably defensive and resistant to change. This can be dangerous since the Game Player uses power and its symbols, often effectively, to marshal support for resistance, or to gain an optimal position in a conflict.

The weaker the leader, the more successful the Game Player. The good manager may not like the Game Player, but can always use him by effective manipulation of status symbols. A poor manager does not recognize that the game is being played, and cannot intellectually separate actual performance from the Game Player's symbols of performance.

Game Players avoid risk by predicting the "right side" of an issue based upon who supports it. Insecure managers—who are frequently Game Players themselves—find the Game Player to be a comfortable couch. These followers comprise the entourage that often surrounds the executive, and they derive much of their power from association with higher-level executives. They will use symbols of power to influence others to perform tasks they consider risky, then carry the successfully completed task forward under the illusion of being the producer.

The Game Player is easy to identify because of his desire for status. Photos with key executives, a wall full of awards and certificates, and the like create the continuing illusion of power and influence. The Game Player usually has formal education and degrees to aid his credibility. Managers are better off without the Game Player. If Game Players are part of their followership, they are easily managed—but never loyal.

The Achiever

The individual who has a high desire for enhancement and is reasonably ready to accept the possibility of failure is the classic Achiever. He loves visible symbols of success and takes risks to get them, but he avoids really big risks. The Achiever is productive, is a goal setter, and desires a great deal of performance feedback.

To many managers, however, the Achiever is also annoying. He is too goal-oriented in an ambigious world, too concerned with the social relativity of symbols of success, and constantly needs feedback. Yet, the Achiever is receptive to, and shows movement toward, organizational change.

The Achiever typically wishes to develop a close personal relationship between himself, the job, and his supervisor. The leader, in the mind of the Achiever, needs to know how to achieve results, or there is a quick loss of respect. This follower requires that the leader demonstrate technical knowledge *and* ability to deliver rewards.

In essence, managing the Achiever requires more excellence than with any other type of follower. An Achiever will not follow a poor manager for very long. The Achiever requires a manager who plans ahead, and is decisive and dynamic. Together they plan for new mountains to climb, execute the plan, and reap the rewards.

The Kamikaze

For this individual, fun, fame, and fortune are the goals—never mind the risks. In situations requiring significant organizational change, the Kamikaze can be a leader's delight. On the other hand, Kamikazes may get themselves, the leader, and the organization into serious trouble. They are typically immature, have little concept of extended self, have not become jaded enough to fear failure, and have tremendous need for symbols of success. Although they alienate those with a greater desire for protection, they are usually productive.

Although often innovative, the Kamikaze generally is not an effective problem solver. The Kamikaze sees a problem, jumps to the first conclusion, and charges forward. His energy and enthusiasm often carry the day. The Kamikaze can quickly create resentment among those he comes in contact with, because he employs politically insensitive methods to accomplish results. Thus, the Kamikaze's supervisor should expect to spend a great deal of time repairing the damage this individual creates.

A manager may effectively appoint a Kamikaze to complete some tasks that create flux in the organization. If the manager has a straightforward task that needs to be accomplished quickly and for which he can offer a visible reward, the Kamikaze is the person to assign.

The Kamikaze is easily managed at the start of a task; however, he is hard to control once underway. Thus, the manager should have some *a priori* plan for removing the Kamikaze from the task.

The Bureaucrat

Typically found in the administrative ranks, the Bureaucrat ranks, the Bureaucrat is the classic "organization man" (or woman). As a category of followership, however, one must remember that this term originated with the work of Max Weber (*The Theory of Social and Economic Organization*), in which bureaucracy was viewed as an ideal form of organization. Thus the Bureaucrat is generally productive, because he enjoys status symbols and the trappings of power—yet understands his role's limitations.

On the other hand, this term has evolved to imply organizational members preoccupied with preserving the current structure. The Bureaucrat is a very low risk taker and, when change is necessary, can become indecisive and procrastinate since failure avoidance is so dominant.

In a slow-growth organization, Bureaucrats are often viewed by their superiors as excellent followers. Their work rate is constant, their behavior predictable. Leaders often find that followers who are predictable, dependable, and moderately productive are a joy to manage. Consequently, leaders create many of them.

But when external or internal threat creates a need for change, these managers offer little. If the leader can offer both a solution and a guarantee of protection, the Bureaucrat will then follow—but only then. These followers are administrators in the very sense of the word: They maintain administrative and bureaucratic systems; cannot tolerate ambiguity; and constantly strive to maintain known environments within which to work.

Bureaucrats are apparently easy to manage, yet their own rigidity can become a severe problem for their leader. While acknowledging change, they do so only superficially and often frustrate the content or function of change.

The Super Follower

This is the ultimate form of followership. This individual desires rewards, although not as much as the Achiever. The Super Follower assumes a position of moderate risk. Thus he is usually quite productive to the organization. The history of great performances rarely includes organizations without members having a tremendous desire for personal enhancement—but that does not say that these organizations did not have plenty of Super Followers.

If there is a followership style that can maintain a high productivity level while remaining self-motivated to change, it is the Super Follower. He can be molded by the leader, yet can act independently in adapting to new situations—while retaining a positive commitment to the organization.

He follows, yet does what is best for the organization, balancing personal gain against organizational gain.

Super Followers are easily managed because they are mature and open, and they have a sense of propriety not found in the Kamikaze or the Game Player. They are true assets and need to be rewarded, both short- and long-term.

The Artist

The Artist bases his decision of what work to pursue on personal and/or professional pleasure or achievement. Such behavior may involve a high level of risk in the eyes of others in the organization (and they may be right). Thus, Artists can be productive, although the leader must allocate time to monitor work direction and risk levels. In addition, the leader must be aware that Artists are also exhibitionists—which implies need for formal recognition by the organization.

The key to motivating an Artist is to find the proper work for him to do. When the leader has a chance to work with the Artist in identifying that "one best task," productivity from the Artist works for the delight of the creation *per se*. He revels in the systems or products of his work, not their outputs or efficiences. This, then, requires the leader's practical hand and guidance.

The Artist poses another problem for the manager: Since he never sees his work as finished, he revises and revises. In the demanding work world, this can be a manager's nightmare.

The Artist is difficult to manage from the manager's plan-execute-results point of view. Artists make significant contributions, but their leaders require an eclectic management style.

The Apathetic

Some desire to participate in the formal system of rewards is necessary for followers' productivity. When the follower has no such desire, coupled with intense desire for protection from failure, he will exhibit insidious behavior—apathy.

Defensiveness, withdrawal, and so on accompany apathy. However, the history of the organization's (or leader's) distribution of rewards, as well as its reaction to failure, may to a certain degree justify this apathy. This may be particularly true when the individual's only perceived source of "protection" is another organization which may be in conflict with the formal organization (such as a union).

To break through the barriers the Apathetic employee constructs, the leader must redesign structural elements of the job that may have served as the source of apathy. Forced assumption of responsibility, training, and job change are some approaches.

This work redesign *must* be attempted, because the Apathetic is an organizational cancer. Not only does this follower not produce, but he hides in the woodwork of the system. Behind the scenes, he fights any changes which he feels may result in his being exposed. This is contagious: Other workers learn that you can beat the system even if you cannot be successful within it. Accountability and its associated visibility are the Apathetic's nemesis.

The Apathetic is difficult if not impossible to lead; the best remedy may be termination.

The Donkey

What distinguishes the Donkey from the Apathetic is the amount of power the organization (or leader) can exert over the individual. The Donkey will respond to change essentially because he has to, but rarely will the response be based on expectation of formal rewards. Thus, the Donkey is characterized by very little movement, unless he is pushed, and low productivity. Again, however, one must assess the organization's effect on these behavior patterns. Certainly, when McGregor defined Theory X (authoritarian management), he was thinking of leaders who *assumed* that their followers were Donkeys.

If you inherit a staff of Donkeys, you will be quite tired at the end of the day. Productivity is achieved by a continuous string of threats and the exercise of power. The donkey does not want what you have to offer and, if he does, he does not expect to get it, given his incremental effort. Establishing credibility takes time (and control over rewards).

The manager's problem is that the donkey thinks effort is performance. Therein lies a related problem: Donkeys expect rewards for effort regardless of outcome.

The Deviant

Since he has no desire to participate in the formal reward system, and is unafraid of the visibility of failure within the organization, the Deviant responds against the organization. This individual could not care less what the leader thinks, and is usually a high-turnover category of employee.

Deviants are like red ants: When you see one, you had better step on it before it bites you. Leaders should not believe that their job is one of a social worker. Time spent on changing this follower is not invested in enhancing of high-performing followers. If the manger finds he has Deviant followers, he had best look to the selection process that is providing them and change entry routes into the organization.

OPERATIONAL PATTERNS

Since these categories of followership are so observable in organizations, they raise two important questions for leaders. First, what organizational/leadership behaviors create (or reinforce) followership categories? Second, how does an individual manager create motivation and change when dealing with specific types of followership?

How closely an organization ties its system of status symbols and rewards to incremental performance and the assumption of responsibility is obviously an important determinant of followership categories and their intensity. Concomitantly, how an organization responds to individual failure serves as a catalyst to developing various types of followers. Let us deal first with the system of status symbols and rewards and its equitability in the organization. As a predictor of emerging followership categories, a careful distinction must be drawn between symbols and rewards associated with position (usually hierarchical level) and rewards associated with incremental performance within position. The "climate" created by variations in these two rewards systems leads to certain followership types. This is outlined in Figure 2. Thus, reward distribution delineates the categories of followership illustrated in the first row of Figure 1.—Game Player, Achiever, and Kamikaze.

Figure 2.

Followership Types Emerging With Reward Distribution

Rewards for incremental
performance within position

		Not High	High
	High	Game Player	Achiever
Rewards for position			
	Not High	?	Kamikaze

Thus, to the extent that the reward system aids high-enhancement followers, the organizational pattern of reaction to failure and its tolerance of self expression serve to separate medium- and low-enhancement followers. This is illustrated in Figure 3.

Figure 3.

Followership Types
Emerging With Failure Reactions and Tolerance of Self Expression

Tolerance of expression

		High	Not High
	High	Bureaucrat	?
Negative reactions to failure			
	Not High	Artist	Super Follower

The last three categories of followership—Apathetic, Donkey, Deviant—can be placed in an organizational context by understanding the distribution of power. Since low-enhancement followers are predicted by (1) little relationship among performance and rewards, (2) high negative reactions to failure (by the organization), and (3) little tolerance for self-expression (by the organization), the amount of power that can be exercised by the organization becomes extremely important.

This is outlined in Figure 4. Our observation is that when there is high countervailing power, typically a union, Apathetics abound—often regardless of the extent of the formal organization's power. On the other hand, when countervailing power is low, the amount of power that can be exerted by the organization, or the leader, becomes the predictor of the emergence of the Donkey or Deviant.

Figure 4.

Follower Types Emerging With Power Distribution

Organizational power

		High	Low
	High	Apathetic	Apathetic
Countervailing power			
	Low	Donkey	Deviant

CREATING MOTIVATION FOR CHANGE

The organization's nature and emergence of followership categories, although based on direct observation, is still tentative. Many other developmental factors external to the organization—social history, marital status (the extended self can be very important), predisposition to achievement motivation—may also predict emergence of follower stereotypes. Thus, no matter how these behaviors emerge, the leader's task is to deal with them as they exist. Introducing change is a critical motivational task facing the leader, relative to many followers categories.

When organizational change is made imperative by either internal or external events, each followership category, as previously discussed, is predisposed to support or resist a new set of behaviors. By identifying the follower's basic tendencies, the leader can more effectively develop a workable change strategy—either for individual or collective followers. We again stress that a manager is not a social worker; the situation may demand change, and the leader must be instrumental in its introduction and implementation.

Conceptually, there are three basic approaches to organizational change: (1) the direct-power approach, (2) the supportive, developmental approach, and (3) the devious, manipulative approach. In fact, all three approaches can be appropriate, depending upon the severity of the change and the targeted followership category.

Figure 5 outlines the basic change approaches that we believe to be the best strategies for each followership category. Since the Super Follower, the

Figure 5.

Basic Change Approaches To Follower Categories

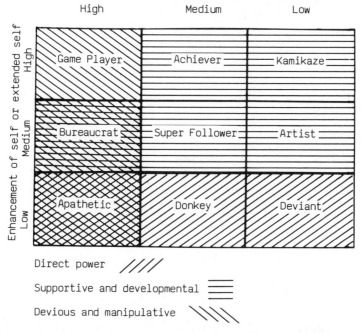

Direct power

Supportive and developmental

Devious and manipulative

Achiever, the Kamikaze, and the Artist are all willing to take and desire enhancement, a supportive and developmental strategy is preferred. Of course the nature of this support, as well as the extent of the leader's direct participation, must vary depending on the category. The Bureaucrat should also receive support, clarity, and development, although the leader should somewhat conceal the fact that change is imminent.

The greater the extent of self protection, the greater the necessity for a manipulative approach where the Game Player is concerned. Also, the less the desire for enhancement, the greater the necessity for a direct power approach. When the follower does not want to participate in the formal reward system (or does not expect to), the leader usually has no other choice than direct power. When a countervailing power (pressure of a union) is significant, a healthy dose of deviousness is usually also required.

Speaking specifically rather than conceptually, we have observed various techniques of introducing change that managers effectively use. These are listed in Figure 6. Of course, the three basic change approaches—direct power, support, manipulation—can be keyed to specific follower types as in Figure 5, thus providing a comprehensive strategy to introducing change among various follower categories.

Figure 6.
Examples of Specific Change Introduction Techniques

Change introduction technique	Basic change approach		
	Direct Power	Support	Manipulation
Dictate	✓		
Discussion/Salesmanship	✓	✓	
Training	✓	✓	✓
Participation		✓	
Rumor			✓
Modeling			
Coworkers		✓	✓
Competition			✓
Create system failure	✓		✓
Surveys		✓	✓
Consultant	✓		✓
Manuals	✓		✓

We should stress that the way change is introduced is more crucial to success than actual implementation. Introductory techniques are what really address resistance, even among those willing to take risks.

RELATIONS AMONG FOLLOWER GROUPS

We are often asked: If leaders segment followers, and vary change strategies depending upon follower categories, will this not create dissatisfaction among some follower groups? The answer is yes—with two important caveats. First, previous success is the ultimate predictor of group satisfaction. Second, managing to motivate is substantively different than managing to minimize dissatisfaction. The former approach can work: the latter never will.

Also, interactions take place among followers simultaneously with manager's actions. These second-order interactions, so to speak, are another set of complications for the manage to understand. These interactions are determined by the make-up of the group (number of different type followers) and can enhance or detract from the manager's actions. Managers must study their followerships' make-up; develop strategies to motivate based on different followership types; and use followers' actions directed at each other to enhance their own strategy.

IMPLICATIONS OF FOLLOWERSHIP

Serious questions emerge throughout the study of followership that reflect on the leader: Can a manager adapt to a diversity of followers? Can management training provide the manager with these skills? Can managers learn new leadership approaches when moving to new levels and therefore new followerships?

Questions relating to organizational systems make the followership examination even more complex, such as: Does company policy allow managers flexibility in followership? Is the compensation system tied to performance so a manager may use it to manage?

Lastly, the study of followership leads to serious questions about selection and turnover. Those chosen today are not necessarily the right people for the organization tomorrow. Security and job longevity are more critical than ever. The need for this followership study reveals that companies often pay scant attention to the future when hiring and very little attention to strategic human resources planning and development.

Some commonly held cultural beliefs and organizational policies remove the organization's ability to optimize leader-followership relations. These policies, such as tenure in a university, remove one complete dimension—job security—of the motivational framework both leader and follower should work within. Moderate job security is one thing; complete employment guarantees regardless of contribution is another.

The followership framework outlined above requires a manager who understands his subordinates, works in a milieu that provides for diversity of management actions, and is allowed to reward his followers to enhance their motivation. Hopefully, more study of the manager-followership interface will lead to better organizational structure without undue concern for existing power relations. All power is a compromise, and the study of followership is aimed at optimizing this compromise so that all can win.

Joseph A. Steger is executive vice president and provost of the University of Cincinnati; George E. Manners, Jr. and Thomas W. Zimmerer are professors of management at Clemson University.

22.
LEADERSHIP, MANAGEMENT, AND THE SEVEN KEYS

Craig M. Watson

> Outstanding companies are distinguished not by the leaders who head them or by the managers who run them, but rather by the manner in which leadership and management are harmonized.

A comparison of traditional organization theory with the 7-S model highlights key differences between mangers and leaders. The distinction may lie in purposeful use of the "soft" tools of style, staff, skills, and shared goals.

In recent years a good deal of excitement has grown around the implications and significance of the 7-S organizational framework,[1] stemming both from the insights the system yields into organizational effectiveness and from the explanation it provides for consistently outstanding performance by excellent companies.[2]

In brief, the theory holds that the traditional view of organizations pivots on three axes: *strategy*, which leads almost implicitly to organization *structure*, and *systems* which orchestrate complex functions resulting in performance. The 7-S construct, by contrast, suggests that four additional S's are critical to achieving and understanding the effectiveness of excellent management: *style*, the patterns of action, symbolic and actual, which top management communicates to the organization at large, and which the organization itself ultimately adopts as a cultural orientation; *staff*, meaning the people side of the organization equation, especially the socialization and development process which molds managers into effective, acculturated performers; *skills*, the company's unique competences and dominating attributes; and *superordinate (or shared) goals*, the set of values or aspirations which underpin what a company stands for and believes in.[3]

The significance of the new framework (as others have stated) is in the attention it draws to the "soft," informal facets of organization which formerly were considered insufficiently systematic or "hard" to be of interest. The traditional approach focuses on the relatively easy-to-change strategy, structure, and systems, while the new approach alerts us to the crucial role played by the more elusive features.

The key factors distinguishing the 7-S framework from the traditional approach to organizational effectiveness, in fact, focus on the change levers which leaders, as distinct from managers, have always manipulated to effect organizational change and to achieve superior performance. By extension, much of what the 7-S approach embodies is the direct result of observing organizations run by leaders as opposed to managers. The implications of this perspective are manifold. For example:

- If one believes that there is a difference between leadership and management, then there is some question as to whether managers can achieve 7-S performance at all.
- Society produces far fewer leaders than it does managers. The socialization process which cultivates managers also reinforces tradition, whereas leaders succeed in making change.
- Some cultures more naturally incline toward utilization of both the hard and the soft levers to effect change and achieve performance. This, in fact, has been called the "art of Japanese management." Does this imply that certain cultures are more naturally adept at creating leaders than others?
- Achieving 7-S management is a long-term undertaking. There is some question as to whether the predominantly short-term orientation of American management can be modified sufficiently to make the transition successfully.
- Finally, our management education system reinforces the traditional view of organization performance. The relative novelty of the 7-S framework makes it unlikely that the approach will be adopted quickly by the educational system.

These issues, while indeed speculative, are worth raising because it is easy to embrace new techniques and approaches as panaceas before fully appreciating their implications. Thus they are put forth as cautions. This having been said, let us return to the distinctions between leadership and management.

The seminal work on the difference between leadership and management is Abraham Zaleznik's 1977 McKinsey award-winning contribution.[4] Zaleznik explores the distinctions in attitudes toward goals, conceptions of work, relations with others, senses of self, and manner of development. Using these basic headings, I will underscore the correspondence between the leader's broad focus on multiple elements of the seven keys, and contrast this with the manager's traditional attention to the more limited set of organization factors.

ATTITUDES TOWARD GOALS

Goal-setting is a central element in the guidance of organizational achievement. Through setting an overall target on performance and focusing group effort, the executive—leader or manager—implicitly concentrates organizational energies in a given direction.

Zaleznik argues that "Managers tend to adopt impersonal, if not passive, attitudes toward goals. Managerial goals arise out of necessities rather than desires, and, therefore, are deeply embedded in the history and culture of the organization."[5] In contrast, leaders "are active instead of reactive, shaping ideas instead of responding to them. Leaders adopt a personal and active attitude toward goals. The influence a leader exerts in altering moods, in evoking images and expectations, and in establishing specific desires and objectives determines the direction a business takes. The net result is to change the way people think about what is desirable, possible and necessary."[6]

This fundamental distinction in goal-setting attitudes is expressed in the way goals are set in organizations and in the goals which result. The *manager* is more likely to identify threats and opportunities and mobilize to respond to them in a systematic fashion through focus on *strategy*. The *leader*, on the other hand, tends to define a *superordinate goal*, such as product leadership, quality, service, or being number one; in working to achieve that goal, the leader commands outstanding performance. To leaders, strategy is the overall pattern of executing goal achievement. Managers are more likely to see strategy, or a component of it, such as product differentiation or lowest cost, as the overriding issue, rather than the corporate goal itself. Semantics plays a part, but not a big one: lowest cost is a strategy; "number one" is a value.

In McKinsey's studies of excellent companies Thomas Peters states, "The operating principle at well-managed companies is to do one thing well. At IBM, the all-pervasive value is customer service. At Dana it is productivity improvement. At 3M and HP it is new product development. At P&G it is product quality. At McDonald's it is customer service, quality, cleanliness and value. . . .At all these companies, the values are pursued with an almost religious zeal . . ."[7]

CONCEPTIONS OF WORK

Irrespective of how goals are set, organizations must deal, operationally, with the mundane details of getting things done. They must organize and execute the thousands of tasks which, collectively, result in performance, for better or for worse. In the course of this activity, there are decisions made, resources allocated, and positions taken which, in substance, form the work of the organization. In this context, Zaleznik underscores distinctions between managers and leaders in the areas of choice and risk-taking.

"In order to get people to accept solutions to problems, managers need to coordinate and balance continually. . . . The manager aims at shifting balances of power toward solutions acceptable as a compromise among conflicting values."[8] The leader, alternatively, "needs to project his ideas into images that excite people, and only then develop choices that give the projected images substance. Consequently, leaders create excitement in work. . . .Unless expectations are aroused and mobilized, with all the expectations inherent in heightened desire, new thinking and new choice can never come to light."[9]

These conceptions of work manifest themselves both in managed and in led organizations: Leaders are inclined to make work exciting by encouraging an organizational *style* that is intuitive, highly personal, and tied in closely to the "carrots" that motivate key players to perform. Moreover, the leader's company is more likely to promote entrepreneurial autonomy at appropriately low levels in the organization, as a way of motivating people to make choices for themselves which, collectively, improve the performance of the whole. Peters reports: "Well-managed companies authorize their managers to act like entrepreneurs. . . .As a result, these managers develop unusual programs with results that far exceed those of a division or corporate staff."[10] In so doing, leaders use *structure* to advantage as a motivational extension of their leadership style.

Inherent in the decentralized structure is a higher level of risk, since the choices made are more removed from the leader's direct control. A higher degree of remoteness from operating decisions is accepted by leaders, because they tend to "work from high-risk positions, indeed often are temporarily disposed to seek out risk and danger, especially where opportunity and reward appear high."[11] Thus, in the leader's *style* we see an inherent capacity to invest faith in people's desire to respond to excitement, risk and opportunity. This faith can only exist, however, when the leader has assembled appropriate staff and skills necessary to ensure high levels of performance. In consequence, the leader is more comfortable placing his faith in his own or in his key executive's judgement than in analysis, quantitative methods, and other potential assurances. He knows the difference between "computer printouts" decisions and "cigar and brandy" decisions and is comfortable with either when he has faith in the people involved or in his own judgement. Because he is willing to take risks on people, the leader depends less on *structure* to dampen the impact of risk, and even less on *systems* to gather information and to make things happen.

Managers, alternatively, in their need to coordinate and balance, place a great deal of faith in *systems* and *structures*. Thus, we see managers' companies *dominated* by planning, forecasting, capital budgeting, and other systems which, at the extreme, can actually supplant judgement.

From the standpoint of risk, Zaleznik points out that for "those who become managers, the instinct for survival dominates their need for risk, and their ability to tolerate mundane, practical work assists their survival."[12] Again we see systems coming to the rescue, with major challenges or unique opportunities continually staffed out for study and analysis, and returned with balanced (read: low-risk) recommendations. Similarly, an overly managerial environment tends to be one in which new ideas wither and die, largely because top management is perceived as so risk-averse that venturesome ideas are viewed as having little chance of approval.

RELATIONS WITH OTHERS

Human relationships, in one form or another, are the essential ingredients of organization performance. The manner in which these relationships unfold and operate in the organization determines the quality of organizational performance. As expected, managers and leaders see their relations with others differently.

Zaleznik tells us managers seek out activities with people, but at the same time, "maintain a low level of emotional involvement in these relationships. . . The manager's orientation to people, as actors in a sequence of events, deflects his or her attention away from the substance of people's concerns and toward their roles in a process."[13] Leaders, on the other hand, empathize. "Empathy is not simply a matter of paying attention to other people. It is also the capacity to take in emotional signals and to make them mean something in a relationship with an individual. . . . The distinction is simply between a manager's attention to *how* things get done and a leader's to *what* the events and decisions mean."[14]

Again, the manager's emphasis is on *systems*, possibly even viewing people as part of a framework of processes, while the leader's focus is on meaning as the foundation of motivation. The ability to empathize, to receive and send signals, and to impute meaning to work are all elements of the leader's *style* and *skill*, constituting his mastery of the soft S's of effectiveness.

Another fact of relationships with others concerns the manager's striving to convert win-lose decisions into win-win situations through compromise. On its face, this seems desirable, but in practice, Zaleznik observes, the results are defective both in the manner of achievement and in the choices which ultimately emerge. Specifically, Zaleznik identifies three tactics by which managers seek to convert win-lose to win-win decisions:

* Focus on procedure, not substance.
* Use of indirect signals rather than direct messages.
* Manipulation of time and delay to reduce the sting of losing.
  The ultimate result is an organization steeped in bureaucracy (emphasis on structure) and political intrigue.

The focus of leadership in the face of win-lose decisions stands in sharp relief. Leaders are more apt to cast situations in their worst case form. They are more likely to face reality, make hard decisions, and absorb their consequences. Perhaps because of this, Zaleznik asserts leaders "attract strong feelings of identity and difference, or love and hate . . . leader-dominated structures often appear turbulent, intense, and at times even disorganized.

Such an atmosphere intensifies individual motivation. . . . "[15] Here, again, the leader's style plays a crucial role.

SENSE OF SELF

Much of the distinction between managers and leaders stems from differences in their perceptions of themselves. "Managers see themselves as conservators and regulators of an existing order of affairs with which they personally identify and from which they gain rewards. Perpetuating and strengthening existing institutions enhances a manager's sense of self-worth: he or she is performing in a role that harmonizes with the ideals of duty and responsibility."[16]

The implication of this is that profound change-perhaps even when it is most emphatically needed for the survival of a company—is not normally within the province of managers. This may be one reason why so often a dramatic shift in corporate focus is accompanied by a wholesale management change, as well. Conversely, when organizations achieve desired levels or performance—for example, after a turnaround or following a period of rapid growth—they appoint managers to install systems, procedures and structures designed to consolidate their positions. Managers, in the traditional sense, are not sought out to make change. In contrast, Zaleznik sees leaders as working in, but never belonging to, organizations. "Their sense of who they are does not depend upon memberships, work roles, or other social indicators of identity. . . .[They] search out opportunities for change. The methods to bring about change may be technological, political, or ideological, but the object is the same: to profoundly alter human economic and political relationships."[17]

In summary, these differences imply that leaders have an inherent inclination to utilize the soft S's of style, skills, staff and shared goals. Managers, alternatively, tend toward reliance on the traditional triad of strategy, structure, and systems. Organizationally, the extreme result is likely to be leader-run companies high in performance, energy, focus and motivation, in contrast to manager-run companies with mediocre performance, bureaucratic structures, and ponderous decision-making systems.

CONFLICT, CONVERGENCE AND CULTURE

Ironically, the 7-S framework offers two contrasting perspectives on the future potential of management.

• First, if the points made in this article are valid, 7-S management is the province of leaders, and managers per se will not ordinarily be capable of achieving sufficient mastery of all seven keys to attain consistently superb performance.

- Alternatively, the framework suggests that the effects of leadership (or, at least, its visible instruments) can possibly be *developed consciously and applied systematically by managers* to beneficial effect, by paying attention to the soft as well as the hard S's.

Proponents of the new framework say it is indeed possible to make managers more effective by focusing attention on the soft seven keys. Conversely, the point can equally be made that leaders can become more effective managers by focusing more effort on the traditional strategy, structure, and systems. In this sense, the 7-S framework underscores the importance of balance, of attention to style, shared values, systems, structure, and so forth equally, in the enlightened interplay of the hard and the soft. The whole can become larger than the sum of the parts; management and leadership can be made to converge.

In practice, the best performing companies have, or have had, leaders at the top reinforcing values, lending style, molding staff, and developing unique skills. At the same time, in rare cases, these leaders also possess superior traditional managerial skills. Where both facets are not present in the same individual, hierarchy assumes great significance. For example, where the leader occupies high position, managers below him are likely to be well-motivated and the organization's performance correspondingly impressive. By contrast, when leader personalities work under traditional managers, there is likely to be friction and frustration, ultimately resulting in high turnover. The key complaints of those leaving are an inability to get ideas heard, perception of threats or opportunities unheeded by the firm at large, and a prevailing managerial attitude prone to delusions about competitive realities or internal capabilities.

It is in countering the negative impact of these potential conflicts that particularly creative organizations are apparently successful. Excellent companies encourage ideas from all quarters. They keep structures lean and simple and encourage operational autonomy.[18]

On the issue of culture and its impact (whether Japan, for example, is more likely to produce leaders than the West), the 7-S framework offers important insights. First good management does not depend on the presence of leadership, although in many cases, it is enhanced by leadership qualities. What is crucial is the presence of the soft and the hard instruments of balance. Second, the Japanese are, apparently, more inclined to use the soft tests of management—as an extension of their cultural norms—than are Western managers whose culture stresses different values.[19] Third, managerial performance is multivariate. Culture certainly plays a part, but what is more significant is that excellent performance in organizations in Japan or in the West depends on achieving harmony among all seven keys to organization.

The awareness created by the 7-S approach to organizational effectiveness should benefit organizations run by either leaders or traditional managers, as we have used the terms. Outstanding companies are distinguished not by the leaders who head them or by the managers who run them, but rather by the manner in which leadership and management are harmonized to create a climate in which work is both uncommonly meaningful and unusually effective.

REFERENCES

1. Robert H. Waterman, Jr., Thomas J. Peters, and Julien R. Phillips, "Structure Is Not Organization," *Business Horizons*, June 1980: 14-26.
2. See, for example, Thomas J. Peters, "Putting Excellence Into Management," *The McKinsey Quarterly*, Autumn 1980: 31-41, and Anthony G. Athos and Richard Pascale, *The Art of Japanese Management* (New York: Simon & Schuster, 1981).
3. Each of the seven S's is defined more fully in "Structure Is Not Organization" (see note 1). Also, see Robert H. Waterman, Jr., "The Seven Elements of Strategic Fit," *The Journal of Business Strategy*, Winter 1982: 69-73.
4. Abraham Zaleznik, "Managers and Leaders: Are They Different?" *Harvard Business Review*, May-June 1977: 67-78.
5. Zaleznik: 70.
6. Zaleznik: 74.
7. Peters: 88.
8. Zaleznik:72.
9. Zaleznik.
10. Peters.
11. Zaleznik.
12. Zaleznik: 73.
13. Zaleznik.
14. Zaleznik: 74.
15. Zaleznik.
16. Zaleznik: 75.
17. Zaleznik.
18. Peters: 32.
19. Athos and Pascale.

Craig M. Watson is Financial Director of Business Projects and Planning for the international division of Merck & Co., Inc.

23.
LEADERSHIP:
SOME PRINCIPLES AND CONCEPTS

Richard I. Lester

The mesage is clear. Leaders are not given esteem along with their rank or position; they earn esteem by manifesting the characteristics of leadership.

When perseverance and a willingness to learn are present, leadership skills can be learned. A familiar sign of the times in the corporate world is the outcry for creative leadership. Some observers believe that the average employee would be unable to respond if Martian spacepeople were to land on a corporate site and demand, "Take us to your leader." Most business people understand the concept of management, but they have problems in the application of leadership because it is more difficult to comprehend. In a theoretical sense, leadership is one of the most discussed and least understood subjects in business.

It can be said that managers are necessary, leaders are essential. Modern business has not given enough attention to this distinction; both business and educational institutions have generally placed more emphasis on management than leadership.

DEFINING LEADERSHIP

Experts generally recognize leadership as the art of influencing and directing people in a manner that wins their obedience, confidence, respect and enthusiastic cooperation in achieving a common objective. Practitioners usually define a leader as a person who applies principles and techniques that insure motivation, discipline and productivity when working with people, tasks and situations in order to accomplish the company's objectives.

Considered in the broadest context, people exercise leadership any time they attempt to change or modify the behavior of an individual or a group of individuals.

To understand the nature of leadership, one must first understand the nature of power, for leadership is a special form of power involving relationships with people. To develop these relationships, leaders must successfully fuse organizational and personal needs in a way that permits people and organizations to reach peaks of mutual achievement and satisfaction. Thus, leaders get things done and make things work. In this context, leaders are facilitators who help to pave the way toward the achievement of corporate goals.

DEVELOPING NEW LEADERS

Some people believe that leadership can be taught, but others contend that an individual can only be taught *about* leadership. If one perceives education as a change in behavior through experience, and effective leadership as a set of behaviors applicable to given situations, then leadership can indeed be taught. Despite the complexity of the leadership role, it can be learned when there is a definite willingness to expend the required time and resources.

Leaders are not born. People can develop and learn leadership just as they learn any other complex skill, but the learning process requires intensive effort, study and continuing application within the work environment. Thus, leaders can be developed. Business must do a better job of finding employees with latent leadership talents, and then training them, if it expects to develop effective leaders.

THE LEADERSHIP TRAINING PROGRAM

Three basic elements of leadership are the leader, the follower and the situation. Leadership programs should emphasize that in accepting their professional obligations and positions of authority, managers should demonstrate leadership qualities in all aspects of work. They should understand that leadership of a business organization can be a most rewarding and exciting experience. Although the primary challenge is successful accomplishment of goals, human resources professionals and managers should emphasize that unsuccessful leaders must never overlook the welfare of their employees. Employees are the most important asset any business has.

Leadership development should also focus on the fact that leaders are judged, for the most part, on the timeliness and soundness of their decisions. Knowledge gained through experience, job-related reading, professional training and specialized education is invaluable. The following may be helpful to remember when developing leadership potential:

Visibility and interaction. People cannot lead effectively from the privacy of their office, regardless of their position. True leaders visit their workers on the job and observe their working conditions firsthand. Highly visible leaders leave their "footprints" everywhere in the organization. An effective manager cannot be a lone wolf and expect to lead the pack.

The attitudes of today's employees underscore the need for leadership skills that insure creativity, efficiency, productivity and vitality in a corporate environment constantly faced with the challenge of doing more with less. To meet this challenge, leaders must know their employees, their problems, interests and needs. And today's leader must understand that employees are more sophisticated, better educated, and more conscious of the limits of corporate discipline. As a rule, these men and women are not motivated by intimidation: they must be lead, rather than be driven. The effective leader must instill a sense of responsibility, loyalty and duty for the corporation in each employee if he or she is to succeed.

Caring. Good business leaders are demanding of themselves and their employees. Their style is a blend of caring, discipline and self-confidence rooted in an unshakeable dedication to their employees and the company. There is ample evidence that something so simple as caring for one's employees improves leadership effectiveness.

Quality versus quantity. Effective leaders concentrate on quantitative and qualitative productivity. All too often, people in leadership positions concern themselves with how much work their employees perform and not with what they produce. Effective leaders recognize no substitutes for hard, productive work, intense concentration, and willingness to assume total responsibility for the work of their employees. Leaders must develop and recognize their employees if they expect to excel over an extended period of time.

Delegation. Leaders must delegate tasks and require their employees to make decisions. The true test of leadership is the behavior reflected among their employees. Thus, employees need to be involved as a first step toward commitment to company goals.

LEADERSHIP STYLES

Leadership styles for influencing employees resemble fingerprints in the sense that each is different. Thus, in studying different leadership styles, managers should learn how to sort the good from the bad, the effective from the ineffective. Through this process of sifting and selecting, they can begin to develop the basics of their own leadership style.

Whatever the style, it should be predicated on sensitivity and appropriate consideration for both human relationships and task completion. Managers who wish to practice effective leadership should apply the behavioral science approach to enhance their leadership effectiveness. And they should stress the pluralistic view of motivation to show that employee behavior stems from many different types of needs.

The following are considered key characteristics of good corporate leaders:

Sense of responsibility. People who aspire to high positions must subordinate their personal desires and, at times, even the desires of their families to the company. The leader recognizes responsibility and relishes the opportunity to display leadership skills.

Leaders must also exercise self-control if they expect to control others, and they must maintain self-control in the most trying situations. Furthermore, they should strive to keep their personal lives under control and never allow personal problems to color decisions made at work.

Technical and professional competence. Employees will give a manager a reasonable period of time to get his or her feet on the ground, but they will not respect the manager who continually relies on others in the company to make decisions or provide guidance.

Enthusiasm. A leader must be genuinely enthusiastic in all the tasks that comprise the goals of the company. Employees will automatically give more of themselves and take more pride in their work if they know their leader is involved, committed and enthusiastic. Some managers are reluctant to delve into areas in which they have no prior experience or qualifications. It is important for a leader to seek new directions and to delve into unfamiliar areas.

Communications skills. Effective communications is a key leadership variable. Verbal, written and nonverbal communications are essential in acquiring employee cooperation. Communications is the adhesive that holds an organization together.

A good leader also remembers to listen, but listening involves more than mere hearing. Successful leaders interpret and evaluate what they hear. They do not permit personal ideas, emotions or prejudices to distort what they hear. Disciplined listening is difficult, but it is a key communication skill.

High ethical standards. Ethics play a key role in the leadership function because they are the basis of all group interaction and decision making. Professional ethics require leaders to maintain high standards of personal conduct and to adhere to those standards in all situations so that employees can rely on their actions. Constructive leaders have well-established value systems that have been tested in a variety of situations. Leaders demonstrate integrity when their concern for company interests is always greater than their personal pride, and when they hold themselves to the same standards even when their superiors may not.

Flexibility. A leader must understand that no two people or situations are ever exactly alike. Yesterday's approach may or may not be the correct approach for today or tomorrow. Effective leaders adapt their approaches to the particular person, group or problem at hand. Leaders should also devote a great deal of thought to understanding the nature of change. Flexibility also implies that adaptable leaders are more capable of managing stress.

Leaders should have the ability to take whatever comes their way and thrive on it.

Vision. Leaders need a visual image of where they see the organization going and how it can get there. Vision is indispensable to organizational progress. Furthermore, effective leaders project ideas and images that excite people and develop choices that are timely and appropriate for the situation at hand. Therefore, leaders with vision inspire their employees to do their best.

The message is clear. Leaders are not given esteem along with their rank or position, they earn esteem by manifesting the characteristics of leadership. They first create a tolerant work environment, develop respect between themselves and their employees, and, consequently, win the esteem of their superiors, peers and employees. It is not an easy task to be an effective leader, but the personal satisfaction and sense of achievement and contribution are great and well worth the effort.

Richard I. Lester is Director of Educational Plans and Programs, Leadership and Management, Development Center, Air University, Maxwell AFB, Alabama.

24.
TIME-SPAN ORIENTATION: A KEY FACTOR OF CONTINGENCY MANAGEMENT

Eugene H. Fram
Andrew J. DuBrin

An underrecognized variable in contingency management is *time-span orientation* (TSO). Simply stated, TSO concerns whether the prevailing leadership emphasis is oriented toward the short or long range.

Knowledge of how managers conduct the process of leadership continues to develop despite over 40,000 published articles and books on the topic. During the last decade, the contingency approach to leadership and management has achieved widespread acceptance.[1] Contingency management is the assumption that how a manager behaves should be contingent upon the situation. Contingency management is therefore sometimes referred to as "it all depends" management. Important situational variables in the contingency approach include the task to be accomplished, types of people to be managed, the manager's job description, and the organizational or technical system under which the manager operates.[2]

An underrecognized variable in contingency management is *time-span orientation* (TSO). Simply stated, TSO concerns whether the prevailing leadership emphasis is oriented toward the short or long range. Managers with short TSO's typically press their employees for quick solutions to problems and demand frequent feedback about the status of problems. Managers with long TSO's operate with a long-range time perspective; they are content with infrequent information and feedback from employees.

For example, an aircraft executive might operate effectively with a long TSO because it can take five years or more to develop a new aircraft. In contrast, a newspaper production executive might need to work with a short TSO since a new product is produced every day.

We can begin to appreciate the importance of TSO in leadership by considering case examples of leadership situations. In the following dialogue, two views of time-span orientation are illustrated.

CASE EXAMPLE: PROJECT MANAGER LARRY

In this management situation, Larry is asked to take a temporary foreign assignment. His present duties as manager of Project Olympia are to be assumed for a few months by the general manager, Ned. After one day of reviewing documentation about the inner workings of Olympia, Ned decided to meet with the two key personnel on the project, Jane, the director of engineering and Mack, the director of manufacturing. Ned decided to take each person to lunch separately in order to hold a general discussion of progress on the project. Ned arranged for a Tuesday luncheon with Jane and a Wednesday luncheon with Mack.

"Jane, the reason I've invited you to lunch," explained Ned, "is that I want to get a handle on how things are going on the project. Olympia is a hot item in our company. If we do well, the heavyweights in Washington will be awarding us follow-up contracts for the next decade. Larry, of course, has kept me informed to some extent. I've also been looking at those PERT charts. But now I want a first hand discussion on what's going on."

"Well, Ned, the engineering group is doing pretty well considering the constraints we're working under. We,re meeting our targets and we've only lost one or two key people so far."

"Hold on Jane, I'm hearing some pretty strong reservations coming through on your part. What seems to be the problem?"

"Ned, please don't think I'm taking the opportunity to talk behind Larry's back just because he's out of the country. I like the guy. In some ways I admire his ability to keep on top of things. But I wonder at times if he knows how to handle professional managers. Sometimes I wonder if he is a professional manager himself."

Puzzled by Jane's comment, Ned inquired, "What do you mean Larry may not know how to handle professional managers, or that he may not be a professional manager?"

"To Larry the long range is three days to one week. Sometimes he makes three phone calls a day asking for answers to picky little problems. If you don't have an answer at your fingertips, he panics. He counters with a barrage of additional questions. I think he'd make a great prosecuting attorney. Maybe that's why Corporate wants him for a trouble shooter. I try to set my objectives for several months out into the future. Sometimes I work by yearly objectives. I tackle the big conceptual issues and leave the fine points and the day-by-day details to my staff. I think a professional manager should focus more on the long and intermediate ranges than the short range."

"But in what way does Larry's approach interfere with your professionalism as a manager?"

"I spend too much time getting ready to answer questions about the tiniest problems. I'll give you a specific example. Every Friday morning I have to spend about an hour sorting through the figures to determine if we're on budget for the week. Larry likes weekly budget figures. I'd much prefer to report on a monthly or bi-monthly basis. Less time with budgets would give me more time to plan for the future."

"Thanks for your candor," commented Ned.

"Now let's talk about some of the technical problems on the project."

The following day at lunch with Mack, Ned asked him how things were going. Mack eagerly responded: "Things are going great on Olympia from a manufacturing standpoint. I hope you've taken time to look at the manufacturing input to the PERT chart. We're going great guns. Please don't think I'm playing office politics while the boss is away, but Larry deserves a lot of credit for our success."

"How's that?" responded Ned.

Mack continued, "Larry is just the style of manager we needed on this project. He's got the rat-tat-tat style that a project manager must have when you're playing with big government bucks. Larry presses me for progress details almost daily. He helps keep me on my toes. Larry manages by the philosophy, 'The best way to eat an elephant is one bite at a time'. I think he's a big improvement over the past."

"What was wrong in the past?"

"Before Olympia, I worked on Project Odyssey. Our project manager was oriented toward the long range. He figured that if he set general guidelines and long range targets, the details would fall into place automatically. To tell the truth, I think I became a little lazy working for him. I lost some of my concern for making sure all our milestones were met on time."

"Very interesting to hear your comments, Mack. Let's talk now about some of the hardware that you have been putting together."

As Mack launched into a description of the major components of the system, Ned thought to himself, "Are these two people talking about the same manager?"

HOW TSO AFFECTS LEADERSHIP STYLE

It is apparent that project manager Larry's two employees prefer their immediate superior to work with different time span orientations. Perhaps Larry's major failure is his inability or unwillingness to communicate his TSO to Jane, the director of engineering. (We also assume here that a short TSO fits the requirements of the firm.) As implied in the case, the underlying difference between the polar ends of TSO relates to a sense of time urgency.

The leader with a short TSO thinks primarily in terms of the "here and now." The leader with a long TSO thinks primarily in terms of the long range. (Intermediate range TSO's of course, are also possible.) Of importance to the practicing manager is the fact that differences in TSO lead to differences in behavior. The following summarizes several important differences in behavior we found between leaders with long and short time-span orientations.

Long vs. Short Time-Span Orientations

Short-Range TSO	Long-Range TSO
Demands frequent information and feedback from employees.	Is content with infrequent information and feedback from employees.
Believes that short-range planning is more vital than long-range planning.	Believes that long-range planning is more vital than short-range planning.
Tends to exert tight controls over employees.	Tends to exert loose controls over employees.
Tends to expect results quickly from employees —even on major projects.	Content to wait a relatively long time for results on major projects.
Tends to focus more on details than on concepts.	Tends to focus more on concepts than details.
Spends considerable time in direct contact with employees.	Spends modest amount of time in contact with employees.
Works to tight deadlines.	Likes to allow a time safety margin and to have projects ready well in advance.
Works well with verbal communications.	Likes to have decisions in writing and confirming memo.

HOW DOES TSO RELATE TO OTHER DIMENSIONS OF LEADERSHIP?

TSO is an additional dimension of leadership that sheds insight on already known leadership styles.

For example, it is conceivable that two managers described as *participative leaders* may differ in time-span orientation. Office Manager A might be quite willing to allow considerable latitude in setting work standards and procedures. His approach is to check with employees frequently on how well they are setting new standards and implementing the standards they have set. Office manager B is also a participative manager who allows employees considerable latitude in setting work standards and procedures. However, she is content to receive infrequent information from employees on how well they are implementing the standards and procedures they helped establish.

The relationship of TSO to the *autocratic leadership style* further illuminates the central concept of this article. Several years ago a long-TSO executive ruled autocratically over a conglomerate in the clothing industry. In his words, "I give my division heads enough rope either to escalate themselves to new heights or to hang themselves. I tell them the figures I expect from them for the year. At the end of the year if they have not made their figures they are through. No second chance, no whimpering. We're in a tough business." Most autocratic managers, however, tend to emphasize short-term results and consequently demand frequent status reports from employees.

HOW DOES TSO CONTRIBUTE TO CONTINGENCY MANAGEMENT?

Sensitivity to TSO enhances the ability of a manager to practice contingency management. TSO is another dimension of leadership that often can be consciously altered, modified, or manipulated to meet the demands of a given leadership situation. To illustrate how TSO can facilitate contingency management, four key variables should be considered: nature of the enterprise, nature of the employee, nature of the responsibility, and extent of a crisis mode.

• Nature of the Enterprise

The nature of the enterprise is an influential variable in choosing an appropriate TSO. The type of business itself will often dictate which TSO is necessary. For example, with a general merchandise retail organization, the typical budget-planning period is six months in length. It is not unusual to establish a budget only several months before it becomes operational. On the other hand, the petroleum industry must work in the long range when exploring for resources—which can take up to a decade. Of course, refinery supervisors in that same industry might have to work with very short TSO's.

• Nature of Employees

Dependent and less than fully competent employees will require a shorter range TSO from their supervisors than will their more independent and competent counterparts. Problem employees too will require a shorter TSO; they need frequent follow-up and guidance. The Situational Leadership Theory advanced by Paul Hersey and Kenneth Blanchard supports this position. They suggest that when a group of people is functioning as independent professionals, they require a minimum of supervision.[3] The effective leader will exert very little direct influence over their activities. He or she can deal with competent professionals with a long time-span orientation.

• Line Versus Staff Authority

Line units deal more frequently with short-range problems while staff units more frequently deal with a long range. Consequently, a manger of a staff unit might rely more often upon a long TSO. Yet there are specific times when a manager of a staff unit might need to operate with a very short TSO in order to be effective. One germane example is the director of a legal services department whose firm is suddenly faced with a lawsuit.

He or she might then manage the department with a TSO not unlike that of a fire station captain.

• The Presence or Absence of a Crisis Mode

Organizations designed to handle crises (such as hospitals and the claims office of a casualty insurance company) foster shorter TSO's among their personnel. The same is true of organizations which constantly deal in a crisis mode, although they are not designed as crisis organizations.

Amusement parks are a case in point because they experience a crisis every summer season: the profits of the business are totally dependent on sales taking place during a two and one half-month period.

THE CHOICE IS IMPORTANT

Selecting the appropriate TSO (long, short, or intermediate) helps a manager practice contingency management. Among the contingency variables influencing which TSO is the most appropriate are (a) nature of the enterprise, (b) nature of the employees, (c) nature of the organizational authority (line versus staff), and (d) presence or absence of a crisis mode. An effective manager selects the most appropriate TSO to meet the demands of a given situation.

REFERENCES

1. An impressive exposition of contingency approaches to many phases of management is by Don Hellriegal and John W. Socum Jr., *Management: Contingency Approaches*, 2nd Edition (Reading, Mass.: Addison-Wesley Publishing Company, 1978).
2. William Glueck, *Management* (Hinsdale, Ill.: Dryden Press, 1977), p. 11.
3. Paul Hersey and Kenneth Blanchard, *Management of Organizational Behavior: Utilizing Human Resources*, 3rd Edition (Englewood Cliffs, New Jersey: Prentice-Hall, 1977), p. 164.

Eugene H. Fram is professor of Marketing, Director, Center for Management Study, College of Business, Rochester Institute of Technology, Rochester, NY. Andrew J. DuBrin is professor of Behavioral Sciences, College of Business, Rochester Institute of Technology, Rochester, NY.

Part IV
MANAGER OR LEADER?

25.
LEADING VS MANAGING: A GUIDE TO SOME CRUCIAL DISTINCTIONS

Roger J. Plachy

> It's difficult, perhaps impossible, to be both leader and manager at the same time, all the time. Managers who remain aware of the key differences in the two roles and respond to them give themselves better opportunities for success in managing . . . and in leading.

If you are trying to be both leader and manager to your employees at the same time, all the time, quit confusing them and yourself. Managership and leadership involve separate and distinct responses to different demands. Managers who perceive and accept this dichotomy are more effective at getting things done through their employees because they avoid the debilitating frustration that follows pursuit of the impossible dream of organizational unity.

When we were children, we sensed the difference between the team captain appointed by the coach and another player whose decision to play enthusiastically or not actually determined team motivation. But as adults we fail to distinguish between the role of manager and that of leader. We blur the distinction constantly; that which should be called leadership, we call management, and vice versa (though clearly we hope for leadership, the charismatic element X that supposedly inspires employees to lofty heights of performance).

LEADERS VS. MANAGERS

A natural process of selection occurs in groups. The member who most clearly epitomizes the characteristics of the individual members is chosen, formally or not, as the leader. The basis of nomination is compatibility with the interests of the individuals. This is how leadership develops.

However, the association of individuals also creates a need to consider the collective good—that is, to decide among individual priorities and to respond

171

to external stimuli. The person who decides what shall be done is called the manager.

For members of the group who agree with what the manager decides, the manager is also their leader because their individual interests are being represented. For the members who disagree, however, the manager is only a manager and not also their leader because the decision goes against their individual needs.

Actually, we haven't lost the distinction discovered in our youthful athletic days. We intuitively know the difference between good managership and good leadership, which means that the difference is perceived on some level, but we still need to articulate it more clearly if we are ever to learn the two skills. Unfortunately, the literature on organization behavior has not always clarified the roles, sometimes using the terms "leader" and "manager" interchangeably and making the differentiation inexact.

Modern management theory generally dictates that the organization manager must be accountable for both organizational accomplishment *and* employee satisfaction simultaneously, a condition that is not necessarily an organizational possibility, responsibility, or right. An employee's needs and goals may be obverse, although not necessarily adverse, to those of the organization. Yet managers are typically directed to suggest to employees that they can best satisfy their needs and individual goals by meeting the needs and pursuing the goals of the organization. If we would differentiate clearly between representing the needs and goals of individuals (leadership), and representing organizational needs and goals (managership), we would be able to serve both our organizations and our employees better.

Too many people suffer from the delusion that leadership is some mystical personal quality, usually inbred, a spark that can ignite fervor in the hearts of followers and without which the manager is doomed to failure. A spiritual search for the missing quality will lead only to frustration for the manager and disillusionment for employees who want capable direction.

Managers who sometimes lose the favor of their followers in order to obtain necessary organizational results should not despair; there are times when organizational needs simply must take precedence over individual desires. Certainly, personal magnetism, elusive as it is, exits, and we should try to learn to understand it better. However, what we usually observe in leader-follower relationships, and call charisma, is rooted in concrete managerial authority.

Winston Churchill's public life provides an excellent example. He was a good manager first. He indentified the problem, considered the alternatives, chose the response he considered most appropriate, and acted accordingly—which often meant calling the people to action at a time when many probably didn't want to go. And here is where a vital distinction between leadership and managership can be seen. For the people who immediately perceived that he was likely to be correct in his assessment and plan of action, Churchill was both manager and leader. But for the dissenter, he was only their manager until the moment when they could agree that what was good for England was also good for them as individuals.

The natural difference between leading and managing has been well-stated by Keith Davis, a leading management author. He defines leadership as the "ability to persuade others to seek defined objectives enthusiastically." Says Davis:

> Management activities such as planning, organizing and decision-making are dormant cocoons until the leader triggers the power of motivation in people and guides them toward goals. The leader's act of motivation is similar in its effect to the secret chemical that turns the insect pupa into the resplendent butterfly with all the beauty that was the pupa's potential turned into reality . . . it is part of management, but not all of it . . . it is something a person does, not something that he or she has.

The leader's sensitive understanding of human nature has been described as more vital to performance than any vast accumulation of knowledge or skills concerning science, technology, statistics or abstract reasoning. It has also been noted that good leadership helps others to arrive at a better understanding of themselves, of others, and of the issues at hand. And it enables them to use this greater understanding to accomplish whatever goals brought the members of the group together in the first place.

In distinguishing management from leadership, Paul Hersey and Kenneth Blanchard point out that a manager can be successful but ineffective: If A's leadership style is not compatible with the expectations of B, and if B is antagonized and does the job only because of A's position power, then we can say that A has been successful but not effective.

I would prefer to distinguish the concepts a bit more. If A's *management* style is not compatible with the expectations of B, and if B is antagonized and does the job only because of A's position power, then we can say that A has been successful *as a manager*, but not effective *as a leader*.

A few authors, in order to persuade a manager to be more of a leader and to counter the retention of authority by the appointed manager of the group, have suggested that the design of work and the focus of decision making be altered so that the work group becomes more responsible for the planning, organization, direction and control of work. They have gone too far. These functions, though many times the product of group members' suggestions solicited by a thoughtful manager, are clearly and classically the responsibility of management, and no one else; the functions should not be given away. When projects fail, workers are not confronted first; managers are. The process of managing can be shared, as we have long understood, but the right to manage must be retained.

Management is the accountability that we have to formulate and achieve the objectives of the organization of which we and our employees are members. Leadership is the responsibility we have to represent our followers' needs and goals and help them achieve what they want. A leader deals in emotions, excites camaraderie and unity, and guides vague notions into concrete actions. A manager determines, organizes, and directs programs, and compromises among differing desires.

LEADING VS. MANAGING: A GUIDE

The managership-leadership dichotomy is a reciprocal relationship: the more you choose to manage, the less you choose to lead. Notice the distinctions in Figure 1.

Figure 1.
A Guide to Problem Solving:
Individuals vs Managers

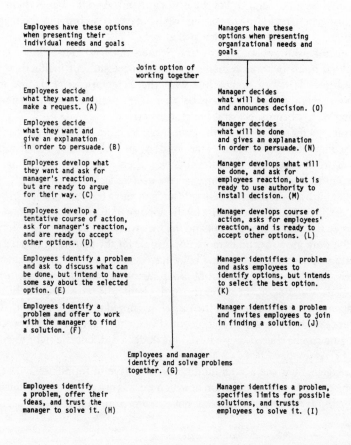

Employees have these options when presenting their individual needs and goals	Joint option of working together	Managers have these options when presenting organizational needs and goals
Employees decide what they want and make a request. (A)		Manager decides what will be done and announces decision. (O)
Employees decide what they want and give an explanation in order to persuade. (B)		Manager decides what will be done and gives an explanation in order to persuade. (N)
Employees develop what they want and ask for manager's reaction, but are ready to argue for their way. (C)		Manager develops what will be done, and ask for employees reaction, but is ready to use authority to install decision. (M)
Employees develop a tentative course of action, ask for manager's reaction, and are ready to accept other options. (D)		Manager develops course of action, asks for employees' reaction, and is ready to accept other options. (L)
Employees identify a problem and ask to discuss what can be done, but intend to have some say about the selected option. (E)		Manager identifies a problem and asks employees to identify options, but intends to select the best option. (K)
Employees identify a problem and offer to work with the manager to find a solution. (F)		Manager identifies a problem and invites employees to join in finding a solution. (J)
	Employees and manager identify and solve problems together. (G)	
Employees identify a problem, offer their ideas, and trust the manager to solve it. (H)		Manager identifies a problem, specifies limits for possible solutions, and trusts employees to solve it. (I)

Let's illustrate the situation of a group of employees who want to change their work schedules and ask to meet with their manager to explain why the change should be instituted, marked on the scale as B in Figure 2. If the manager can agree to their request, he or she has helped employees meet their needs and goals and has responded as a leader. (In this instance, because the response was organizationally sound, the manager, in effect, is meeting both individual and organizational needs and thus has functioned as both manager and leader.)

Figure 2.
Plotting
Managership and Leadership

1. A leadership decision

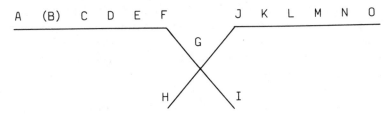

2. A managership decision

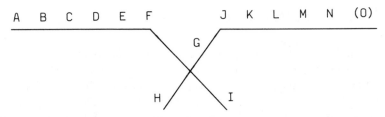

3. A balanced decision

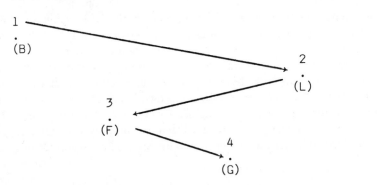

However, organizational needs may force a manager to ignore his leadership responsibilities in favor of his managerial obligations, shown as response O in Figure 2.

The intervening postures C through N we note as skipped. A manager who wants to prevent the loss of leadership status whenever possible would review these postures to ensure that no opportunity for rapport (leadership) has been missed.

Suppose the manager cannot agree with the original request, but doesn't want to ignore the needs of the employees. In an effort to provide as much leadership as possible, the manager can take the posture (L) to signal a willingness to talk about the situation, which may produce an amelioration of the employees' position to (F), and ultimately a resolution at (G). (See Figure 2.)

The philosophical direction on the scale is toward the center—a balancing, so to speak, between individual and organizational needs. Interaction between manager and employees in the central positions means collaboration for the common good. Postures H and I show the greatest degree of trust as manager and employees are willing to allow the other wide latitude in solving problems and pursuing opportunities, and may be viewed figuratively as the bases of the scale. The more distance a manager finds between his or her positions and the positions taken by employees, tipping the scale toward one faction or the other, the more the manager needs to find ways to listen to what employees have to say about their problems and desires as well as to tell employees about the requirements and objectives of the organization.

THE OPTIMUM MOMENT

The challenge before management is to identify and practice the ways in which it can bridge the conflicting needs and goals of the organization and employees. The blatant reality that people are motivated differently, producing natural human discord, cannot be ignored. There is no fundamental truth that will show us once and for all how to manage people, especially when they do not completely agree with our decisions. Such a search for understanding, particularly for charismatic leadership, is an illusion. The optimum moment of organizational effectiveness, when the needs and goals of the organization and the participating members are identical, when everyone wants to do the same thing, even for different reasons, is best viewed as a coincidence.

Our attempts to induce managers to seek optimization at every turn only contributes to mental stress. Managers are not managers unless they are continually creating "disgruntlements" by choosing between conflicting demands. The solution to the puzzle of managing effectively is not to force managers to be leaders when management is required but to allow the coincidence of managership and leadership to occur naturally through honest consideration of both perspectives. The result is that participating members will be more willing to temper their goals so that optimum moments can occur more frequently.

Roger J. Plachy is a management consultant specializing in interpersonal behavior and development of communications skills, particularly in the manager-employee relationship. His organization, Plachy Associates, is headquartered in Winston-Salem, North Carolina.

26.
THE IMPORTANCE OF
STRATEGIC LEADERSHIP

LaRue Tone Hosmer

For decades, business executives have concentrated on the art and techniques of management. But in today's competitive times, more is required. Successful executives must be leaders as well.

Leadership has been defined by many different disciplines in the past. There are psychological, interpersonal, and sociological concepts of leadership in the behavioral sciences; there are historical, allegorical, and fictional examples in the humanities; and there are obvious assumptions in microeconomics, operations research, and quantitative finance. It is strange that strategic management, which purports to center on the duties and responsibilities of the general manager,[1] has never defined leadership.

I should like to propose a strategic definition of leadership, but first I should like to review some of the behavioral models and describe some of the organizational functions. Leadership is important; it is not an outmoded concept from a less scientific and more romantic age, and there is a need for leaders, properly defined, within an organization to make strategic planning something more than "muddling through"[2] or an "incremental process."[3] I would assume that we all accept the accuracy of James Bryan Quinn's observation that formal planning methods based upon an analysis of the gap between expected and desired results do not lead to strategic changes, just as we earlier accepted the justice of Joseph Bower's statement[4] that capital budgeting models based on projections of discounted cash flows just aren't the way investment decisions are made in large organizations. There are interpersonal and intergroup forces that swirl around these normative procedures, and prevent their "working" the way their designers intended. Leadership cannot control, but it does recognize and reduce those forces.

LEADERSHIP THEORIES

Organizational theorists have provided a number of explanations of leadership.[5] These behavioral models are often conflicting, occasionally weak, and seldom supported by empirical data. In a cheerfully cynical statement, Walter Bennis wrote: "Of all the hazy and confounding areas in social psychology, leadership theory undoubtedly contends for the top nomination. And ironically, probably more has been written and less known about leadership than about any other topic in the behavioral sciences."[6] This pessimism comes from an acknowledged inability to prepare a research design that will identify measurable characteristics of leaders (who they are) or leadership (what they do), and then relate those characteristics to various dimensions representing the success or failure of an organization. This is, of course, a problem with which researchers in strategy are not entirely unfamiliar. Both leadership theory and strategy formulation have multiple sets of variables, complex inter-relationships among those variables, and imprecise or unreliable measures of organizational performance. Despite these empirical problems, both leadership theory and strategy formulation have developed conceptual frameworks that are useful and probably valid. These frameworks in leadership theory can be divided into four basic categories.

Personal

The personal theory of leadership is that there are distinguishing characteristics or traits of personality that usually accompany a leadership role; these traits are personal intelligence, self-assurance, physical size, technical knowledge, emotional stability, etc. These traits may combine in a personal style that is anticipative (foresee changes and act in advance to prepare the organization) or reactive (observe changes and act afterward to adjust the organization), and the motives that often attend these traits may be measured as personal drives for power, for achievement or for affiliation.[7]

Interpersonal

The interpersonal theory of leadership is that there are distinguishing characteristics in the patterns of interactions with others that usually accompany a leadership role; these patterns range from outward friendliness and respect to inward suspicion and distrust. The interpersonal styles that result from these patterns may be exploitive (direct others without regard to their individual needs or values), benevolent (direct others with regard to their perceived needs and values), consultative (direct others after consideration of their opinions and beliefs), or participative (direct one's self and others after joint consideration of the group's opinions and beliefs). The managerial styles that are a result of the interpersonal patterns of behavior have been measured as a concern for tasks or a concern for people.[8]

Positional

The positional theory of leadership is that there are distinguishing characteristics in the ability to use the structure and systems of an organization which usually accompany a leadership role. The organizational structure, of course, provides the relative rankings in the authority hierarchy, while the managerial systems generate the sanctions/rewards of the control and motivational processes. Organizational styles of leadership range from coercive (using the sanctions, such as discharge or demotion), to authoritative (using the position, and the common acceptance of that position), to incentive (using the rewards, such as salary increases or promotion).[9]

Social

The social theory of leadership is that there are distinguishing characteristics in the ability to use the power relationships among the subgroups of an organization. The subgroups form coalitions that can exercise power due to their possible refusal to continue contributing either effort or expertise to the organization, which would bring a lowering of the competitive position and economic performance of the company, and could cause a breakup of the organization.[10] Social styles of leadership range from political (using the subgroups) to apolitical (ignoring the subgroups).

Combination

Leadership is viewed by almost all of the behavioral theorists as a complex phenomenon. Most of the traits of individual personality, the patterns of interpersonal competence, the uses of organizational processes, and the manipulation of political subgroups appear to be present, in varying degrees, in all leadership roles, and leadership styles seem to be a composite of the personal, interpersonal, positional and social alternatives.

There is an inherent preference among behavioral researchers for the participative/incentive/apolitical style of leadership—an academic hope the nice guys, both male and female, truly will finish first—but unfortunately there are numerous examples of the success of the exploitive/coercive/political mode of behavior. For people who have taught in a business policy course, the names of John Connolly, chairman of Crown Cork and Seal,[11] and David Goodman and Doris Goodman-Bethea, president and treasurer, respectively, of the Goodman Machine and Foundry,[12] come to mind as people who apparently spent little time facilitating group decisions, building organizational cohesiveness, establishing open relationships, and generally acting in a considerate, supportive manner. In financial terms, however, they were outstandingly successful.

CONTINGENCY THEORY

Exhibit 1

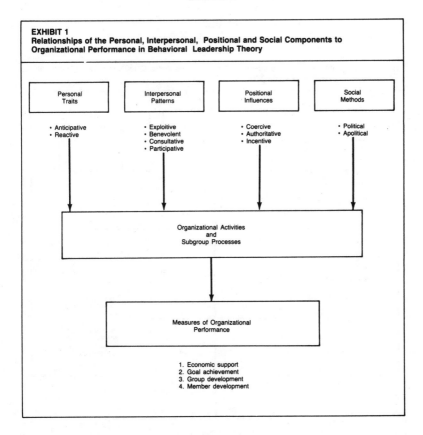

EXHIBIT 1
Relationships of the Personal, Interpersonal, Positional and Social Components to Organizational Performance in Behavioral Leadership Theory

The existence of contrary examples—managers who succeed in spite of their defiance or disregard of the normative prescriptions and who occur with embarrassing frequency in empirical research studies as well as business policy areas—has led to the development of contingency theories of leadership. Contingency theories, of course, state that "it all depends," and in leadership contingency theory it all depends upon intervening variables of group effectiveness in problem-solving activity and on exogenous variables of problem complexity. The intervening variables that are selected often include such factors as technical/functional skills and physical/financial assets and approach the strengths and weaknesses of strategy formulation. The exogenous variables that are chosen include such elements as market/economic trends, functional/ technical requirements and legal/political constraints and approach the opportunities and risks of formulation theory. The resultant model is not entirely dissimilar to the strategy formulation framework.

The contingency theory of leadership seems, to people trained in strategy, to be incomplete. There is no explanation for the level of individual effort and

Exhibit 2

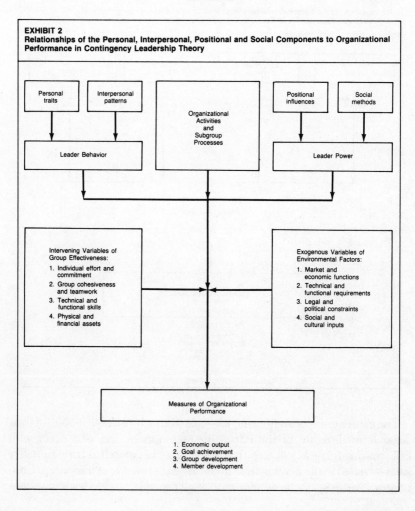

EXHIBIT 2
Relationships of the Personal, Interpersonal, Positional and Social Components to Organizational Performance in Contingency Leadership Theory

| Personal traits | Interpersonal patterns | | Positional influences | Social methods |

Organizational Activities and Subgroup Processes

Leader Behavior   Leader Power

Intervening Variables of Group Effectiveness:
1. Individual effort and commitment
2. Group cohesiveness and teamwork
3. Technical and functional skills
4. Physical and financial assets

Exogenous Variables of Environmental Factors:
1. Market and economic functions
2. Technical and functional requirements
3. Legal and political constraints
4. Social and cultural inputs

Measures of Organizational Performance

1. Economic output
2. Goal achievement
3. Group development
4. Member development

commitment, or the stage of group cohesiveness and teamwork, beyond the behavior and power of the leader, and there is no recognition of the relative position of the organization within an industry of competing firms, or an association of contending nonprofit institutions.

There has been considerable empirical research in strategy that indicates that the competitive position within an industry, or between industries in the case of diversification, is an important determinant of the success or failure of an organization,[13] and should be included in any model that attempts to relate individual, organizational and environmental factors to group performance.

STRATEGIC THEORY

A strategic model of organizational performance does include the competitive position of a firm within an industry and does provide a reason, through the planning, control, and motivation systems, for the individual effort and group cohesiveness. To demonstrate this totality, and to start in the strategic definition of leadership, let us look at a routine outline of the strategy formulation process.[14]

There is no need to define the terms in this model: they are certainly familiar to strategy researchers and management practioners. The mechanism is an iterative decision process: a range of strategic alternatives, representing different methods of competition that are open to the firm at both the divisional and corporate levels. The alternatives are then compared to the specific opportunities and risks from the environment and to the explicit strengths and weaknesses of the corporation. Then a single strategy is selected based upon criteria developed through a comparison of the corporate performance and position with the organizational mission or charter and the managerial values and attitudes. Strategy formulation is conceptually simple, pragmatically complex, and only a part of the general management function. The other part is, of course, strategy implementation; there is also a routine and generally accepted outline of that process.[15]

Again, there is little need to explain terms. The implementation mechanism is a sequential decision process: the selected strategy of the firm is translated into a series of statements on the goals and objectives, policies and procedures, programs and plans, and immediate actions for each of the divisions within the corporation, and then for the functional and technical units within the divisions. In turn, these objectives, policies, programs, and actions define the individual tasks that are essential for strategic success, and the organizational structure and managerial systems can then be designed to coordinate and integrate the performance of those tasks.

Strategic management cannot, in practice, be separated into the twin halves of formulation and implementation because the selected methods of competition, or formulated strategy, can only be expressed in terms of the implement-

Exhibit 3

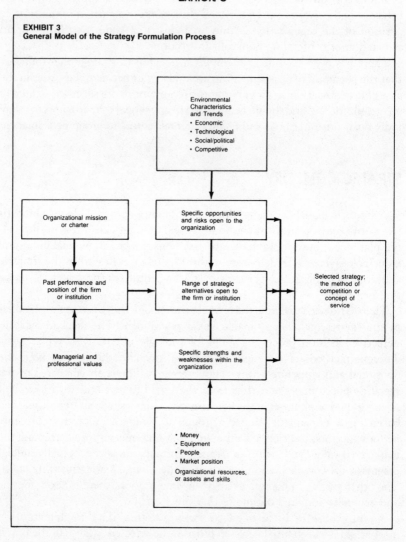

EXHIBIT 3
General Model of the Strategy Formulation Process

Environmental
Characteristics
and Trends
• Economic
• Technological
• Social/political
• Competitive

Organizational mission
or charter

Specific opportunities
and risks open to the
organization

Selected strategy;
the method of
competition or
concept of
service

Past performance and
position of the firm
or institution

Range of strategic
alternatives open to
the firm or institution

Managerial and
professional values

Specific strengths and
weaknesses within the
organization

• Money
• Equipment
• People
• Market position
Organizational resources,
or assets and skills

ing objectives, policies, programs, and actions, and because the strategic
alternatives can only be considered in terms of the information provided and
the performance recorded by the existing structure and systems. Strategic
management is not a divided process; it is the simultaneous consideration of
the formulation and implementation of strategy, and this consideration is
essential for the success of the company due to the continual process of change
in the environment and in the organization which must be reflected in the

Exhibit 4

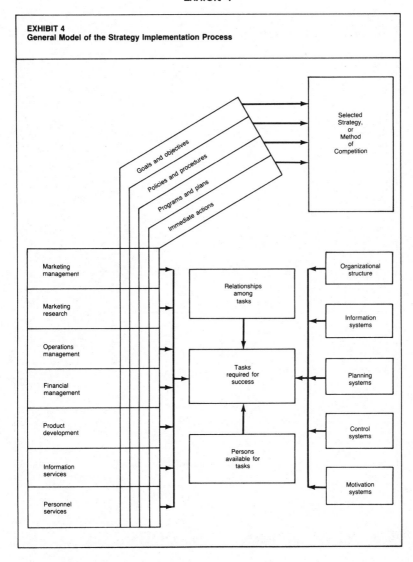

EXHIBIT 4
General Model of the Strategy Implementation Process

method of competition for the firm. This simultaneous consideration of the formulation and implementation of strategy is the responsibility of the general manager, whose function is to combine and direct the efforts and activities of the other members of the organization toward the successful achievement of an improved competitive position for a business firm, or a better service posture for a nonprofit institution. The simultaneous consideration of the formulation and implementation of strategy can also be depicted graphically.[16]

Exhibit 5

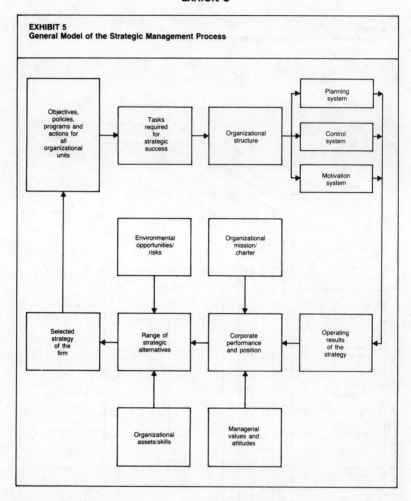

EXHIBIT 5
General Model of the Strategic Management Process

PROBLEMS OF GENERAL MANAGEMENT

Strategic management is the responsibility of the general manager of an organization, but the task cannot be accomplished by a single person. The amount of information needed to evaluate each alternative, the number of alternatives to be considered, the detail in the statements on objectives, policies, programs, and actions, the precision in the definition of the critical tasks, and the variations in the design of the organizational structure and managerial systems are simply too great. Strategic management has to be an organizational task, not an individual effort.[17]

Strategic management is an organizational task and requires an integrated effort by all members of the organization for successful completion, yet there are behavioral barriers to this integration. Organizations are composed of individuals, and these individuals differ on a number of behavioral characteristics or dimensions. These characteristics include interpersonal relationships (formal to informal), individual orientations (tasks vs. people), risk preferences (low to high), time orientation (short to long), uncertainty tolerance (minimal to complete), goal orientation (corporate to individual), and problem-solving style (intuitive to analytical). These individuals also differ in memberships of the functional and technical subgroups, or organizational units, and in levels on the authority hierarchy, from corporate headquarters to product division to operating unit.[18] Each of these personal characteristics, group memberships, and hierarchical levels create a slightly different view of the position, performance, and problems of the organization, and therefore a slightly different view of the need for change in the strategy, structure and systems. The selection of the strategy and the design of the structure and systems cannot be done individually because of the great complexity of the process and must be the result of a coordinated and integrated group effort, despite the diverse personal interests, behavioral characteristics, group memberships, and hierarchical levels of the members. To bring about this integrated and coordinated group effort, there is a need for a strategic leader, not a general manager.

DEFINING STRATEGIC LEADERSHIP

The leader of an organization is responsible for the strategic management process, from formulation to implementation to performance and then back to formulation, on a continual basis to adjust for changes in the environmental characteristics, the organizational resources, and the managerial attitudes. He or she has to ensure that this management process is completed by members of the organization, despite their differences in personal interests, behavioral patterns, group memberships, and hierarchical levels. This is the role of a leader, not a manager. A leader is an individual within an organization who is able to influence the attitudes and opinions of others within the organization; a manager is merely able to influence their actions and decisions.[19] Leadership is not a synonym for management: it is a higher order of capability.

Leadership brings a member of the organization to say, "I'll do it because I think you're right"; management may bring the same person just to say, "I'll do it even though I know you're wrong." The difference between the enthusiasm and reluctance of those two statements is often the difference between the success and failure of an organization.

It is a difficult task to influence the attitudes and opinions of others within an organization in order to achieve the coordinated and integrated group effort that is needed for strategy formulation and implementation, and to avoid the incrementalism and muddling through that is so common in organizational processes. It is a particularly difficult task because of the diversity of behavioral characteristics represented within every organization and the range of functional and technical responsibilities contained in every organization. The selection of the strategy and the design of the structure and systems must be the result of an integrated and coordinated group effort, because one person does not have the information, the competence, or the time to do it individually, but his group effort is hindered by the different viewpoints imposed by the diverse personal interests, behavioral characteristics, functional responsibilities, technical specialties, group loyalties, and positional levels of the members. To overcome these differences and to bring about this integrated and coordinated effort in strategy formulation and implementation, it is necessary to create an overall sense of direction and purpose.

CREATING DIRECTION AND PURPOSE

The general manager of an organization has a limited number of methods to create this sense of direction and purpose, beyond his or her constrained positional and social power, except for one critical technique, and that technique is consistency in strategy, structure, and systems design. The leader has the final decision on these components that can change a formless and directionless assembly of people into a formed and directed organization, and that final decision should be used to achieve consistency. Consistency generates the sense of direction and purpose among the members of the organization; this can be seen by looking at the impact of the strategy, structure, and systems upon the members. This is the reverse of the usual method of examining the strategy, structure, and systems of an organization from the impersonal and "top down" view of the general manager. Instead, let us look at these processes from the very personal, "bottom up" view of the individual member, and recognize that each member may have three very different versions of the strategy of the organization:

- The "proper" strategy for the organization. Each member, depending upon his or her position within the organization, is able to gauge the current performance and position of the business firm or service agency and has some understanding of the environmental opportunities and risks and the organizational strengths and weaknesses. Each member, therefore, has a concept of what the organization ought to be doing.

- The "present" strategy of the organization. Each member, again depending upon his or her position within the firm or agency, has some contact with the goals and objectives, policies and procedures, programs and plans, and

Exhibit 6

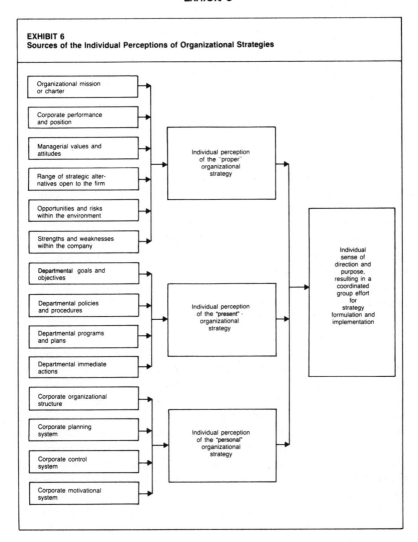

EXHIBIT 6
Sources of the Individual Perceptions of Organizational Strategies

current actions of the product divisions and the functional and technical departments all of which are, or should be, based upon the selected strategy of the company. Each member, therefore, has a concept of what the organization presently is doing.

- The "personal" strategy of the organization. Each member within the organization is affected by the organizational structure and by the managerial systems for planning, control, and motivation. The relationships imposed by the structure and the behavior encouraged by the systems give each person a concept of what he or she should be doing for organizational performance and personal self-interest.

FORMULATING AND IMPLEMENTING STRATEGY

The source of these three individual concepts or perceptions of the organizational strategy are obviously related to the strategy formulation and implementation processes (Exhibits 3 and 4) and can also be shown in schematic form.[20]

The three perceptions of the organizational strategy by the individual members of that organization should be consistent for improved corporate performance and a strengthened competitive position. Members of an organization who believe that what the organization ought to be doing, what the organization is doing, and what it is in their best interests to be doing are not only approximate or parallel but identical will base their decisions and action in line with that sense of direction and purpose. This sense of direction and purpose can generate the coordinated and integrated group effort that is needed for strategy formulation and implementation.

Identical perception of the direction and purpose of an organization by all members of that organization is an impossibility, but an impossibility which can be approached. The approach requires a consistent selection of the strategy from the current performance and position of the firm relative to the environmental opportunities and risks, the organizational assets and skills, and the individual values and attitudes; a consistent statement of the selected strategy in terms of the goals and objectives, policies and procedures, programs and plans, and immediate actions that are generated for each of the product divisions and the functional and technical units; and a consistent design of the organizational structure and planning, control, and motivational systems. This strategy selection, translation, and implementation process cannot be performed by one person, but one person can monitor the sequence and inspire consistency. A consistent analytical and developmental approach to the strategy, structure, and systems of an organization is the true responsibility of the general manager of that organization and is the definition proposed for strategic leadership.

REFERENCES

1. E. P. Learned, C. R. Christensen, K. R. Andrews, and W. P. Guth, *Business Policy: Text and Cases* (Homewood, Ill., Richard D. Irwin, 1965), p. 3.
2. C. E. Lindblom, "The Science of Muddling Through," *Public Administration Review*, Spring 1959, pp. 79-88.

3. J. B. Quinn, *Strategies for Change: Logical Incrementalism* (Homewood, Ill., Richard D. Irwin, 1980).

4. J. L. Bower, *Managing the Resource Allocation Process: A Study of Corporate Planning and Investment* (Homewood, Ill., Richard D. Irwin, 1970).

5. G. A. Yuki, *Leadership in Organizations* (Englewood Cliffs, N.J.: Prentice-Hall, 1981), provides a well-structured introduction to the organizational theories of leadership.

6. W. G. Bennis, "Leadership Theory and Administrative Behavior: The Problem of Authority," *Administrative Science Quarterly*, Winter 1959, p. 259.

7. D. C. McClelland, "N-Achievement and Entrepreneurship: A Longitudinal Study," *Journal of Personality and Social Psychology*, Winter 1965, pp. 389-392.

8. R. R. Blake and J. S. Moulton, *The Managerial Grid* (Houston, Tex.: Gulf Publishing Company, 1965).

9. L. T. Hosmer, *Strategic Management: Text and Cases on Business Policy* (Englewood Cliffs, N.J.: Prentice-Hall, 1963).

10. R. M. Cyert and J. G. March, *A Behavioral Theory of the Firm* (Englewood Cliffs, N.J.: Prentice-Hall, 1963).

11. Intercollegiate Case Clearing House No. 10G13, 1965.

12. University of Michigan Case Distribution No. CM-1048, 1979.

13. R. D. Rumelt, "Strategy and Economic Performance," Division of Research, Graduate School of Business Administration, Harvard University, 1974.

14. L. T. Hosmer, note 9 *supra*.

15. Id.

16. Id.

17. Id.

18. P. R. Lawrence and J. W. Lorsch, Organization and Environment: Managing Differentiation and Integration, Division of Research, Graduate School of Business Administration, Harvard University, 1967.

19. L. T. Hosmer, note 9 *supra*.

20. Id.

LaRue Tone Hosmer is Visiting Professor of Policy, School of Organization and Management, Yale University.

27.
ARE YOU A MANAGER OR A LEADER?

William B. Martin

> Leadership is something distinct, something special, something that goes beyond mere management skill. Do you have what it takes to be a leader? Here's one way to find out: Test yourself on the *Leadership Effectiveness Scale*.

It has taken Ralph twenty years to build a relatively small local manufacturing plant into a multimillion dollar, nationwide business. He prides himself on the way he has nurtured a solid and supportive management team. Ralph attributes much of his company's growth and success to this team. Now it's time for Ralph to step down as an active president and CEO. The demands of the job require a younger person to run the business on a day-to-day basis.

But Ralph is distressed. After reviewing his management staff, he can't find fault with the management ability of his team members, but he doesn't have a *leader* among them. He is finding it difficult to identify the "right" person—one who will be able to take charge and steer the company in the direction it needs to go for the next decade.

Ralph has discovered that good managers are not necessarily good leaders. How can this be?

Jan's quandary: It is time once again for the semiannual performance evaluations within a chain of retail stores. Jan, a regional supervisor, normally has no difficulties performing this job; but now the evaluation of one store manager is giving her fits. It's not that Bob, the manager, is doing a poor job. Quite the contrary. Sales are up in his store. The profit margin is satisfactory. Bob runs his store in an efficient and organized way. He seems to do everything by the book.

However, there seems to be something missing. Bob's employees do their jobs, but don't seem to be excited about their jobs or the company. Bob's employee turnover is above average for the chain. What's missing? Bob seems to be running a textbook operation. Could it be that Bob is a great manager but a lousy leader?

Fred's failure: Fred is on the fast track to success—or so he thinks. His friends call him a natural leader. He was captain of the football team and president of his fraternity in college. Fred is naturally gregarious and likable. Furthermore, having a clear sense of purpose and direction, Fred is decisive and knows what he wants. However, Fred's boss plans to call him into the office today—and fire him.

Although Fred is great with people, he just doesn't follow through on details. He over-extends himself and, hence, finds it difficult to get things done. The bottom line? Fred is an *ineffective manager*. Despite his charismatic qualities, any leadership potential that Fred may possess is in jeopardy because of his ineptitude.

IS LEADERSHIP DIFFERENT?

What do these three cases tell us? What is the common thread running through each one? Ralph is discovering that building strong managers does not necessarily build strong leaders. Bob is a textbook manager, but lacks leadership skill to pull his employees together. Hopefully, Fred will eventually realize that great leadership potential may be lost without solid management skills to back it up.

Management and leadership skills, though closely interwoven, are, in fact, separate and distinct. Often the difference is subtle, but it's there.

Elwood N. Chapman, in his book, *Put More Leadership Into Your Style* (Science Research Associates Inc., 1984), describes the difference this way: "Management is keeping people productive, maintaining optimal working conditions, and making the best possible use of all resources. . . .It is holding things together. Leadership . . . takes a broader view. Leadership takes you into new territory. As a manager you may be content to work primarily inside the framework of your organization; as a leader, you become increasingly concerned with the direction the organization itself is taking."

What Mr. Chapman discovered after interviewing more than sixty acknowledged leaders in business, education, and government is that true leadership behavior transcends management behavior. Not only do effective leaders behave differently than non-leaders, but *effective leadership behavior also can be adapted to any management style*. The practical application of this principle lies in the ability of managers to improve upon their leadership abilities.

Mr. Chapman has concluded that effective leadership is dependent upon a

LEADERSHIP EFFECTIVENESS SCALE

Instructions: This rating form describes 30 practices that are commonly demonstrated by acknowledged leaders. Please read each statement carefully. Then decide the extent to which the person being rated demonstrates that practice. Indicate your decision by checking the appropriate column. (To score the results, see below.)

The Person Being Rated:	Usually If Not Always	Fairly Often	Occasionally	Rarely If Ever
1. Keeps group members informed.				
2. Expresses thoughts clearly and forcefully.				
3. Speaks well from a platform.				
4. Is a good listener.				
5. Attracts others to want to hear what he/she has to say.				
6. Communicates a sense of "being in charge."				
7. Encourages upward communication from followers.				
8. Demonstrates compassion for others.				
9. Provides rewards that are important to followers.				
10. Is sensitive to the needs of others.				
11. Attracts others to want to join his/her group.				
12. Has the full backing of all those who work under him/her.				
13. Provides enough structure to create a cohesive feeling among his/her subordinates.				

194

14. Establishes an authority line that is clear, consistent, and appropriate for the situation.

15. Strives to win by allowing subordinates to also win.

16. Gets tough when necessary.

17. Is respected by subordinates when authority is used.

18. Uses the power that he/she has with firmness, but also with sensitivity.

19. Consults with others before making important decisions.

20. Has a strong track record for making important decisions.

21. Follows a logical pattern in making decisions.

22. Communicates decisions with pride and decisiveness.

23. Is able to admit mistakes whe he/she makes them.

24. Faces up to and makes hard decisions.

25. Gets others caught up in his/her positive forces.

26. Creates an active tempo that others emulate.

27. Communicates a positive attitude during difficult or tough times.

28. Always put his/her best foot forward.

29. Articulates an inspiring mission for the group.

30. Generates a feeling of pride and accomplishment in his/her followers.

solid manager base: "You can be an excellent manager without becoming a good leader; but you cannot be an excellent leader without becoming a good manager."

RATE YOURSELF

If you are serious about improving your leadership abilities, the first step is to identify the areas in which you are performing well so that you can continue to perfect those skills. The next step is to uncover areas in which you are not performing up to your potential—where improvements can be made. The *Leadership Effectiveness Scale* can help you with both of these steps.

For the optimum benefit rate yourself as a leader first. Then invite business colleagues to respond to the *Leadership Effectiveness Scale* with you in mind. From your input and theirs, you should be able to arrive at a fairly accurate profile of your strengths and weaknesses.

How did you rate? To calculate your score on the Leadership Effectiveness Scale, give yourself 4 points for every Usually If Not Always, 3 points for every Fairly Often, 2 points for every Occasionally, 1 point for every Rarely If Ever.

Record the subtotal of each category in the corresponding section below:

Communicator:	Questions 1-6	Subtotal——————
Mutual Rewarder:	Questions 7-12	Subtotal——————
Power Figure:	Questions 13-18	Subtotal——————
Decision Maker:	Questions 19-24	Subtotal——————
Positive Force:	Questions 25-30	Subtotal——————

Leadership Effectiveness   Total——————

Scoring scale: 105-120 Strong leader; 90-104 Good leader; 75-89 Fair leader; Under 75 Improvement needed.

WHAT LEADERS DO DIFFERENTLY

Because effective leadership depends on a solid managerial base, Mr. Chapman derived a formula for leadership, consisting of five foundations. These foundations can be conceptualized in pyramid form, with each layer building on the one below it. Although each of the five foundations is considered separate and distinct from management skills, the formula builds in sound management principles.

First Foundation: Leader as communicator. It's *how* they communicate that ultimately moves managers into the realm of leadership. When leaders communicate, there is little doubt about who is in command. Followers want to hear what they have to say. Moreover, leaders are superior listeners. They can absorb what it is that their followers want, enabling them to know *where* and *how* to lead.

Second Foundation: Leader as mutual rewarder. Followers provide rewards to leaders through their support, loyalty, and performance. But the hard part for the leader is knowing and providing what it is that followers want. Leaders must use their communication and listening skills to provide the right mix of rewards at the right time. Ironically, good leadership itself may be the primary reward that leaders *give* to followers.

Third Foundation: Leader as power figure. Regardless of the source, when effective leaders use the power that they have, they do so with care. Power is never flaunted for its own sake. Rather, it is used as a tool to maintain standards and accomplish goals. When power is used appropriately it is respected and welcomed by followers. In sum, the way in which you demonstrate your power can make the difference as to whether or not you have any followers.

Fourth Foundation: Leader as decision-maker. Leaders have an ability to make the right decision at the right time. Making right decisions, in turn, increases followers' support. Effective leaders tend to follow a logical process for making the right decision, knowing when to involve others in the decision-making process. Effective leaders also understand the need to change course as soon as possible when a misjudgement has been made. They are able to admit mistakes and then get on with the business at hand. Further, effective decision-making requires courage. And effective leaders are able to take a stand that may not be popular—and stand by it when they know it represents the best course of action.

Fifth Foundation: Leader as positive force. Acting as a positive force represents the apex of the leadership formula. Effective leaders are able, in some way, to generate a positive force in which others get caught up. They project strength, vigor, and vitality—something good, something positive. Followers, in turn, are proud to identify with effective leaders because they transmit a sense of accomplishment and purpose. Effective leaders also generate a positive force by articulating an inspiring mission for the group. An inspiring mission goes beyond common statements of profit and growth goals by reflecting the essence of what the group or organization is all about.

LESSONS

Even though Ralph, Bob, and Fred all have lessons to learn about leadership, their potential for success remains high. Once the unique requirements are understood, plans can be made to put them into practice. Just like learning how to play tennis, play the piano, or paint a picture, learning the craft of leadership requires the will to learn and a great deal of practice.

After calculating your score on the *Leadership Effectiveness Scale*, formulate an action plan for your own improvement. Establish realistic goals. Work on one foundation at a time until you can blend them all together into a comfortable and effective leadership style. You may be pleasantly surprised to find that you *can* put more leadership into your style.

William B. Martin heads his own management-consulting firm, William B. Martin Associates, Claremont, Calif., which specializes in management training and development.

28.
REALITY SUPERVISION

Harry Nelson

There is no one style of supervision. You as a perceptive supervisor should base your approach on the realities of the situation and the personalities and needs of the employees involved.

It is understandable why supervisors, who are new at the position, have doubts and confusion regarding the "right" supervisory style to use. One reason is due to there being a wide range of supervisory approaches which have been used since time immemorial. These supervisory leadership concepts run the gamut from authoritarian to permissive as reflected on the continuum shown:

Autocratic   Benevolent
Sea Captain   Authoritarian
Participative   Democratic
Laissez Faire

The stereotyped sea captain approach is, "Do it," the benevolent authoritarian is along the fatherly approach, "Let us do it my way, I know best." In the participative, the supervisor ask the subordinates to participate in the decision-making process; although there are some who comment this is a facade in some cases, as the decision has already been made in the supervisor's mind. In the democratic approach, one asks for input and puts into practice any feasible suggestions which are advanced by subordinates. In the last approach, laissez-faire, one simply turns the job over to the subordinates and walks away, saying in effect, "Do it any way you wish."

In using a realistic supervisory approach, it is acknowledged that the major motivation for most of us to show up for work each day is the salary or wage involved. There are some supervisors who state flatly that is the only reason people work and base their supervisory approach to their employees on that view. They operate solely from the authoritarian sea captain approach and their assumption is very well expressed by a supervisor who commented, "The only reasons people work are fear, need or greed!" In his case, his style has been successful, due to the type of job involved and the personalities of the workers in the plant. There are some work places in which that structured authoritarian style meets the needs of the employees; but in many other work situations the workers would resent it as it did not meet their job expectations. In those cases, realistic supervision would be of value to both the employee and the supervisor.

JOB EXPECTATIONS

In recent years, the concept has been given greater acceptance by supervisors and managers alike, that there are employees who have expectations from the job other than just a wage, there are other basic needs they would like to have met on the job. These views are not new, it is simply that with the more humanistic approach used in many organizations today, these views with the encouragement of the behavioral scientists are, through the medium of seminars and supervisory classes, being brought to the attention of more supervisors. The behavioral scientists maintain that among the job expectations and needs some workers have are such things as a desire for more job responsibility, job enrichment, being able to see the end results of their work, being permitted to participate to some degree in decision-making and knowing how well they are doing on their job. A point to remember when looking over these studies made by behavioral scientists is that they reflect the needs which are important to them as behavioral scientists; that is why they themselves became involved in their particular line of endeavor. It does not mean that every person in the work force puts the same value on having these particular needs met!

USE PRACTICAL APPROACHES

This comment is not at all meant to belittle the supervisory styles they advocate, these styles are more than buzzwords, they are practical approaches, but like medical prescriptions they do not work for everyone. Realizing the differences workers hold regarding job expectations is the basis of reality supervision. It calls for the supervisor to be realistic and take the time to learn what each individual's traits and needs are. Then the supervisor must adapt a supervisory style some place along the continuum which will enable him/her to use that specific individual's traits and needs to the best advantage of the organization and the worker.

As a supervisor, you soon became aware that not all workers have the same job expectations and that they react differently to your supervisory style. You have employees to whom working is living, it is a major part of their life; and there are others who see the job simply as a means to get sufficient money to find fulfillment off the job. You cannot treat them both alike; the first group will probably be eager to accept responsibility and will want to make suggestions, while the second group will be more comfortable in a structured environment—one in which you as supervisor tell them how to do the job. Don't think the second type of employee is undesirable, both types fill a need in the operation, having one type could hamper production. Be realistic, then you will use the supervisory style along the continuum which uses each worker's individual skills and personality to the best possible advantage of your department.

STYLE OF LEADERSHIP

Just as you, the supervisor, may feel more at ease using one specific style of leadership, so will the workers feel more comfortable when you use a supervisory approach which takes into account their needs. However, you in employing reality supervision normally do not have the luxury of using just one style. During the course of a workday, you may find yourself operating at different points along the continuum, depending on the personnel involved and the job.

At the same time, were an emergency to face you, such as an accident or a fire, in all probability you would take over, regardless of who was in you crew, and supervise in an autocratic manner. For in that situation, one person would have to take over and make the decisions.

YOU CAN'T CHANGE HUMAN NATURE

Some may view it as an imposition to expect the supervisor to, when necessary, use a different supervisory approach with different members of the work crew, believing it is up to the worker to adjust to the supervisor's style. However, you cannot change human nature; you may make the workers feel sorry they did not change, but that is not the best technique to use. It will be simpler, and you will get more cooperation and productivity if you are tolerant of these differences in your workers and by using reality supervision you go along with these differences and have them work for you, not against you!

Two examples will serve to point this out: a new supervisor was put in charge of a medical clinic in which all the nurses had been used to a boss with a democratic leadership style. The new supervisor had an inflexible authoritarian style and within six months of his taking over, eighty percent of the staff had quit. In the five previous years, the turnover rate had been nil; the new supervisor was fired in one year! The second example involves an overseas operation, new management had taken over and supervisory staff were informed that from then on they were to use a democratic approach with the workers.

The supervisor/manager did not realize that the cultural background of the native workers had led them to expect to be told what to do: they were more comfortable with an authoritarian approach. With the new style of leadership in effect, the majority of the workers quit, their views being, "If the people who run the operation don't know what to do, we don't want to work there!" It would seem that in neither of these cases was realistic supervision being practiced.

SUMMARY

In summation, reality supervision accepts that money is the major motivator for employees; however, there are some who have other needs they would like to have met on the job, among them recognition, a feeling of responsibility, a sense of participation. The supervisor practicing reality supervision would be aware of the specific needs of the employees and, if possible, meet those needs.

There is no *one* style of supervision which fits all job situations, so do not feel ill at ease if your style does not jibe with what is being used in another department. You as a perceptive supervisor would base your approach on the realities of the situation and the personalities and needs of the employees involved. However, regardless of the style or styles you use, if your company is meeting its goals and you are treating your people as best you can and meeting their needs on the job; you are then using reality supervision. You are doing well!

29.
I HAVE MET THE ENEMY

Paul Elsasser

> How you perceive yourself will most definitely affect your performance as
> a manager. Leadership is not a collection of public relations tricks, it's a
> state of mind.

Remember that declaration made famous by Pogo? "We have met the enemy
and he is us." Well, unfortunately that aphorism too often describes some of
the difficulties we make for ourselves in our daily lives. If I were to paraphrase
it: "I have met the enemy and he is me," it would illustrate the mental quagmire
we sometimes make of our self-image. Nowhere is this tendency to become our
own worst enemies more evident, nor more crucial to our effective functioning, than during that transformation from hourly worker to supervisory position. Make no mistake about it—how you perceive yourself will most definitely
affect your performance as a manager/supervisor.

Why? Because leadership is not just a collection of public relations tricks, it's
also a state of mind. One of the reasons that people follow leaders is that they
perceive a special something in those leaders . . . an apparent sense of
purposeful direction and—more importantly—*self-confidence*. Think back to
supervisors you have admired: What is it that made you want to follow them?
Right, they seemed to know where they were going and how they were going to
get there. As you'll find out, appearances can be deceptive. At times, you
won't really feel as confident about the outcome of your decisions as your
subordinates may think. In fact, as you move up, and observe the mechanics of
upper management from close range, you'll see that even *up there*, they are not
supernaturally enlightened, either. But if you have faith in yourself, you'll be
calm and clearheaded enough to make the best possible decision under the
circumstances. That is what the people who follow you will see—a leader who
appears confident of the right course and unafraid of difficult choices. By
cultivating that kind of confidence, your batting average of correct decisions
will improve rapidly.

So it's important (before you take that giant step into supervision) to come to terms with yourself, take an honest inventory of your capabilities and your new responsibilities.

First, the inventory of your own abilities. As for technical ability, you shouldn't have any worries on that score; management doesn't choose supervisors on a whim. They are convinced you can do the job. Let's face it, your boss has a vested interest in your success. How about drive and a sense of responsibility to the company? Would you have come to the notice of management if you didn't have the drive to do a better than average job? Of course not, that's what made you stand out from the rest in the first place. Now, what about that intangible leadership? The big question: "Can I be an effective leader?" There are natural leaders but they're few and far between. Mostly, people grow into leadership through a desire to influence events around them and a faith in themselves. So you can do it if you believe in yourself.

Why is faith in yourself so important? Because in every one of us, there is a tendency to paint our self-image with the brush strokes of other people's perceptions of us. Or more accurately, what we think other people's perceptions are. That can be damaging to your self-respect and ability to function as an effective supervisor. When you step into that new role, you will find that your circle of friends has shrunk considerably. Have you ever seen that commercial on TV? The one where the newly promoted production foreman spends one minute and forty-five seconds of the two-minute slot fending off the backpats and handshakes of his former co-workers. They can't wait for the production line to shut down so they can take the boss out to get a beer—after all, *one of them* has finally made it; there is some justice in the world, after all. Such unrestrained joy, such love.

Forget it. Chances are, what a cross section of those people out there will feel for you will be: respect (they know you earned the promotion, and they don't begrudge you that); a sense of loss, by a few (I mean, he's one of *them* now); hope, on the part of some, that you'll carry the message from the troops into the management bunker, be their champion; and outright, squinty-eyed suspicion on the part of others that you've just turned on them, sold your soul to management (the first tough decision you have to make, they will say, "See! See, I told you.") You'll find, after an initial "honeymoon" period, that the decisions will get tougher, and your loneliness will become more apparent. There will be times when it will be tempting to run away from your responsibility rather than risk the disapproval of people you worked with closely for years. So tempting to cast yourself in the guise of the well-intentioned messenger of ill tidings (the friend of the people caught between the heartlessness of management and the plight of his true friends) instead of making that tough, but correct, decision—or standing behind a decision made by management (of which you are now a member). That's when faith in yourself will be like money in the bank.

PUT IT IN WRITING

Now an inventory of your responsibilities. The first thing you must pin down—after the initial euphoria has worn off—is exactly what are your responsibilities and what is your span of authority? I can't stress this enough. Many companies, especially the larger, older firms, will have made available to you a company policy and procedure manual which will contain a job description of your function and a detailed description of your authority and the appropriate personnel procedures. Of course, no company can give you a catalog of duties and responses to cover every conceivable situation. The company considers—and quite rightly, in my view—that, as a member of management, you are getting paid for making judgements and forging decisions under pressure. Management is an art, not a science, and you create as you go along. But I have seen a lot of pain, uncertainty and inefficiency result from fuzzy or nonexistent supervisory guidelines. So if your company is one of those without established, printed procedures, I urge you to do this: Agree verbally with your boss just what your span of responsibility is and exactly what areas of the operation you are responsible for—*and then put it in writing*. Write a detailed letter to your immediate supervisor detailing your understanding of your responsibilities and authority (keep a copy for yourself, of course). This will serve as a rough guideline through the potential minefields. Your boss won't be upset by your wanting to delineate your responsibilities, he'll probably respect your organizational sense. Who knows you may even have instigated a new company or departmental manual for supervisors.

So what have we got? You've taken an assessment of yourself and seen that you're not such a bad candidate for promotion, after all. In fact, you may just be the best possible person for that supervisor's position. You know there'll be rough periods ahead. We all crave the approval of our fellows. You know now that you will be alone a good part of the time, but you also feel confident of handling the situations without losing your self-respect. Too, you know exactly what's expected of you by your supervisor. You know just how far your authority reaches before it infringes on someone else's turf. In short, you're ready to do that job that fate—and your own abilities—has placed in your path. So go to it!

30.
10 REASONS WHY EXECUTIVES FAIL

Jeffrey L. Kovach

"Failure" is a harsh word. But it's also a harsh reality for executives who are "coerced into transition." Competence is no guarantee of longevity.

Executives rarely, if ever, *fail*. Granted, they may find themselves outplaced, prematurely retired, phased out, temporarily reassigned, or even in "coerced transition"—but *fail?* Not to hear them tell it.

But never mind the ego-buffering euphemisms which dominate today's executory argot. Neil S. MacKenna and Richard L. Jandl of MacKenna, Jandl & Associates Inc., a Lynnfield, Mass., outplacement and executive counseling firm, tell a different story.

"We spend the better part of each day dealing with executives who had failed in their previous jobs and were subsequently fired," says Mr. MacKenna. "These are individuals who have to face up to the fact that it simply hasn't worked out. Our job is to conduct an in-depth analysis to determine both why it didn't work out—and what can be done to make sure it won't happen again."

After years of listening to involuntarily unemployed executives vent their trials and tribulations, Messrs. MacKenna and Jandl have discerned a "recurring pattern to executive failure."

EXECUTIVES FAIL . . .

. . . when a new boss arrives on the scene. In almost every case, a change at the top is made to effect positive change in an organization.

Unfortunately, since the new boss may be under the impression that hand-picked managers will be more loyal, the transition is often made at the expense of competent, self-motivated managers already in place. "Who needs someone around who seems to be fighting what the new boss wants to accomplish?" asks Mr. MacKenna.

. . . by playing "Prince Hamlet." Hesitating before taking corrective action is the downfall of many executives. "If the boss says, 'Get rid of George,' a common response may be to first defend good old George, and then delay taking action as long as possible, hoping the problem will just go away," observes Mr. MacKenna. "I've seen executives drag their feet, eventually fire George, and then be fired themselves for acting too slowly."

. . . when they rise to the level of their incompetence. Executives are usually told—not asked—about their promotions. "We live in a society that believes that being a manager of managers is what it's all about," says Mr. Jandl. Hence, since very few promotions are ever challenged by executives who may have been perfectly content in their previous positions, both the promoted individuals and their companies often suffer.

"For example, take a supersaleman who is promoted to a management position," says Mr. MacKenna. "If he doesn't succeed in the new unfamiliar position, chances are good he'll leave the company rather than return to his former position because of the stigma of failure."

. . . by striving to be liked rather than respected. Successful executives must make the tough decisions. If executives adopt "ownership attitudes" toward their companies, advises Mr. MacKenna, doing what the *situation* commands (rather than what their personal feelings suggest) will begin to come naturally.

. . . when their behavior is consistently inconsistent. Treating occurrence "A" with anger today, but with smiles tomorrow, greatly diminishes an executive's managerial effectiveness.

. . . by not incorporating themselves into the corporate culture. There are some things "you're just supposed to know" about a company's executive hierarchy, says Mr. Jandl. To succeed in some companies, for example, executives must know that only white shirts should be worn, brown suits are anathema, and divorce is "out of the question."

. . . when they don't realize why they were hired in the first place. In short, "executives aren't hired for their magnetic personalities," quips Mr. MacKenna. "They're hired to help their bosses achieve determined objectives."

. . . when they inadvisedly take co-workers into their confidence. There's no such thing as "off-the-record criticism of a boss" within a company, notes Mr. MacKenna. Loose lips have sunk plenty of executive careers.

. . . by demanding changes in subordinates' work habits without first attempting to alter their belief systems. Both Mr. MacKenna and Mr. Jandl agree that most U.S. managers aren't aware of the critical role that belief systems play in worker productivity, motivation, and satisfaction —although this awareness is slowly increasing.

. . . by deluding themselves that it's always the other guy who fails—or, should we say "doesn't succeed."

31.
LEADERSHIP THROUGH FOLLOWERSHIP

William Litzinger
Thomas Schaefer

Does the "right" choice of a leadership pattern presuppose that subordinates must have learned to choose the "right" followership pattern?

Not long ago, we posed a question to a group of officers, most of whom were on the West Point faculty, and many of whom were themselves graduates of the Academy. "Since developing leadership is what this place is all about," we asked, "how do you go about doing that task?" Their answer surprised us. "We begin by teaching them to be followers."

This insight prompted us to undertake a study, not of the nature of leadership but of the notion that leadership may be chiefly an achievement of followers—that able leaders may emerge only from the ranks of able followers. Because of the genesis of our idea, we call it the West Point Thesis. Our concern is the developmental question of how leaders emerge and, particularly, how the mastery of followership may prepare and qualify one for leadership.

Contemporary authors seem to say little or nothing about what leaders must have done yesterday to become leaders today. Yet the ground of leadership can lie only in the leader's personal history.

Much earlier writers seem to have realized this. Plato's *Republic* analyzes what the king must do from his earliest years to become the sovereign. In the *Politics*, Aristotle laments the rarity of virtue among aspirants to statemanship, and insists that only by training from youth may subjects grow to leadership. Much later, the philosopher Hegel required of the mature leader the most intimate understanding of his followers, achievable only by passage through the experience of servitude. In his *Phenomenology of Mind*, Hegel so strongly affirms the mastery of followership as the sine qua non of leadership—our "West Point Thesis"—that an outline of his idea is critical here.

LEADERSHIP/FOLLOWERSHIP

Hegel's "dialectic of master and slave" is a significant episode in the history of leadership theory. Leadership is possible, says Hegel, not only on the condition that followership has been learned, but on the more radical condition that the leader has known subjection and thralldom. The mature leader not only must have know the travail of the follower; he must here and now incorporate within himself all that the follower is. The school for leadership is indeed followership, a followership that is fully preserved within leadership, but transformed for having moved beyond itself. The leaders in short, must not merely have been a follower. He must, here and now, be a follower in the fullest sense; in a sense, paradoxically, that the follower cannot be. The leader is more a follower than the follower.

In the curious Hegelian dialectic, where opposites pass constantly into one another, the recognition that there is "followership in the leader" demands the recognition that there is "leadership in the follower." Believers in participative leadership would agree; "management by objectives," especially, through insisting that none manage "by objectives" who do not "control themselves," affirms a need for "leadership in the follower."[1] In MBO, leadership is a shared effort in which all, leader and follower alike, not only struggle for goals, but also set them. A central purpose of MBO is to substitute for the supervisor's role of judge that of "helper." This connects the "followership of the leader" with the "leadership of the follower." MBO receives "good grades" in the school of Hegel.

The paradoxes of Hegel's thought may be less unsettling when we recall how the Pope of the Catholic church designates his own leadership; he is "The Servant of the Servants of God." Where leader and follower alike are held to obedience to define doctrine, neither may act on his own autonomous will alone. Leadership endures so long as it assumes a posture of humility, a spirit of followership.

EPITOMIZING THE GROUP'S VALUES

Argument from authority is notoriously weak. Plato and Aristotle, Hegel and others have propounded the "thesis," but does it prove out in practice?

In fact, many fine leaders *have* been excellent followers. The young Churchill distinguished himself as a faithful taker of orders, as did the young Bismarck, and the youthful Caesar. Even figures who are despised because they were not good followers of societal norms—such as Stalin, Hitler, Idi Amin—were good followers of some other code. Though he "marched to a different drummer," Hitler was an excellent "follower" of National Socialism in Germany. He was not above showing obsequiousness to those whom he judged to be arbiters of his rise to power. Mussolini, beloved of the Fascists, was a beast to the Allies, as was Genghis Khan to the people of Europe.

The leader, then, appears to be a poor follower when judged by norms other than his own. When perceived in the context of his own organization, he is its obedient servant. Adversary organizations (gangs, revolutionary groups) demand more rigid conformity to group norms than do their legitimate counterparts. In prison societies, for example, an "inmate code" demands that leaders conform more perfectly to group norms than do their followers. Leaders who were notoriously "poor followers" of societal norms are typically heads of opposition groups that replaced, or threatened, another regime. They are, of course, poor followers of the enemy regime, but excellent followers of their own. "Mavericks," like Zapata, who became leaders, may appear to have been bad followers. They are, in fact, good followers of an orthodoxy other than the one by which the majority judges them. Zapata's organization exacted the strictest possible obedience from all, including Zapata himself.

Whether adversary or orthodox, an organization demands common acceptance of values. In this lies the link between obedience and command. The commander cannot break the link without destroying the legitimacy of his rule. Richard Nixon broke the link and had to relinquish command. In this sense, surely, followership is the school of leaders. To have internalized an organization's values, to have become, even, an embodiment of them, is to have the potential to be a leader. And, assuming an infallible awareness among the organizations's members that one among them is an incarnation of its values, that member will be elected to leadership. No less certainly will abandonment of these values by the leader bring his decline and eventual fall.

There has been broad recognition of what we are calling the West Point Thesis throughout history. For centuries in China, leaders were chosen on the basis of their obedience to and knowledge of Confucian principles. The British Civil Service, like virtually all armies, has linked faithful service at the lower ranks to advancement to leadership. The idea, in fact, is inseparable from the conception of hierarchy. To stand at the pinnacle, one must have ascended some series of steps. Ascent demands not merely effort but upward progress. This occurs by gaining a foothold at each level, mastering each higher step. It requires the art of followership.

APPLYING THE WEST POINT THESIS

How might the West Point Thesis mesh with present day concepts? Chester Barnard's well-known Acceptance Theory of Authority strongly asserts the follower-leadership link.

"The decision as to whether an order has authority or not lies with the persons to whom it is addressed, and does not reside in 'persons of authority' or those who issue these orders."[2]

With the ground of authority in the followers' granting or withholding obedience, leaders are constrained to lead in ways construed by followers to be consistent with the goals of the organization. "A person will accept a communication as authoritative only when . . . he believes that it is not inconsistent with the purposes of the organization," says Barnard. The leader, then, must also "follow," that is, follow goals as understood by those under him. Followers hold power over the leader since they judge whether the leader leads, that is, conducts them to their goal.

The leader turns out to be a follower, and "a truer follower than the followers" in that he is held to a greater fidelity in followership than are the followers. So great is the requirement of faithful followership for the leader that he ceases to exercise command the moment this "faith" is judged wanting by his followers. Such a situation arises when a command lies outside the "zone of indifference," that group of commands which are unquestionably acceptable. Presumably, if the follower perceives an order as conducive to the goal and *still* disobeys, the threat to organization is not nearly so great as it is when the leader commands action that does not conform to the goal. Again: mastery of followership is even more important in the leader than in the follower.

Barnard's ideas, then, support the West Point Thesis. Our thesis would illuminate the Acceptance Theory by focusing on the followership exercised by the leader. How is the leader's followership like, and how is it unlike, that of the followers? Pursuit of these questions could be fruitful in clarifying the Acceptance Theory, and in drawing out the meaning of the West Point Thesis. In any case, if followership as a subordinate is a propaedeutic for followership as a leader, then surely, as Aristotle claimed, "who would learn to command must first of all learn to obey."

Theorists are well aware of the "reciprocality" between leader and follower, realizing that "poor" subordinates affect leadership style profoundly.

Yet the kind of follower the leader was may affect how he leads as significantly as the kinds of followers the leader now commands. We argue here that this dimension should be brought into any dialogue about leadership.

How might a more explicit awareness of "The West Point Thesis" enrich modern theories of leadership? We now grope for some idea of how "the thesis" might open some dimensions within existing theory.

"X AND Y-STYLE" FOLLOWERSHIP?

McGregor's distinction invites concern over which leadership style is best in particular circumstances. Whatever style may be appropriate, however, distinct styles of leadership must elicit distinct styles of followership. Appropriate types of followership will be expected as responses to, and support for, particular styles of leadership. Should we designate a follower's response to autocratic leaders as "X-style followership," or would the nuances of the concept require a separate designation? Whatever the answer, identifying followership styles seems a condition for understanding the kind of follower the leader was, which is crucial for knowing the kind of leader he is now. The most appropriate followership training needed for a specific style of leadership will probably depend on the style of leadership in question.

The ways in which the arts of followership and leadership are related will probably vary as a function of the degree of centralization, extent of specialization, type of technology, location on the product-life cycle trajectory, and other factors in the organization. A past mastery of followership probably would be increasingly important for leadership as one moves along a continuum from loosely controlled, decentralized organization to tightly controlled, centralized types. While the followership and leadership arts would prove always linked in some way, logic suggests that in the tightly structured organization the link would be very strong, while in the loosely structured organization, with decision-making at the lowest possible levels, the link would be found weaker.

CHOICE OF A FOLLOWERSHIP PATTERN

Does the "right" choice of a leadership pattern presuppose that subordinates must have learned to choose a "right" followership pattern? Is flexibility in the choice of "followership style" possible in anything like the way in which flexibility is possible in choosing one's leadership style? Although followership may be a necessary prelude to leadership in some organizations, is it necessary in all?

This last question prompts the reflection that, while a personal history of good followership may be one significant factor in leadership, it is not the final determinant of leadership success. Some mastery of followership is a *necessary* condition for leadership, but not a *sufficient* condition. A good record of followership is far from a guarantee that one will make a fine leader. Something more than being an "obedient servant" is needed to create the leader. There were others among the tribes of Israel as obedient as Moses, but none with his "fire."

Still, followership deserves a larger place among those items now attracting the attention of leadership theorists. The perennial affirmation of the idea through history should be enough to prompt more serious consideration of it. Its greater integration into contemporary theory will provide new insights into the phenomena of leadership.

REFERENCES

1. In the chapter, "Management by Objectives and Self-Control" in *The Practice of Management* (New York: Harper and Row, 1954), Peter Drucker

affirms this point strongly: "It [MBO] motivates the manager to action not because somebody tells him to do something . . . but because the objective needs of his task demand it. He acts not because somebody wants him to but because he himself decides that he has to—he acts, in other words, as a free man.": 136.

2. Chester I. Barnard, *The Functions of the Executive* (Cambridge, Mass.: Harvard University Press, 1938): 82.

William Litzinger is Director of the Division of Management and Marketing at the University of Texas at San Antonio. Thomas Schaefer is Professor of Management at the University of Texas of the Permian Basin.

32.
MIND GAMES

Gary Benson

Inherent in modern management is the separation between supervisor
and subordinate. Over the years, unfortunately, this schism has bred contempt and distrust.

Douglas McGregor explained Theory X and Theory Y as the assumptions
managers make about employees. Often overlooked, however, is the role
employee assumptions play in shaping managerial behavior.

McGregor defined an assumption as an unconscious acceptance of certain
basic conceptions of one's world. Managers react not to an objective world, but
to one fashioned out of their own perceptions, assumptions and beliefs.
Managers, he argued, are often trapped by their own assumptions about human
behavior.

What is, perhaps, most misleading is the popular tendency to associate
Theory X with "hard management" and Theory Y with "soft management."
McGregor rejected both labels. They were intended not to be descriptions of
opposing management styles, but rather to describe alternative sets of
assumptions that managers make about people.

McGregor's theories were formulated on his observation that most
organizations and managers operate under one set of assumptions or the other.
For example, assumptions McGregor embodied in Theory X view employees as
disliking work so much that they must be coerced, controlled, and directed
toward organizational goals. On these assumptions, managers try to control
employees' behavior through a system of external constraints, such as the
power to give and withhold financial rewards.

However, employees, in an attempt to make the organization aware of and
responsive to their needs, withhold their total commitment and produce at
minimally acceptable levels. Managers, in turn, exert more constraints. Consequently, when employees behave on assumptions of Theory X, managers
point to this behavior to justify additional coercive efforts to get satisfactory
performance.

McGregor viewed this self-defeating atmosphere of distrust and competition not only as degrading and wasteful, but also as unnecessary. An often overlooked, but extremely valuable, contribution of McGregor's theory is that he argued that employees learn unproductive behavior as a response to managers' efforts to control their behavior.

Hence, the manager's behavior, stemming from a set of assumptions, influences the behavior and performance of subordinates. The behavior of managers determines the behavior of employees.

Employee assumptions. Related to managerial assumptions are employee assumptions. These important but previously overlooked assumptions are those which employees hold with respect to managers' behavior. Just as McGregor argued that employees learn their behavior patterns from managers, it can be argued that managers learn their behavior patterns from their employees.

If employees' assumptions and expectations are that managers are autocratic and hard-nosed, then the employees behave accordingly, and that managerial style and behavior will be reinforced and further elicited. The behavior of the employees thus determines the behavior of the manager.

An attitudinal study of a variety of respondents including entrepreneurs, managers, students, nurses, supervisors and production-line workers revealed two sets of employee assumptions about managers. These parallel the assumptions of managers about employees. The first category included the following responses to the "managers are" section of the questionnaire.

• Managers are generally considerate and objective in their relations with workers;
• energetic and imaginative;
• respected by subordinates;
• intelligent and competent;
• cooperative and open-minded; and
• determined and goal directed.

The second category of assumptions is included in the following responses to the "managers are" section of the questionnaire.

• Managers are inherently distrustful of workers;
• not respected by their subordinates;
• narrow-minded and inconsiderate;
• incompetent and lacking in creativity; and
• egotistical and dictatorial.

Two views of managers. The two sets of assumptions seem to represent the two alternative views of managers held by people in general and workers in particular. Just as McGregor argued that employees are often lazy, indifferent, uncooperative, and uncreative because they learn these behaviors as a response to managers' assumptions, managers may behave according to employee assumptions.

If the assumptions that managers hold about employees determine employee behavior, and vice versa, then the only way to improve performance is through total organizational development. Much time has been spent on management development, leaving a void in employee development.

There are innumerable development and training programs to assist managers in adopting alternative sets of assumptions or to change from being task and production oriented to being more human relations oriented. However, little has been done to assist employees to adopt alternative sets of assumptions about their managers.

Inherent in much of modern management is the separation between supervisors and subordinates. Over the years, unfortunately, this schism has bred contempt and distrust between the two factions.

A committed effort to total organizational development is needed, including extensive employee development along with management development. Such employee development activities might include programs and training in the following areas: team building; quality circles; productivity teams; job enrichment; management by objectives; and career and life development.

Through these and other similar programs, employees may learn to put themselves in the shoes of management for a greater understanding of the position and responsibilities of management. This promotes a "We're all in this together, so let's do the best job we can" attitude.

Employee development programs should focus not only on technical job training, they should encourage the awareness of how employee assumptions can shape managers' behavior and vice versa.

By participating in such programs, employees may learn that most managers do not distrust employees and are not narrow-minded and inconsiderate. Rather, they will learn to have a much greater appreciation and understanding of the importance of management in the organization. This will foster a greater spirit of cooperation and teamwork between supervisory and nonsupervisory employees.

Dr. Gary Benson is coordinator of business programs at the University of Wyoming, Casper Campus, Casper, Wyo.

Part V
LEADERSHIP THEORY AND TRAINING

33.

THE RIGHT STUFF

Charles A. Garfield

A distinct combination of "learnable" qualities places excellent managers ahead of the pack.

Peak-performing managers are trained, not born.

This conclusion is based upon 18 years of research into peak performance in corporations, and training programs that have been an outgrowth of these studies.

Some managers seem intuitively to possess the specific skills and leadership behaviors that enhance productivity. But thousands of others exhibit major increases in their performance levels by taking steps to successfully acquire these valuable skills. The most successful managers possess particular characteristics that allow them to perform optimally, and these qualities are learnable.

This research, which has been coordinated at the Performance Sciences Institute in Berkeley, California, began during NASA's Apollo project and has continued for more than 18 years. Recently, in-depth interviews have been conducted with more than 300 managers as part of a study of over 1,500 peak performers. Interviewees have been selected from not only the business world, but in fields ranging from medicine and the sciences to sports and the arts. In evaluating the content of these interviews, particular themes and skills appear repeatedly among optimal achievers.

TEN COMMON TRAITS

The highest-performing managers, we have discovered, possess the following 10 qualities that contribute significantly to their success.

1. Peak-performing managers exhibit *foresight and the ability to execute effective strategic planning*. Consequently, they are less consumed by short term gain at the expense of long-term planning.

2. They *decide in advance* what staffing, equipment, finances, and other resources they will need to successfully complete a project. This is in marked contrast to their less productive peers, who often zealously launch into a project only to discover halfway that additional resources or skills are necessary.

3. These managers *refuse to become entrapped* at any particular plateau for very long. They consistently aim toward higher levels of accomplishment by committing themselves to ever-increasing excellence in addition to attaining specific end points or goals.

4. Top managers posses a *superior ability to take creative risks,* thus avoiding prolonged "comfort zones" where fears of success and failure limit productivity. They are not content with safe, predictable performance, but rather insist on stretching beyond their current levels.

   High-achieving managers often assess their risk taking through a technique called a "catastrophe report" or "worst-case scenario." In this procedure, they imagine the worst possible consequences of a particular risk. "What's the worst thing that could possibly happen?" "What action would I take if it did?"

   If they can develop an action plan that allows them to deal with this scenario, they often engage the risk with significantly reduced apprehensions and increased self-confidence. However, if the catastrophe report is too overwhelming, they abandon it and seek a different course of action. In essence, this is a process designed for making rational decisions without becoming paralyzed by unnecessary fears of risk taking.

5. High-performing managers demonstrate *extremely high levels of self-confidence and self-worth.* Any failure or rejection is treated only as a temporary setback, and outside criticism that is not constructive affects them much less than it does their peers.

6. Not surprisingly, high-achieving leaders have a *significant need for responsibility and control.* They are not afraid to take action, and seldom feel victimized by their circumstances. They often rely on superior communication and "sales" skills to generate new options for solving old problems.

7. High-achieving managers *mentally rehearse situations.* Many managers, for example, before entering an important meeting, envision both the process and the desired outcome, thus imprinting successful actions (and the feelings that accompany them) into their psyches.

8. High-performing managers tend to engage in their work for the *art and passion* of it. Their "mission" matters to them, and they approach it with enthusiasm. They have what is known as an "internal locus of control," and need less outside praise or recognition to feel validated and self-confident.

9. These managers concentrate on *solving problems rather than placing blame.* As a consequence, they avoid behaviors that are self- defeating and

counterproductive. They do this largely by seeking feedback for the purpose of self-correction, usually from a network of people whose opinions they respect.

Top-performing managers tend to approach problem solving by asking such key questions as, "What is the current situation?" "Where are we going? "How do we get there?" In the process, these managers end up with subordinates who act and take risks, and who are not afraid to contribute to solutions.

By contrast, lower achievers channel much of their energy into discovering who and what caused the problem, diverting their attention away from the situation at hand. They remain isolated from subordinates who may be able to assist them in getting back on course.

10. High-achieving managers demonstrate a *proprietary attitude*—that is, they have a tendency to assume ownership of their ideas and products. They prefer to act upon well-considered ideas, testing them to their upper limits, rather than retreating into a new-ending "feasibility" mode.

These skills surfaced again and again in interviews with top-flight managers.

LIFE AT THE TOP

With this information in hand, we next examined the skills of peak-performing managers in senior positions. During these interviews, six additional skills surfaced, detected repeatedly among the highest-performing senior managers.

- These men and women are motivated as much or more by quality-driven rather than merely quantity-driven sensibilities.
- Peak-performing senior managers endeavor to increase productivity through effective human resource development. These leaders perceive their employees as valuable resources who, when working at their own peak, can contribute significantly to bottom-line increases in productivity.
- High-performing senior managers understand and implement an effective balance of autonomy and direction to encourage productivity. True, their managers and employees are held to goals, but there is flexibility on procedures, and innovation in attaining these objectives.
- Senior managers typically assign their subordinates to small, independent entrepreneurial units.
- Successful senior managers do not allow themselves to be undermined by the "paralysis of perfectionism." In aligning themselves with action-oriented procedures, their modus operandi is best described as, "Do research . . . try it out . . . modify and self-correct." The peak-performing manager recognizes that perfection is an illusion, and aims instead at ever increasing levels of excellence. In the process, he or she frequently reaches the very high standards that intimidate many of his or her peers.

Peak-performing senior managers understand the need for systematic training of other managers, particularly in the human side of organizational functioning. Providing superior management training is most often viewed as a vital aspect of leadership excellence.

TRAINING PEAK PERFORMERS

Management training remains a widely misunderstood field. Some insist that such training is absolutely unnecessary—that men and women from sales or technical areas should be promoted to managerial ranks and allowed to "sink or swim," learning to be managers through their own mistakes. That approach vastly underestimates the demands of management.

There are other people, however, who elevate training to the other extreme. They believe that an effective manager must come equipped with graduate degrees and tremendously sophisticated schooling and instruction. We have found that a middle ground is the most practical and effective approach.

One of the most important aspects of our research in corporate settings has been to analyze how well companies are functioning. In the process, we examined the developmental hurdles that sometimes prevent even the best-equipped managers from excelling.

Repeatedly, we see a few managers who possess the skills and characteristics described earlier, but who still run a poorly functioning team. They may build a cadre of less-motivated and less-skilled people than themselves, and then complain of overwork. Even the most brilliant, highly motivated individuals, it seems, can sometimes become thwarted. Most often, their own fears, ridigity, compulsiveness and even oppressive, domineering behavior are to blame.

These individuals are guided through a self-analysis process in which they first identify their own counterproductive activity—from an unwillingness to delegate responsibility to a reluctance to bridge communications gaps with subordinates. Then the reasons that such self-defeating behaviors have surfaced are examined. For example, in some cases, it may be because their primary motivation is, in fact, power and dominance rather than achievement. One manager, for example, recognized that control over his staff was highly valued in the corporate culture in which he worked, and thus he sought a significant amount of dominance over those beneath him.

Finally, it is important to help individuals perceive that their difficulties may stem from specific obstacles arising naturally in the development of a peak-performing manager. In fact, there are five distinct stages in the evolution of high-achieving managers. Knowing these stages can help managers recognize and move past the blocks that can abort their career development. Those organizations that anticipate these stages and teach their managers to proceed through them successfully will benefit, often considerably, through increased productivity and performance.

1. In the *initiation stage*, a new manager must, first and foremost, learn to identify him or herself with the role of manger after a nonmanagerial history (as a salesperson, engineer, student). Until he or she does, the individual may find him or herself brainstorming excessively, displaying anxiety around subordinates, and procrastinating.

2. At the next level, the *fear of success stage*, the new manager may begin to perform so well that he or she actually becomes afraid of prospering on the job, apprehensive of what the consequences of this success may be. He or she may unconsciously fear both increased recognition and expanded responsibilities, which may lead to failure to capitalize on proven, tangible successes.

3. The *team-building stage* is next, at which point the manager has successfully conquered the earlier obstacles, and is now fully committed to the management position. However, he or she suddenly has difficulty generating new leaders among key subordinates, and forming a tightly knit team among personnel. Unable to replenish excessive control, the manager inhibits the development of the group into a peak-performing team.

4. The manager next approaches the *affiliation stage*, where the individual realizes that while his or her productivity is dependent upon the work of others, the responsibility for managerial performance remains his or hers alone. The task then becomes developing higher-level leadership capabilities. He or she has to relate effectively to both upper and lower levels of the organization, and needs to acknowledge the increased importance of people-oriented leadership skills, particularly delegation.

5. The last hurdle is the *elevation-seniority* stage, where the individual is tapped for a senior-management post. As a result, the manager must learn to successfully handle the increased responsibility and separation from subordinates that accompany the promotion. He or she must negotiate a shift in focus from people to organization, and from products and projects to money issues. Difficulties at this stage are most often associated with the transition from more human-focused concerns to more abstract financial and strategic planning concerns.

Just as there are stages in the normal development of adults, so too with managers. Growing numbers of corporations are now acknowledging and making provisions for learning these developmental stages in the context of specially designed management training programs. When this happens, employees are managed better, and productivity increases.

Dr. Charles A. Garfield is president of Performance Sciences, Inc., Berkeley, California.

34.
A REAPPRAISAL OF LEADERSHIP THEORY AND TRAINING

James Owens

> Over the last two decades top managements have exhibited a kind of
> blind, if not desperate, faith in management training, as if such faith
> would produce a miracle.

Much leadership and management training today reflects vague or confused
theoretical foundations, resulting in somewhat aimless training efforts. The
seasoned eye can usually detect the implied theoretical base (or often several of
them) underlying a particular training design and its published agenda.
Frequently the program design and its parts are drawn, with no one seemingly
aware of it, from fragments of theory buried in three pervasive theories of
leadership dominating this century: trait, behavior and contingency theories.
But these fragments seem selected casually, at random (cafeteria style) or for
personal reasons (hunch, personnel preferences, good-old-boy network, etc.)
rather than by conscious design based on the integration of clear program goals
and subordinated, explicitly chosen, means.[1]

For example, a vague grasp of underlying theory (even with clear program
goals) led to the following common and typical case of a management training
program's parts subverting—rather then supporting—its set goals: with
production and performance on the job as its main goal, a participative
leadership style became a central part of a foreman-training program which,
later, revealed a *negative* relationship between that goal and that leadership
style. Much wasted, costly and even counterproductive training ensued based
on a fragment of behavior leadership theory which was popular at the time
(participative leadership).[2] Today's management training professional,
familiar with certain key aspects of the contingency theory of leadership, would
easily and knowingly avoid such a training design.

OFF-THE-SHELF TRAINING

The enormous volume of highly-advertised off-the-shelf training materials must be carefully scrutinized for its underlying theoretical base(s) and whether, or how, it will support a program design's ultimate objectives. Similar scrutiny applies as well to the multitude of public and standardized off-the-shelf training programs, usually hotel-based, three-day seminars which are heavily advertised in the training media and by direct mail. These, and all components of any training program design, should not be isolated design decisions but rather decisions explicitly governed by ultimate goals (strategic); these to be gained by well-understood and appropriate means (tactics). Effective decisions about management training designs are impossible (except by chance) without a working knowledge of recent leadership theory and its findings.

The purpose of this article is to review and organize modern leadership theories, as well as their current status and specific findings about leadership, as a conceptual resource for the increasing number of management training professionals responsible for the training of the nation's future managers.[3]

A chronological picture of the development of modern leadership theory will be sketched, highlighting the major innovators, theories, research findings and turning-points and the significance of all of these. It is the sense of the history and meaning of leadership theory that we are after as an understandable framework for training professionals as they make program design decisions.

TRAIT THEORY OF LEADERSHIP

Trait theorists contended early in this century that there was a finite set of personal characteristics, inner traits, which distinguished effective from ineffective leaders. Just determine statistically which traits were associated, consistently and exclusively, with de facto demonstrably effective leaders. Then standard psychometric tests could be devised to identify and select high-leadership-potential people at an early point in their lives or careers. These select few would be given intensive leadership training. Trait theorists had no illusions about the difficulty of the research undertaking and knew it would require enormous effort, funding, patient research and time. But they seemed to know, too, that the trait hypothesis was simple and sure in principle, richly practical to solve real leadership needs as soon as this trait theory was proven and ready for use and ultimately certain to be validated within the most rigorous standards of scientific research methods. Trait research began about 1904 and systematically expanded for almost fifty years into a giant body of findings, information and theory.

RESEARCH METHODS AND RESULTS

Hundreds of research models and methods were devised over these years to find the sought-after set of leadership traits. Only a few, as illustrations, can be mentioned here.[4] In many studies, members of a group would be asked to indicate who they preferred to be leader and what traits influenced their choice of leader. In other studies, individuals were nominated as outstanding leaders in their fields and traits common among these samples of effective leaders were identified and classified into leadership profiles (Thurstone did this with highly-placed government administrators in his 1944 study).[5]

The early-century optimism and confidence about trait theory soured into disappointment and confusion by mid-century (about the time of Heath's 1946 military study).[6] After almost a half-century of intensive research, no scientific consensus had emerged to establish trait theory or the expected standardized uses of the theory to produce effective leaders. The field of leadership had become a mass of traits, vying with each other from one research study to another for priority in the maze of lists of leader traits. There was little consistency in the many studies and resulting lists of key traits. Stogdill found only three traits ranking consistently high in the many lists of effective leader traits of that period: intelligence, initiative and responsibility.[4]

LEADERS ARE BORN, NOT MADE?

Many trait researchers, more interested in the practical fruits of trait theory than the theory itself, had long hoped for a highly-predictable method of selecting leaders. Jennings (1943)[7] and many others urged that, given the development of sound criteria for psychological testing, selecting leaders would be far easier and more certain than the usually hopeless attempt to train non-leaders to become leaders. In his view, leaders are born, naturally endowed as leaders by innate traits; they cannot be made such by training courses. However, by mid-century, it was clear that the desired criteria (traits) for leader-selection were undiscovered, probably undiscoverable. Hope for reliable methods of selecting leaders dimmed along with trait theory itself.

BEHAVIOR THEORY OF LEADERSHIP

Trait theory did not die nor, to my knowledge, has any noteworthy researcher ever repudiated the trait approach *per se*. Intuitively, the central idea of trait theory, that traits are the roots at the very bottom of a human personality determining everything including leadership effectiveness, remains vivid. It just can't be or at least hasn't been proved. Among its adherents, it remains a matter of faith rather than rational demonstration. But leadership researchers, determined to make leadership a matter of science and proof, gradually changed course and, by mid-century, were looking for behaviors (rather than traits) associated with effective leaders. Behavior, unlike traits, was observable, more exactly definable and thus more amenable to the methods of empirical science. Without abandoning trait theory as a valuable, but metaphysical, intuition, science-oriented researchers increasingly dedicated themselves and their research efforts to the new behavior approach. Thus trait research did not just end at mid-century and behavior research begin then. Instead, the two approaches overlapped, trait research waning and behavior research rising into prominence. The same overlapping pattern would soon recur when contingency theory began to displace behavior theory.

Even in the midst of the early-century emphasis upon traits as the key to leadership, a few researchers were experimenting with leadership behavior, and classifications of it, as a sounder focus. Bogardus, for example, in 1918,[8] classified leadership behaviors into four types: autocratic, executive, democratic and reflective. During the early years, the main thrust of behavior theory was the development of a typology of leader behavior. Many classifications of leadership styles emerged. Influenced greatly by the work of Lewin, Lippitt and Bradford, beginning in 1938,[8] these styles settled finally into a classification of six generally accepted by mid-century for behavior research:

Autocratic   Issue orders, tell subordinates what to do.

Bureaucratic   Develop and enforce rules to govern all
                      behavior and situations.

Diplomatic   Persuade and motivate subordinates, sell
                      them on ideas and orders.

Consultative   Solicit ideas from, consult with,
                      subordinates before final decisions.

Democratic   Discuss decisions with subordinates seeking
                      consensus or majority view.

Free Rein   Set goals for subordinates, then give them as
                      much freedom as possible.

Later, Schmidt and Tennenbaum converted the six stereotypical classes of leader behavior into a continuum, ranging in degrees from high-leader-authority on the left side of the continuum to high-subordinate-freedom on the right end.[9] Approximate points on the continuum were still labeled for convenience of reference to them: autocratic leader at the extreme left and free-rein leader at the extreme right. But the continuum and the concept underlying it, emphasized the reality that actual leaders do not fall conveniently into just six categories but operate at dozens, even hundreds, of subtly differing degrees or points on the continuum from authority-oriented to freedom-oriented leadership styles.

The Ohio State Leadership Studies: Beginning in 1945, a group of researchers at Ohio State University developed a list of 1,800 descriptions of leadership behavior, each very specific. A particular supervisor could be rated by subordinates, peers or superiors as high or low (usually on a scale from one to five) on each of the leadership descriptions. For example, a typical description might be stated as: "He lets you ask questions after giving you an order" (always, usually, sometimes, seldom, never); the rater would circle one of the above. Ultimately, the original 1,800 descriptions were reduced to 150, classified into nine categories, by eliminating duplicate descriptions. This became the first format of the "LBDQ" (Leader Behavior Description Questionnaire) and, soon, with experience in using the LBDQ, the nine general categories of leader behavior became reduced to just two: "initiating structure" and "consideration."

Structure or initiating structure is an abbreviation for that category of leader behaviors by which the leader clearly states goals to be achieved, the structure and work assignments involved and exactly what is expected of each individual subordinate. People working for a high-structure leader know their goals clearly, how they are doing and where they stand.

Consideration includes all the LBDQ behaviors which manifest concern for and personal interest in subordinates and their welfare. About the same time, Fleishman developed the "LOQ" (Leadership Opinion Questionnaire) which measured responses about people's expectations as to what a leader ought to be.[10]

The LBDQ was originally, and extensively, used in military studies. For example: it was found that upper-level superiors rated high-structure crew commanders high while rating low those scoring strongly on consideration; the reverse was true for crew members whose job satisfaction was positively related to consideration on the part of the commander and negatively related to his initiation of structure, that is, while in training; later, in combat conditions, both consideration and structure by commanders were positively related to crew members' satisfaction.[11] (Another hint of contingency theory soon to come.) Apparently, when effective performance and task results were critical to crew members themselves, like personal survival, they preferred a considerate commander but also one who knew what he was doing and provided clear plans and structure for everyone and his role. Other studies found that military supervisors manifested both higher structure and higher consideration than their civilian counterparts in large air force headquarters.[12] Other studies showed no correlation at all among the key variables of consideration, structure, job satisfaction and performance.

Similar ambiguous results were reported in studies of educational institutions.[13]

TESTING SITES

But factories and other industrial settings became the main testing sites for the behavior theorists. Increased emphasis was placed on trying to relate the central LBDQ variables, consideration and structure, to bottom-line performance results such as production, job satisfaction (observable on-the-job motivation) and production-related variables such as turnover, absenteeism, employee grievances and so on. Some studies showed that high-consideration supervisors and managements experienced significantly low absenteeism and employee turnover while high-structure management increased absenteeism, turnover and grievances. But often high-structure supervision was positively related to employee job satisfaction and, very importantly, to group effectiveness and productivity. Apparently, workers feel better when management is considerate but work better when it structures goals clearly and makes everyone know what is expected of him. Often, however, opposite and contradictory relationships were found among these key variables as leadership behavior studies multiplied in the late 1950s and the 1960s.[14]

Two very interesting examples of unexpected results were Stogdill's 1965 study of 27 organizations and the 1971 study of three by House, Filley and Kerr in which consideration and structure were both related positively to high levels of employee morale and job performance.[15]

Even in the early 1960s, many behavior theorists began to abandon the two-factor LBDQ (structure and consideration) as too simplistic for researching the increasingly complex phenomenon that leadership was coming to be.[16,17] The LBDQ, and decades of research based on it, was sadly becoming a garbage collector of information instead of the logically structured and scientific framework originally envisioned.[18] After a quarter-century of behavior approach to the leadership question, behavior theorists seemed to have fared no better than their earlier brethren, the trait theorists.

The Institute for Social Research, University of Michigan. Paralleling the Ohio State studies and other behavior research, the Institute for Social Research led by Rensis Likert developed different theories and methods in its behavior research. Instead of the LBDQ's two, and then varying numbers of factors, Likert's system contained four which he called "Systems of Management 1, 2, 3 and 4" (respectively, exploitive authoritative, benevolent authoritative, consultative and participative). Although classified as four leader styles, they were treated in research as points on a continuum, à la the Schmidt-Tannenbaum continuum above,[9] ranging from high leader authority to high subordinate freedom and involvement in decision-making and management of an organization. Likert hypothesized, and clearly believed that the Institute's research would prove, the effective leader to be high on the continuum (a "system 3" or "system 4" manager). Certainly research reported in Likert's 1961 300-page book[19] seemed to confirm the effectiveness of consultative and participative management climates, even using the hard, bottom-line criteria of performance, production and mean productivity (pp. 124-128). But certainly too, Likert's conclusions were not being consistently replicated or confirmed by other contemporary research.

Other Views of Directive vs Participative Styles of Leadership. The first systematic study of management and organizations began about 1900. For the first quarter-century, at least in America, Taylor's scientific management dominated management research. The theory was, and it worked, that there was some one best way, method or system for accomplishing any task, and this could be discovered by scientific method.[20] The scientific method was the supreme guide to success and efficiency, no matter how small or large the task. Taylor and his staff spent five months testing for, and found, the most efficient way to do the task of shoveling of coal vs iron ore vs a variety of lighter materials. Gilbreth, and his wife, reduced every job to its series of single elements which they called "therbligs". Gantt devoted virtually a lifetime to developing his "Gantt charts", still a fundamental concept in the training of modern industrial engineers.[21]

But, still, many industrial observers complained about the low levels of productivity, interest and incentive on the part of the average industrial and government worker. The famous Hawthorne experiments were launched to investigate this problem.

HAWTHORNE STUDIES

The significance of the Hawthorne studies in the history of modern management and ultimately leadership theory cannot be exaggerated. Sited at the Hawthorne Works of the Western Electric Company in Chicago, the nine-year study (1924-1932) began a most sophisticated experiment in the best tradition of scientific management. For years, precise records were accumulated concerning the productivity of assembly-line workers (assembling telephones) under carefully altered combinations of such physical working conditions as lighting, room temperature, spacing of fatigue breaks and so on. In order to develop realistic options about such combinations of working conditions, the workers (whose productivity was being measured) were frequently involved in planning meetings with Western Electric managers and the two Harvard University professors (Elton Mayo and F.J. Roethlisberger) who were in charge of the design and conduct of the study. Often the suggestions of the workers, especially those of the girls working in the Relay Assembly Room, were welcomed and implemented as part of the study's design. Productivity soared throughout most phases of the study; but, frustrating to the managers and Harvard professors, there was no correlation between productivity and the variety of physical conditions installed. Later interviewing studies (1928-1932), in which workers were urged to declare their attitudes and opinions about the high-productivity work results, revealed the reasons for the otherwise unexplained and consistent increases in productivity: during the studies, while being frequently consulted for ideas and thereby made to feel important and recognized as people that count, the incentive and inner motivation of these involved workers had changed drastically as had their attitude toward their work and their (new) desires for personal worth in higher productivity. There was obviously nothing of "scientific management" to account for the high productivity at Hawthorne; rather, it was due to a new variable: human attitude, incentive and positive feeling about their job.[22] In terms of later behavior theory, the key to the Hawthorne productivity was a participative management style and climate.

TWO-DIMENSIONAL MANAGERS

Although controversy still exists about the specific conclusions of the Hawthorne studies, and of many attempted replications of them in the form of behavior research into "participative" management, the Hawthorne studies constituted a major turning point. After Hawthorne, every serious study of management had to be two-dimensional, confronting not only the physical properties of the workplace and the worker (the main thrust of "scientific management") but also the psychological and human aspects as well. Organizational psychology had been born about a quarter-century after management "science". Naturally, like any new thing, the just-discovered human side of management was driven by some extremes: for example, the doctrinaire "human relations" movement dedicated to making all workers happy all the time, contented and free of grievances (quite apart from getting a job done efficiently or even done at all). Personnel departments were created or expanded in most organizations then and were often accused of such doctrinaire views and practices. The developing labor unions, especially their more tendentious leaders, latched on to the new human dimension as an increasingly popular rationale for their purposes. During the years immediately following

Hawthorne (the depression years), the two dimensions of organizational practices were sharply polarized and set against each other: consideration of human welfare versus organizational efficiency and productivity. It occurred to very few theorists of that time that the two opposing thrusts could, or should, be integrated (i.e. that each could be made to contribute to, rather than detract from the other, concern for people increasing productivity and the latter in turn contributing to human satisfaction of workers).

After the depression and World War II, the leadership studies at Ohio State University, the University of Michigan and elsewhere often found the two dimensions (then termed initiating structure and consideration) not opposed at all but mutually supportive. But the tension, often strident, between the two sets of interests continued for decades and still exists as an ideological conflict between the advocates of "quality of life in the workplace" and adherents of the traditional American ideal of hard work, thrift, individual responsibility and productivity. Over these decades, the emphasis, like a pendulum, moved from one extreme to the other but differently at the same time in different intellectual circles: the new "management science" of the 1960s and 1970s, based upon sophisticated mathematical models and quantum leaps occurring in computer science, drove mechanically onward toward optimum industrial efficiency, productivity and quality control (i.e. of the products, not people); at the opposite extreme, sensitivity training for managers caught on as the way to expand consciousness and understanding of co-workers and employees (usually quite unrelated to any kind of job results or productivity).[23] Recent efforts in a new field, termed OD (Organizational Development), are trying to integrate the two elements: improve a manager's interpersonal competence but with the explicit objective being to use such competence toward "bottom-line" production results.[24,25] OD specialists feel convinced they are beginning to merge structure and consideration into a new organizational synergy, maximizing at the same time both production results and personal worker satisfaction.[26]

But, comparing the results of hundreds of behavior research studies into the 1970s, Stogdill had to conclude: "Group productivity does not vary consistently with directive and participative styles of leader behavior. There is a slight tendency for satisfaction to be related to participative leadership as well as group cohesiveness (p.392).[4] Behavior theory, like trait theory before it, had failed to solve the leadership enigma.

CONTINGENCY THEORY OF LEADERSHIP

From the beginnings of leadership research in this century, even early trait theorists had noted as an obstacle in the search for a universal set of leadership traits that traits required in a leader seem to depend, to some extent, on the demands of the particular situation and specific classes of followers. The factor of situation, the particular environment in which the leader happened to be, had been purposely eliminated from the research designs of both the trait and behavior theorists. The ideal they sought was a leader profile (a set of traits or behaviors), *universally* valid as a predictor or descriptor of what a leader is, *independently* of changing circumstances or followers or situation; just as qualities such as human courage, self-confidence, physical strength or communication skill operate and continue to be useful in all situations. The original expectation in leadership research was that leadership was that kind of universal quality; it needed only to be specifically described in terms of traits or, later, behaviors. As we have seen, 50 or more years of intensive research efforts found leadership as a universal set of either traits or behaviors non-existent. Finally, the situation factor had to be faced directly.

VARYING BEHAVIOR AND STYLES

By the 1960s, some researchers had begun to capitulate by specifically including, rather then excluding, situational factors in their studies. This made research designs far more complex. Originally simplicity had been envisioned and the complexity of situational factors studiously avoided. Now, with the essential failure of both trait and behavior theories, many felt that the last alternative was to confront the phenomenon of effective leadership as dependent upon two series of variables: varying leader behavior and styles as well as varying situations and follower groups.[27]

Fiedler's Contingency Studies. Fred Fiedler (1967) is usually credited with the first major studies to use situation as a main factor.[28] Fiedler used the original two factors of the Ohio State studies (structure and consideration) as his basic two leaderships styles but hypothesized that neither style was effective or ineffective per se; its effectiveness depended, or was contingent upon, three situational factors: 1. *leader-member relations* (open and trusting vs defensive or hostile, etc.); 2. *task structure* (the job itself routine vs complex and variable, etc.); and 3. *position power* (degree of real authority of the leader, especially power to reward or punish). More convenient terms came into use for the two styles: Task-oriented leader as equivalent to one who initiates structure; and employee-oriented leader as one high in consideration. Also, new psychological measuring instruments were developed to rate leaders as predominantly task- or employee-oriented (the LPC instruments).[28] The results of Fiedler's studies and those of other contingency theorists were consistently valid as to the main contingency theses: that effective leadership style was not a single "right" one, but was contingent upon situational factors. For example, a task-oriented leader style generally worked best when the task was routine and the leader-member relations were good or when the task was complex, provided the leader's power position was strong: if it were weak, employee-oriented leaders succeeded best in complex job situations. And so on.[29] However, it was not such specific illustrations or combinations of variables that held true throughout the contingency studies (for example, R. J. House and others found in many studies that workers in routine jobs resented a task-oriented boss, whose orders were redundant and unnecessary for workers who could do the routine jobs in their sleep and exhibited higher satisfaction and productivity with an employee-oriented leader).[30] Rather, the essential validity being found in the contingency studies was about contingency itself: the effective leader style depended, in every situation with all the variables in it, on that particular situation; there is no one, single effective leadership style.

This author's survey of hundreds of recent, practicing managers (1973) is one of many reality-oriented confirmations of the contingency thesis.[31] These managers expressed a virtual consensus that, based on their actual experience, each situation they handled demanded a different leadership style. No single style could suffice under the day-by-day, even minute-by-minute varying conditions of different personalities and moods among their employees, routine process vs changing or sudden deadlines, new and ever-changing government regulations and paperwork, ambiguous roles of workers, wide ranges in job complexity from simple to innovation-demanding, changes in organizational structure and markets and task technologies and so on. Contingency theory has come to mean, therefore, that the effective manager has, and knows how to use, many leadership styles as each is appropriate to a particular situation.

PATH-GOAL LEADERSHIP

The Path-Goal Contingency Theory of Leadership. R. J. House and his colleagues expanded the contingency theory of leadership to include the psychological processes underlying it.[30] Vroom's earlier "Expectancy Theory of Motivation", not of leadership, according to which workers will strive for management goals to the extent they can expect personal rewards for it, provided the basis for the new refinement of contingency theory of leadership.[32] Path-goal leadership theory, as House termed it and as it has dominated the research journals currently, states that "the functions of a leader consist largely of increasing personal rewards to subordinates for goal attainment and of making the path to these rewards easier to travel by clarifying it, reducing roadblocks and pitfalls and increasing the opportunities for personal satisfaction enroute." The central concept is that the chief motivation inducing a worker to perform an action (desirable by management) is a combination of the worker's expectation that his action will result in a specific, and certain, outcome and that this outcome will be of personal value and advantage. According to House, the more complex or uncertain the task, the more positive the relation between task-oriented leadership and employee satisfaction. The reverse will, however, often occur when the worker is highly-motivated and a self-starter (a freer or participative style is more appropriate to this situation).

These and other contingency approaches continue into the 1980s, confirming the essential theme of situational factors as inherent within any act of effective leadership. The research will become increasingly complex as models are attempted which identify, classify and relate the multitude of situational variables (size of organization, followers' ages or levels of education, kinds of tasks, even the economic state of a company, and so on).

MANAGEMENT TRAINING BASED ON TRAIT OR BEHAVIOR THEORY

Until about 1970, virtually all management or leadership training was guided in its design and practice by the tentative conclusions of trait theory slightly and behavior theory predominantly, controlled by the research findings prevalent in the journals of a particular decade. Moreover, when the national demand for leaders awakened interest in leadership-training (the World War II years), behavior theory and research were in vogue and dominated the design and practice of such training. Methods included texts, lectures, case studies, films, discussion and, later, role playing psychodrama and behavior experimentation. Emphasis on the latter, combined with the then faith in democratic leader style as the key to effective leadership, launched the wave of "sensitivity training".[33] Interpersonal skills and group process became ends in themselves, unrelated to task goals such as performance, productivity or profit. Most leadership training programs, however, were less intensive human relations courses aimed at making foremen and managers more employee-oriented and less task-oriented. One- and two-day training programs extolling the virtues of participative leadership were commonplace (many major universities mass-produced, and marketed, materials for such programs in the 1960s. I was one of the purchasers, as well as one of the human relations and sensitivity trainers then), but its training was based upon flawed theory, never to become validated and later to be replaced by contingency theory.

And yet, it is not unusual to find in one's mail or on one's desk, even today, training program announcements or ads obviously based on eclectic fragments or large chunks of now-obsolete behavior leadership theory. For example, most management training professionals, now reading this article, could easily find in their file of such program announcements many that promise behavior (and even attitude) changes, on the part of foremen and managers, in the direction of "employee-centeredness", etc., not to mention those advocating single-solution themes such as Semantics, TA (Transactional Analysis), AT (Assertiveness Training), MBO, PERT and variations of sensitivity training in their more doctrinaire forms.

NO SINGLE SOLUTIONS

The flaws in management training endure because of habit and old-familiar ways. It must be immediately noted that no criticism of such constructs as TA, MBO or OD is implied in the above statements. This writer uses all of them and admires their originators; the essential point is that they must be used as subordinate contributions to a larger contingency-oriented training design, not as single-solutions or cults as too often is the case.

The alert management training professional of today, guided by a sense of the history of leadership theory and training, will quickly spot the above mentioned kinks or flaws in training proposals, or at least raise sharp questions about their possibility in his programs. And any up-to-date professional offering management training services should be able to provide satisfactory answers to such questions.

Despite conceptual problems about management training, however, it has enjoyed since its beginnings tenacious support by top managements of most organizations (i.e. dollars to back it and the hunch that it might work). Over the last two decades, particularly, top managements have exhibited a kind of blind, if not desperate, faith in management training as if such faith would produce a miracle and give them the sorely-needed effective managers.

Sound theory was simply not available then; it is today in the form of contingency theory of leadership, despite the many refinements of it still to be researched and made available for use in management training. Current OD training programs (team building), for example, are tightly determined in their design and every movement by the contingencies and very specific situational factors of the client organization and, especially, of its members actually participating in the program. As mentioned above, OD centers on task results in a particular, real situation; employee satisfaction, group cohesiveness and team-spirit are means to that end, never ends in themselves (as was the case in sensitivity training).

Training prior to contingency theory was summarized: "leadership training has failed to address itself to the most crucial problems of leadership—consequences of training . . . and the effects of leadership on group performance and member satisfaction. Training that ignores these issues can hardly be called training in leadership" (Stogdill, p. 199).[4] Today, a now-valid contingency theory, as the theory-base underlying leadership training, directly counters these criticisms. Management training professionals, in charge of programs, should be looking for it.

MANAGEMENT TRAINING BASED ON CONTINGENCY THEORY

What are some of the identifying characteristics of management or leadership training based on the contingency approach?

First, there are no absolutes, no one right way or single and lasting method (formula) for managing people toward the twin goals of employee productivity and personal job satisfaction (and in that order, although the latter is often critical to consistent productivity and to that extent employee-centeredness can be a valid program design component). It is hard to live and operate without absolutes—nature abhors a vacuum and the human mind abhors uncertainty and thus is often prey to illusions that promise comfort and security in single, certain solutions. The longing for such pervaded the first half-century of leadership research and still lingers in many management training designs. But contingency theory accepts the uncomfortable reality about leadership, that it is complex and dependent upon many situational variables. A training program outstandingly effective in one place might be, in a different place with different kinds of work and workers, counterproductive or even dangerous. (I am reminded of a recent MBO program, obligatory for all managers, in which their pay was directly tied to easily quantifiable profit and cost results; the situation in some key departments, such as R & D and Quality Control, drove managers to ignore all-important qualitative and long-range factors not easily quantified; they worked the new, universal system by its own rules, got their pay increases and soon after the company came close to bankruptcy.)

Secondly, contingency theory totally abandons the presumption of any single best leadership style, although we must still live with the pejorative overtones of names like autocrat and bureaucrat inherited from the behavior theory period. The best leadership style varies and "depends on a) the individual personality of the manager himself b) the individual followers, the kind of people they are and the kind of work they do, and c) the particular situation and circumstances on any given day or hour."[31] In short, no cookbook or formalized recipe for effective leaders exists—it never did, although some still believe in or market theirs. For example, in several situations I've seen recently (one a government intelligence agency and the other a central bank, both requiring absolute fool-proof provisions to avoid fatal errors), an essential element of bureaucratic safety rules and precautions was rightly demanded by those situations—everyone understood this and none resented it. In a different situation, for example R & D, a bureaucratic leader, operating by that style needlessly, would be ineffective. Similarly, a friendly and supportive autocrat is often the necessary "helping hand" for some who, by this only, can cope and function as satisfied and productive workers. One among us coined the term "tool-box" approach for this varying use, by the same leader, of different leader styles, as tools, depending on the particular situation confronting him at a particular time and place. (There is no such thing as a best tool; it depends: a hammer is best for driving a nail, an aspirin for lowering a high temperature.)

SETTING SPECIFIC GOALS

Thirdly, a training design, based on contingency theory, usually exhibits these days a clear-cut MBO flavor; specific training goals are set in terms of specific, real situations; means are chosen (the program design) or rejected insofar as they contribute to the goals; these goals and means, as sub-goals, are made clear standards for evaluation and re-design, if necessary, of the training program. This process has become quite routine and many excellent tests exist detailing the steps involved in it.[34]

Other things to look for, which characterize contingency-based management training, are: trainer attitudes (alert and adjustable to your situation vs set on his standards or off-the-shelf program design and supplementing training materials); trainer's classroom style (promise of absolute answers and solutions vs an objective analysis of leadership styles, motivation methods and other management techniques as options, stressing the pros and cons of each, urging final judgement about the use of any options as a particular manager's as he faces particular situations) and a multitude of other signals, based on the sense of the history of leadership research, that easily identify the theory anyone is in or is coming from: trait, behavior, or contingency theory.

New work and refinements of contingency theory appear monthly in the management science journals, but the essential concept of contingency theory and how management training designers use it can today be declared a sound, validated and long-needed approach to the increasingly urgent and costly task of training and producing effective managers.

REFERENCES

1. Such a system is precisely what is meant by "training-by-objectives," advocated formally as early as 1967 (American Society for Training and Development, *Training and Development Handbook*, McGraw-Hill, edited by R. Craig and L. Bittel). See Chapter 2 and 5.
2. For example, see the study by Dunteman, G., and B. Bass, "Supervisory and Engineering Success," *Personnel Psychology*, 1963, 16; and many other studies during this period.
3. The commonly accepted definition of "leader" is used: one who achieves goals through the directed efforts of followers.
4. See *Handbook for Leadership* for the most detailed history of the literature from 1900 till the early 1970s.
5. Thurstone, L.L., *Factorial Study of Perception*, University of Chicago Press, 1944.
6. Heath, C. W., Gregory, L. W., *Infantry Journal*, 1946, No. 58.
7. Jennings, H. H., *Leadership and Isolation*, Longmans-Green, 1943.
8. Lewin, K., and Lippitt, R., "An experimental approach to the study of autocracy and democracy," *Sociometry* (1938, No. 1); Bradford, L. and Lippitt, R., "Building a democratic work group," *Personnel* (Nov. 1945); Bogardus, E. S., *Essentials of Social Psychology*, 1918).
9. Schmidt, W. H. and Tannenbaum, R. "How to choose a leadership pattern," *Harvard Business Review*, March 1958.

10. For a detailed history of the development of the LBDQ, see the articles by Hemphill, J. K. and Coons, A. D. and by Fleishman, E. A., in *Leader Behavior: Its Description and Management* (ed. by Stogdill, R. M. and Coons, A. E., Ohio State University, Bureau of Business Research, 1957); and *Manual for the Leader Behavior Description Questionnaire* (Ohio State University, 1957) by Halpin, A. W.

11. Halpin, A. W., "The leadership behavior and combat performance of airplane commanders," *Journal of Abnormal and Social Psychology*, 1954, No. 49.

12. Holloman, C. R., "Perceived leadership role of military and civilian supervisors," *Personnel Psychology*, 1967, No. 20.

13. For example, Hemphill, J. K., in *Journal of Educational Psychology* (1955, 46, pp. 385-401) and Fast, R. G., *The Leader Behavior of Principals* (University of Alberta Press, 1964).

14. See abstracts of studies by Korman, Fleishman, Evans, Skinner, House, Filley, Kerr and others in Stogdill's *Handbook of Leadership*, pp. 133-140.

15. Stogdill, R. M., *Managers, Employees, Organizations*, Ohio State, 1965, and House, R. J., et al, "Relation of leader consideration and structure to R & D subordinates' satisfaction," *Administrative Science Quarterly* (1971, 16, pp. 19-30).

16. Halpin, A. W., and Croft, D. B., *Organizational Climate of Schools*, Washington, St. Louis, 1962.

17. Stogdill, p. 143

18. Saris, R. J., *The 13th Subscale to the LBDQ*, University of Idaho, 1969 and Yuki, G., "Toward a behavior theory of leadership," *Organizational Behavior and Human Performance* (1971, No. 6).

19. See Likert's two major books for details: *New Patterns of Management* (McGraw-Hill, 1961), especially pp. 222-233 about the four systems and their components, pp. 113-121 for his underlying theory and "linking pin concept of group processes" and *The Human Organization* (McGraw-Hill, 1967).

20. Today's industrial engineering and psychology (time-motion-methods experts) prove it.

21. See, for details, Boorstin, D., *The Americans: The Democratic Experience* (Random House, 1973, pp. 363-371) and *Classics in Management*, edited by Merrill, H. F. (American Management Association, NY, 1960), especially chapter on Owen, Taylor, Fayol, Gantt and Gilbreth.

22. The best account of the Hawthorne experience is by Roethlisberger, F. J., *Management and the Worker* (Harvard Press, 1939). Mayo's later book (1945), *Social Problems of an Industrial Civilization*, is also worth consulting.

23. Odiorne, G., in *Training Director Journal* (1963, 17, pp. 9-20), analyzed over 100 articles reporting sensitivity training results and found none demonstrating any useful change of behavior productivity "back on the job." Sensitivity training made managers understanding and functional

in the training classroom but weakened their task-orientation when they returned to the job; it seemed to cultivate leader "softness rather than ability to cope with tough realities of the job environment." A more comprehensive, but concise, account of sensitivity training and its results is in Stogdill's *Handbook of Leadership* (pp. 183-190), Free Press, 1974; Stogdill's conclusions about sensitivity training, drawn from a much broader base of research findings, were the same as Odiorne's.

24.   A key work in this field is Lippitt's, G., *Organizational Renewal* (Appleton-Century, 1969). See also the excellent history of OD by W. French and C. Bell (*Organizational Development*, Prentice-Hall, 2nd Edition, 1978).

25.   McGregor, Douglas, *The Human Side of Enterprise* (1960) and *The Professional Manager* (1967).

26.   Blake, R. and Mouton, J., *Grid Organizational Development*, Addison-Wesley, 1969.

27.   Note that a third series of variables (traits) was excluded. Still, and deeply, based in the new contingency theory, David McClellan and his Boston-based (McBer Inc.) colleagues are combining behaviors and traits (which they call "competencies") to train effective leaders in very specific and defined situations. It seems to be working. (*American Psychologist*, 1973, 28, pp. 1-14; and see *Psychology Today*, Jan. 1981).

28.   LPC tested a leader's perception of his least preferred coworker. High LPC leaders tend to be friendly, considerate and employee-oriented; low LPCs are task-oriented, objective and impersonal. See Fiedler, F. D., *A Theory of Leadership Effectiveness*. McGraw-Hill, 1967.

29.   See corroborating studies (abstracts) in Stogdill's *Handbook of Leadership* (pp. 335-9). 1974.

30.   R. J. House, "A path-goal theory of leader effectiveness," *Administrative Science Quarterly*, 1971., Vol 16 and see the House & Dessler article in *Contingency Approaches to Leadership*, edited by Hunt, J. G. and Larson, L. T., Southern Illinois Press, 1974, and the Dessler & Valenzi article in the June 1977 issue of the *Academy of Management Journal* (Vol. 20, No. 2); the quotation used is on page 25, including the italics.

31.   Owens, J., "The Uses of Leadership Theory," *Michigan Business Review*, Jan. 1973.

32.   Vroom, V. H., *Work and Motivation*, Wiley, 1964.

33.   The R. Lippitt & R. White (1943) study of democratic leader style was probably most influential along with other articles in *Child Behavior and Development* (1943) by R. Baker.

34.   An excellent recent example: G. Nixon's *People, Evaluation and Achievement*, sponsored by the American Society for Training and Development, Gulf Press, 1973.

Dr. James Owens is professor of management at the American University, College of Business, Washington DC. He is the author of The Effective Manager, *published by Management Education Ltd.*

35.
A NEW LOOK AT LEADERSHIP

Irvin McMaster

There is no successful leadership "type." Each supervisor must recognize certain qualities of leadership before making the transition from boss to leader.

The qualities of leadership can be elusive and difficult to develop. In fact, many new supervisors discover to their chagrin that being a "manager" and being a "leader" can actually be two completely different things.

Even supervisors of long experience, with obvious leadership qualities, find it difficult to explain the reasons for their success. A supervisor or foreman may become highly skilled in quality control, methods improvement, federal regulations and many other aspects of management without ever developing proficiency in the art of leadership.

"Art" is the key word, for leadership is indeed an art, rather than a skill or science. This is the reason different supervisors or managers often take different approaches to their responsibilities. One may be a "top sergeant" type, another may be a "big brother" type, while still another may be a "football coach" type.

Each of them, in his or her own way, is trying to solve the problems of leadership without realizing that no successful "type" of leader exists. Good leadership has been defined as the ability to weld a group of individuals together into a productive team or unit for successfully accomplishing objectives. This definition will apply to a football coach, a first-line supervisor, a commanding officer, a department manager or any other person who guides and directs a group of individuals into the successful accomplishment of predetermined goals.

For the qualities of leadership remain the same, no matter how varied the situation or circumstances.

Fortunately, the qualities of good leadership can be developed by most people, and for this reason, the ability to develop into a leader is neither an intangible nor unattainable goal for the average, competent supervisor.

All that's required is for the supervisor to recognize the qualities of leadership and understand how to develop them. When you do—whether you're new in your field or a person of long experience—you have taken the first step from being a "boss" to becoming a leader.

When a company appoints a person to supervision, that person is given tremendous responsibility. The leadership required to successfully meet this responsibility is a real challenge. Some supervisors are able to meet this challenge, and some are not; but those who meet it are those who are best able to develop the qualities of leadership.

Obviously, there are many qualities of leadership. And the qualities required for success may vary with the type of responsibility and the circumstances. Generally speaking, however, there are five basic qualities which seem to be present in all successful leaders:

Integrity. The good leader is a person of integrity, for it's one of the most important qualities of leadership. Leaders who have integrity always maintain high standards of conduct and performance both for themselves and others. They always set good examples and never ask others to meet standards which they don't meet themselves.

They accept their duties and responsibilities willingly. If the job calls for them to be the first one in and the last one out, they accept it as part of their responsibility and don't begrudge the extra time or work. Good leaders never take special privileges or abuse the position. They don't set double standards (one for supervisors and one for employees), for most people can spot a phony, and a phony leader is the most transparent of all.

Good leaders are always equitable and just, for these attributes are an essential part of integrity.

Accordingly, they are fair minded and give credit where credit is due. They express their appreciation with sincerity. They say "thank you" and don't ration their smiles. They never stoop to pettiness or maliciousness; they forgive what has happened in the past and never hold grudges. The good leader is always big enough to admit a mistake and to say, "I was wrong."

Intelligence. The good leader doesn't have to be a genius but is obviously a person of intelligence. Good leaders are smart enough to recognize their own shortcomings and to realize that they don't know everything. (Only the ignorant believe they know everything!) Good leaders don't necessarily have extensive formal education, but they have enough perception to constantly strive for self-development. For example, a man may sign up for some evening courses in psychology because he realizes that he is weak in human relations. A woman may take engineering courses because such areas of study weren't popular for women when she was in school.

Even with a college degree and extensive on-the-job experience, a good leader will strive to avoid obsolescence and have the intelligence to realize the need for constant self-improvement.

Accordingly, good leaders are always flexible. They keep abreast of change and adjust quickly to new methods. They are often the first to pioneer and introduce new systems in their departments.

Good leaders are well read and knowledgeable of changing conditions and new developments in their fields. They follow the trade and business publications.

They ask to be put on the routing lists of such publications that are routed through their plant or they take personal subscriptions. For example, the low subscription cost of a magazine such as "Supervision" is an excellent investment in developing leadership qualities and advancing your career. It's smart planning to keep a personal file of back issues for ready reference.

Courage. The good leader is obviously a person of courage, with the resoluteness to stand behind his or her actions and decisions and to stand up for what is right.

Good leaders have self-confidence and an inner reliance on their own ability. They may not be known as a "buddy" to employees and may not win a popularity contest, but their courage and self-determination inspire the confidence and respect of the people who work for them.

Accordingly, good leaders are able to develop teamwork and motivate others. They don't procrastinate. They don't pass the buck . . . they tackle it head-on.

Initiative. Good leaders display initiative in many ways. They are resourceful, ingenious and adroit. They always display enthusiasm and imagination.

Good leaders take command. They don't hesitate to step forward when leadership is needed. They have the initiative to take swift action in emergencies. Accordingly, they are masters of their own actions and have unusual skill in developing the cooperation and efforts of others.

Judgement. The good leader is at all times a person of judgement; for in the final analysis, judgement must determine all of his or her actions and decisions.

Judgement gives good leaders an awareness of their own impact on their employees and the situations which surround them. Judgement provides insight into the needs of the situation and the directions and actions which must be taken. Judgement provides a perception for proper action—when to be friendly and when to be stern, when to negotiate and when to stand firm.

Most important of all, judgement enables the leader to make sound management decisions. Accordingly, judgement might be defined as a depth of reasoning power and a sense of perception, insight and understanding that are beyond the grasp of the average person.

Can you develop leadership skills? These five qualities of leadership are well known to management experts. The question is: Can you develop them yourself? Of course you can! But you must remember that there are no shortcuts to achieving proficiency in supervisory leadership.

Skill in this field, as in all professions, requires hard work and extensive effort—but the results are worth it. Anything that's easy to achieve can hardly be considered an achievement. And the long work and training involved are among the most distinguishing differences between a profession and an ordinary job.

For these reasons, if you make a determined effort to develop supervisory leadership, you will soon distinguish yourself from those who don't have the stamina or determination to succeed. And as you develop the skills of leadership you will be preparing yourself for higher levels of responsibility.

36.
HOW COMPANIES USE
UNIVERSITY-BASED EXECUTIVE
DEVELOPMENT PROGRAMS

Albert W. Schrader

University-based executive development programs are popular. But very little research has been done to evaluate these programs. This University of Michigan study came up with some surprising results, with major implications for both business and academe.

Executive development programs are an important investment in a company's future leadership. They provide state-of-the-art training that is designed to fill in gaps in an executive's knowledge (for example, an engineering manager may be introduced to unfamiliar financial concepts and techniques) or update a manager whose formal education was completed ten or fifteen years ago. Unlike the in-house program that often tells "how we do it here at our company," university programs expose executives to two viewpoints that may be very different from their own: the *academic viewpoint* of faculty who are unfettered by company policies or pressures of the managerial job, and the *viewpoint of professional counterparts*—classmates with broad and diverse experiences they can share in solving classroom problems and in informal discussions outside the classroom.

For the university business schools that conduct them, executive development programs (EDPs) are an important bridge between academia and the world of the practicing manager. The programs keep faculty up to date on the problems and challenges facing companies and the executives who run them. They are also an important source of revenue to pump into research, student services, facilities, materials development, or other programs that require external funding. Many business schools are considering expanding their executive development activities as demographics lead to lower enrollments in traditional degree programs and as demand for MBAs begins to slacken.

THE RESEARCH PROJECT

Because the programs are important to both companies and universities, it would follow that companies do everything possible to use them well and that universities would engage in activities designed to contribute to executives' educational objectives as well as to their own institutions' goals. To learn to what degree this is true, questionnaires were sent to three sample groups.

The *first* group consisted of two-hundred personnel/human resource professionals in large companies that make use of EDPs. A wide diversity of industry sectors was represented, and the sample included several European firms that send executives to programs in the U.S.; one-hundred-six replies (fifty-three percent) were received. These respondents had job titles such as corporate vice-president of human resources, director of executive development, personnel director, manager of organization and management development, and manager of career planning and development. They reported that their companies had been sending people to EDPs for anywhere from one year to forty-five years. The average was 20.1 years.

The *second* group consisted of four-hundred-fifty alumni of eighteen EDPs offered by sixteen universities; three-hundred-twelve of them (69.3 percent) replied. These executives, selected randomly by university program directors from programs conducted during the 1978-82 period, have general management responsibilities or senior positions in all the major functional areas—finance, marketing, production, and so forth. At the time they attended a program, nearly seventy percent of them had been with their company for more than ten years; approximately two-thirds had been on the job they then held from one to five years. They work for large and small companies and for public sector organizations. Responses were received from throughout the U.S. and six other countries.

The *third* group was made up of forty-five directors of executive programs offered by universities in the United States and Canada; thirty-one (61.8 percent) of the directors responded. The programs they direct have these characteristics:

- They are formal (classroom-based) programs;
- Enrollment in them is open to the public—they are not in-company programs conducted by the university for a single firm;
- The subject matter is general management—they are not limited to one function (such as marketing or finance); and
- They are at least two weeks long.

Most previous studies of executive development programs have focused on the question, "Do EDPs work?" Although the various studies have defined success in different ways, the general conclusion seems to be that EDPs are an effective way of educating executives. The present study focuses on two other kinds of issues. First, it is designed to *examine some rather fundamental questions* such as:

* Why are people sent to programs? That is, what benefits are sought?
* Who are sent to programs? What does the profile of program participants look like?
* How are programs selected? Who selects them? What is important in selecting or evaluating a program?

The second kind of question has to do with *what companies and universities can do the make the programs of greater benefit to the executive and his or her firm.* The respondents were asked, for example:

* What is done to prepare an executive to get the most out of a program?
* What kind of debriefing is done by the company when the executive returns to the company?
* What is done by the company and the university to facilitate use of that which is taught in the programs?

WHO ATTENDS EDPs?

When asked to describe the benefits of attending an EDP, program alumni cited most frequently (63 percent) a major benefit that had nothing to do with course content or objectives. They said, "It gave me a chance to meet other executives and learn that they have much in common with me." Personnel/HR professionals agree. Seventy-three percent of them said a description of who attends is of vital or considerable importance in selecting and evaluating a program. University program directors also place considerable emphasis on the make-up of a class. "We want people who will contribute as much to a program as they will take away from it," one director said. A second reason for the directors' concern is the effect of the participant profile on program curriculum.

Most EDPs were founded in the early 1950s to meet a specific and (at that time) widespread need. Most executive-level managers of that era did not have a formal education in business or management. Accordingly, most EDPs were mini-MBA programs. They contained segments of each of the major academic disciplines found in a business school curriculum: accounting, finance, personnel, marketing, and so forth. Because these topics were new to most of the executive-students, they were presented as "introductions to" each of the disciplines and were not necessarily well integrated into a coherent whole. The intent was to give executives just enough information about fields other than their own specialties to broaden and familiarize them with the other components of "the big picture."

But now university business schools are producing more than sixty-thousand MBAs per year. Many of these graduates have now reached executive-level jobs and are returning to campus. For them, mini-MBA programs are inappropriate. They are ready for a more advanced, integrated body of information. This was true for thirty-seven percent of the respondents in this survey who had business degrees. But before we conclude that the content of programs should be more advanced, we must remember that sixty-three percent of the respondents did not have formal training in business.

For the program director and faculty, this dichotomy poses a severe problem. Should the course be designed for the individual who has had no formal training in, let us say, accounting, for someone who has had graduate training in accounting, or for the person whose training lies somewhere between these two extremes? The same kind of decision must be made about each of the other topics taught in an EDP, making the program design decision quite complex. Participants may sit through elementary lectures on their own field one moment and then be overwhelmed by unfamiliar, complicated topics, usually delivered at a rather rapid pace, the next. Those who select programs would be well advised to learn from universities how or whether a program's design is affected by the formal education of those who attend. In this regard, it should be noted that seventy-one percent of the program directors said the candidate's formal education was only slightly important in making a decision to admit that person to a program.

The personnel/HR respondents were asked what percent of the people they send to EDPs are fast-track, high-potential people. On the average, sixty-eight percent were described as being in this category, and forty-seven percent were said to be slated for promotion within one year. But the range was very broad in both cases. One company said only five percent of the people it sends are in the high-potential category; several companies said one-hundred percent are. Some companies said none of the people it sends to EDPs will be promoted within a year; two said ninety percent of its people would be promoted within one year of attending a program.

WHY ARE THEY SENT?

Executive programs have long had as one of their major purposes broadening an individual. This is still the primary reason companies send executives to programs. More than ninety percent of the personnel/HR professionals cited broadening and showing the individual the "big picture" as very important reasons for sending people to EDPs. And, as noted earlier, "the chance to meet other executives; to learn they have much in common with their counterparts in other firms" is also an important reason; fifty-eight percent of the personnel/HR professionals designated this as a very important reason. Other reasons are less frequently cited. Less than half (forty-eight percent) said a very important reason is "to give the opportunity to learn how other companies solve problems of the sort we have." Enabling the individual to gain new and specific information (for example, how the Euromarkets work) was cited as a very important reason by forty-five percent. Improving decision making and problem solving skills was given as a very important reason by forty-four percent. None of these respondents felt an important reason should be to reward an executive for long or good performance, and none saw the programs as an important way to establish or strengthen the company's relationship with a university.

In general, the program alumni concurred with their colleagues in personnel/HR. In one instance, though, there was disagreement. "Getting away from it all" and seeing things from a new perspective was ranked as a very important benefit by fifty-seven percent of the program alumni; only thirty-one percent of the personnel/HR professionals felt it was very important. The executives' belief is supported by comments they made:

"I believe the best approach is 6-10 weeks away from the office to get back into the academic environment in a worthwhile learning experience." —Director of technology.

"[I appreciated the] exposure to the broad economic, political, social environments . . . it develops a clearer understanding of your own values and beliefs."—Director of national accounts.

"A course should be long enough to permit it to become part of the student's life rather then an interlude."—Vice president.

These comments highlight an important issue: the interrelationship of program length, content, and purpose. Program alumni were asked to describe a hypothetical "best" program to which they might send their subordinates. What would such a course teach? According to some survey participants, just about everything. The list of subjects desired was diverse and virtually endless: tax law, labor relations, speed reading, discounted cash flow analysis, people management, use of personal computers, telecommunications, organization design, statistical decision making models, stress management, macroeconomics, international business, negotiating skills, new product development, the role of government, long-range planning, public relations, and personal investments. A program containing this kind of topic array, some respondents said, would last ideally not more than four weeks. Three weeks would be better.

Some universities have responded to this sentiment, but with mixed results. First, many topics receive very little, even superficial treatment. Second, the workload—especially the reading assignments—is truly staggering for the student. Not surprisingly, this has engendered a backlash of sorts. One banking executive said: "With current programs there seems to be a desire to put the participants under pressure involving them in as heavy a workload as possible. It should be borne in mind that the participants selected are all 'proven performers' or they would not be in the program, and there is no need to place them under this artificial pressure. More benefit would be obtained by using the program as a medium to enable thought to be given to problems. This is something most of the participants are unable to do in their everyday life."

The pressure termed "artificial contrived" was in fact the school's way of responding to the many requests that had been made by past generations of participants. Companies also pressure universities to impose heavy workloads. The reasoning for this seems to be that the company wants as much for its money (in terms of topics taught and hours of instruction provided) as the university can provide. Neither party, though, seem to pay enough attention to whether the executives can assimilate the ensuing avalanche of information. One executive said: "The workload was heavy to the extent of 'over-kill.' At approximately forty percent of the way through the program I noted that 80-90 percent of the students had realized this and had simply given up."

Other executives who had attended other programs echoed his comment. Companies and universities alike should give careful consideration to the learning experience the executive will actually encounter. Will it be a demanding dawn-to-dusk (and beyond) examination of nearly every possible subject area? Or will it be a more focused experience at a less arduous pace that gives time for reflection?

Program "character," which is in part determined by the interplay of scope, length, and workload, varies from course to course. Although this feature is sometimes difficult to perceive (and communicate) in materials describing programs, university brochures do give some information that can help in selecting a program. Many schools reproduce a portion of the program schedule in their brochures.

HOW ARE PROGRAMS SELECTED?

The director of a university executive development program shares a problem with all others who have a product or service to sell: identifying the customer. For the program director, the problem manifests itself in the question, "Who decides which program executive X will attend?" Does X decide? Does the personnel/HR department decide? Does someone else? Even more fundamentally, who decides that X will go to *any* program?

Table 1 shows the responses of program alumni when asked, "Who identified you as a candidate for an EDP?"

Table 1.

"Who Identified Candidate?"—

	Program Alumni Response
25%	I did
45%	My immediate supervisor
27%	Someone else
3%	I don't know

Personnel/HR professionals said that in forty-three percent of the cases more than one person or group was involved. Table 2 shows how personnel/HR professionals say that candidates were identified.

Table 2.

"Who Identified Candidate?"
Personnel/HR Professionals Response

18%	Individual identified self as a candidate
56%	Identified by immediate supervisor
14%	Identified by top management
66%	Identified by personnel/HR department as it engages in manpower planning or succession planning.

Table 3 shows how the two groups responded to the question, "Who selects the program?" As the second column of the table suggests, the personnel/HR respondents said the decision was made jointly (sixty-eight percent of the time). Once again there is greater involvement by personnel/HR than reported by the program participants. To shed further light on their role, personnel/HR respondents were asked to describe their involvement in program selection. They said:

9%—I am an information clearinghouse. Others come to me for information about EDPs, but I do not make any recommendations or evaluate statements about programs. I am neutral.

53%—I evaluate programs. I recommend certain programs (or a specific program), but others make the actual decision.

38%—I evaluate programs. I choose certain programs (or a specific program), and my choice is invariably agreed with by others.

Table 3.

Program Participants	Personnel/HR Professionals	Program Selected By
35%	30%	Participant
15%	15%	Immediate supervisor
—	26%	Unit manager
20%	39%	Top management
17%	69%	Personnel/HR department
4%	1%	Other
8%	—	All attend same program
4%	—	Don't know

Program directors were asked, "In selling your program, how important is each of the following individuals or groups; how great an effort is directed at each of them?" Table 4 shows the percentage who said that the indicated target audience was very important.

Table 4.

Very Important Target Audience

45%	Potential participants
42%	Potential participants' supervisors
55%	VP of personnel/HR
74%	Director of management/executive development
55%	Top management
23%	Alumni of my school or university
71%	Past participants in my program

One wonders whether to critize these program directors for their lack of focus—they seem to sell hard to nearly everyone—or to laud them for recognizing and responding to the many different buyers in the marketplace.

Two other factors complicate the program directors' communication/selling task: finding out which information sources are important to their prospective customers and determining what it is about a program that is important to them in evaluating/selecting it.

SOURCES OF INFORMATION

Personnel/HR professionals and program participants who selected the program they attended were asked to identify information sources that were important to them in learning about programs. Sixty-one percent of the program participants said the university's brochures were important sources of information, and forty-five percent cited reports made by others who had attended programs in the past.

Personnel/HR professionals, often regarded as senders by university programs directors, look to many sources of information before they decide between Program A, Program B, or Program C. Unquestionably, though, their primary source of information is their own executives who have first-hand knowledge of a program. Companies make an extensive effort to gain this information. Sixty percent of the personnel/HR professionals said they discuss the program with the returning executive. Fifty-five percent of the executives meet and discuss the program with their immediate supervisors, and thirteen percent meet with top management. Moreover, in forty-three percent of the companies, structured evaluation forms (for example, questionnaires) are filled out and filed with personnel/HR. Written but unstructured reports for the personnel/HR department are required in thirty-six percent of the companies, and executives submit written reports to their immediate supervisors in thirty-one percent of the companies. In only eight percent of the companies is no systematic evaluation made.

While returning executives undeniably represent an important source of information, relying solely on them has two limitations. First, according to the executives themselves, the companies don't really get all the information that the figures in the preceding paragraph would suggest. Two-thirds of them said they did discuss the program with their immediate supervisor, but only eighteen percent, not forty-three percent, reported filling out a questionnaire; fourteen percent, not thirty-six percent, said they filed an unstructured, written report with personnel/HR; and a third—not sixty percent, as reported above—discussed the program with the personnel/HR department. Fifteen percent said they wrote a report to their boss, and thirty-seven percent reported discussing their experience with top management. But in twenty-two percent of the companies, according to the executives, no systematic evaluation at all is made.

The second limitation has to do with returning executives' frames of reference. By definition, graduates of Program A have first-hand knowledge only of Program A. They have no experience that will enable them to compare the program they attended to Programs B, C, or D.

To the degree that companies rely on executives' subjective reactions, *all* programs probably would be deemed good. When asked to identify the major shortcoming of the program they attended, the most frequent response was "there were none." And when asked to describe the features of a "best" program to which they might send their own subordinates, many executives gave answers like these:

"I would want a general type program and I don't believe I could improve on Emory's.—Assistant vice president.

"As with the program I attended (the University of Pittsburgh's Management Program for Executives), the program must be viewed as a 'total experience,' for a broad view of business. If this is the need, I would not change anything."—Director of marketing.

"MIT's program is an excellent model to follow. Because it is broad based and provides exposure to a mixture of theory and practice, it is very helpful to someone in a general management position."—Assistant to the CEO.

But two or three executives gave answers similar to this one:

"There is no one program for all. Each executive should be matched to a program which will challenge him in new areas and increase his awareness of management tools and executive styles. It should be a program that offers many diverse areas of study so that he can concentrate on subjects of personal interest. From a company perspective, it would be best to pick and choose among a number of alternative programs. This would allow better matching of executives and programs—and enhance the motivation that comes from attending."—Vice president of marketing.

PROGRAM SELECTION CRITERIA

How are executives and programs matched in actual practice? Personnel/HR professionals and program participants who selected the program they attended said they considered the factors shown in Table 5. To learn if the university program directors were attuned to the interests of their clientele, they too were asked to give their estimate of criteria companies use to pick a program. The figures shown are the percentage of respondents in each group who said the indicated variable was of vital or considerable importance in making a selection.

Table 5.

Selection Factors of Vital or Considerable Importance

Personnel/HR Professionals	Program Participants	Program Directors	Factor Considered
97	96	90	Program content
93	93	68	Program objectives
88	88	94	University's reputation
79	64	84	Program length
73	38	71	Who attends
67	57	29	Instructional method
56	44	52	Dates offered
52	67	55	Who teaches
51	50	45	Unique features
48	51	16	Class size
43	—	48	Facilities
44	39	16	Workload, daily schedule
—	16	—	Location
34	16	13	Price
—	10	—	Personal affiliation with university (for example, a graduate)

Perhaps the most remarkable finding is that, except in two or three cases, all responded so similarly. In one of the instances where not all three groups responded alike, narrative comments belie the figures. Only thirty-eight percent of the participants said who attends is of vital or considerable importance. Yet in enumerating program short-comings or describing the hypothethical "best" course, the executives repeatedly made reference to the make up of a class. An energy company executive said: "I felt that the student cross section might have been just a little too diverse for my particular liking from both a personal interest and knowledge standpoint . . . Some were there for a vacation. Others possessed a great deal of management experience and were looking to hone their skills with advanced concepts. And yet there were several people who had never had any prior supervisory/managerial training... I think a more experienced and knowledgeable student cross section would have promoted a more spirited exchange of ideas and would have provided an opportunity to dwell longer on advanced principles."

Although a majority of the company respondents say instructional method is important, their narrative replies make it clear that it is the *quality* of instruction, not the method, that is critical. Poor instruction was overwhelmingly the most frequently cited shortcoming reported. Nor was this criticism leveled at only a few programs. On the contrary, only two or three schools escaped the tongue-lashings that less-than-acceptable teaching engendered: "Keep the rookies and inexperienced academics out of the EDPs. It is an insult to exploit the participants' time and money for training of underutilized faculty!"

"I had the impression that this was an annual break for some of the profs; i.e., that they felt they could 'wing it' and handle the classroom in good shape without bothering to update their materials and reading assignments."

"Some of the professors were too occupied with consulting arrangements— flying out after class, etc.—to pay attention to us."

"There were days when I wondered if the program was to benefit starving accounting professors who speak in a monotone."

Several judged the faculty's ability in relation to the qualifications and abilities of the class members. A vice-president of an agribusiness company said, "The only weak segments were those presented by weak teachers. The program demands the best. If the best are not available the program will fail. The group is highly professional. Therefore, the teaching staff must be equally good. Subject matter was good but in one or two cases the teachers were mediocre."

His last sentence makes an important point. While there was widespread criticism of short-comings in teaching, the criticism was invariably directed at only one or two of a program's faculty team. Executives, who in their back-home setting are constantly evaluating others on their ability to communicate, are as demanding in the classroom as they are in the boardroom.

PROGRAM FACULTY

University program directors were asked to describe their schools' staffing policies, practices, and goals. Their answers have important implications for companies that are evaluating different programs.

Not surprisingly, EDPs are taught primarily (but not always) by professors. These professors are not always on the faculty of the university that offers the program. Thus, those who say "the university's reputation" is a vitally or considerably important criterion in selecting a program (eighty-eight percent of the company respondents did) should realize that it may be erroneous to equate the university's reputation with the program faculty's capabilities. On the average, two-thirds of the instructors in a university's program are members of that university's faculty. At one university only ten percent of the program instructors come from the sponsoring institution. The others are faculty from other universities (ten percent), consultants (fifty percent), practicing managers (twenty percent), and government officials (ten percent).

While no other program matches this ten percent inside/90 percent outside ratio, it is not uncommon for program directors to go outside to staff substantial portions of their programs. They do this because they are faced with demands for "only the best" and there is a shortage of talented faculty in their own schools. (But schools that use this strategy don't escape participant criticism for poor teaching.) Of the program directors who responded, forty-three percent said they wanted to staff their programs exclusively (or mostly) with faculty from their own schools but that they have difficulty in doing so. Among the reasons given are that some faculty members are not interested in teaching executives, some are not particularly good at it, and workload limitations preclude their participation. Another twenty-six percent don't even have as a goal staffing their programs primarily with their own faculty.

All the program directors said that faculty were evaluated by program participants. This evaluation has two purposes: (1) to enable the individual instructor to gain feedback that can be used to revise and improve his or her presentations in future sessions of the program, and (2) to help the program director to decide whether to expand, reduce, or eliminate the instructor's participation in future sessions.

Noticeably absent from the evaluation process were the school's administrative and academic leadership. More specifically, in only three of the thirty-one responding schools did the school's dean or a faculty committee evaluate faculty performance in EDPs for the purpose of making decisions about promotion, tenure, or base salary. Put another way, in all but three of the responding institutions, teaching in EDPs is solely an add-on assignment—a marginal effort for marginal compensation. The long-term career rewards of promotion, tenure, and increases in base salary can have a tremendous influence on the efforts an individual faculty member will expend on teaching in EDPs. But most schools have chosen not to recognize EDP teaching as a highly regarded faculty responsibility. This policy can lead a professor to conclude that excellent performance really isn't required or properly rewarded. Schools that want to compete more effectively in the executive education marketplace would be well advised to review their policy on this issue. Companies considering alternate university programs might want to inquire as to what value the institutions themselves place on good teaching in EDPs.

INPUT AND OUTPUT: PROGRAM ADMISSIONS AND RETURNING TO THE JOB

Just as companies want to do a good job of matching program with executive, so do universities want to have the best possible students in the classroom.

The most important criteria used for accept/reject decisions were ranked by university program directors as follows:

- The candidate's potential as described by the company;
- The candidate's organizational level;

- The candidate's title;
- The candidate's job history;
- An endorsement or letter of recommendation by the company;
- The candidate's stated goals in attending.

Beyond these criteria, though, is the university's desire to have the right *mix* of executive-students. The University of Michigan's brochure notes, "The school regrets that due to class size constraints and the desire to have a balanced mixture of backgrounds, not all applicants, even some of those fully qualified, can be admitted to the program."

The quality of a class is influenced by the relationship program directors have with their clientele and, in some cases, by the admissions process itself. The University of Virginia requires that a candidate's suitability be discussed with the associate dean for external relations before application is made and discussions are initiated with the applicant.

Companies rely on such advance contacts. Fifty-seven percent of the personnel/HR professionals said that they communicate orally (usually by telephone) with the university, describing the candidate, in order to find out whether the application will be accepted by the university. Thus, by the time an application is formally submitted, there often has been agreement between the company and the university that the individual will attend and be accepted into the program.

PRE-PROGRAM BRIEFING

Companies do a less than thorough job of informing people as to why they are being sent to an EDP. Personnel/HR professionals said that in only six percent of the cases were executives *not* told why they were being sent to an EDP. But nineteen percent of the executives said they were not told the reasons for their attendance. The discrepancy exists partly because personnel/HR thinks the executives' supervisor or higher-level managers are giving this information. Table 6 shows responses of the two groups to the question, "If the

Table 6

"Who Tells Candidate Reasons for EDP?"

Program Participants	Personnel/HR Professionals	Source of Information
49%	69%	Immediate supervisor
8%	29%	Candidate's unit head
28%	21%	Someone in top management
12%	21%	Someone in personnel/HR
3%	0%	A committee, other

Table 7

Reasons Given for Being Sent to EDP

Program Participants	Personnel/HR Professionals	Reason Given for Being Sent
54%	50%	"To prepare you for the future"
10%	23%	"To prepare you for your next job, which will be . . ."
65%	56%	"To broaden you"
19%	43%	"To help you do your present job better"
15%	42%	"To permit you to get knowledge/information you didn't get in your formal education"
9%	29%	"To help you brush up on your skills in . . ."
5%	20%	"To get information and/or ideas the company needs for specific, planned endeavor in the future (for example, "We want you to learn about acquisition strategies so we can become a more diversified company.")"

candidate is told why he/she is going to and EDP, who gives this information to the candidate?"

The problem is aggravated by another perceptual mismatch. Table 7 shows the response of the two groups when asked, "What reasons are given to executives for being sent to an EDP?"

In addition to the several instances of the two groups failing to report comparable data, two points deserve mention. First, the personnel/HR professionals seem to emphasize short-term performance ("to help you do your present job better," "To help you brush up your skills in . . .") whereas the stated purpose of most EDPs is preparation for the future. Second, although personnel/HR professionals earlier in the questionnaire reported that forty-seven percent of the executives sent to EDPs are slated for promotion within one year, they now say they inform the executives of this only twenty-three percent of the time. Only ten percent of the executives report that they are told of their forthcoming promotion at the time they are sent to a program. One wonders how much better executives could function in their new jobs if they were able to use the program to prepare for them.

Some universities make explicit the need to prepare executives for their educational experience. This statement appears in the brochure describing MIT's Program for Senior Executives: "Sponsoring organizations are urged to brief their Senior Executives before they come to MIT. They should receive some focus, guidance, or general mission from their sponsors, not a narrow assignment but some general objectives relevant to the problems and goals of the sponsoring organization. An appropriate question for the organization to ask its returning Senior Executives is: What do you think we should be doing differently—particularly in view of the organization's need we discussed before you went to MIT?"

Just as the two groups fail to agree about pre-program preparation, so is there lack of congruence about what happens upon return to the organization. Table 8 shows responses of the two groups when asked how the company makes use of the knowledge, ideas, and skills the individual acquired in an EDP.

These are not encouraging figures. It would appear that the course of action taken by companies most often is inaction; they permit executives to behave differently but don't stimulate or initiate change. Perhaps the companies expect "good" executives to exercise initiative and act upon what they have learned in an EDP. But the observations of one banker reveal that returning alumni need some help: "A few days should be set aside following the course to assess the knowledge acquired and reflect on how it might be assimilated quickly into our working habits. After a period of absence from the office most of us return to a heavy workload which usually demands our immediate attention. We are inclined to set aside incorporating our new knowledge into firmly

Table 8

How Companies Make Use of What Is Learned In EDPs

Program Participants	Personnel/HR Professionals	Methods Used
3%	20%	Given a project that makes use of information gained in program
12%	40%	Assigned to a new job
6%	17%	Present job is changed
2%	27%	Makes a formal presentation to others so they can share information
66%	77%	May choose to use information but no systematic effort is made to change procedures, systems, organizational structure, and so forth
17%	0%	Other

established habits. We have the best intentions of doing so as and when time permits. Sometimes, that opportunity does not present itself."

Several program alumni express disappointment that more isn't done to capitalize on their enthusiasm and newly-acquired knowledge. An aerospace project manager said, "They really didn't think through and prepare for my return, especially my changed expectations." Many of the "other" responses in Table 8 were similar to the statement of a marketing manager who reported, "There was little or no follow-up use [of what I had learned.]" A public utility financial executive said, "I wasn't permitted to use what I learned. It was too radical for the company."

Universities can do more to help make the transition back to the job more productive. Less than half include presentations in their programs about "re-entry." A third ask participants to develop a plan or project that incorporates what was taught in the program. Six of the schools say they communicate with the participant's immediate supervisor, describing the program and encouraging application of what is taught. Five of the responding schools conduct follow-up programs that give participants an opportunity to describe how they applied what they learned in the program. These sessions are intended to increase the probability that what is taught in the program will be applied. Sometimes the transition back to the job starts before the program is even conducted. As part of their admission process, four schools ask the company to specify how the individual's future responsibilities will change to incorporate what is taught in the program. One school reports that it sets up two visits per year with participants' managers, but eight of the thirty-one responding schools say they make no effort to facilitate participants' back-home use of the ideas, knowledge, and skills acquired in a program.

FUTURE USE OF PROGRAMS

Even though it appears companies are not doing all they could to maximize the benefit they receive from EDPs, the value of the programs is apparently great enough to warrant continued or increased use of them in the future. Forty-nine percent of the personnel/HR professionals said their participation will remain at about the same level during the next one to five years, thirty-five percent forecast a modest increase, and another nine percent said there will be a substantial increase in the number of executives they send to EDPs. Six percent predicted a modest decrease in program use, and one firm planned a substantial decrease.

The business community's positive attitude toward university-based executive development programs perhaps can be summed up best by the statements of two program alumni. One of them, a director of planning in a telecommunications company, described his experience this way: "The program I attended incorporated all the factors I think are essential: It was aimed at general management, covered all issues facing general managers, and required a high degree of participation. The faculty were very experienced in actual business activity through consultation, directorships and management proprietorships. The participants were fairly uniform in responsibility and years of experience but widely varied in industry, function, nationality, etc. Because there was a large group of participants, I made many good business contacts. It involved many high-level businessmen as guest lecturers and discussants, and the university offers considerable resources for the future."

A banker put it more succinctly: "I consider this program the finest classroom education to which I have ever been exposed, and consider having attended it a special privilege."

Their comments attest to how valuable EDPs can be. They also serve as a challenge to universities and companies alike. For companies, the challenge is to make certain this potential value is realized. They can meet this challenge by having clearly defined reasons for sending an executive to a program, sharing those reasons with the individual, selecting a program that will contribute most to this goal, and then giving the executive ample opportunity to apply what was learned in the program. For universities, the challenge is to deliver high-quality programs that are attuned to the needs of executives and their sponsoring organizations. Meeting this challenge will require schools to make substantial investments in executive development and to provide career incentives that will lead to greater faculty involvement in this increasingly vital dimension of management education.

Albert W. Schrader is president of the Kerf Corporation in Ann Arbor, formerly Associate Dean for Management Education at the University of Michigan Graduate School of Business Administration.

37.
DEVELOPING LEADERSHIP POTENTIAL

Marsha Sinetar

Sound leadership development programs must have both educational and behavioral foundations.

The heart of effective management is effective leadership. Yet in most organizations a high percentage of managerial promotions are made in a haphazard way—almost as though a clear definition of leadership and its function were lacking.

Defining leadership involves an examination both of what a leader *is* (i.e., personal attributes, physical traits, energy levels, abilities, etc.) and of what a leader *does* under particular circumstances.

Although most of us think we understand what leaders do, few of us have clear knowledge about what we mean by "leadership." The problem with our fuzzy definition is that we become clumsy in both the recognition and selection processes when appointing persons to leadership functions. When a person becomes a manager, even though much can be done to enhance his or her leadership abilities through developmental programs, that manager is generally left to his or her resourcefulness to cultivate leadership qualities. Most organizations do not have developmental programs for leaders because traits and skills which comprise leadership functions have not been clearly specified and are not adequately understood.

New managers who have not yet developed their own qualities for sound leadership stand less than a fair chance for consistent success when faced with management's everyday situational problems. The same managers have a much higher probability of managerial success if they bring to their positions some inherent leadership characteristics. Organizational success also increases measurably if the selection process at managerial levels is based on a clear conception of what a leader looks like and how a leader behaves.

The fact remains that many first line managers are initially selected in a subjective way and eventually (through either seniority, chance, normal attrition or lack of better alternatives) glide into top managerial spots where leadership skills play a crucial role in the vertical determination of organizational growth and prosperity.

A DEFINITION OF LEADERSHIP

Leadership is not only dependent upon a person's characteristics, but also on the situation in which an individual finds himself. Leadership should be removed from the broad and often vaguely defined area of purely social interaction and integrated with work performance and working relationships. Leadership is both a function of personality structure and situational interaction.

Leadership, seen functionally, is associated with those behaviors which reinforce the security of a group, or help bring about integration of the diverse elements of a group. The opposite type of behavior, namely "nonleadership-like" action, seems to have a disruptive effect on group solidarity, and seems to be caused by the nonleader's own stress levels, inability to function smoothly in tense situations and a lack of adroitness with situational issues. Leaders can be defined as those persons who show a pattern and/or a potential for having both a purpose and a following. Leadership can be taught to and developed in persons of average or above average intelligence. Leadership is not a position one has by "divine right" of birth or personality.

On the other hand, the trait theory of leadership (i.e., that certain traits, such as intelligence, risk taking, flexibility, verbal facility, etc., show a consistent relationship with leadership status) may prove valuable in identifying those individuals who aspire to leadership roles. Organizations which have a clear understanding of the trait clusters which seem to show a consistent relationship to leadership functioning can more easily and effectively locate individuals with high leadership quotients and thus promote their abilities instead of stultifying them.

Very often, in the promotional process, our intuitive reactions come into play. This is excellent and just as it should be. However, we may not get intuitive guidance from our internal machinery. All too often, when faced with a choice between several qualified persons for managerial positions, we select someone who might have the most seniority or someone who is technically competent in his or her specific field, rather than individuals with leadership qualities. Those of us who have lived with our incorrect choices are aware of the risk of promoting someone according to these objective, but often irrelevant, factors.

LEADERSHIP SKILLS AND TRAITS

In late 1979, a group of social scientists and educators met in Sacramento, California, at the request of the California State Department of Education, to see if a definitive profile of leadership traits might be established. From that meeting, the following characteristics of high leadership potential were identified:[1]

- Is respected by peers; others seek his/her ideas
- Is a risk-taker, independent
- Is energetic, enthusiastic, persevering
- Knows what is going on; is aware of nuances in environment and others
- Influences, may dominate; enjoys power
- Is self-confident
- Is responsible
- Has many new ideas or insights
- Is assertive
- Is diplomatic in group and peer relations
- Is structured, organized
- Is flexible

LEADERSHIP BEHAVIOR

How does a person with such leadership traits behave? Since there are different areas of behavior, it seems appropriate to cluster a few behaviors into at least three behavioral categories: intellectual; personal; and interpersonal or group behaviors.[2]

- **Intellectual/Cognitive Skills of a Leader**

1. Figures out what is wrong; show others how to solve problems
2. Handles abstract ideas and sees a broad perspective; sees the whole picture, while others may focus on parts
3. Plans and follows through
4. Projects into future, seeing consequences of decisions

- **Personal Skills of a Leader**

1. Judges appropriateness of own decisions, directions or suggestions; gauges appropriateness of own timing in these same areas
2. Copes with unpleasantness
3. Is able to absorb interpersonal stress
4. Is able to tolerate ambiguity, delay, frustration

- **Interpersonal Skills of a Leader**

1. Listens to, observes and recognizes the skills and abilities of others

2. Interacts with others easily; has the ability to inspire confidence in others
3. Perceives and articulates unstated feelings; recognizes and states goals, problems, ideas and interests of group
4. Has the capacity to structure social interaction systems for specific purposes
5. Follows well
6. Supports members of the group; accepts responsibility; is able to determine appropriate behaviors and courses of action
7. Organizes others, directs activities, delegates responsibility and establishes the mood of the group

CAN LEADERSHIP BE TAUGHT?

There is evidence throughout the literature that leadership can be taught or developed. It does not appear that any one type of person holds a monopoly on knowing it all. Rather, leadership is an evolution and a combination of skills, experience, knowledge and intuitive understandings. Certain situations seem to bring about leadership-like personality traits or innate abilities, allowing an individual to solve problems for others as an outgrowth of a given time or place.

An organization's ability to develop each manager's human awareness and self-awareness will to a large extent determine the quality of working life within that facility. People are quick to respond to leaders who establish a climate of basic trust, mutual respect and support. They are equally quick to balk at directives from managers with whom they have little rapport.

Many organizations have not yet bought this idea. Leadership development programs within such establishments are likely to be absent, or perhaps token efforts at best. It is not unusual to hear graduates of such programs using the latest psychological buzz-words, as if trying a new tactic on the the troops.

Stressing the behavior aspects of leadership development programs is a must if human resources development strategies are to reach into the uppermost ranks of organizational life. In terms of developing leadership, it seems insufficient to send a manager to a one day seminar on leadership. This type of activity, so prevalent in today's organizational development programs, illustrates a superficial understanding of human growth or development needs.

LEADERSHIP TRAINING CRITERIA

Sound leadership development programs must have both education and behavioral foundations. Such programs should:

- Provide a climate in which participants feel free to discuss and express themselves
- Develop an atmosphere of mutual interests, problem-solving and mutual respect among members—a support group, as it were, for all participants, in which each willingly assists the other's growth and is helped by others in his/her own growth
- Obtain an initial needs assessment in order to develop the programs to meet the requirements and interests of all the members of the particular group
- Continually clarify developmental goals through mutual discussions, practices and surveys
- Relate the program to actual work situations
- Utilize role playing to allow for as much open discussion as appropriate and to maintain an arena in which human feelings and attitudes are regenerated
- Structure the experience to achieve specific behavioral goals, with the structure coming from sound psychological principles and sound managerial philosophy
- Utilize one-on-one counseling methods to augment the developmental programs, thus developing a sense of "self" within each individual.

SELECTION AND TRAINING OF LEADERS

It is from a sense of self that leadership behaviors emerge. Self-confidence and assertion—natural partners to effective management—come both from experience and personal development. Personal development can be greatly assisted by developmental programs which nurture the participant's self-awareness and understanding of his or her relationship styles to others.

Pre-packaged leadership programs may well have their place in reinforcing the skills, ideas and behaviors necessary for sustained long-range efforts. It is also likely that each time a participant attends one of these brief programs, he or she will come into contact with someone who models leadership traits and who can, in that mode, also serve the developmental function. A one-day program, however, does not constitute "leadership development," unless it is part of an ongoing process.

The acceptance of one's self, which is at the heart of courageous leadership, comes primarily though self-understanding and through developmental programs which are grounded in a sound behavioral framework. Our instant gratification urge, so prevalent in the culture at large, also seems to have infiltrated human resource programs. Programs which have depth and which are individualized to the specific needs and unique perceptions of persons in question are not instant.

Selecting managers with high leadership quotients is only part of an organization's task. The other part—a developmental process—is not immediately actualized. Grooming managers for effective interpersonal functioning is a key adjunct to any selection process. This involves knowing what traits and skills are to be enhanced, and then designing programs which cultivate a deep understanding of human nature and of each individual participant's own self.

REFERENCES

1. California State Department of Education, Management Team Conference for Education of the Gifted, Leadership Committee, December 1979.
2. Mitchell, T.R., "The Construct Validity of Three Dimensions of Leadership Research," *Journal of Social Psychology*, 1970, pp. 89-94.

Dr. Marsha Sinetar is a consulting psychologist specializing in industrial human resources development. Dr. Sinetar also serves as a special consultant to Loyola-Marymount University's Industrial Relations Center in Los Angeles.

38.
LET MANAGEMENT DEVELOPMENT SCORE FOR YOUR ORGANIZATION

Richard W. Scholl
Winifred W. Brownell

> Management development should involve not only improvement of individual skills, but development of the group as an effective problem-solving unit.

Success depends on avoiding the pitfalls that plague most programs. While differing predictions regarding the future abound, most agree that managing in the '80s will require a renewed emphasis on efficiency and cost cutting. With increased pressures for efficiency and the need to get the most out of invested dollars, the need for skilled management becomes greater as managers search for new and improved strategies to motivate individuals and improve managerial decision-making. Although we expect top management to turn to management development as a source of solutions to complex organizational problems, many firms are actually looking to their management development programs as places in which to cut their budgets.

When managers are faced with increased pressures to produce and increased pressures on their time, why is an important source of potential help often eliminated? Why don't organizations look to management development as a source of solutions for organizational problems when times are difficult?

A SOLUTION TO ORGANIZATIONAL PROBLEMS?

In the past, management development has not always brought about desired results. Participating managers often reported that they enjoyed a program and considered it successful; but as they returned to their departments, little change in behavior or improvement in results actually took place. Thus, the problems facing their departments continued as before. As a result, although many fine programs have been developed based on the latest theory and research, many top managers are becoming skeptical of the promised program benefits. What we find them looking for are programs that actually improve organizational, departmental, or individual performance.

We have identified four potential reasons why many management development programs have failed to deliver expected results: 1) ambiguous goals; 2) incomplete program development and design; 3) inattention to models of behavioral change; and 4) emphasis on the inappropriate units of analysis.

AMBIGUOUS GOALS

One of the reasons why management development programs do not deliver the results top managers might expect is that they were not designed with immediate problem-solving in mind. We have accumulated a list of frequently cited goals of management development programs:

- increased sensitivity and self-awareness
- increased understanding of the human element, generally through enhanced knowledge of the concepts and theories or organizational behavior
- improved decision-making skills
- increased motivation to manage
- change in behavior from one leadership style to another
- acquaintance with "state of the art" techniques of management
- development of technical skills relevant to individual's function within the organization

While these are admirable goals, they fall short of stating what changes or improvements are expected in terms of organizational performance. Implicit in all of these goals is the assumption that individuals will use what they have gained in the program to solve problems and make decisions. In reality, what we desire is increased performance that comes about through improved decision-making and problem-solving.

If we view the problem-solving process in four stages—1) problem identification; 2) problem diagnosis; 3) solution generation and implementation; and 4) evaluation—we can see how the stated goals should fit into this process. For example, increased self-awareness and sensitivity should make individuals more aware of their biases in identifying and diagnosing problems. Understanding of the human element should make diagnosing of the causes of departmental or individual performance problems easier and more accurate. Increased motivation to manage should increase the manager's motivation to identify, confront, and solve problems, rather than allow them to increase in magnitude. State of the art techniques and new leadership styles should expand the manager's repertoire of potential solutions.

The problem with setting goals is that the connection between these goals and improved problem-solving and performance is left to chance and the ability of the manager to make this connection. In addition, when the problem is centered at the departmental or organizational level and involves a number of managers, it requires simultaneous improvements. Most programs place little focus on helping managers transfer the training to their specific work situations.

INCOMPLETE PROGRAM DEVELOPMENT AND DESIGN

The first and often the most important step in designing a training program should be an assessment of training needs. Hopefully, this needs assessment is more than a sorting through of the assortment of seminar announcements received by the training director.

David J. Stein has outlined two approaches to needs assessment: 1) the felt-needs training approach, and 2) the prescriptive training needs approach.[1] The felt-needs approach uses a survey to determine what prospective participants would like to see covered in the program. The prescriptive approach starts by identifying performance deficiencies and identifies what training is required to correct each deficiency. The prescriptive approach may take on a number of forms. One prescriptive method is to use job analysis to identify skills, abilities, and knowledge that participants require to perform adequately. Another method is to do a behavioral analysis that compares current behavioral patterns (e.g., leadership style, conflict resolution style, etc.) with some normative behavioral model. These areas where the current pattern of behavior differs from the pattern prescribed by the normative model would be keyed as areas for training.

PROBLEM IDENTIFICATION

A final prescriptive method involves identification of organizational, departmental, or individual problems. Problems are identified and an analysis is made to determine the root causes of these problems. Once causes are determined, training is designed to solve the problems by training managers in areas that relate to the identified causes. For example, if a problem of low productivity is identified, and it is determined that employee motivation is the root of the problem, the training would focus on the topic of employee motivation.

Dennis C. Kinlaw and Donna R. Christensen argue that one of the critical factors in gaining the support of both top management and participants is whether or not they believe that the program will improve performance.[2] We not only agree, but would argue also that if the management development program is to have any effect on organizational, departmental, or individual performance, the needs assessment must be prescriptive and must identify specific areas of performance that are in need of improvement.

Once needs are identified, most trainers attempt to develop a list of topics that fit the training needs. The result of this process usually resembles a syllabus from a university management course; that is, the list of topics, moving from session to session, addressing one area at a time. For example, the program may start with motivation and then move on to leadership and communication, with each session being a self-contained module including a discussion of models, theories, tools, and techniques related to the topic.

Here lies one of the major problems with management development and, for that matter, management education in general. Topics are taught from a "forward theory building" perspective. This perspective presents models of motivation and leadership that show the relationship between independent variables such as job design, rewards systems, and leadership style, and dependent variables such as employee performance, satisfaction, and attachment. Our purpose is not to quarrel with the accuracy of the models, but to point out that managers have a difficult time using these models to do what they do most of the time: solve problems.

Problems lie in the dependent variables. A manager may have to deal with low productivity, poor product quality, or high turnover. To deal with these types of problems, managers need to take a "reverse theory building" perspective. For example, let's assume that a manager is faced with the problem that his or her department is continually late in meeting deadlines. Is this problem the result of low motivation, poor leadership, organizational structure inadequacies, poor communication, or a combination of all of these? The point is that forward theory does not directly address this issue, nor help the manager to diagnose the causes of a problem.

In addition, when topics are taught sequentially, it becomes difficult to see the interrelationships among processes. Reverse theory starts with dependent variables and examines the potential causes of problems in these areas, providing guidelines for determining where the roots of the problems lie.

We start by assuming that improvement in performance requires some type of behavioral change on the part of managers, whether it be in leadership style, decision-making approach, or problem-solving style. If behavioral change is desired, the ability of management development programs to facilitate this change must be examined. Does management development clearly address the three stages of the behavioral change process; that is, 1) developing the motivation to change; 2) providing a model for change; and 3) reinforcing the change?

What motivates a manager to actively participate in a management development program? Kinlaw and Christensen argue that participant support and motivation is a function of whether the participants believe that the program will help to improve performance and that it is worth their time. Participants must be interested in improving some dimension of unit performance and believe that their behavior is at least in part contributing to the current performance level. Thus, managers must believe that some change in their behavior is necessary for desired performance improvement to take place. Many programs fail to consider this step.

Needs assessments that do not identify and focus on areas of low performance often leave managers with the belief that the program material is for others, or it is nice to know if a problem should ever arise. The first step in a successful management development program is to develop the motivation to change. This can often be accomplished by focusing on problems that participating managers identify with and feel a need to solve.

MODELS AND REINFORCEMENT

The participant must become familiar with new behaviors, techniques, or styles of management and see the link between these new approaches and improved performance. More importantly, the manager must know in what situations the new approach will and will not be successful. This requires not only knowledge of the new approach, but the ability to diagnose the causes of problems in order to determine the appropriateness of potential solutions. By focusing on problem areas rather than topics, the goal of developing diagnostic skills is better served.

Once new behaviors or a change in style or even structural change is implemented, there must be some type of feedback that informs the participant that performance is improving or the problems identified are being eliminated. Few management development programs provide this structured feedback. Some of the behavioral modeling programs are notable exceptions.[3]

John H. Zenger and Kenneth Hargis made a strong case for more effort in the evaluation of management training.[4] Not only would this evaluation provide useful information to program designers and training directors, but it could also be used to provide structured feedback to participants on the effectiveness of new behaviors.

Stanley D. Truskie contends that when training is evaluated, the evaluation focuses on reaction or level of learning, rather than behavioral change or organizational results.[5] It is difficult to provide the structured feedback that participants need when there is no careful assessment of the program results. This can be accomplished when future performance is compared to needs assessment data. In summary, for behavioral change to take place, three conditions must be met:

1. Managers must desire improvements in performance and believe that a change in their behavior is necessary to bring about improvements.
2. The program must provide a basis for diagnosing problems and an array of strategies for improvement.
3. Feedback that performance is improving is necessary for continued improvement.

THE ROOT OF THE PROBLEM

Many organizational problems are rooted in a number of processes and positions within the organization. Programs aimed at the individual level may not lead to improved performance simply because participants returning to their work roles cannot implement changes independently. They often meet resistance from those who were not part of the program or have not participated in the diagnosis that led to a proposed change.

We are becoming increasingly aware that team or group performance is more than the combined individual efforts of its members. Management development should involve not only improvement of individual skills, but development of the group as an effective problem-solving unit. It has become important for groups to practice problem-solving as an integral part of the management development program.

OVERCOMING TRADITIONAL ROADBLOCKS

In order to overcome some of the problems inherent in traditionally designed management development programs, we borrowed concepts from team building and action research and developed a process of management development that is centered around recurring organizational problems in the client organization. This process includes three steps: needs assessments, program development, and evaluation.

The first step of the needs assessment is to develop a set of performance pressures for the focal work unit. Generally, an analysis of the external and internal claimants on the unit is necessary to perform this step. In general, ask what dimensions of organizational performance are important for the continued success of this focal unit. Once performance pressures—which are generally some combination of quality, cost, service, and time variables—are identified, an attempt is made to determine dimensions where improvement is needed. Areas where the unit is not meeting claimant expectations are identified as problems.

Thus, if an organization competes largely on service, and it becomes clear that service standards and customer expectations are not being met, this is identified as one of the problems that will be focused on in the program. While some needs assessment approaches will continue to diagnose the causes of the service problem to identify training topics, we stop the needs assessment at the problem identification stage, leaving the diagnosis for the participants in the program.

FROM SYLLABUS TO MODULE

The program syllabus should simply become a series of modules designed around identified problems. Each module may last for three or four sessions, during which we explore the processes that underlie the problem. We often cover many parts of traditional management development topics in one module, as we examine the motivation and structural roots of the problem.

The major benefits of this part of the process is that managers see the link between outcomes and processes and are exposed to behavioral models in a reverse theory manner. We believe this process aids in the development of diagnostic skills. In addition to diagnosing the problem, potential intervention strategies are discussed. Management techniques are examined with respect to their usefulness in addressing the focal problem. Before the module is concluded, specific plans for action are developed, along with timetables, goals, and individual assignments.

EVALUATING THE BENEFITS

The evaluation performs two functions. The first is to assess how effective the program was in delivering results. The second is to provide reinforcement to participants. Effectiveness is measured by conducting another assessment of work unit performance and comparing the results of this assessment with those obtained in the needs assessment. As with the action research process, this second assessment provides the basis to continued change and development.

We have identified three major benefits of this process over traditional processes. First, the performance oriented needs assessment provides a motivation to change. We have often found a low motivation to change when current behavior is compared to some ideal managerial behavior when there is no indication of performance problems. The performance problems provide the basis for a clear set of program goals.

Second, many of the problems of transference of training issues are eliminated because participants are not forced to make the connection between the acquired knowledge and the problem-solving process on their own. Finally, evaluation is designed to provide feedback and reinforcement of any change implemented.

REFERENCES

1. Stein, David J. "Designing Performance Oriented Training Programs," *Training and Development Journal* (January 1981), pp. 12-16.
2. Kinlaw, Dennis C., and Christensen, Donna R. "Ways of Winning Motivational Support for Management Education Programs," *Personnel* (March-April 1982), pp. 64-80.
3. Burnaska, Robert F. "The Effect of Behavioral Modeling Training Upon Managers' Behaviors and Employees' Perceptions," *Personnel Psychology* (Autumn 1976), pp. 329-335.
4. Zenger, John H., and Hargis, Kenneth. "Assessing Training Results: It's Time to Take the Plunge," *Training and Development Journal* (January 1982), pp. 10-16.
5. Truskie, Stanley D. "Getting the Most From Management Development Programs," *Personnel Journal* (January 1982), pp. 66-68.

Richard W. Scholl is assistant professor of Management, Department of Management. Winifred W. Brownell is associate professor of Speech Communication, Department of Speech Communication. Both are with the University of Rhode Island, Kingston, Rhode Island.

39.
A CHECKLIST OF QUALITIES THAT MAKE A GOOD BOSS

Nation's Business

A study showed that subordinates have strong and surprisingly consistent opinions, not only on what makes a good manager, but on just how well their own boss is doing.

A successful manager has ten qualities that are the same in a wide range of industries and occupations.

So says Harbridge House, a Boston consulting firm, which drew its profile of a successful manager from interviews with more than five thousand employers that it serves.

The answers were consistent "regardless of the age or sex of the manager, or the industry, size, location, organizational structure or corporate culture of the company," says Ernest Glickman, Harbridge executive vice president.

Employees are asked what qualities they think their own bosses need. They also are asked how their bosses measure up. The answers help the consulting firm shape its management training programs to the specific needs of each organization.

In each company a questionnaire is developed listing as many as fifty manager qualities. Employees are asked to pick from the list the qualities they consider most important for a manager to be effective. Then they are asked to rate their own boss against the list.

Despite the diversity of occupations and the differences in individual managers, the study showed that the men and women who reported on their bosses hold strong and surprisingly consistent opinions, not only on what makes a good manager, but on just how well their own bosses are doing.

This is what a good manager must do, the study concludes:

1.   Provide clear direction. An effective manager needs to establish clear goals and standards for people. He must communicate group goals, not just individual goals. He must involve people in setting these goals, and not simply

dictate them himself. He must be clear and thorough in delegating responsibility.

2.   Encourage open communication. The manager must be candid in dealing with people. He must be honest, direct and to the point. "People want straight information from their bosses," the study says, "and managers must establish a climate of openness and trust."

3.   Be willing to coach and to support people. This means being helpful to others, working constructively to correct performance problems and going to bat for subordinates with superiors. This last practice "was consistently rated as one of the most important aspects of effective leadership." says Robert Stringer, senior vice president of Harbridge, who supervised the survey.

4.   Provide objective recognition. The manager must recognize people for good performance more often than criticizing them for performance problems. Rewards must be related to the excellence of job performance, not to seniority or personal relationships. "Most managers don't realize how much criticism they give," the study says. "They do it to be helpful, but positive recognition is what really motivates people."

5.   Establish on-going controls. This means following up on important issues and actions and giving subordinates feedback on how they are doing.

6.   Select the right people to staff the organization.

7.   Understand the financial implications of decisions. This quality is considered important even for functional managers who do not have responsibility for the bottom line.

8.   Encourage innovation and new ideas. Employees rate this quality important in even the most traditional or conservative organizations.

9.   Give subordinates clear-cut decisions when they are needed. "Employees want a say in things," the report says, "but they don't want endless debate. There's a time to get on with things, and the best managers know when that time comes."

10. Consistently demonstrate a high level of integrity. The study shows that most employees want to work for a manager they can respect.

For the study, Harbridge House used computerized data acquired during research for clients.

The consultant firm regularly conducts anonymous polls of employees as part of a program of improving the effectiveness of managers.

Stringer says: "When you start getting thousands of employees in a disparate group of organizations coming up with essentially the same profile of a successful manager, you can safely conclude there is some validity to the information they are giving you."

In view of how often managers themselves disagree on questions of management style, Stringer says he was impressed by the near-unanimity of the answers given by employees.

Is there one quality that stood out above all others in employee's responses? "It's amazing," he says, "how important open and honest communication is to employees."

40.
MANAGEMENT RESOURCE PLANNING: KEYS TO SUCCESS

James F. Bolt

In the future, management quality and depth may be the source of a competitive advantage. Management resources is a serious business at all progressive companies—as well it should be.

What do IBM, GE, DuPont, Exxon, and Xerox all have in common? Despite their obvious diversity, they have in common a deep concern for the development of their management resources (MR). There is nothing new about that. No self-respecting CEO or other senior executive would argue against the fact that the long-term growth and success of their enterprise requires a certain number and quality of seasoned managers to run the organization. In recent surveys, CEO's and personnel executives ranked this subject as the most critical issue facing their organization. However, the expressed concerns regarding this subject seem to be taking on a sense of urgency. The reason is straightforward enough—competition! Whether it's from the Japanese, the Germans or newer U.S. competitors, the competition is significantly better than we've ever faced before. One reason is the narrowing of the technology gap. Even though these large corporations generally have superior resources to apply to R&D, much of the new computer technology cannot easily be protected by patents. Also, some previous technological advantages have been lost through legal action, e.g. in 1975 Xerox was required by the FTC to license virtually anyone who wished to use its copier technology.

In addition to the narrowing technology gap, many of these competitors are very well managed. The management gap may also be narrowing. In fact, many of the successful new companies in the computer industry have been started by young entrepreneurs who came from large organizations where it was difficult to express their entrepreneurial spirit and skills. It's only recently that

American businessmen have come to realize that a major reason for the Japanese success is excellent management practices.

Lastly, the average level of education has improved so that the MBA is almost common now. Combining these elements, it can be argued that technological superiority is declining and that among the companies competing, the quality of management is more even than in the past. Therefore, a significant competitive edge that these large companies must have is superior management talent in their key management positions and superior bench strength to fill those positions when vacated.

Management quality and depth may be more the source of competitive advantage than it has been in the past. Thus, the intense interest in this subject, in terms of being required for survival versus the general statements one often hears. Rather than expounding on the importance of the subject, this article deals with the common and critical elements in management resource planning (MRP) processes currently in place in major corporations and will then explore some of the persistent problems in this field. The following case is used to illustrate a typical Management Resource Planning system of a major corporation.

THE CASE

J. B. Carlisle, CEO, was about to go into the monthly meeting of the corporate management review committee (CMRC). Carlisle chaired this committee which was made up of the top six senior executives of the company. This group also formed the central policy committee which met weekly on matters of key policy and operational significance. Management development is an important subject at this company as evidenced by the fact that this committee exists and that they recently decided to expand the amount of time dedicated to management resource planning (MRP) considerably. The purpose of the CMRC was to review the key management positions and people in the company in terms of their performance and developmental needs, and to plan the replacements for these key people/jobs.

Top management felt that MRP was an important part of their responsibility. Carlisle felt especially strong about this. In fact, he was personally responsible for setting up the extensive process used throughout the company nearly eight years ago. XYZ, a four billion dollar company, had nearly 70,000 employees and was organized on a divisional basis. Every effort was made to provide the divisions with maximum autonomy. The MRP process was a bottom-up approach, not complicated but time consuming. It was corporate policy that all divisions use the same process for middle-level management positions and above. Therefore, once each year the process was reviewed and updated for all middle manager positions and above. The division had an option to do the same for lower levels of management. There were two fairly simple forms. One was completed by the employees and contained a summary of their work experience and their career goals. The second form was filled out by their managers and summarized current performance levels, long-term potential, specified the most likely next jobs for each person, identified specific developmental needs as well as appropriate developmental actions such as special assignments or training. It also specified the names of two to three people who could replace the incumbent.

The division presidents were responsible for management succession within their organization and were required to use the corporate system. Most of the division presidents had formed their own version of the CMRC with their division senior executives, performing similar functions as the corporate committee but within their division. Beyond that, in several of the divisions, such committees were common at lower levels, e.g. the manufacturing plant manager headed a committee which oversaw all management succession activities for management positions in that plant. No assignment could be made without their review and approval. This was done in order to assure that management development needs (not just the immediate needs of the business) were a primary factor in assignments. The plant manager felt that this was important because there was a natural tendency for managers to fill critical jobs with the most qualified candidate due to the pressure in meeting near-term business objectives. Naturally, these were the assignments which were also best for testing younger managers who showed exceptional potential.

The divisions have considerable autonomy in their management resource activities. However, in addition to the requirement to use the corporate process and forms, there were other corporate "demands." Once each year, the division presidents had to visit corporate headquarters specifically to review their management resources with the CMRC. It was required that they review each of the senior positions reporting to the division president. Those reviews covered the incumbent's management resource information as well as the two most likely replacements for each of those positions. It was common for these meetings to be lively since many of these people were known by the members of the CMRC, and these meetings had to end in agreement on the next moves, replacements and development for each person and position reviewed.

It was also required at these meetings that the division presidents discuss lower level "high-potential" managers who would be put through special developmental experiences to test, challenge and prepare them for senior division positions within the next ten years. Lastly, each division president was required to review people who had been identified as having the potential to fill the most senior corporate positions within the next ten to fifteen years. The CMRC took great interest in this group because they were potentially their replacements. Once they were approved by the committee, these people became "corporate resources" and all developmental plans, job assignments and compensation actions had to be approved by the CMRC.

Carlisle felt that this was necessary in order to assure the identification and long-term development and preparation of the future senior executives. It was natural for the division presidents to want to keep their best people within the division. In fact, many of them felt that they could provide these people with adequate development opportunities within their division without any corporate involvement. Carlisle strongly disagreed. He believed that future senior executives needed assignments in several businesses and functions, in at least two different divisions and preferably an international assignment, to have the thorough understanding and knowledge of all key aspects of the business and to have a broad perspective. Therefore, these corporate high potentials became part of a separate process. This process was administered by the Manager, Management Resources on the Corporate Personnel staff. He was responsible for coordinating all the management resource actions for the corporate high potentials, which involved about 200 people. More detailed, long-term developmental plans were created for each of these people. These long-term plans were created by the division but required the approval of both the Manager, Management Resources and the CMRC.

In reflecting on the meeting he was about to start, Carlisle was proud of the company's program and of his own foresight in setting it up despite cries of corporate bureaucracy from the divisions, and the fact that it was established when the company was much smaller and the need less clear. Of course there were some problems, but for the most part he felt it had worked quite well as evidenced by the fact that in the last three years they only had to go outside the company twice to fill key executive positions.

However, he knew this meeting would be a difficult one. The president of the largest division was in for his annual MRP review. Carlisle knew he had some specific gripes which would be aired in the meeting. First of all, he and his senior people were upset because a new senior corporate position had recently been created to manage a new acquisition and the job had been filled from outside the company because "we didn't feel anyone inside had the appropriate understanding of the technology needed in the newly acquired company." Secondly, the division did not meet its sales and profit margin for the year and the division president felt it was partly because two of his most talented people in critical assignments had been moved for developmental purposes to other divisions. The performance of their organization had declined during the transition to their replacements.

Carlisle was not satisfied with the number of minority and female names on the division's management resource review last year and was looking for significant improvements. Also, during the past year, Carlisle had received an open-door letter from a middle manager in that division who "sensed there were very few opportunities for development in that division and wanted to know what top management could do about it." A similar letter was received from a manager who had been there for twenty years and who felt that the division management resource process was discriminatory because none of the division high potentials were over forty years of age.

CRITICAL ELEMENTS OF A MAJOR
MANAGEMENT RESOURCE PLANNING EFFORT

This case is not representative of a specific company, but is a composite made up from a study of the processes used in several major corporations. As such, it provides a useful way to illustrate elements which seem to be common and which apparently are critical to successful programs. Although these represent large companies' practices, I'm sure it will be clear that the principles would apply to many small and medium-sized companies as well, although perhaps in a scaled-down version. What, then, are these keys to success or critical, common elements?

Extensive Involvement of Senior Management

The CEO sets the example by his or her personal involvement in the process. Often the CEO is the head of the system and the most prominent proponent of the Management Resource Process. Senior line managers see themselves as being responsible for management resources with the staff (usually the Personnel function), playing a supportive role and being responsible for administration of the process. In other words, the development of management resources is clearly seen as the responsibility of line managers versus the staff role of advising and managing the process or system. In many cases, the CEO personally approves the replacement plans for the key positions and the long-term development plans and assignments of high potential employees. Typically the CEO and his equivalent of the CPC spends 40 to 50 hours per year in formal management resource reviews with the operating divisions.

An Institutional Process

A single, consistent process, institutionalized over time, is used throughout the company. Divisions have the responsibility for the development of management resources with their divisions, but they have little choice in the process or system used, which is mandated by corporate headquarters. There are written development plans for all people included in the program. The MR process has become a way of life in the company, almost ritualistic and a part of the corporate culture. There are dedicated support staffs. No one debates the value or need for management resources, it's just done as part of the ongoing management process.

An Overall MR Strategy

The long-term development resources in these companies is usually only a part of a broader management resource strategy, although it is infrequently articulated or even conceived as such. There is an overall strategy based on the basic philosophy that it is better to grow your own management talent than to hire from outside. Recognizing that there are some risks to this approach, e.g. possibly less creativity than might result from infusing the organization with outside talent, they are willing to accept these risks in exchange for what they feel are off-setting benefits. Namely, the motivational aspects of reserving promotional opportunities for their own employees and the ability to "grown their own," steeped in their corporate culture, values, management philosophy and practices. Their overall strategy, not necessarily articulated as a coherent, comprehensive strategy, is to grow their own talent. This normally includes a promotion-from-within policy backed up by a practice of assuring that external hires are generally recent college graduates who can advance as their talent and experience allows. Many even have dedicated college relations staffs to assure that they get their share of the best college graduates. These graduates can then be groomed over a long period of time for managerial responsibilities.

Formal, mandatory internal management orientation and training programs are used to teach management philosophy, skills and practices. This is seen and used as a way of imbuing new managers with the corporate philosophy, values and key management practices. Subsequently, advanced internal management training programs purposely review and reinforce these values and philosophies throughout the manager's career.

These companies tend to pay their employees very well compared to other companies in their industry and have executive compensation practices which are designed to retain their management talent. At the same time, there is strong emphasis on a merit pay system in order to reward performance.

Lastly, the importance of developing management resources is reinforced through the reward and incentive systems in general. Typically, the performance appraisal for all managers must appraise the managers on how well they have done in this area, and specifically in coaching, counselling and developing their own employees.

MR Committees Throughout the Organization

It is common in these major corporations that MR committees have expanded below the level of top management. Frequently there are a series of committees performing much like the CMRC illustrated in the case. Table I illustrates a typical system. In this example the Division President serves as a member of the CMRC. He is also the Chairman of the Division MR Committee which oversears the MRP for the division and approves all key developmental plans and assignments for managers who are in the MRP. In this example, the V.P., Manufacturing is a member of the Division MRC but is also Chairman of the Manufacturing MRC. The Plant Manager is a member of the Manufacturing MRC as well as Chairman of the Plant MRC, etc. There is a "layer" of line committees which meet regularly to plan and manage the development of their management resources.

Table I

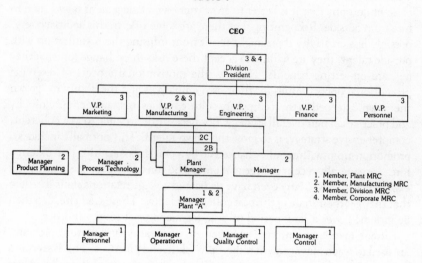

Special Process for High Potentials

Both in the divisions and at corporate headquarters, there is a special effort made beyond the normal replacement planning process. This effort is aimed at identifying managers early in their careers who have the potential to fill key senior leadership positions in the future and to plan developmental experiences over a relatively long period of time (approximately 10 to 20 years). These experiences are designed to test and help prepare these high potential managers. In the divisions, people are identified who can eventually fill the senior division jobs. At corporate headquarters, a pool of "corporate resources" are identified who have the potential to fill the key corporate jobs including president and CEO. Generally, these corporate plans assure developmental assignments across functions, within different divisions and internationally, to assure sufficient breadth, perspective and understanding of the entire enterprise.

Internal Management Training

Although these companies believe that development occurs primarily on the job, all of them have extensive internal management training programs to support and supplement on-the-job development. These programs are generally designed and run internally simply because the company feels it can do it better then any outside organization could. There is usually a series of programs offered (attendance is mandatory) at key career points. This includes programs for newly appointed managers, programs for middle-level managers who must manage other managers and then programs for more senior managers and executives as they move into positions requiring responsibility for policy and/or understanding of the management of multiple functions or businesses. The programs are aimed primarily at reviewing and reinforcing key corporate values, management philosophy and practices, and at providing training on the management knowledge and skills required at that management level. The lower level programs, offered early in the management career, tend to be highly oriented towards skill building, whereas the senior level programs are less so and more focused on building a broad perspective of the company and the outside world, e.g., world economic factors, government relations, environmental factors affecting the business, etc. In other words, these programs are designed as a series of learning experiences to supplement on-the-job development. They are aimed at imbuing the values, philosophy and management practices which are felt to be needed throughout the company and at imparting the key knowledge and skills required on the job. They also help broaden the perspectives of those moving into more senior positions. It is not unusual for the most senior level programs to be run by outside faculty from major business schools.

Executive Education

All of these companies use external executive education programs such as Harvard's AMP and PMD, MIT's Program for Senior Executives, and the Stanford Executive Program, to supplement job assignments and their internal management training. These are used as a planned part of the management resource process versus having people attend on an ad hoc basis. These companies seem to feel that they are most valuable for the development of a general management perspective. That includes developing a broad knowledge and understanding of all major functions of the business, reviewing major world economic, political and social issues, and exposing executives to their counterparts from other organizations from which much of the learning comes. These programs are invaluable for senior managers or those about to become senior managers whose work experience has been totally or primarily in one functional area. Surprisingly, this is the case in many major corporations. These programs are expensive and time consuming. The programs run from 8 to 14 weeks.

SOME PERSISTENT PROBLEMS

If these are the common and critical elements in a major MRP effort, what are the persistent problems which seem to negatively impact the effectiveness of such programs?

The Basic Conflict: Short-Term Versus Long-Term

As illustrated in the case, there always has been and perhaps always will be a troublesome conflict between a bottom line, near-term, results oriented management focus and the necessary long-term developmental process of management resources planning. Operating managers are driven to meet this year's (often this quarter's) product, sales or profit targets, and in order to do so, require the best available management talent in their key positions. Because they are key positions, they are usually the best developmental assignments for high potential managers in terms of testing their mettle and providing a significant learning experience.

However, frequently the developmental assignee has little or no previous experience in that function. Therefore, he or she is unlikely to perform at the level of performance the division would get if it put in the person most qualified, if they were solely concerned about meeting their performance targets. That's the heart of the issue. Human nature causes an obvious tendency to take the actions which result in the most positive, near-term consequences. The natural pull is for filling critical assignments with the best qualified candidate for that position now versus the developmental candidate. Despite long-term efforts to make management resources more important to the line managers, such as making it a part of the performance appraisal and bonus plan, seldom are these efforts strong enough to overcome the pressure and importance of meeting this year's bottom-line results. Stories of managers being promoted because they did an exceptional job at management resource development, even though they missed their bottom-line sales or profit targets, are few and far between.

This difficulty is evidenced by the fact that even when these key assignments get reviewed by a group like the CMRC, a near-term business "crisis" sometimes gets the nod over previously agreed to, long-term developmental assignments. Is there a way to satisfactorily resolve or eliminate this issue so that these needs are not in conflict? Probably not. The only answer seems to be brute force. The CMRC must assure that the long-term developmental needs are met by insisting on following long-term developmental plans for the division and corporate high potentials. They must review and approve all assignments for these key people and for all key positions. This will often not be satisfactory to the divisions since the short-term results may suffer, but it will assure that the long-term corporate management resource needs take precedence over short-term division requirements. Also, it sets an important example for managers in the division. This kind of action on the part of CMRC is more important to the organization than anything they say about management resources. In other words, it demonstrates their interest and belief in the importance of this subject.

Identification of Potential

Obviously, a critical factor in these MR processes is the accurate and early identification of people with exceptional potential for advancement. Despite the obvious importance of this, relatively little progress has been made. In most cases, there are virtually no criteria for including people in the MR process other than being at a certain job level and/or being "seen as a potential replacement" for a key job. Nor are there hard criteria for selecting people to be included in the high potential process. Some work has been done in the area of written tests. Generally, however, these companies do not use such devices. The assessment center approach, where potential is assessed by having people work in simulated management situations which are related to satisfactory performance in the future job, has tremendous face validity and when done correctly seems to actually work much better than more traditional methods of screening out or selecting people. Nevertheless, other than AT&T, few major corporations seem to use this process widely, In fact, even where these methods are used, the trend has been away from using them to select people and more towards their use for developmental purposes, i. e. to identify developmental needs and plan developmental activities.

A major reason for not using assessment centers more often seems to be that they are costly and time consuming. Yet they are surely less so than the disruptiveness and cost of management failures caused by poor selection processes. Is there an answer to this persistent problem? Probably. There is certainly little excuse for the relative lack of the use of assessment techniques. These processes must be based on actual studies of the key positions in question to identify the key success factors in the job. The technologies are available to build assessment programs or processes to test candidates through job simulation. Part of the problem is that many managers don't like it. They got ahead under the old system and they pride themselves on being able to spot talent. The facts suggest that the use of assessment technology is more accurate. There are significant front-end and ongoing costs involved. But it only takes a handful of avoided management failures to defray these costs. The avoidance of the morale problems of management failures is also significant.

Other related techniques such as panel interviews, where several managers interview potential candidates based on a study of job factors which are critical, have also proven to be statistically more effective than traditional methods. Those methods which are based on a study of the actual job are more likely to be legally defensible since they reduce bias and increase objectivity in the selection process.

It is still commonly believed that the best test is the challenge of a new and difficult assignment. Being tested under a variety of managers reduces personal bias and provides the opportunity to work under different types of managers. It also provides the opportunity to be tested under different, challenging types of assignments, different functional areas, line as well as staff, etc. Not only is this a good test of abilities, but it is excellent in developmental aspects. What should be, and in some cases is, being done is more frequent rotational assignments, especially across functional lines and starting much earlier in a manager's career, often right after the first management assignment. Even when this approach is used now, it is often started late in the managers' careers after they have proven themselves for many years in a specific function and become overspecialized.

Planning for Long-Term Needs Versus Replacement Planning

Most of these elaborate MR systems are designed to identify and develop the replacement for current organizational positions and do it quite well. Generally, however, they do a poor job of planning future organizational requirements. In this case, Carlisle went outside to fill a key job because they did not anticipate the acquisition far enough in advance to identify and develop a manager internally. Unfortunately, this problem is not caused by or even aggravated by a weakness in their MR process. It is fundamentally a weakness in the business planning process. Even these major corporations are not as good as they'd like to be in business and strategic planning and, therefore, are generally unable to accurately predict significant organizational shifts which would require different types of technical skills or managers far enough in advance (ten years) to adequately prepare people internally.

Unless long-term business/strategic planning improves significantly, this problem is one we must live with. What can be done to alleviate it? First of all, it's essential that the MRP and business planning processes are clearly and actively linked so that the MRP can at least be as good as the business planning processes. In fact, it is wise to specifically require that division and corporate long-term plans include a section forecasting management resources requirements even if it has to be a little blue-sky.

If the other long-term developmental actions are taken as noted elsewhere in this article, there should be very few jobs that a manager who's proven himself/ herself in assignments in several functions, divisions, in line and staff as well as international assignment, couldn't handle. Therefore, the replacement planning process coupled with long-term developmental plans would handle most cases. This would assure that external hiring would be only as a last resort to meet specific technical requirements which could not be forecasted or, perhaps, to occasionally bring in a fresh or innovative perspective.

It's best to not oversell your promotion-from-within policy or practices. People should understand that under certain, critical circumstances you will go outside so that when it does happen, it isn't read as hypocritical or a betrayal of a corporate promise.

CONCLUSION

Management resources is a serious business at these major companies and clearly should be. Extensive, comprehensive Management Resource Planning systems have been developed and are in place and work pretty well. The larger and more diverse the company, the more MRP is seen as essential to the long-term growth and survival of the enterprise. There's much to be learned from what's being done in these companies.

In general, their MRP processes include all management positions at a certain level and above, and require planning of assignments and the development of the incumbents of each job as well as their replacements. Senior level positions and high potentials are reviewed annually and approved by the CMRC. This includes the identification of people with high potential to fill the senior corporate positions. Developmental plans, compensation and all assignments are then approved by the CMRC for these people. The role of the CEO and other chief executives is prominent.

There are some persistent problems. Short-term business needs versus long-term developmental needs and the identification of potential seem to be manageable with special effort, time and financial resources. The difficulties caused by insufficient, long-term business and strategic planning can be alleviated with careful management attention. The emerging issues of the 80's and 90's need to be carefully studied and plans put in place to deal with them. This type of forecasting of emerging issues and contingency planning should be an integral part of the planning systems rather than waiting until the issues are upon us when only a reactive position can be taken.

In summary, applying to your own organization a careful planning and development process for your management resources is clearly an opportunity to make management talent a true competitive advantage.

James F. Bolt is director of Human Resource Planning and Development with Xerox Corporation, Stamford, Connecticut.

Part VI
LEADERSHIP IN TRANS-
FORMATION

41.
THE LEADERSHIP CHALLENGE—
A CALL FOR THE
TRANSFORMATIONAL LEADER

Noel M. Tichy
David O. Ulrich

Based on the premise that the pressure for basic organizational change will intensify and not diminish, tranformational leadership, not transactional management, is required for revitalizing our organizations. Ultimately, it is up to our leaders to choose the right kind of leadership and corporate lifestyle.

Some optimists are heralding in the age of higher productivity, a transition to a service economy, and a brighter competitive picture for U.S. corporations in world markets. We certainly would like to believe that the future will be brighter, but our temperament is more cautious. We feel that the years it took for most companies to get "fat and flabby" are not going to be reversed by a crash diet for one or two years. Whether we continue to gradually decline as a world competitive economy will largely be determined by the quality of leadership in the top echelons of our business and government organizations. Thus, it is our belief that now is the time for organizations to change their corporate lifestyles.

To revitalize organizations such as General Motors, American Telephone and Telegraph, General Electric, Honeywell, Ford, Burroughs, Chase Manhattan Bank, Citibank, U.S. Steel, Union Carbide, Texas Instruments, and Control Data—just to mention a few companies currently undergoing major transformations—a new brand of leadership is necessary. Instead of managers who continue to move along historical tracks, the new leaders must *transform* the organizations and head them down new tracks. What is required of this kind of leader is an ability to help the organization develop a vision of what it can be to mobilize the organization to accept and work toward achieving the new vision, and to institutionalize the changes that must last over time.

Unless the creation of this breed of leaders becomes a national agenda, we are not very optimistic about the revitalization of the U.S. economy.

We call these new leaders transformational leaders, for they must create something new out of something old: out of an old vision, they must develop and communicate a new vision and get others not only to see the vision but also to commit themselves to it. Where transactional managers make only minor adjustments in the organization's mission, structure, and human resources management, transformational leaders not only make major changes in these three areas but they also evoke fundamental changes in the basic political and cultural systems of the organization. The revamping of the political and cultural systems is what most distinguishes the transformational leader from the transactional one.

LEE IACOCCA: A TRANSFORMATIONAL LEADER

One of the most dramatic examples of transformational leadership and organizational revitalization in the early 1980s has been the leadership of Lee Iacocca, the chairman of Chrysler Corporation. He provided the leadership to transform a company from the brink of bankruptcy to profitability. He created a vision of success and mobilized large factions of key employees toward enacting that vision while simultaneously downsizing the workforce by 60,000 employees. As a result of Iacocca's leadership, by 1984 Chrysler had earned record profits, had attained high levels of employee morale, and had helped employees generate a sense of meaning in their work.

Until Lee Iacocca took over at Chrysler, the basic internal political structure had been unchanged for decades. It was clear who reaped what benefits from the organization, how the pie was to be divided, and who could exercise what power. Nonetheless, Mr. Iacocca knew he needed to alter these political traditions, starting with a new definition of Chrysler's link to external stakeholders. Therefore, the government was given a great deal of control over Chrysler in return for the guaranteed loan that staved off bankruptcy. Modification of the political system required adjustments, including the "trimming of fat" in the management ranks, limiting financial rewards for all employees, and receiving major concessions from the UAW. An indicator of a significant political shift was the inclusion of Douglas Frazer on the Chrysler Board of Directors as part of UAW concessions.

Equally dramatic was the change in the organization's cultural system. First, the company had to recognize its unique status as a recipient of a federal bailout. This bailout came with a stigma, thus Mr. Iacocca's job was to change the company's cultural values from a loser's to a winner's feeling. Still, he realized that employees were not going to be winners unless they could, in cultural norms, be more efficient and innovative than their competitors. The molding and shaping of the new culture was clearly and visibly led by Mr.

Iacocca, who not only used internal communication as a vehicle to signal change but also used his own personal appearance in Chrysler ads to reinforce these changes. Quickly, the internal culture was transformed to that of a lean and hungry team looking for victory. Whether Chrysler will be able to sustain this organizational phenomenon over time remains to be seen. If it does, it will provide a solid corporate example of what Burns referred to as a transforming leader. [1]

Lee Iacocca's high visibility and notoriety may be the important missing elements in management today: there seems to be a paucity of transformation leader role models at all levels of the organization.

ORGANIZATIONAL DYNAMICS OF CHANGE

Assumption One: Trigger Events Indicate Change Is Needed. Organizations do not change unless there is a trigger which indicates change is needed. This trigger can be as extreme as the Chrysler impending bankruptcy or as moderate as an abstract future-oriented fear that an organization may lose its competitiveness. For example, General Electric's trigger for change is a view that by 1990 the company will not be world competitive unless major changes occur in productivity, innovation, and marketing. Thus, Chairman Jack Welch sees his role as that of transforming GE even though it does not face imminent doom. Nonetheless, the trick for him is to activate the trigger; otherwise, complacency may prevail. Similarly, for AT&T, technological, competitive, and political forces have led it to undertake its massive transformation. For General Motors, economic factors of world competition, shifting consumer preferences, and technological change have driven it to change.

In a decade of increased information, international competition, and technological advances, triggers for change have become commonplace and very pressing. However, not all potential trigger events lead to organizational responses, and not all triggers lead to change. Nonetheless, the trigger must create a *felt* need in organizational leaders. Without this felt need, the "boiled frog phenomenon" is likely to occur.

The Boiled Frog. This phenomenon is based on a classic experiment in biology. A frog which is placed in a pan of cold water but which still has the freedom to jump out can be boiled if the temperature change is gradual, for it is not aware of the barely detectable changing heat threshold. In contrast, a frog dropped in a pot of boiling water will immediately jump out: it has a felt need to survive. In a similar vein, many organizations that are insensitive to gradually changing organizational thresholds are likely to become "boiled frogs"; they act in ignorant bliss of environmental triggers and eventually are doomed to failure. This failure, in part, is a result of the organization having no felt need to change.

Assumption Two: A Change Unleashes Mixed Feelings. A felt need for change unleashes a mix of forces, both a positive impetus for change as well as a strong negative individual and organizational resistance. These forces of resistance are generated in each of three interrelated systems—technical, political, cultural—which must be managed in the process of organizational transitions (see Table 1).[2] Individual and organizational resistance to change in these three systems must be overcome if an organization is to be revitalized.[3]

Table 1

A List of Technical, Political, and Cultural System Resistances

Technical System Resistances include:

Habit and inertia. Habit and inertia cause task-related resistance to change. Individuals, who have always done things one way may not be politically or culturally resistant to change, but may have trouble, for technical reasons, changing behavior patterns. Example: some office workers may have difficulty shifting from electric typewriters to word processors.

Fear of the unknown or loss of organizational predictability. Not knowing or difficulty in predicting the future creates anxiety and hence resistance in many individuals. Example: the introduction of automated office equipment has often been accompanied by such resistance.

Sunk costs. Organizations, even when realizing that there are potential payoffs from a change, are often unable to enact a change because of the sunk costs of the organizations' resources in the old way of doing things.

Political System Resistances include:

Powerful coalitions. A common threat is found in the conflict between the old guard and the new guard. One interpretation of the exit of Archie McGill, former president of the newly formed AT&T American Bell, is that the backlash of the old-guard coalition exacted its price on the leader of the new-guard coalition.

Resource limitations. In the days when the economic pie was steadily expanding and resources were much less limited, change was easier to enact as every party could gain—such was the nature of labor management agreements in the auto industry for decades. Now that the pie is shrinking decisions need to be made as to who shares a smaller set of resources. These zero-sum decisions are much more politically difficult. As more and more U.S. companies deal with productivity, downsizing, and divestiture, political resistance will be triggered.

Indictment quality of change. Perhaps the most significant resistance to change comes from leaders having to indict their own past decisions and behaviors to bring about a change. Example: Roger Smith, chairman and CEO of GM, must implicitly indict his own past behavior as a member of senior management when he suggests changes in GM's operations. Psychologically, it is very difficult for people to change when they were party to creating the problems they are trying to change. It is much easier for a leader from the outside, such as Lee Iacocca, who does not have to indict himself every time he says something is wrong with the organization.

Cultural System Resistances include:

Selective perception (cultural filters). An organization's culture may highlight certain elements of the organization, making it difficult for members to conceive of other ways of doing things. An organization's culture channels that which people perceive as possible, thus, innovation may come from outsiders or deviants who are not as channeled in their perceptions.

Security based on the past. Transition requires people to give up the old ways of doing things. There is security in the past, and one of the problems is getting people to overcome the tendency to want to return to the "good old days." Example: today, there are still significant members of the white-collar workforce at GM who are waiting for the "good old days" to return.

Lack of climate for change. Organizations often vary in their conduciveness to change. Cultures that require a great deal of conformity often lack much receptivity to change. Example: GM with its years of internally developed managers must overcome a limited climate for change.

Managing technical systems refers to managing the coordination of technology, capital, information, and people in order to produce products or services desired and used in the external marketplace. Managing political systems refers to managing the allocation of organizational rewards such as money, status, power, and career opportunities and to exercising power so employees and departments perceive equity and justice. Managing cultural systems refers to managing the set of shared values and norms which guides the behavior of members of the organization.

When a needed change is perceived by the organizational leaders, the dominant group in the organization must experience a dissatisfaction with the status quo. For example, in the late 1970s John DeButts, chairman and chief executive officer of AT&T, was not satisfied with the long-term viability of AT&T as a regulated telephone monopoly in the age of computers and satellite communication systems. Likewise, when Roger Smith became CEO at

General Motors in the early 1980s, he could hardly be satisfied with presiding over GM's first financial loss since the depression. In these two cases, the felt need provided the impetus for transition; yet, such impetus is not uniformly positive.

The technical, political, and cultural resistances are most evident during early stages of an organizational transformation. At GM the early 1980s were marked by tremendous uncertainty concerning many technical issues such as marketing strategy, production strategy, organization design, factory automation, and development of international management. Politically, many powerful coalitions were threatened. The UAW was forced to make wage concessions and accept staffing reductions. The white-collar workers saw their benefits being cut and witnessed major layoffs within the managerial ranks. Culturally, the once dominant managerial style no longer fit the environmental pressures for change: the "GM way" was no longer the right way.

One must be wary of these resistances to change as they can lead to organizational stagnation rather than revitalization. In fact, some managers at GM in late 1983 were waiting for "the good old days" to return. Such resistance exemplifies a dysfunctional reaction to the felt need. As indicated in Figure 1, a key to whether resistant forces will lead to little or inadequate change and hence organizational decline or revitalization lies in an organization's leadership. Defensive, transactional leadership will not rechannel the resistant forces. A case in point is International Harvester which appears to have had a defensive transactional leadership. Thus, in the early 1980s, International Harvester lacked a new vision which would inspire employees to engage in new behaviors. In contrast, Lee Iacocca has been a transformational leader at Chrysler by creating a vision, mobilizing employees, and working toward the institutionalization of Chrysler's transition.

Assumption Three: Quick-Fix Leadership Leads to Decline. Overcoming resistance to change requires transformational leadership, not defensive, transactional managers who are in search of the one minute quick fix. The transformational leader needs to avoid the trap of simple, quick-fix solutions to major organizational problems. Today, many versions of this quick-fix mentality abound: the book, *One Minute Manager*, has become a best seller in companies in need of basic transformation.[4] Likewise, *In Search of Excellence* has become a cookbook for change.[5] In fact, a number of CEOs have taken the eight characteristics of the "excellent" companies and are trying to blindly impose them on their organizations without first examining their appropriateness. For example, many faltering organizations try to copy such company practices as Hewlett-Packard's (HP) statement of company values. Because they read that HP has a clearly articulated statement of company values—the HP equivalent of the ten commandments—they want to create their list of ten commandments. The scenario which has been carried out in

Figure 1.
Transformational Leadership

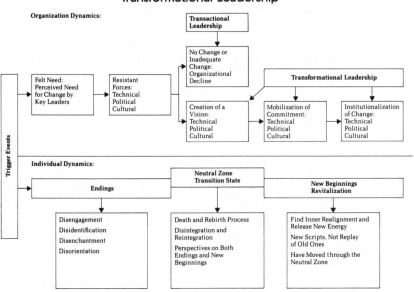

many major U.S. firms in the past year goes something like this: the CEO wants to develop the company value statement, so he organizes an off-site meeting in order to spend a couple of days developing the company XYZ corporate value statement. The session is usually quite enlightening—managers become quite thoughtful, and soul-searching takes place. At the end of the session, the group is able to list the XYZ company's "ten commandments." The CEO is delighted that they are now well on the way to major cultural change. He brings the ten commandments back to the corporation and calls in the staff to begin the communication program so that all company employees can learn the new cultural values. This about ends the transformational process.

The problem with the ten-commandments quick-fix is that the CEOs tend to overlook the lesson Moses learned several thousand years ago—namely, getting the ten commandments written down and communicated is the easy part; getting them implemented is the challenge. How many thousands of years has it been since Moses received the ten commandments, and yet today there still seems to be an implementation challenge. Transformational leadership is different from defensive, transactional leadership. Lee Iacocca did not have to read about what others did to find a recipe for his company's success.

Assumption Four: Revitalization Requires Transformational Leadership. There are three identifiable programs of activity associated with transformational leadership.

1. **Creation of a vision.** The transformational leader must provide the organization with a vision of a desired future state. While this task may be shared with other key members of the organization, the vision remains the core responsibility of the transformal leader. The leader needs to integrate analytic, creative, intuitive, and deductive thinking. Each leader must create a vision which gives direction to the organization while being congruent with the leader's and the organization's philosophy and style.

For example, in the early 1980s at GM, after several years of committee work and staff analysis, a vision of the future was drafted which included a mission statement and eight objectives for the company. This statement was the first articulation of a strategic vision for General Motors since Alfred Sloan's leadership. This new vision was developed consistently with the leadership philosophy and style of Roger Smith. Many people were involved in carefully assessing opportunities and constraints for General Motors. Meticulous staff work culminated in committee discussions to evoke agreement and commitment to the mission statement. Through this process a vision was created which paved the way for the next phases of the transformation at GM.

At Chrysler, Lee Iacocca developed a vision without committee work or heavy staff involvement. Instead, he relied more on his intuitive and directive leadership, philosophy, and style. Both GM and Chrysler ended up with a new vision because of transformational leaders proactively shaping a new organization mission and vision. The long-term challenge to organizational revitalization is not "how" the visions are created but the extent to which the visions correctly respond to environmental pressures and transition within the organization.

2. **Mobilization of Commitment.** Here, the organization, or at least a critical mass of it, accepts the new mission and vision and makes it happen. At General Motors, Roger Smith took his top 900 executives on a five-day retreat to share and discuss the vision. The event lasted five days not because it takes that long to share a one-paragraph mission statement and eight objectives, but because the process of evolving commitment and mobilizing support requires a great deal of dialogue and exchange. It should be noted that mobilization of commitment must go well beyond five-day retreats; nevertheless, it is in this phase that transformational leaders get deeper understanding of their *followers*. Maccoby acknowledges that leaders who guide organizations through revitalization are distinct from previous leaders and gamesmen who spearheaded managers to be winners in the growth days of the 1960s and early 1970s. Today Maccoby argues:

> The positive traits of the gamesman, enthusiasm, risk taking, meritocratic fairness, fit America in a period of unlimited economic growth, hunger for novelty, and an unquestioned career ethic. The negative traits of manipulation, seduction, and the perpetual adolescent need for adventure were always problems, causing distrust and unnecessary crises. The gamesman's daring, the willingness to innovate and take risks

are still needed. Companies that rely on conservative company men in finance to run technically based organizations (for example, auto and steel) lose the competitive edge. But unless their negative traits are transformed or controlled, even gifted gamesmen become liabilities as leaders in a new economic reality. A period of limited resources and cutbacks, when the team can no longer be controlled by the promise of more, and one person's gains may be another's loss, leadership with values of caring and integrity and a vision of self-development must create the trust that no one will be penalized for cooperation and that sacrifice as well as rewards are equitable.[6]

After transformational leaders create a vision and mobilize commitment, they must determine how to institutionalize the new mission and vision.

3. **Institutionalization of Change.** Organizations will not be revitalized unless new patterns of behavior within the organization are adopted. Transformational leaders need to transmit their vision into reality, their mission into action, their philosophy into practice. New realities, action, and practices must be shared throughout the organization. Alterations in communication, decision making, and problem-solving systems are tools through which transitions are shared so that visions become a reality. At a deeper level, institutionalization of change requires shaping and reinforcement of a new culture that fits with the revitalized organization. The human resource systems of selection, development, appraisal, and reward are major levers for institutionalizing change.

INDIVIDUAL DYNAMICS OF CHANGE

The previous section outlined requisite processes for organizational revitalization. Although organizational steps are necessary, they are not sufficient in creating and implementing change. In managing transitions, a more problematic set of forces which focuses on individual psychodynamics of change must be understood and managed. Major transitions unleash powerful conflicting forces in people. The change invokes simultaneous positive and negative personal feelings of fear and hope, anxiety and relief, pressure and stimulation, leaving the old and accepting a new direction, loss of meaning and new meaning, threat to self-esteem and new sense of value. The challenge for transformational leaders is to recognize these mixed emotions, act to help people move from negative to positive emotions, and mobilize and focus energy that is necessary for individual renewal and organizational revitalization.

Figure 1 provides a set of concepts for understanding the individual dynamics of transitions. The concepts, drawn from the work by Bridges, propose a three-phase process of individual change: first come endings, followed by neutral zones, and then new beginnings.[7] During each of these phases, an identifiable set of psychological tasks can be identified which individuals need to successfully complete in order to accept change.

THE THREE-PHASE PROCESS

Endings. All individual transitions start with endings. Endings must be accepted and understood before transitions can begin. Employees who refuse to accept the fact that traditional behaviors have ended will be unable to adopt new behaviors. The first task is to disengage which often accompanies a physical transaction. For example, when transferring from one job to another, individuals must learn to accept the new physical setting and disengage from the old position: when transferred employees continually return to visit former colleagues, this is a sign that they have inadequately disengaged. The second task is to disidentify. Individual self-identity is often tied to a job position in such a way that when a plant manager is transferred to corporate staff to work in the marketing department he or she must disidentify with the plant and its people and with the self-esteem felt as a plant manager. At a deeper personal level, individual transactions require disenchantment. Disenchantment entails recognizing that the enchantment or positive feelings associated with past situations will not be possible to replicate in the future. Chrysler, GM, AT&T, or U.S. Steel employees who remember the "good old days" need to become disenchanted with those feelings: the present reality is different and self-worth cannot be recaptured by longing for or thinking about the past. A new enchantment centered on new circumstances needs to be built. Finally, individuals need to experience and work through disorientation which reflects the loss of familiar trappings. As mature organizations become revitalized, individuals must disengage, disidentify, disenchant, and disorient with past practices and discover in new organizations a new sense of worth or value.

To help individuals cope with endings, transformational leaders need to replace past glories with future opportunities. However, leaders must also acknowledge individual resistances and senses of loss in a transitional period while encouraging employees to face and accept failures as learning opportunities. Holding on to past accomplishments and memories without coming to grips with failure and the need to change may be why companies such as W.T. Grant, International Harvester, and Braniff were unsuccessful at revitalization. There is a sense of dying in all endings, and it does not help to treat transactions as if the past can be buried without effort. Yet, one should see the past as providing new directions.

Neutral Zone. The key to individuals being able to fully change may be in the second phase which Bridges terms the neutral zone.[8] This phase can be interpreted as a seemingly unproductive "time out" when individuals feel disconnected from people and things of the past and emotionally unconnected with the present. In reality, this phase is a time of reorientation where individuals complete endings and begin new patterns of behavior. Often Western culture, especially in the U.S., avoids this experience and treats the neutral zone like a busy street, to be crossed as fast as possible and certainly not a place to contemplate and experience. However, running across the neutral zone too hurriedly does not allow the ending to occur nor the new beginning to properly start. A death and rebirth process is necessary so that organizational members can work through the disintegration and reintegration. To pass through the neutral zone requires taking the time and thought to gain perspective on both the ending—what went wrong, why it needs to be changed, and what must be overcome in both attitude and behavioral change—and the new beginning—what the new priorities are, why they are needed, and what new attitudes and behaviors will be required. It is in this phase that the most skillful transformational leadership is called upon.

A timid, bureaucratic leader who often reels in the good old days will not provide the needed support to help individuals cross through the neutral zone. On the other hand, the militaristic dictatorial leader who tries to force a "new beginning" and does not allow people to work through their own feelings and emotions may also fail to bring about change. The purported backlash toward the "brash" Archie McGill at American Bell in June 1983 may have been an example of trying to force people through the neutral zone in order to get to a new beginning. Archie McGill was know to rant and rave about the stodgy, old fashioned, and noninnovative "bell-shaped men" at AT&T. While he was trying to help and lead individuals to become innovative and marketing orientated, he may not have allowed them to accept the endings inherent in the transition. Although his enthusiasm may have been well placed, he may have lacked the sensitivity to individual endings and neutral phases of transactions.

Failure to lead individuals through the neutral zone may result in aborted new beginnings. In 1983, International Harvester appeared to be stuck in the neutral zone. In order for International Harvester to make a new beginning, it must enable people to find a new identification with the future organization while accepting the end of the old organization. Such a transformation has successfully occurred at Chrysler Corporation where morale and *esprit de corps* grew with the new vision implanted by Lee Iacocca. In the end, organizational revitalization can only occur if individuals accept past failures and engage in new behaviors and attitudes.

New Beginnings. After individuals accept endings by working through neutral zones, they are able to work with new enthusiasm and commitment. New beginnings are characterized by employees learning from the past rather than reveling in it, looking for new scripts rather than acting out old ones, and being positive and excited about current and future work opportunities rather than dwelling on past successes or failures. When Mr. Iacocca implemented his vision at Chrysler, many long-term employees discovered new beginnings. They saw the new Chrysler as an opportunity to succeed, and they worked with a renewed vigor.

WHAT QUALITIES DO TRANSFORMATIONAL LEADERS POSSESS?

So what does it take to transform an organization's technical, political, and cultural systems? The transformational leader must possess a deep understanding, whether it be intuitive or learned, of organizations and their place both in society at large and in the lives of individuals. The ability to build a new institution requires the kind of political dialogue our founding fathers had when Jefferson, Hamilton, Adams, and others debated issues of justice, equity, separation of powers, checks and balances, and freedom. This language may sound foreign to corporate settings but when major organization revitalization is being undertaken, all of these concepts merit some level of examination. At Chrysler, issues of equity, justice, power, and freedom underlay many of Mr. Iacocca's decisions. Thus, as a start, transformational leaders need to understand concepts of equity, power, freedom, and the dynamics of decision making. In addition to modifying systems, transformational leaders must understand and realign cultural systems.

In addition to managing political and cultural systems, transformational leaders must make difficult decisions quickly. Leaders need to know when to push and when to back off. Finally, transformational leaders are often seen as creators of their own luck. These leaders seize opportunities and know when to act so that casual observers may perceive luck as a plausible explanation for their success; whereas, in reality it is a transformational leader who knows when to jump and when not to jump. Again, Mr. Iacocca can be viewed either as a very lucky person or as the possessor of a great ability to judge when to act and when not to act.

THE SIGNIFICANCE OF CORPORATE CULTURE

Much has been written about organizational cultures in recent years.[9] We suggest that every organization has a culture, or a patterned set of activities that reflects the organization's underlying values. Cultures don't occur randomly. They occur because leaders spend time on and reward some behaviors and practices more than others. These practices become the foundation of the organization's culture. At HP, for example, Bill Hewlett and Dave Packard spent time wandering around, informally meeting with and talking to employees. Such leadership behavior set the HP cultural tone of caring about and listening to people. Similarly, Tom Watson, Sr., at IBM spent a great deal of time with customers. His practice led to a company culture of commitment to customers. Indeed, corporate cultures exist. Leaders can shape cultures by carefully monitoring where and how they spend their time and by encouraging and rewarding employees to behave in certain ways.

Culture plays two central roles in organizations. First, it provides organizational members with a way of understanding and making sense of events and symbols. Thus, when employees are confronted with certain complex problems, they "know" how to approach them the "right" way. Like the Eskimos who have a vocabulary that differentiates the five types of snow, organizations create vocabularies to describe how things are done in the organization. At IBM, it is very clear to all insiders how to form a task force and to solve problems since task forces and problem solving are a way of life in IBM's culture.

Second, culture provides meaning. It embodies a set of values which helps justify why certain behaviors are encouraged at the exclusion of other behaviors. Companies with strong cultures have been able to commit people to the organization and have them identify very personally and closely with the organization's success. Superficially, this is seen in the "hoopla" activities associated with an IBM sales meeting, a Tupperware party, or an Amway distributor meeting. Outsiders often ridicule such activities, yet they are part of the process by which some successful companies manage cultural meaning. On one level, corporate culture is analogous to rituals carried out in religious groups. The key point in assessing culture is to realize that in order to transform an organization the culture that provides meaning must be assessed and revamped. The transformational leader needs to articulate new values and norms and then to use multiple change levers ranging from role modeling, symbolic acts, creation of rituals, and revamping of human resource systems and management processes to support new cultural messages.

CONCLUSION

Based on the premise that the pressure for basic organizational change will intensify and not diminish, we strongly believe that transformational leadership, not transactional management, is required for revitalizing our organizations. Ultimately, it is up to our leaders to choose the right kind of leadership and corporate lifestyle.

REFERENCES

1. J. M. Burns, *Leadership* (New York: Harper & Row, 1978).
2. N. M. Tichy, *Managing Strategic Change: Technical, Political and Cultural Dynamics* (New York: John Wiley & Sons, 1983).
3. *Ibid.*
4. K. H. Blanchard and S. Johnson, *The One Minute Manager* (New York: Berkley Books, 1982).
5. T. J. Peters and R. J. Waterman, Jr., *In Search of Excellence* (New York: Harper & Row, 1982).

6. M. Maccoby, *The Leader* (New York: Ballantine Books, 1981).
7. W. Bridges, *Making Sense of Life's Transitions* (New York: Addision-Wesley, 1980).
8. *Ibid.*
9. T. E. Deal and A. A. Kennedy, *Corporate Cultures* (Reading, MA: Addison-Wesley, 1982); "Corporate Culture: The Hard-to-Change Values That Spell Success or Failure," *Business Week*, 27 October 1980, pp. 148-160; W. Ulrich, "HRM and Culture: History, Rituals, and Myths," *Human Resource Management* (23/2), Summer 1984.

Noel M. Tichy is professor of Organizational Behavior and Industrial Relations at the University of Michigan's Graduate School of Business Administration. He is the editor of the journal Human Resources Management. *Dr. David O. Ulrich is assistant professor of Organizational Behavior and Faculty Associate at the Institute for Social Research, the University of Michigan. He has a Ph.D. degree from the University of California, Los Angeles.*

42.
STRATEGIES FOR SUCCESSFUL LEADERSHIP IN CHANGING TIMES

Michael Bisesi

> Less control, more flexibility, and greater attention to people in the organization and to the environment outside the organization may be the keys to successful leadership.

Leadership is one of those nagging ideals that frequently defy definition. People play leadership roles, regardless of their official position or titles, in groups, organizations, and nations. What makes the elusive "leadership" role all the more critical is the changing, unpredictable environment in which we live. Tomorrow's leaders, and those who aspire to leadership, must, therefore, become comfortable with the volatile, uncertain times, must be willing to acquire and develop skills that may not make an overt impact on the bottom line, and must promote career development activities for themselves and others.

For the moment, consider James MacGregor Burns's definition: "Leadership over human beings is exercised when persons with certain motives and purposes mobilize, in competition or conflict with others, institutional, political, psychological, and other resources so as to arouse, engage, and satisfy the motives of followers."[1] In light of this definition, leadership does not exist without followership, and is dependent on a setting that promotes growth and development. The key here is the active relationship in which leaders muster resources to accomplish objectives through, and for, other people. The success of this mobilization effort will depend, first of all, on the leader's ability to understand and accept uncertainty.

CHANGING CONDITIONS

We are often guilty of "frozen evaluation." Once we have found cozy niches for people, organizations, or societies, we fix those descriptions in our minds as immutable reference points. But we are not permitted that satisfaction for very long. Irresistible forces are continuously transforming our lives, ranging from the development of information as a strategic resource to the evolution of a global economy to the decentralization and deinstitutionalization of American life. More people are rejecting the "one life/one-career" concept and are beginning to see their lives as a series of stages. The contradictions that are inherent in a simultaneous desire for a strong economy and expanded social service programs have finally caught up with us, suggesting that our dreams for the future must be tempered by an acceptance of limits. The United States has become highly regionalized, as illustrated by the "Frostbelt-Sunbelt" debate in Congress that has been fueled by the population shifts of the last decade. It is also clear that unemployment in the upper Midwest is tied to an active Japanese export policy; that American farm income is related to Soviet weather; that driving one's car or heating one's home may depend on the political stability of a desert kingdom; and that European war might have started because of a labor union in Poland. The "American Century" is fast waning, and the "global village," though hardly unified, is a reality.

WHAT MAKES A SUCCESSFUL LEADER?

In the face of uncertainty, we all have a natural desire to tame the environment or to control its impact on us. We may lobby for protectionist trade laws, we may try to tighten financial controls, or we may attempt to monitor the behavior or employees. But, quite frankly, we often move in the wrong direction. We sometimes mistake tools of decision making (particularly technological ones) as tools of salvation. We frequently enhance the "hardware" of our organizations—physical plant, computers, public image—when we should be bolstering the "software"—people.

The prescription for a leader who wants to be successful must have two main ingredients: he or she must view an organization as part of a total system; and he or she must cultivate people as the most important resource of the organization.

THE ORGANIZATION AS PART OF A TOTAL SYSTEM

If "no man is an island," then no organization is autonomous. Organizations are part of a large environment that interact with elements of that environment and that are composed of people from the environment who belong to other groups and organizations. An organization must thus be willing and able to ask what business it is in. If, however, the question is asked at all, it is usually only in lip service to strategic planning. For this reason, a leader must be willing to ask what is going on, either through regular sessions with peers and subordinates or through periodic off-site retreats.

But all of this means nothing unless the leader recognizes the most important element of an organization—that is, its people. Without followership, there is no leadership. And without people, there is no organization.

PEOPLE AS THE MOST IMPORTANT RESOURCE

This is *not* a soft-hearted plea, but an argument for a hard and practical approach to cultivate people. It must be recognized that leaders have a responsibility to their followers and that productivity is directly tied to a leader's relationship to his or her followers.

No one knows a job better than the person who performs it, but no one knows how and why that job fits into the overall scheme of things better than the leader. Unfortunately, few organizations make a concerted effort to explain how different jobs contribute to the total effort, which usually results in dysfunctional consequences. Orientation sessions often concentrate on health insurance and other benefits, with a little corporate history thrown in merely for show. Staff development, in-service training, and other updating activities vary widely in quality and quantity. Nevertheless, an effective leader is one who helps people understand how their work contributes to the objectives of the total organization. New employees should be shown how their jobs contribute to their unit and to the total organization. Training and development programs should focus on changes in the organization and the environment, and should reinforce the employee's role in the productivity of the organization.

THE CHARACTERISTICS OF AN EFFECTIVE LEADER

Groups within organizations often compete for attention and resources. A leader must be willing to negotiate, often through informal networks that do not appear on any organizational chart, to get individuals and groups to accomplish goals. This may mean encouraging employees to seek novel ways of completing tasks, particularly in nonroutine situations.

A leader must have a heightened sense of corporate social responsibility. In other words, whether an organization is a closely held corporation or a government agency, it is part of the larger society. A leader therefore must not be afraid to say "no" when "yes" (or no response) would be so much easier, particularly in a case involving the kind of sexual prejudice that was displayed in the fabled Mary Cunningham episode.

A leader must also be willing to give up some authority. Many organizations have instituted "quality circles" or employee involvement groups. Although this process may cause some short-term discomfort among middle managers, it will empower employees to be more productive. In any case, the key is both to redirect leadership in order to mobilize people to accomplish organizational objectives and to help people attain their own goals in the workplace. (This last point is an important element in the Burns definition of leadership.)

Finally, a leader must take greater responsibility for the career development of his or her people. He or she must recognize that successful work is accomplished when there is a match between the requirements of the job and the talents of the individual. Thus, a leader must be willing to "let go" of valuable staff members who have outgrown their jobs. A successful career as a leader can be assured to those who recognize that their own success depends on the success of their employees.

CONCLUSION

The rate of social change, the volatility of technological innovation, and the instability of political governance all contribute to doubts about the future. Nevertheless, successful leaders must ultimately take responsibility for their own development and the development of their people and organizations in the following ways:

Learn more about people and how they work in groups and organizations. It is always interesting to observe that financial administration is a relatively high status unit in most organizations and that personnel administration (including training and development) is usually a low-status one. Yet the ability of people to work effectively with one another will determine the success or failure of the organization. This is not to suggest investing in "sensitivity training." Rather, it is to suggest spending some time studying task-oriented behavioral sciences and other disciplines that probably do not appear in the financial reports. Leaders must recognize that motivation, group dynamics, and interpersonal communication make a significant difference in the assessment of profit or loss.

Talk with people about their careers. Leaders are obliged to know if their employees are properly matched with the requirements of their jobs. They also have an obligation to recognize when people have grown out of particular positions. Thus, performance appraisal should be as much a discussion of a person's next job as it is an assessment of how he or she is doing in the current role. If a person has exploited all the possibilities of the current position, the leader should either expand the scope of the job or help the person move on to a more challenging position.

Hire broadly educated people. Regardless of the position, the more people know, the more they will contribute to the organization. Broadly educated people with diverse interests will contribute a great deal. Organizations have a compelling need for flexible people who are qualified to move beyond entry-level jobs. Hiring practices, however, often emphasize technical skills to the exclusion of all else. James O'Toole argues that:

> People who are vocationally trained to unquestioningly perform a single task are manifestly unprepared to design their own work, participate in decision-making, assume control over their own working conditions, work as members of a community of equals, or take responsibility for the quality of their own work when a boss is not looking over their shoulders. Like narrowly trained managers, these workers feel easily threatened by change and act defensively, inflexibly, and in ways society deems irresponsible when circumstances require them to adapt.[2]

Leaders who make or influence hiring decisions should take stock of their priorities. Deemphasizing BBAs is one possible approach that makes a great deal of sense. Another approach is to take a second look at the undergraduate preparation of MBAs. Almost *any* bachelor's degree, combined with an MBA that emphasizes flexibility and organizational behavior, is preferable to a BBA-MBA combination. Medical schools welcome nonscience majors (as long as they meet the science requirements). Law schools do not encourage undergraduate "law" courses. The American Assembly of Collegiate Schools of Business and graduate schools of business should likewise encourage broader preparation in MBA admission requirements, which ultimately may make the hiring of broadly educated people an easier task.

Don't become obsolete—or worse, dull. Since successful leaders often have the characteristics of good teachers, one should remember that successful teachers are also lifelong learners. A college degree is just an introduction to a continuing professional education. Beyond the obvious methods of reading professional journals and attending professional meetings, leaders should also stretch beyond the confines of their businesses. They should attend people-oriented conferences and read a diversity of nonbusiness periodicals to help put the world in a new perspective.

Keep a low profile. Everyone has a complex combination of motives for working, and Burns's definition of leadership suggests that leaders who capitalize on employee motives will be ahead of the game. But people who aspire to leadership often have well-developed egos, and consequently like to let people know who is in charge. However, the leader who may be the most successful is the one described by Lao-tzu and reported by Michael Maccoby in *The Leader*:

> The best of all leaders is the one who helps people so that eventually they don't need him.

Then comes the one they love and admire.

Then comes the one they fear.

The worst is the one who lets people push him around.

Where there is no trust, people will act in bad faith.

The best leader doesn't say much, but what he says carries weight.

When he is finished with his work, the people say, "It happened naturally."[3]

REFERENCES

1. J. M. Burns, *Leadership* (New York: Harper Colophon Books, 1978), p. 18.
2. J. O'Toole, *Making America Work: Productivity and Responsibility* (New York: Continuum, 1981), p. 182.
3. M. Maccoby, *The Leader: A New Face for American Management* (New York: Simon and Schuster, 1981), p. 11.

ADDITIONAL SOURCES

T. E. Deal and A. A. Kennedy, *Corporate Cultures: The Rites and Rituals of Corporate Life* (Reading, MA: Addison-Wesley, 1982).

P. Drucker, *The Changing World of the Executive* (New York: Truman Talley/Times Books, 1982).

J. Garreau, *The Nine Nations of North America* (Boston: Houghton Mifflin, 1981).

R.E. Kaplan and M. Mazique, *The Manager's Network of Relationships* (Greensboro, NC: Center for Creative Leadership, 1983).

J. Kotter, *The General Managers* (New York: The Free Press, 1982).

H. Levinson, *Executive* (Cambridge, MA: Harvard University Press, 1981).

M.W. McCall, Jr., *Leadership and the Professional* (Greensboro, NC: Center for Creative Leadership, 1981).

J. Naisbitt, *Megatrends: Ten Directions Transforming Our Lives* (New York: Warner, 1982).

W. Ouchi, *Theory Z: How American Business Can Meet the Japanese Challenge* (Reading, MA: Addison-Wesley, 1982).

E. H. Schein, *Career Dynamics* (Reading, MA: Addison-Wesley, 1978).

D. Yankelovich, *New Rules: Searching for Self-Fulfillment in a World Turned Upside Down* (New York: Random House, 1981).

43.
LEADERSHIP IN
A DECLINING WORK ETHIC

Ann Howard
James A. Wilson

The first to lead others may soon be rekindled under a reformulated ethos, but the legacy of these shifting values in our culture may be a firm warning that corporations and organizations in general can no longer take employees' loyalty and involvement for granted.

In the last decade, as the baby boom generation entered adulthood, one fact has emerged. This post-war generation, born in the joy of victory and a surge of unprecedented affluence, represents a sharp change in the social fabric of American life. In stark contrast to the overly ambitious hopes of their parents, the baby boomers are less motivated toward success, less optimistic, and certainly less committed to the large institutions that make up this society than any previous generation of Americans.

Nowhere does this sharp break with traditional values cause more consternation than in the U.S. corporate world, which built its strength on competition and on the Horatio Alger myth of personal success through the scramble for leadership. As the baby boom generation meets the corporation, one wonders. Is this the proverbial clash of irresistible force and immovable object? Will the corporation change to accommodate these young people weaned on immediate gratification and wedded to notions of rampant individualism, or are these youngsters in anomie simply aliens passing through without leaving a mark on the corporation? Will a renewed emphasis on participative management engage the hearts and minds of these disaffected young people or will the team approach simply hasten the demise of the work ethic? Can organizations negotiate a safe journey through the turbulent times ahead if leadership falls to those who would rather not lead?

HARD DATA FROM AT&T

In the late 1970s the American Telephone and Telegraph Company began its second major longitudinal study of managers, eager to see if new college graduates entering the management work force of the Bell System's twenty-three operating companies were comparable to a similar group of twenty years before. Ability measures used in the study brought good news: the new generation did indeed match the former managerial group. But when it came to measures of motivation, the research data delivered a formidable shock. By and large the new recruits were inclined neither to push their way up the organizational hierarchy nor to lead others. In short, the new managers weren't motivated to act like managers.

The data producing these startling conclusions were extensive and comprehensive. The original longitudinal study of managers, the Management Progress Study (MPS), was initiated at AT&T in 1956 by Dr. Douglas W. Bray, who continues to direct it as the participants crest middle age and prepare for retirement. The second project, the Management Continuity Study (MCS), which Bray and the senior author of this article began in 1977, was designed to parallel the college graduate subsample of MPS as closely as possible. Participants in both studies constituted those newly hired into first level general management jobs.

The MPS sample was selected from six Bell operating companies; the average age was twenty-four. The later MCS group came from a broader range of thirteen telephone companies, and the average age was twenty-five. The new sample was better educated; forty-five percent had attempted post-graduate training compared with only eleven percent of the previous cohort. The two hundred seventy-four participants in the earlier study were all white males, but by the time of the new study, the management population was more diverse, including other race groups and females. Consequently, of the two hundred four participants in the MCS sample, one-half were women and one-third minorities, a reflection of the hiring mix in the Bell companies.

For both longitudinal studies, data collection began with three days at an assessment center. Participants were evaluated by a team of assessors after completing a variety of exercises, including ability tests, personality, motivation and attitude questionnaires, simulations and group discussions, and interviews and projective techniques. For both samples, the assessors were psychologists from both inside and outside the Bell System. Three of the eight assessors employed each year were the same as for the MPS group (assess 1956-1960) and the MCS group (assessed 1977-1979), and efforts were made to keep standards identical across both samples.

Narrative reports and quantitative results of the assessment process were read aloud at staff integration sessions, and the assessors rated each participant on twenty-six dimensions that were considered critical to managerial ability and motivation. In addition, predictions were made as to whether each assessee had the potential for middle management and whether he or she could be expected to remain with the Bell System for a normal career life. Follow-ups have included a number of interviews with participants and their bosses and two three-day reassessments eight and twenty years later for the original MPS men.

The two samples were not dissimilar in all aspects of motivation. In what might be called motivation for accomplishment, they were remarkably alike. For example, on the Edwards Personal Preference Schedule (a forced-choice questionnaire based on Henry Murray's "needs") scale measuring "need for achievement," both groups were similar in their preferences for goals such as accomplishing something of great significance or doing a difficult job well. The focus in the scale is on mastery of challenging tasks, with no assumptions about extrinsic or accompanying rewards like money or promotions. A comparison of the two samples showed no significant differences in average score on this scale; the MPS (1950s) participants scored at the sixty-second percentile and the MCS (1970s) at the sixtieth of 1958 Bell System college recruit norms.

After the assessment staff heard all data regarding motivation for accomplishment, they rated assessees on the dimension "inner work standards," the extent to which the individual would want to do a good job even if a less good one were acceptable to the boss and others. Here, too, there was no difference in average rating between the two cohorts. To the extent that performance on management jobs provides challenge and a sense of accomplishment, the new group of recruits should be as motivated to perform well as the former. Yet is is important not to be misled by the willingness of the young people to "work hard," for, as we shall see, their reasons for doing so differ from those that operated in the past.

Moreover, high standards for task accomplishment, while essential for the technical specialist, may not be as critical for the general manager. What differentiates the manager is that he or she is expected to rise to higher and higher levels within the company, directing others and taking the broad view of the organization, rather than focusing on individual task goals. On exercises designed to measure the desire to advance oneself, however, the 1970s recruits showed a disappointing lack of interest.

One of these exercises was a short questionnaire measuring desires for upward mobility or motivation toward powerful, high status and well paying positions. As the left side of Figure 1. illustrates, the average score for the 1950s MPS participants on the questionnaire was at the fifty-second percentile; twenty years later the MCS average was at the twenty-ninth percentile of the same MPS norms, a statistically significant difference. The 1970s participants scored significantly lower than those of the 1950s on all the advancement items in the questionnaire as well as on half the general and money-related items. Although the new recruits seemed to be motivated internally toward task accomplishment, if the challenge they seek in their work is not readily available, it is unlikely that money or advancement opportunities will inspire their work efforts.

Figure 1.

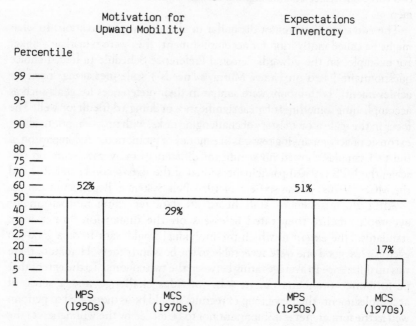

Career Orientation
Average Score

| Motivation for Upward Mobility | Expectations Inventory |

Percentile

MPS college norms N=274 group differences p <.001

This seeming apathy toward climbing the corporate ladder was matched by a decline in the new recruits' expectation level. In an expectations inventory, the recruits were asked to speculate five years ahead and indicate what they foresaw for a variety of situations. The items concerned not only advancement and salary but more generalized aspects of managerial life, such as intellectual stimulation from peers, access to company information and resources, and geographic desirability of work location.

The average MCS (1970s) score, shown on the right-hand side of Figure 1., was only at the seventeenth percentile of the 1950s MPS norms. In fairness, this score should not be interpreted as unbridled negativism toward the corporation but rather a dampened optimism toward many aspects of work life. The questionnaire explored beliefs or attitudes and the participants in one or both samples could be misreading the system. Alternatively, they could have been moved to provide "socially acceptable" responses, acceptable for their own times.

But for whatever reasons, the new recruits indicated beliefs that the future has less to offer. For example, while sixty percent of the 1950s sample strongly affirmed that in five years they would hold a challenging job with the opportunity to learn and accomplish new things, only forty-five percent of the 1970s group were this positive. Of the expectation that the company would make a strong effort to furnish all the resources needed to do a good job, fifty-eight percent of the 1950s group were strongly positive compared to only twenty-seven percent of the latter group. Even with respect to building deep friendships with at least two or three work associates, seventy-five percent of the last generation had the highest expectations compared to only forty-six of the current one.

When asked to list which of the expectations inventory items they most wanted to be true, about the same proportion of MCS and MPS participants claimed they wanted a challenging job and one that would pay at least a middle manager's salary. But fifty-four percent of the 1950s sample also chose advancing to middle management as something they most wanted, while only thirty-four percent of the latter sample chose that item. Clearly, the new generation doesn't want as much from a managerial career and doesn't expect as much.

Other assessment center exercises confirmed the generational differences in motivation. Projective techniques, including two incomplete sentence tests and stories written to six Thematic Apperception Test (TAT) cards, revealed that while the newest recruits were as directed as the former toward individual task accomplishment, they were less concerned about personal advancement. Personal interviews also revealed negativism toward advancement. Illustrative was the comment, "The higher you go up in management, the more time you have to put in your work. I plan to do my job the best I can, but my loyalty is to my family."

Interview comments revealed less commitment to a business career as such, which is, perhaps, consistent with the less favorable responses to the expectations inventory. Many of the new recruits expressed their intention to return to graduate school, thus implying that neither their formal education nor their career plans were as yet final. One, explaining his reluctance to form a close allegiance with a large organization, said, "I want to lead a life style that isn't all work." He claimed he would secretly "like to be an actor or an artist."

Any comparison of the MPS and MCS participants should, of course, take into account the impact of race and sex differences within the MCS sample. With respect to task accomplishment, career advancement, and expectations, sex differences were negligible and not statistically significant. The only meaningful difference here was that more women were expecting to leave the company voluntarily since they anticipated career/family conflicts in the years to come. The minorities scored significantly higher than whites in advancement motivation and expectations. But interview information, as well as an examination of the relevant items in the questionnaire measure of upward mobility, revealed that the primary motivation of the minority group was not for the power or challenge associated with advancement, but to gain financial rewards. Flagging ambitions were somewhat more a white phenomenon than a minority trait, and a comparison of whites alone across the two generations signalled even greater disparities.

Advancement in a managerial career nearly always results in assuming leadership responsibilities and directing others in the organization. A hierarchical organizational structure requires that fewer and fewer managers at higher levels be accountable for greater and greater numbers of managers and workers at lower levels. It is imperative that an upwardly mobile manager appreciate, respond to, and indeed thrive on leadership responsibilities.

One measure of the motivation toward leadership comes from the "dominance" scale of the Edwards Personal Preference Schedule. Respondents indicate on this scale their preferences for such activities as leading and directing others, assuming leadership of groups to which they belong, and persuading and influencing others to follow their wishes. As shown in Figure 2, the MCS (1970s) managers were much less favorably inclined toward these items than were the MPS (1950s) managers, producing an average score at only the twenty-second percentile compared to the forty-ninth percentile for their predecessors. The females were partially responsible for this downward shift, as they scored significantly lower than the males, but that was only a small part of

Figure 2.

Average Score on Dominance

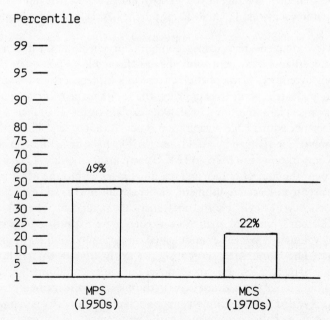

Edwards personal preference schedule. 1958 Bell system college recruit norms N=585 group differences p <.001

the difference. The average "dominance" score for the MCS males was only at the twenty-eighth percentile, still markedly lower than the scores of their MPS counterparts. Race differences on the scale were not significant.

The desire to lead and direct others expressed on the dominance scale should not be construed as a predilection for an authoritarian, rule-oriented, inflexible use of power. In fact, on a revised version of the California F-scale measuring authoritarianism, the MCS recruits were not any less rigid or dogmatic than their peers of the previous generation. The new managers appear to reject leadership roles regardless of leadership style.

Their rejection of leadership does not necessarily imply a preference for followership. On the Edwards scale of "deference," indicating a tendency to follow instructions, follow others, and defer to if not revere those in higher positions, the MCS (1970s) managers also scored lower than their MPS (1950s) counterparts, although this difference was not quite statistically significant, primarily because the minority males were more deferent than others in the group. More convincing evidence of the lack of deference came from the interviews and projective tests, so that the rating of the assessors on the dimension "need for superior approval," shown in Table 1, showed a marked discrepancy between the two generations.

Table 1.

Followership: Assessment Dimension,
Need for Superior Approval

	MPS (1950s)	MCS (1970s)
High	68%	37%
Moderate	21%	39%
Low	11%	24%
	100%	100%
N	274%	204%

Group Differences p < .004

While sixty-eight percent of the MPS participants had been rated high on this dimension, only thrity-seven percent of the MCS participants were judged this way, with no significant race or sex differences. Said one participant, describing his reluctant acceptance of the subordinate role, "People with authority often earn it with time rather than ability. My ambition is to never have a company, government, or person capture my soul and spirit because of financial shackles."

The organizational hierarchy seems to have been attacked from both flanks. The new managers neither aspire to higher-level jobs nor defer to those who have them. To paraphrase Shakespeare's Polonius, the philosophy of this generation might be "Neither a follower nor a leader be." This evidence does not clearly indicate what these young managers do want. Since the Edwards test is a forced-choice questionnaire, less desire for some scales is necessarily counterbalanced by stronger desire for others. The two scales that are notably higher for the new managers both relate to emotional support. Providing such support is the content domain of the "nurturance" scale, shown on the left side of Figure 3.

Items refer to assisting others less fortunate, treating others with kindness and sympathy, or being generous with others. The MCS (1970s) recruits scored significantly higher than MPS (1950s) on this scale; their average was at the seventy-fourth percentile compared to the forty-ninth for the previous generation. Race and sex differences were inconsistent, since among whites the males scored slightly higher and among minorities the females scored higher.

The new managers apparently want to receive as well as to give emotional support. This is reflected in the Edwards "succorance" scale, shown on the right side of Figure 3. Scale items reflect wanting others to offer help when in

Figure 3.

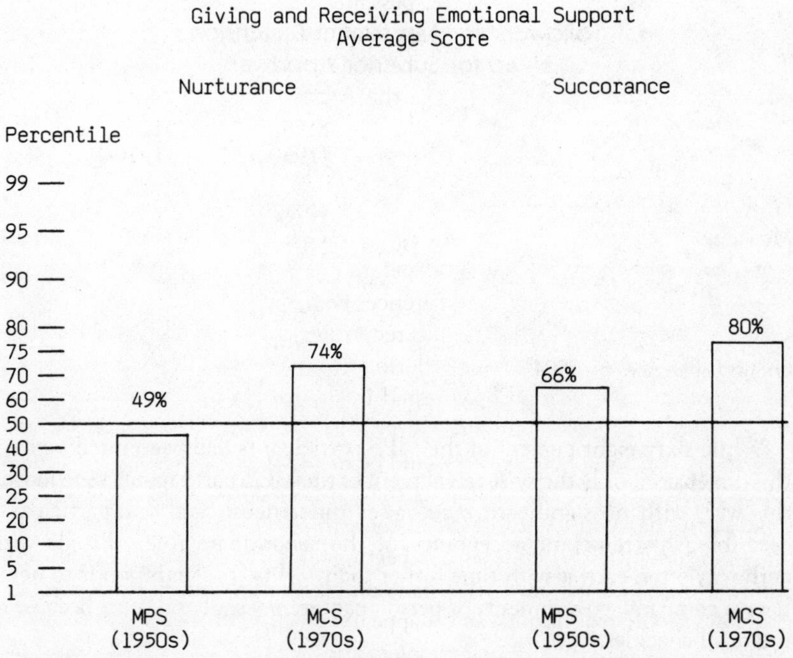

Giving and Receiving Emotional Support
Average Score

Nurturance   Succorance

Percentile

```
99 —

95 —

90 —

80 —                                                80%
75 —              74%
70 —                                     66%
60 —    49%
50 ————————————————————————————————————————————
40 —
30 —
25 —
20 —
10 —
 5 —
 1 ——————————————————————————————————————————————
      MPS        MCS          MPS        MCS
    (1950s)    (1970s)      (1950s)    (1970s)
```

Edwards personal preference schedule. 1958 Bell System college recruit norms N=585 group difference p < .001

trouble, seeking encouragement from others and gaining their sympathy and understanding for personal problems. Again, the 1970s managers scored high compared to those in the past, their average score topping the eightieth percentile compared to an average score at the sixty-sixth percentile for the 1950s group. There were no race differences but a small significant sex difference; still, the MCS males logged in an average score at the seventy-sixth percentile, a significant increase over the previous group of males.

Those who view business executives as cold-hearted, status-oriented, impersonal machines will no doubt rejoice at this apparent shift toward humanism. These new managers may reject the exercise of authority and offer their subordinates instead an atmosphere of collegial sharing of emotions and feelings that will lead to the release of spontaneous creativity. But a practical organization with goals of efficient production and service might well wonder if these young managers will occupy themselves with the personal problems of their subordinates to the neglect of legitimate business concerns. Moreover, the aura of pessimism that pervades the responses of the recruits suggests that their embrace of emotional supportiveness may be more a cry of anguish than a business goal that they seek on the basis of moral principles.

One reading of these data could be that a dispirited new generation of managers, unsure of future direction, wants primarily an interesting job and emotional sustenance from peers, with no heavy commitment to the organization. With little desire to advance, pessimism about organizational rewards, little inclination to assume leadership and equal disdain for following others, these new college graduates may not be well suited to managing a large, traditional, hierarchical organization like the current Bell System.

THE CULTURE BEYOND

In looking at these two widely disparate groups of Bell System employees, one must question whether the differences between the two groups were not a function of the Bell System itself—its recruiting practices over the years or the type of college graduate it attracted during the 1950s and the 1970s. Though it may be true that those most interested in power and quick business success would probably choose individual ventures rather than a large corporation, there is no reason to believe this would be more true in the 1970s than in the 1950s. Moreover, the Bell System of the 1950s had something of a homelike small town character in its individual companies not present today, when the corporation's monopoly status has been challenged and it is learning to compete in world markets. Thus, noncompetitive, security-oriented college graduates should have found it more appealing in the past than in the present.

To find out whether similar problems are being experienced elsewhere, AT&T researchers have invited other organizations to participate in an inter-business testing study. Although the data are just beginning to come in, the initial results show a similar pattern of differences between younger and older managers. In the meantime, other evidence also suggests that the MCS findings reflect a trend broader than the experience of just one corporate entity.

In 1974, Dr. John Miner predicted a shortage of individuals with the personality traits needed to manage large hierarchical, bureaucratic organizations.[1] He based his predictions on responses from college students, usually those in undergraduate business courses, using the Miner Sentence Completion Scale. This projective instrument is predicated on the notion that certain motivational patterns should match up with the role prescriptions of hierarchical organizations. These motivations include a favorable attitude toward people in authority positions and the desire to complete, to exercise power over others, to assert oneself, to stand out from a group, and to perform routine administrative duties responsibly.

Data using the Miner scale have now been extended to more than twenty-five different samples, geographically dispersed and traversing a period of twenty years from 1960 to 1980.[2] A decline in scores first appeared in 1962 or 1963 with younger students and continued for a period of ten years. Scores remained at this plateau until 1980, with the average student responding negatively to managerial cues more often than positively. Female students, though originally significantly below the males, dropped relatively less over time, so that in 1980 the two sexes were indistinguishable in terms of their managerial motivation—they were equally low.

The thrust of the results with the Miner Scale not only confirms the Bell findings in a much broader context, but suggests the problem may have manifested itself in new management recruits before 1977 had such characteristics been explored. The combination of the two sets of results suggest potential problems for business with respect to leadership in the coming years.

The declining desire to manage is no doubt related to the emergence of a new breed of workers described recently by the survey firm of Yankelovich, Skelly and White.[3] Their research points to a declining work ethic in which loyalty to the organization has been replaced by loyalty to the self, where concern for work has been superseded by concern for leisure, and identification with a work role has devolved to preoccupation with individual needs and pleasures. Respect for authority and a belief in the importance of rules, once taken for granted in the corporate setting, are increasingly drowned in a pool of skepticism and cynicism. The firm's survey results also indicate a challenge to the time-honored reward system of work. Belief in meritocracy has been upstaged by a psychology of entitlements, so that rewards are no longer reserved for the deserving. In the current value system, such things as a good job, health care, and a secure retirement are considered inalienable rights. As government guarantees of financial subsistence plus two-paycheck families mitigate the threat of job loss, traditional penalties for poor performance become impotent. Money is less a symbol of success than a facilitator of one's leisure activities and personal life style. Present sacrifice and hard work as a means to later rewards is now thought to be foolish; immediate gratification and living for today set the style. Goals in life are described subjectively in terms of fulfilling one's own potential with little respect for the outward manifestations of success, such as money or social and organizational status.

Other accounts in the popular literature bolster these findings and impressions. A survey of *Esquire* readers in 1979 found that men under thirty wanted more time for what they called "personal growth," though they did not want to work hard.[4] They aspired to a life perfectly balanced between love, leisure, and personal expression; they rejected ambition and effective leadership skills as important values in life. The most negative prospect to these men was to follow their father's footsteps in a pattern of early marriage, family responsibilities, and long years on a narrow corporate track in hope of some later rewards.

About the same time, *Technology Review* reported that MBAs at even the most prestigious schools placed a premium on individual values,[5] and *U. S. News and World Report* noted that money and power were losing favor as motivators at work.[6] In 1980 *Fortune*, in a report of new high potential twenty-five-year-olds in business, found them arrogantly confident that they would rise to high places.[7] To these young achievers, business was a quick means to gratify frankly materialistic requirements. The group considered corporate loyalty a misfortune suffered by their parents and many sought to begin their own businesses in their early thirties. This, they believed, would best help them realize their goals of self-actualization, autonomy, and freedom from monetary worries.

It appears that many young people today are encapsulated in the notion of privatism, avoiding involvement in anything beyond their immediate interests. Since they believe their "real life" begins after work hours, there is sometimes painful fragmentation between work and leisure. If work is not life, then commitment to the institution providing work seems ill considered.

The corporation is not the only institution spurned by the value system of the emerging young adult population. Church, family, the political arena, government, and military all come in for well-aimed scorn as they face challenges to their authority and increasing skepticism about the institution's ability to solve society's problems and offer hope for the future. They, too, detect a flowering of narcissism among the "Me Generation," a crisis of authority, and an age of cynics.

The signs of value change and discontent extend beyond U.S. borders. Recently, youth in Switzerland pressed their demands for a youth center by raining destruction on the Bahnhofstrasse. As reported in *New York Times Magazine*, this "movement of the discontented" rebelled against conformity, materialism, militarism, and male chauvinism.[8] Though fiercely critical of older values and "bourgeois ambition," their own values and motivations were unclear and nebulous except for the certainty that they did not want to waste themselves in hard work. A problem for the authorities in dealing with them was that their motto was "No leaders"—there were no spokespersons or structure with whom to negotiate.

These various accounts of new values share common themes: pervasive cynicism, self-righteous individualism, and condemnation of the values of the previous generation. One must conclude that sometime between the days of the MPS recruitment (1950-1960) and that of MCS (1977-1979), the cultural environment, especially values, shifted sharply. We assume that the characteristics of the Bell System's new managers, described previously, are not substantively different from those of new managers elsewhere in large U. S. organizations; all seem to be cut from the same cloth.

HISTORICAL DEVELOPMENTS

The causes of cultural change dwell somewhere in the realm of theory. Explanations are merely speculations, but the effort can allay the discomforts of ignorance. Writers indulge in the art of clarifying what seems illogical by reordering history to their own ends. We, too, will indulge.

Most historians, economists, writers, social critics, and others attempting to explain the source of the new values begin with the post-World War II period. Up until that time, dating at least from the Reformation, the dominant value scheme in Western civilization was what Max Weber called the "Protestant work ethic." Religious in basis, the Protestant work ethic equated hard work and self-denial with walking in the paths of righteousness. The Calvinists, in fact, practiced austere asceticism as a measure of spiritual discipline. Man was urged to advance by habits of industry, sobriety, moderation, self-discipline, and avoidance of debt. Self-indulgence was considered not only socially undesirable but morally reprehensible.

Masculinity, in this scheme, was intertwined with being a good provider, and loss of one's job was akin to loss of social respectability. Under these traditional values, women stayed home if they could afford to and dedicated themselves to housewifery and motherhood. Men, in turn, directed their efforts to providing for their families. They expected security from the jobs and hoped for money and status as well. They repaid the corporation with their loyalty, tolerating its various drawbacks, inconveniences, and work requirements. They postponed their gratifications and rewards, working in preparation for some distant future by patient and painstaking accumulation of skills, credibility, and cash. Following World War II, in a country elated by victory and sudden prosperity, Americans approached life with a new confidence in the future. The idea that women's role was solely to bear and rear children so dominated this time of affluence that it resulted in the largest baby boom in the nation's history. From 1946 (peaking in 1957) until its decline in the early 1960s, an ethic of procreation permeated every race, class, and education group. Elaborating on the theory of economist Richard Easterlin, Landon Jones, in his book *Great Expectations*, described how the sheer size of this new generation has affected everything from cultural values to divorce rates and crime statistics.[9]

To the baby boom parents of the late 1940s and 1950s (themselves emerging from the Great Depression), familial life was equated with material possession; their children were to have everything. Never would they know the deprivation and hardship experienced by their parents. Hand in hand with this child-centeredness went progressive education. Whether a reaction to war, a revolt against the strict scheduling of Watson's behaviorism, or something else not yet suspected, permissiveness characterized modern child-rearing practices. Schools emphasized social values of getting along (perhaps as a way to manage the great influx of children), and academic standards declined. This permissiveness and emphasis on social interaction, in turn, began to undermine the Protestant work ethic. Although, at the emotional level, parents may have wanted their children to accept their values, practices recommended by Dr. Spock and progressive educators may have undermined their efforts to instill them.

Thanks to the achievements of the still hard-working older generation, consumer goods abounded and an upwardly spiraling standard of living sharply challenged the ethic of deferred gratification. The new American, courted by advertising, became even more sought after as consumer than as producer. Labor was no longer a moral obligation for a life of righteousness; its value lay in providing the means to purchase the accoutrements of the good life.

According to Jones, as this enormous and pampered cohort of boom babies advance through adolescence into college in unprecedented numbers, they became competitors for the scarce resources of an academic community unprepared for the influx. Their response was reaction, as they became "the most fiercely anti-competitive generation in our history."[10] The turbulence and conflicts of the sixties, fueled by events like the Kennedy assassination and the Vietnam War, may have been by-products of the massive size of this youthful generation struggling in prolonged adolescence. Ultimately, they began to create a culture of their own.

The Flower Children were the extreme expression of this anticompetitive culture. Repulsed by their parents' overstriving and disillusioned by the war in Vietnam, they rejected hard work as an unfulfilling and meaningless activity. In fact, true to the absolutist thinking of youth, their rejection of parental values was total. Condemning the older generation's world as militaristic, repressive, corrupt, materialistic, and joyless, they defined their own values in direct opposition, loudly proclaiming adherence to personal freedom, openness, joy, and love. The achievement ethic was replaced by the pleasure principle. Their hedonistic indulgences in sex, drugs, and "rap sessions" stressed a togetherness which required neither labor nor commitment.

The extremes of the hippie counterculture did not last, but a quieter challenge has replaced them. The dramatic clash between the Protestant work ethic of their parents' generation and the hippie counterculture intensified the struggle of the young to fashion an identity of their own. Lacking the religious and moral fervor of their parents, they nevertheless found little that was viable in the counterculture. Sexual freedom brought sophistication but little intimacy and an inability to commit to others or to specific ideals. The ties of marriage and children were often postponed or broken. Similarly, they reasoned that jobs which became boring could simply be changed.

The boom generation, in an existential crisis with no clear alternatives, is still plagued by uncertainty about what it should be or become. Wandering in anomie, finding no suitable role models, this generation has been forced to look inside itself. This focus on self developed in the 1970s into the narcissistic excesses of the Me Decade. If the Calvinists were compulsively industrious in their flights from sin, the narcissistic were equally obsessive in attempting to infuse their aimless lives with meaning.[11] Their flirtations with cults, drugs, therapies, sports, and diversions can be viewed as desperate attempts at self-definition. With their avoidance of genuine commitment or strong family ties, their emotional outreachings seem less a goal than a sustenance.

Just as the original altruism has turned to narcissism, early optimism has turned to pessimism. The anticompetitiveness bred in crowded colleges was reinforced when the boom generation faced their peers again in the employment market. Many could not find jobs or learned that a college education brought fewer rewards than their parents had promised. Promotions seemed less probable when so many of this generation vied for them. According to Jones, the realization that the unrealistic high parental dreams for this affluent, educated generation were unachievable resulted in lowered expectations and an unwillingness to truly compete. They appear less ambitious, have lesser expectations, and are apathetic about advancing in organizational life.

They must face not only the realization that their numbers put them at a disadvantage in the competition of the work environment, but that the earth's resources are limited too. These children of affluence will have to adjust to a world of scarcity. While the energy crisis continues and inflation erodes investments and savings, the call to buy now and pay later seems ever more sensible. Said historian Christopher Lasch, "As the future becomes menacing and uncertain, only fools put off until tomorrow the fun they can have today."[12]

The result is that the new narcissists have learned to live for the moment. History, rather than providing a reservoir of experience from which to guide their lives, has become irrelevant, and the future looks too dismal and unpredictable to warrant attention. Immediate gratification is the new order of the day as society shifts from the ascendance of superego values and self-restraint to the self-indulgence of the id.

Today, the affluence this generation experienced early in life has been translated into a psychology of entitlements, with little appreciation for the role of sacrifice and commitment. Perhaps fueled by the government follies of Vietnam and Watergate, today's young generation has little respect for authority or experience as stabilizing elements in life. Yet it is the older adults, acting out of their own historic forces, who failed to convince the younger generation of their capacity to lead the country toward moral and incorruptible goals. And now it is the older adults who will have to fill the leadership vacuum in organizations, for those in the younger generation are preoccupied with themselves.

FUTURE DIRECTIONS

Though private industry may bemoan its destiny, there are those who will welcome and laud the turning away from materialism, power-seeking, upward-striving, and competition and the movement toward individual freedom, leisure, and cooperation. Environmentalists and others have questioned the imperatives of economic progress, high technology, and material abundance. Simultaneously, social movements have emphasized relaxation, inner peace, and harmony rather than the conquest of nature. The orientation of these social movements was illustrated when the MCS (1970s) recruits ranked eighteen terminal values on the Rokeach Values Inventory. When compared with seventy-one older (by fifteen years, on the average) fourth- and fifth-level high-potential Bell managers, the MCS managers gave significantly higher ranks to "inner harmony," "wisdom," and "true friendship." The older managers scored higher on "conquer the environment" type values—"a sense of accomplishment," "freedom," and "an exciting life."

With forces pulling in both directions, our culture may be at a turning point. Sociologist Amitai Etzioni has suggested three possible future directions for Americans.[13] In his first scenario, the erosion of modernity, the pace of the economy would slow, with people becoming less driven to achieve. This could yield greater pleasure and relaxation but also result in lowered productivity, less efficiency, and, perhaps, more corruption. The Fall-of-Rome alternative is unlikely to be popular with the older generation.

The second scenario, reindustralization or restoration, is a return to the past, where old virtues and taboos take on a new urgency. This would satisfy the longing many feel to return to a respect for authority, rules, and responsibilities. Accompanying this would be development of energy sources and a rededication to efficiency, productivity, and economic progress. This approach is exemplified by the Reagan administration's "New Beginning" and the conservative temper. Business should be pleased by the economic possibilities, but a return to sexual and social repressions could create a serious backlash, particularly among the freedom-loving and socially tolerant young. Perhaps more significantly, elimination of such social programs as job training, income supports, and mass transit funding could lead to a new backlash from the underprivileged.

The third scenario, a quality-of-life society, would focus more on culture and recreation and less on materialism, more on living in harmony with the environment and less on a conquest of the environment or exploitation of nature. Social progress would get more attention than economic progress. In a similar fusion, Yankelovich argues for an ethic of commitment, away from both self-denial (old values) and self-fulfillment (new values) and toward a connectedness with others.[14] He visualizes integrating the instrumental and expressive sides of life, just as others have rejected old, "macho" values in favor of an androgynous blend of the traditionally masculine with the traditionally feminine.

Aspects of Etzioni's third scenario have been pursued in various forms by quality-of-life enthusiasts in industry with the thought that more fulfilling work or shorter working hours might lead to a revitalized interest in work and more productivity. Changing work values are cited increasingly by these supporters to justify their pleas for greater worker participation in decision making and democracy in the work place. Recent questionnaires show growing favor for the notion that workers should take part in decisions affecting their jobs—not surprising considering the declining voice of authority and rising psychology of entitlements.

An organizational approach to coming to terms with the new values may consist of restructuring the organization, reducing the hierarchical impact, and dispersing power and authority to a wider segment of the work force. Some organizations have introduced matrix management, worker councils, sociotechnical systems, autonomous work groups, quality circles, and other versions of "industrial democracy" which increase worker participation and reduce the need for extended chains of command.

These measures have not won unqualified acceptance. Some, including union leaders, have criticized efforts at humanizing the work place for creating a false image of democracy while actually leaving workers in a more helpless position than before. Lasch claims that the decline of authority at work, just as in the family, leads not to the collapse of restraints but to depriving them of a rational basis. The so-called democratic techniques soften the adversary relationship between supervisor and subordinate (as between management and labor) and make it more difficult for the workers to resist the demands of the corporation.[15] Thus, the "workers' control" movement, ostensibly aimed at a redistribution of power, has been castigated as but a more sophisticated method used by the truly powerful to pressure workers toward greater production.

Without considering the merit or demonstrated effectiveness of the industrial democracy alternatives, it could be argued that they do not adequately address the current generation's lack of interest in leadership or advancement. These methods have been tried primarily with nonmanagement employees, who may or may not share the new values of their college-educated peers. While production workers may replace some lower-level managers, the motivation to manage is less critical for this group. The real problem in this new approach is that quality circles or similar self-regulating groups and committees create an even greater demand for social and leadership skills and managerial motivation among those who remain in the higher echelons.

Other organization changes in the quality of work life domain may raise the work satisfaction of new-values employees and perhaps even foster loyalty. Suppose an organization were avant garde with respect to sex roles and decided neither women nor men employees should have to sacrifice family for career. By offering a package of alternatives such as flex-time, shared jobs geographical moves geared to couples, child care, and paternity leaves the organization might find itself in a buyer's market for managerial and professional talent. Similarly, "cafeteria" benefit plans and various time options, like sabbaticals, flexiyear contracts, and trade-offs of time and income, could replace rewards like money and advancement in vying for workers' commitment. Of course, there is no guarantee that any new consonance between individual values and an organization's benefits would result in higher productivity or performance. Like many well-meant social engineering schemes, this could, in fact, boomerang into a tangle of expensive and difficult to administer human resource programs that attract the laziest and least promising employees and encourage the achievers to follow suit.

Though some organizations may be willing to adjust their implied psychological contracts with employees, resistance to major structure change is apt to be intense, especially if change were to threaten traditional power and authority relationships. Coming from an age in which humans were to serve the organization, it is heresy to suggest that organizations serve the people within them. Realistically, some organizations, like the Marine Corps, may be incapable of functioning participatively, or at least so we believe. Moreover, in those organizations already threatened by outside forces, radical change may be particularly ill advised. The Bell System, currently in the throes of a major government-ordered restructuring into separate subsidiaries, comes to mind. One might argue, in fact, that never before has Bell had so great a need for strong traditional forms of leadership.

If the organization cannot or will not undergo a major transformation to accommodate the new values, what alternatives remain for meeting the potential leadership crisis? One classic approach is to cull the applicant population, using advanced personnel selection techniques, for managers whose values are more old than new. One Bell System division traditionally has looked for only the most advancement-oriented recruits, luring them with promises of better positions and higher starting salaries at the second rather than the first level of management. The commitment is to a fast track of promotions for those who prove their merit and dismissal for those who don't.

Twenty-two such recruits were assessed with the MCS participants in the late 1970s; the results showed that the selection process had indeed been working. They outshone their peers on nineteen of the twenty-six managerial dimensions, including very high needs for advancement and strong leadership skills and motivation. Not all young people are alike, and sophisticated organizations can still skim the cream off the top if they can muster the recruiters and incentives to capture what may be, or become, a rare breed. Yet even among this elite, upwardly mobile group, some of the new values crept through: they were more noticeably selfish than their peers, equally low on deference to superiors, and some blatantly planned to exploit the company for a brief experience before moving on to something else, such as starting their own business.

There are reasons to hope that in a few years there may be more of the traditionally motivated young people in the applicant pool. Several questionnaire studies on college campuses show a slight upturn in responses to questions about interest in business, administrative positions, or making money. A recent readministration of the Miner test to business students also hinted that the downward trend in managerial motivation may at least be reversing itself.[16] The trials of the first baby boomers may have exhausted the pendulum swing toward nonwork anomie as their younger siblings realize they have to eat. Social change is often dialectic, and perhaps it is time for a return swing to a more moderate position.

In the meantime, what to do with the dispirited cohort already lolling in the ranges of management? Perhaps their motivation for challenge and accomplishment, thankfully still alive, could be tied to the carrot of advancement. Or perhaps the special attention of an early career development program might be warranted. Young people may have to be taught the meanings, virtues and strengths of power and leadership, their value in instilling good ideas, making positive things happen and directing organizations and society toward new goals as well as old. Sympathetic mentors, role models, and counselors may help by giving feedback and advice as well as interpreting and reaching the values and mores of the firm. Opportunities to learn about their own and other organizations and cultures, by formal development programs or temporary assignments in other organizations or overseas, may help put self- and organization-oriented goals in perspective while fostering creative approaches to management. If the new managers are unconvinced that higher management jobs will on balance, offer them more of the good life than "merely" higher status, perhaps we should be grateful for what remains of the work ethic and hope that a new crop of recruits can be found to pass them by on the hierarchical success ladder.

To adapt to the new values of young managers one can change the organization, change the reward system, recruit differently, or provide early career development experience. But this holds all variables constant, in a sense. Both human institutions and human motivations flow from the spiritual ethos or Zeitgeist created by conditions of the times. As the culture evolves, so do people, values, and organizations so that new people and new modes of work can exist in a reformulated consonance.

At first blush it might appear that the quality-of-life reformers and new-values employees were made for each other. Yet the root ideas for humanizing the work place are not really new. During the 1940s, when Abraham Maslow and Carl Rogers began to speak of man's actualizing tendency, participative management was introduced into a pajama factory. Efforts in this vein did not entirely die out, and in the early 1970s, the quality-of-life movement was revitalized as a system approach.

Still, it is no more plausible to say that quality-of-life reforms were a response to new workers' demands than to hypothesize that the young people of the 1970s, in their existential angst were easy prey for the quality-of-life reformers. More likely both emanated from a common evolving Zeitgeist, reflecting two sides of the same coin. Whether this coin can buy much-needed productivity is the critical but unanswered question. That organizations and current personal value systems are out of phase suggests an effort should be made to restore the balance lest we sacrifice the viability of contemporary organizations. Yet because of cultural drives toward homeostasis, it may not be mere wishful thinking to expect a naturally evolving balance.

Calvinism once united virtue, salvation, work, and motivation in a productive package, but that package has come undone. Perhaps people now look only to themselves for the motivation that used to be supplied externally and emerge prisoners of their own insularity. The fire to lead others may soon be rekindled under a reformulate ethos, but the legacy of these shifting values in our culture may be a firm warning from humans that corporations and organizations in general can no longer with impunity take their loyalty and involvement for granted.

REFERENCES

1. John B. Miner, *The Human Constraint: The Coming Shortage of Managerial Talent* (Washington, D.C.: The Bureau of National Affairs, 1974).
2. John B. Miner, "The Human Constraint over Twenty Years," presentation at American Psychological Association Convention, Montreal (1980).
3. Daniel Yankelovich, "The New Psychological Contracts at Work," *Psychology Today* (May 1978).
4. Gail Sheehy, "Introducing the Postponing Generation," *Esquire* (October 1979), pp. 25-33.
5. "Technology and the Workplace—Changing Values of the MBA," *Technology Review* (June/July 1979), p. 78.
6. "Why 'Success' Isn't What It Used to Be," *U.S. News and World Report* (30 July 1979), p. 48.
7. Gwen Kinkead, "On a Fast Track to the Good Life," *Fortune* (7 April 1980), pp. 74-84.
8. Paul Hofmann, "The Swiss Malaise," *The New York Times Magazine* (8 February 1981), pp. 35 ff.

Leadership

9. Landon Y. Jones, *Great Expectations: America and the Baby Boom Generation* (New York: Coward, McCann, and Geoghegan, 1980).

10. *Ibid.*, p. 84.

11. Christopher Lasch, *The Culture of Narcissism: American Life in an Age of Diminishing Expectations* (New York: W. W. Norton and Company, 1978).

12. *Ibid.*, p. 53.

13. Amitai Etzioni, "Work in the American Future: Reindustralization or Quality of Life," in Clark Kerr and Jerome M. Rosow (eds.), *Work in America: The Decade Ahead* (New York: Van Nostrand Reinhold, 1979).

14. Daniel Yankelovich, *New Rules: Searching for Self-Fulfillment in a World Turned Upside Down* (New York: Random House, 1981).

15. Lasch, *op. cit.*

16. K. M. Bartol, C. R. Anderson, and C. E. Schneier, "Motivation to Manage Among Business Students: A Reassessment," *Journal of Vocational Behavior*, Vol. 17 (1980), pp. 22-32.

Dr. Ann Howard is the manager of basic human resources research at the American Telephone and Telegraph Company. She holds a Ph.D. in industrial psychology from the University of Maryland. Dr. James A. Wilson is an associate professor of business administration and assistant to the dean for planning and development at the Graduate School of Business, University of Pittsburgh. Dr. Wilson holds a Ph.D in psychology from Queens University, Belfast, U.K.

44.
PROSPECTUS FOR
CORPORATE LEADERSHIP

Charles T. Hutchinson

> Corporations need to build on existing values, concepts, and
> technologies to evolve a new model of progressive corporate leadership,
> for their own sake as much as for that of society.

Let me walk you through a compelling prospectus: a model of American
corporate leadership in the 1980s and beyond. There are tremendous benefits
to be gained from taking this model as a goal and expending corporate energy
on achieving it, particularly in view of the prevailing views of the citizenry of
the business community.

PERCEPTIONS OF CORPORATE LEADERSHIP

Opinion Research Corporation, in a recent study, found overall approval
sadly lacking for business and, by implication, business leadership. Seventy
percent of Americans polled gave *little* approval to business, an all-time record;
only one in fourteen gave it high approval. Compared to other institutions
being evaluated on the degree of trust and confidence they enjoy, large
corporations rated near the bottom of the list and were on a trend line headed
downward. Yankelovich, Skelly and White recently found that fewer than one
in five Americans thinks business is doing what it should be doing. In a word,
that's where the total audience stands.

If we move closer and focus on the segment of society comprising
organizations that interact regularly with business, we get a different picture.
This audience, more knowledgeable about the intricacies and imperatives of
business operations, tends not to look with disfavor on business per se. Being
itself immersed in the business process, this group takes a more selective view,
differentiating corporation by corporation across a whole spectrum of

leadership characteristics and capabilities, some seen as good, some as not so good; ratings are often heavily influenced by perceived bottom-line results.

If we move still closer, all the way to the leadership group of a single corporation, we get yet another view. Inferentially, they believe that, through their leadership, their business is doing precisely what, under its circumstances, it should be doing. If they didn't believe that, you can almost hear them say, they would change things so that it was.

Thus we see a broad range of business leadership perceptions. At the two extremes: the decidedly favorable view of internal senior management and the decidedly negative view of American society as a whole.

Can either extreme be right? Both obviously think they are. Both perceptions are realities, the considered views of rational, well-intentioned people.

Such a divergence of views invites examination.

Those of society are formed in large measure by the outward signs of corporate activity—layoffs, plant closings, pollution, discrimination, shoddy or unsafe products, disputed takeovers, spiraling prices, windfall profits. Many of these evidences reach society through the media, through what James Reston terms "police blotter" reporting; not what's right, but what's wrong.

The impressions created are reinforced by repeated television and movie characterizations of the corporate "heavy" and of worker exploitation, both generally overdrawn. And, of course, people remember even more vividly events they may observe affecting their communities, their families, and their friends.

In addition, the people of our society, by reason of circumstances, have never for the most part been charged with making a business enterprise go. They haven't been at the helm. Indeed, many are engaged in pursuits bankrolled by wealth-generating corporations, activities that simply redistribute one way or another the already generated wealth. They don't know what it's like at the top of the corporate heap; generally, they don't *want* to know.

For their part, corporate leaders know all too well the crunch, the agony, and the high associated with making an enterprise go. Moreover, they have a deep vested interest in doing so. As to their training, over the years they, their predecessors, and their successors, legions of them, have been "carefully taught," in Hammerstein's phrase, that "profit is the name of the game." Given that conditioning, they would view as an unavoidable necessity an event that society might term calculating, self-serving, even heartless. They would also characterize much of what assorted constituencies would have them start doing or stop doing as intrusive on the ability of the corporation to do what, in their eyes, it is supposed to do.

To the best of my knowledge, there has never been a survey in which corporate leaders rated society on what it is doing to or for business. If there were, the rating would be comparable to society's rating of business.

NEW CORPORATE LEADERSHIP EMERGING

These thoroughly imbedded, widespread views notwithstanding, evidence mounts of initiatives which collectively seem to suggest that change in the perceptions of corporate leadership will one day evolve. Certain major corporations have instituted innovative practices that potentially could modify the overall dichotomy we have thus far seen. By way of illustration:

Bank America Corporation adopted a voluntary disclosure code over recent years shaped by this guiding principle: "The corporation's various constituencies (customers, investors, employees and anyone concerned with its activities) are entitled, within reasonable limits, to have available the information that *they* think *they* need to judge its activities by *their* standards." Seventy separate categories of information are regularly open to public gaze.

International Business Machines Corporation maintains a privacy code for employees, a model many other Fortune 500 companies have followed, that limits personal information it can request upon employment and makes available most information recorded while employed. Cummins Engine Company provides employees with a printout of their personnel files annually. Atlantic Richfield Company has invited employee whistle-blowing wherever chemicals used might threaten health or the environment.

Amercian Center for the Quality of Work Life, American Productivity Center, and similarly dedicated groups work with an increasing number of corporations evolving cooperative work cultures and structuring opportunities for personnel at all levels to become actively involved in solving work-related problems, "to be of service . . . not subservient," in the words of one General Motors employee.

The issue of corporate governance has come to the fore, in the course of which the Business Roundtable has been moved to issue a set of guidelines for boards of directors; the New York Stock Exchange has made the presence of a board audit committee a condition of Exchange membership; the makeup of boards has shifted strongly toward a majority of outside directors; and dramatic growth has occurred in the number of board-level public policy committees.

These and other signs point to an evolving and profound new assessment of the role of the corporation in our society.

MISSION OF THE U.S. CORPORATION

Spokesmen for corporations on the leading edge have felt moved to capture and articulate the role of the corporation in society. Some samplings:

"The basic goal of private enterprise remains what it has always been—to produce needed goods, earn a fair return on investment and succeed as an economic institution. But the new dimensions that must be observed—a new bottom line for business, really—is social approval. Without it, economic victory would by Pyrrhic indeed"—Thornton Bradshaw, RCA.

"Society granted our corporate charter . . . clearly this is a privilege subject to whatever requirements it decides to impose. We will continue in business only as long as we reasonably meet those requirements" - Coy G. Eklund, Equitable Life Assurance Society of the United States.

"I do not believe society will tolerate permanently a major institution in its midst which justifies itself solely on economic terms. Nor do I believe that people who staff the entity will be able indefinitely to pursue conduct in their business relationship which is not consistent with other dimensions of their lives"—Harold M. Williams, The J. Paul Getty Trust.

"In industry, we have long accepted the fact that if a corporation cannot compete effectively in the marketplace, it will fail; we are less ready to accept the fact that the justification for our existence depends also on meeting the requirements set by the societies in which we operate.

"Within that view, the corporation is seen as both dependent on and responsible to the full range of people whose lives it affects"—Henry B. Schacht, Cummins Engine Company.

"We believe that business exists for one purpose only: to serve society. Profit is our reward for serving society well"—William A. Andres, Dayton Hudson Corporation.

Clearly, as each of these statements in its own way attests, society holds the franchise on business. That's the way it is; it can't be any other way. Equally, clearly, the mission of the U.S. corporation, stated in its broadest form, must be as Mr. Andres said, "to serve society." That, too, can't be any other way.

Parenthetically, I suggest that such a statement of mission is one that which society itself will agree. Here we have the bedrock foundation from which mutual respect and accord, one for the other, can one day rise.

A key task thus becomes identifying and describing the primary components or elements through which this mission will be fulfilled. I submit that such fulfillment occurs when the five following fundamental corporate purposes are mutually and optimally served:

Purpose 1: To provide socially needed goods and services of acceptable quality at reasonable prices.

Purpose 2: To create and maintain an internal organization and culture in which personal and group achievement, growth and fulfillment thrive.

Purpose 3: To attain and sustain net income sufficient both to perpetuate the enterprise and yield a return on investment satisfactory to the stockholders involved.

Purpose 4: To protect, preserve, and enhance social, cultural, and physical environmental conditions wherever the operations of the enterprise are located and wherever its products and services may go.

Purpose 5: To communicate openly, honestly, and voluntarily relevant information concerning all of these activities to all constituencies concerned.

Firguratively speaking those five basic statements of purpose box the corporate compass.

They are listed in the sequence that calls to mind advice from General Electric's Chairman John F. Welch, Jr.: "Try to design an industrial enterprise from the customer backward into the factory, rather than from the production process forward."

But the phrase "mutually and optimally served" was also used by design. In no sense is this sequence a ranking. Each purpose is an essential part of the whole. Each relies on, reinforces and, at the same time, places restraints on each of the others. No one of them can dominate or be pursued to the lasting detriment of any or all of the others. A dynamic balance must evolve.

Connecticut General Insurance Company Presiding Director Henry R. Roberts, who helped develop CG's statement of corporate purpose, comments on this interrelationship. "These . . . elements of corporate purpose," he writes of CG's statement, "are seen as inseparable. To be acceptable, a given policy or course of action may relate to some of them more than others, but would not be in conflict with any of them."

It seems reasonable to expect that corporations fulfilling their mission to serve society through such a blend of purpose would be performing in a manner which an informed society could support.

At this stage, we are still dealing with broad, sweeping statements of corporate purpose. Inevitably, they must be translated into specific actions.

CORPORATE LEADERSHIP MODEL OF TOMORROW

The evolving leadership role for a corporate enterprise can best be described by illustrating what in general terms its most senior leaders will do, given the foregoing mission. I speak here of those leaders whose duties and responsibilities entirely or in large part transcend the functional realm and span the enterprise as a whole, management in the true sense.

Who they are will vary by organization size and structure, and how they do things will vary by personal style; but, working in concert with supporting staffs, all will have in common a proactive dedication and commitment to these concerns and pursuits.

• This leadership group will select those society segments the enterprise will seek to serve. Be they consumers, industrial groups or other entities, it will gain an intimate knowledge of those segments and the people in them—their demographics, interests, needs and expectations. It will also know their aspirations and apprehensions, where they think they are headed, and what that suggests to them for the future. It will see them not as groups from which to extract revenue but as segments of society to be served.

It will fashion product or service offerings of genuine value carefully tailored to meet selected present and emerging interests and needs of these target groups and will repeatedly assure that they are in fact being met. It will cause those offerings to change as change evolves in the interests and needs of those being served. It will also have an intimate knowledge of who else is serving those segments and with what.

It will closely track the portions of the target segments already being served by the enterprise and will increase steadily the size of those shares.

It will provide the necessary physical facilities through which to produce those offerings in required volumes currently and in the future.

It will identify other segments to serve, other products or services to offer as the well-being of the enterprise may warrant or require.

• The leadership group will develop and maintain an organization that *wants* to and *can* admirably fulfill the selected interests and needs of these segments through the products or services offered. It will assure for each member that responsibilities are defined, expectations are clear, and performance against expectations is known. It will encourage and support participative practices that enhance the quality of work life and foster individual and group productivity, providing opportunities for problem solving at all levels and feedback on results attained. It will reach out, learn participants' interests and needs, involve them in the decision-making process of matters affecting them. It will stimulate personal growth and development. It will assure equitable rewards for services performed, including incentives based, not on profits, but on mission achievements. It will continuously endeavor to meet all of the reasonable expectations of those participating in the enterprise, the society within, engendering mutual trust and respect.

• The leadership group will husband the financial resources of the enterprise, managing its assets, controlling its liabilities, maintaining a balance sheet suited to its present and future financial needs. It will emphasize the long-term rather than the short-term best interests of the enterprise. It will cause to be controlled and quantified the current and expected effects of the activities of the enterprise in revenues received, costs expended, net earnings, and return on investment achieved. It will seek alternative plans and programs when these results fall seriously below needed levels or, conversely, greatly exceed them.

Like the customer being served, it will also know the stockholders very well, their interests, their needs, their expectations; and it will dutifully factor these into its stewardship of the enterprise their investment supports.

• The leadership group will be extremely aware of and sensitive to the larger environment. It will be sensitive, first, to conditions in that environment affected by the enterprise itself, and second, to those affecting the enterprise.

It will be well informed and play a lively and constructive role in the resolution of environmental issues as they develop.

For its own part, it will adopt the rule of thumb precept that the enterprise will endeavor to leave that environment as good as or better than it found it.

To that end, it will formulate and carry out strategies and plans that go beyond mere compliance with legislated and regulated requirements. These may include, for reasons of corporate conviction, protecting and enhancing measures that exceed legal requirements in selected situations.

The leadership will also consider and participate in those environmental concerns less directly related to the primary economic thrust of the enterprise, but of substantial interest to the people, the communities, and the constituencies with and among whom the enterprise lives. These may range through a broad realm of social concerns including but not limited to education, health care, social services, the arts, economic aid, community development and other pursuits dedicated to the betterment of the human condition.

• The leadership group will follow an open, voluntary communications policy with all constituencies concerning the relevant plans, actions, interests, and concerns of the enterprise. In all of these areas and with all of these constituencies, it will be straight-forward and credible, will tell it like it is, whether the news be good or bad. It will assure that these communications, whatever their forms, combine to provide a balanced, objective, play-by-play report on the fulfillment of all elements of the corporation's stated mission. In so doing, it will respect at all times that the enterprise is in effect, a public institution.

REWARD OF THE MISSION SERVED

Assuming the quality of strategic and tactical decisions taken along the way has been reasonably good, we have here a thriving business enterprise. Moreover, we have one that will out perform competitors in the same circumstances.

What sets it apart is the internal culture generated by assiduously and effectively pursuing—*simultaneously* and in a *balanced* way—a five-fold set of purposes to which both the society within and the society without can relate:

• providing needed goods and services;
• maintaining productive, rewarding internal relations;
• attaining sufficient earnings;
• protecting surrounding environments; and
• talking openly about it all.

The culture generated by that combination of pursuits is charged with energy, creativity, commitment, resolve, zeal. It becomes a vital, vibrant force. An internal dynamism evolves that progressively lifts individual contributions and ultimately those of the whole organization to levels of excellence never before achieved.

The basis of this achievement is the alignment of corporate purpose and performance with informed social expectations. The potency of the resulting human interaction cannot be overstated. The postulate is simply this: when, through fulfillment of stated purposes, the informed expectations of all constituencies are reasonably and continuously met, then the corporation's maximum human resource capabilities are released.

We noted earlier the huge dichotomy between perceptions of corporate leadership today. We read of other economies where the dichotomy is much reduced and where, concurrently and not coincidentally, productivity is much greater. What we are gaining here is a beginning insight into the tremendous *internal* benefits for the American corporation of closing that gap.

There are obvious external benefits as well, most notably a developing trust and respect.

While this "state of the art" corporate leadership model may in some respects seem new, it is more accurately described as simply an evolution from all that has gone before. It builds on existing values, concepts, and technologies, becoming their logical extension and thus the leading edge of an expanding continuum whose other parts comprise established, proven leadership practices of the present and the past.

Given that perspective, this model is within the grasp of many progressive corporate leaderships today.

Charles Hutchinson is assistant to the President of the American Thread Company. He is a Fellow of the Center for the Study of Values at the University of Delaware and also a management consultant.

45.
ANTICIPATORY MANAGEMENT OR VISIONARY LEADERSHIP: A DEBATE

Jay S. Mendell
Herbert G. Gerjuoy

The visionary get excited about an idea and tries to make it work without considering all the pitfalls and side effects, and the anticipatory manager misses many ideas because he does not have room to speculate.

Thesis Statement by Jay S. Mendell: *Anticipatory Management Is an Excuse for Avoiding Transformation.* Visionary leadership is humankind's process of effecting necessary transformation in the face of overwhelming need to change, and anticipatory management is administration's method of holding on to what it has by making incremental changes. The first is a "process" through which practically anything may happen, and the other is a method of making sure that things happens within limits. Both may effect change: one effects needed transformation and the other avoids it.

In the visionary process, people open themselves up to all sorts of ideas and information—pleasant and unpleasant ideas, information that confirms or disconfirms their preconceptions, even information that questions the ability of their organization to survive. In the visionary process people tolerate uncertainty and ambiguity for the longest time until a sense of purpose, direction and vocation emerges. Visionaries exist in what George Prince has called the "experimental self": they feel, take risks, break rules, see connections, recognize patterns, play, speculate, are curious, see the fun in things, like surprises, are open to anything, make impossible wishes, do not mind being wrong, do not mind being confused, see images, think intuitively, are impetuous, are in touch with their subconscious minds, are in touch with their total experience, use seeming irrelevance, and use their dreams. (I'm paraphrasing Dudley Lynch, who paraphrased George Prince in *Focus Creativity.*)

This experimental mindset often results in a shift in the way they construct their mental maps of the world and the way they direct the traffic of their minds. After tolerating a sense of directionlessness for months or years, they snap over, feel a spinal tingle, and develop a sense of excitement about something new. And sometimes they try this "something new" within established systems of governance or management; but sometimes they legitimize their own informal leadership and try to take over the direction of their organization. Their guarantor of success is excitement and commitment, not rationality: they cannot prove they are on the right track—but nowadays, who can?

Anticipatory management is the "official" approach of people who want to know where they are going, the approach of professors of management, for instance, and their graduates, and executives for whom looking sophisticated is more important than doing good work. The people who give the go-ahead to launch anticipatory management (who control the money and personnel) expect *not* to be told that the future has no place for them and their organization. They don't want disruption: they want rationality. So anticipatory management is a systematic approach to forecasting and strategy that leads to actions within established governance and is not likely to delegitimize the people who authorize it. Daring transformations of worldview and exciting enterpreneurial developments occur only if vision contaminates the system.

Anticipatory management necessarily deals with little bits of the big picture, suppresses tension, and represses emotional reactions to exciting opportunities by smothering them in feasibility analyses that are *a priori* rigged against the unconventional. The anticipatory manager is stuck in George Prince's "safekeeping" mindset: he censors, evaluates, reassures and supports the establishment, analyzes, guides, is realistic, avoids surprises, avoids wrongness, avoids risks, makes and accepts rules, is serious, is cautious, is suspicious, is fearful, punishes mistakes, punishes wrongness, and probably punishes what his parents would have disapproved of. (Again, I'm paraphrasing Dudley Lynch prarphrasing George Prince.)

Neither the rational anticipatory manager nor the visionary leader takes everything into account. The visionary gets excited about an idea and tries to make it work without considering all the pitfalls and side effects, and the anticipatory manager misses many ideas because he does not have room to speculate.

Antithesis Statement by Herbert G. Gerjuoy: *Anticipatory Management Is Visionary Leadership Made Reliable.* I see this debate as focusing on education and selection of managers. Should we try to train them to be visionaries, or should we train them to use well-understood, albeit humdrum, step-by-step procedures? Should we select managers for their creativity or for their reliability? I feel that in the long run Mendell's vision will come true: we will eventually improve the quality of management by increasing the contribution of intuition to managerial performance, thus making management more visionary. But today, and for the rest of this century, I feel we must focus on strengthening our managerial routines, our explicit, step-by-step, algorithmic, verbally comprehendable methods. At this time, this is what we can teach, transmit from generation to generation, from mentor to novice. Until we can reliably and effectively teach visionary leadership, it would be suicidal to seek prematurely to develop a managerial tradition dominated by intuition and visionary charisma.

Fundamentally, Mendell and I have no quarrel. It is a silly mistake to believe that anticipatory management and visionary leadership are mutually exclusive. Rather, they are complementary. Management without visionary leadership lacks the vitality to survive; intuitive management that disregards methodical preparation for the future very swiftly fails. The less a visionary leader considers future possibilities, the more suicidal it is to follow her or him. The more charismatic and persuasive such a leader is, the more likely she or he is to lead her or his fellow lemmings into the sea.

The contrast between anticipatory management and visionary leadership resembles the contrast between:

- digital and analog
- verbal and nonverbal
- explicit and implicit

It also resembles the pseudoneurological modern phrenological contrast between the left and right cerebral hemispheres. We need both digital and analog thinking, both "left brain" and "right brain." To enlarge on the phrenological metaphor, rather than needing conflict between the two hemispheres, we need enhancement of the functions of the corpus callosum; we need better bridging between the hemispheres. We need to articulate our intuitions more effectively, and we need to be more intuitive in selecting what to articulate.

Anticipatory management, since it is digital and verbal, makes use of managerial algorithms, explicit programs or recipes for accomplishing managerial tasks. But algorithms do not make it possible for us to dispense with human judgment, nor do they seek or purport to do so. We must use judgment to decide which algorithms to use, when and how to use them, what data inputs to provide, and how to interpret the output. This is true, whether the algorithms are embodied, as they so often are nowadays, in computer programs or are embodied in formal social decision systems, such as procedural codes for organizational decisionmaking.

To renounce explicit, formal, digital, managerial methods is romantic and antirational. It is consistent with the recent mood, in some circles, of intellectual despair and disillusionment with nineteenth century visions of rational progress. It is ironic, of course, that extremism in favor of visionary leadership derives from the failure of an early visionary ideal.

The march of civilization has been largely a process of algorithmicizing performances initially achieved through genius. Human survival required that the kindling of fire not require rare triumphs of insight. Rather, it was necessary that people become able to start and maintain fires even when they did not understand how fires burn and even when they lacked the creative empathy necessary to tune non-verbally into the combustion process. You and I do fairly well many things that once only rare geniuses did—albeit superlatively. Anticipatory management exemplifies such necessary routinization.

Of course, it would be better if we all could function at the genius level. If a method could be developed for making genius less rare, then perhaps visionary leadership could suffice without anticipatory management.

How much less rare? It is in the spirit of anticipatory management that I feel constrained to be precise about the prerequisites for successful visionary leadership, even if this precision makes any argument more vulnerable. I think that if at least ten percent of managers were mistresses or master of intuition, then visionary leadership would be the method to nurture in our schools of management, and it would be the method to select when managers are hired.

However, I feel that achieving this necessary minimum of ten percent genius in the ranks of managers is too visionary to be anticipated in this century. Of course, nurturing creativity, insightfulness, and even genius, is not, in principle, impossible. John Stuart Mill and Norbert Wiener were both products of reasonably deliberate and explicit attempts to do so. Note that it is by no means contradictory that creativity be taught by explicit, algorithmic methods. Indeed, it is probably desirable that creativity and insightfulness be achieved this way, to avoid paradoxes of self-reference. My disagreement with Mendell is mainly about time scale, about rate of change to be anticipated. This disagreement underlies our disagreement about the strategies for selection and development of managers during the rest of this century. Because I think the necessary intellectual infrastructure for effective visionary leadership is now too rare, I think we should, in the short run, concentrate on developing better anticipatory management—of course, doing so in a way that facilitates the long-run evolution of a unified managerial style that adds to the pedestrian (but workable) methods of anticipatory management the dash and depth of (presently impractical) visionary leadership.

Premature focus on visionary leadership at the expense of anticipatory management can give us a managerial climate that favors intuition un-supported by reliable, replicable procedures, and managerial methods that are neither communicable nor transmissable. If we are serious about seeking to move toward a more nonverbal, intuitive, visionary management style, then we should focus on widespread implementation of the second prerequisite for turning from anticipatory management to visionary leadership: developing methods for transmitting from effective practitioner to novice the necessary habits of orderly thought that enable a creative individual to avoid drowning in his or her creative productivity.

Our thoughts naturally transcend logic and order. We literally can and do, from time to time, leap from two-plus-two to the square root of negative one. But such leaps are far more likely to be in the wrong directions than in the right. The random element in our thinking makes our thinking a Darwinian process. Our thoughts are replete with mutations, and like most mutations in complex systems, they are usually unfavorable. Without adequate corrective feedback from the environment, we naturally drift toward paranoia. The more creative we are, the more likely it is that our notions about the world will reflect our inner selves rather than the true structure out there. Foolish original ideas are natural: the consequences of avoiding all foolish originality is avoidance of worthwhile originality as well.

Therefore, another prerequisite for moving from anticipatory management to visionary leadership is development of an adequate social infrastructure for helping individuals weed out their many foolish and even mad ideas, and selectively nurturing the necessarily rare good ones. I think that Mendell's notions about visionary leadership are a good example. The notions are not fundamentally unsound, but they need corrective feedback. They must be tempered with the caution that comes from concern with the details essential to avoidance of the many pitfalls on the faint path between today's humdrum anticipatory management and tomorrow's hoped-for visionary leadership.

REBUTTAL BY JAY MENDELL

I concede that my "anticipatory management" and "visionary leadership" are extreme ideal cases that cannot exist in pure form. A little bit of vision creeps into every rational management scheme and lifts it out of its ruts. Its presence is not acknowledged, let alone its importance, but it's there. And visionary leaders need the skills of anticipatory management to use when they choose to.

It's the tendency of, the necessity for, in fact, one scheme to contaminate the other, that makes me laugh out loud when Herb Gerjuoy talks about replicability and teachability of anticipatory management. Once a little bit of vision creeps into the rationality, the replicability flies out the window. Rational management is structured: that much I'll concede. But it is cleverly (perversely) structured to permit just enough vision to make the system work and to give the appearance of foresight, but not enough vision to scare people.

What's all this talk about the riskiness of mistakes? Generating ideas is bare creativity. Making initially improbable ideas work is visionary leadership, and it operates best in the crepuscular area that anticipatory managers dismiss as infeasible. There is too much concern about absolutes of right and wrong: the safekeeping mind is in control.

I have experienced no insuperable obstacles in training business, government, and educational leaders to be more visionary. Visionary leadership is, after all, the method that humankind has used to transform civilization since long before management existed. Rational management is a Johnny-Come-Lately fad. All I have to do is to *undo* some of the harm of five years of formal management education. How I do it is beyond the scope of this article. But I do it in my graduate course in "Visionary Management."

Finally, while I concede there is a need for the visionary in the rational and the rational in the visionary, I suspect that organizations will usually select less vision than they need and more structure. So visionary leadership will remain a guerrilla activity carried out by disillusioned anticipatory managers for the hell of it, carried out by people who think that their organizations need nothing less than the opportunity for transformation.

REBUTTAL BY HERB GERJUOY

When Mendell defines visionary leadership and anticipatory management, he begs the question. May not something resembling "visionary leadership" occur even though change is unnecessary? If visionary leadership is a process "through which practically anything may happen," are we to believe that practically anything that may happen will prove to have been desirable? I prefer setting limits on what may happen. Jay assumes that setting limits avoids needed transformations. May not setting limits also avoid unneeded or undesirable transformations? Or is change always good?

Not all problems have quick solutions. Not all have fun solutions. We have to be able to deal successfully with problems that must be solved without a spinal tingle.

Mendell is correct: we cannot prove we are on the right track—that is to say, we cannot ever establish with absolute certainty that we are on the right track. But in the spirit of St. Korzybski of the Differential, I must point out that there are many alternatives to being able to "prove" we are on the right track. We may, for example, be able to demonstrate that probably we are on the right track—albeit not certainly. Unreliability is not all-or-none. It is possible to be a little unreliable, or moderately unreliable, and so on. The digital, algorithmic methods of management science make possible reliable, precise measurement of degree of unreliability. Consequently, while perfect replicability is impossible without (unattainable) perfect reliability, acceptable replicability may be achieved and verified, despite some unreliability. Adding a little visionary leadership to anticipatory management need not reduce its reliability and replicability to zero.

Incremental, rational methods can give rise to surprise and excitement; example: a masterful mathematical proof in which astonishing theorems are logically, rationally, and delightfully derived from basic postulates. Incremental, rational methods need not suppress tension and smother innovation; example: the exciting, innovative moon landings, which required painfully detailed rational analyses. Many scientific triumphs reflect major thought mutations; example: Kekule's discovery of the ring structure of benzene. Many other triumphs were achieved after many small incremental steps; example: development of modern antibiotics after the first breakthroughs. The latter example illustrates the natural, healthy interplay between major creative leaps, such as Ehrlich's original insight or Fleming's serendipitous observations, and later incremental improvements and enhancements, such as the successful though tedious trial-and-error search for new and better mycins.

It is true that rational management is a Johnny-Come-Lately. It arrived in time to contribute to the past century's great leap upward in human productivity. Visionary leadership, in contrast, is the age-old tried-and-true method used by such visionaries as Genghis Khan and Hitler, and—of course—the founders of all major religions; it was also used by the innumerable legions of failed would-be messiahs and world conquerors that fill history's dusty trash heap.

The spirit of anticipatory management—pragmatic, circumspect, modest, self-restrained, and open to criticism—causes me to doubt that the issues discussed in this debate can be resolved by debate. We need facts, not rhetoric. Our disagreement has clear operational implications. If Mendell can, indeed, effectively teach or trigger creativity in, say, ten percent of his students, that should be demonstrated. Of course, the demonstration, to be acceptable to me, would have to conform to the accepted canons of science—canons that are fundamentally explicit, digital, and "right-brained." Therefore, it is to be hoped that Mendell and I are not about to shift our focus of disagreement away from training and selection of managers to a parallel debate about anticipatory versus visionary psychosocial research on management training. It would be far better if Mendell and I would stop squabbling, and he would teach me (and the rest of the world) how reliably and replicably to make people more visionary.

Jay S. Mendell is Professor of Business in the School of Public Administration at Florida Atlantic University in Boca Raton. He is the editor of Foresight In Business, *published by Greenwood Press, and is the author of numerous business articles and the author of a syndicated column for college and university papers on "adapting to change." Herbert G. Gerjuoy is president of Program Strategics Inc. of West Hartford, Connecticut. He hold a Ph.D. degree in human psychology.*

46.
HAZARDS AT THE TOP

James Braham

Yes, CEOs face occupational hazards, too. Plenty of them. There's the "self-made-man syndrome"—the boss thinks he's irreplaceble. Or the "isolation-booth syndrome"—the CEO locked in an ivory tower. Or the executive who's so good that he's bad. And the list goes on. . . .

Sometimes the very traits that propel a man to the top can eventually cause his fall—and weaken the company he helped to build. Like everyone else, even chief executive officers have to contend with "occupational hazards."

Consider, for example, the self-made-man syndrome. Most corporate chiefs have dominant, independent personalities. Some feel they got there the hard way—succeeding on their own, and, by golly, so can the next fellow. Such CEO's often fail to groom successors, and that's a prime occupational hazard. "The most abdicated responsibility in American management is the development and nurture of subordinates," notes Neil S. MacKenna, a partner in MacKenna, Jandl & Associates, a Lynnfield, Mass., outplacement firm.

The "self-made-man" syndrome is reflected by an aura of "almost papal infallability," adds Deborah J. Cornwall, senior vice president of Harbridge House, a Boston-based management consultant. "I [the executive] was smart enough to make it on my own. If you want to make it, junior, you've got to have the talent to figure it out yourself."

Since developing successors is a cardinal business rule, why wouldn't a CEO oblige? "Train the man and he becomes a threat," replies Dwight Prouty III, senior consultant with Fuch, Cuthrell & Co., a New York out-placement firm. "They [top brass] try to avoid that. It happens a lot. Any good firm will say, 'We never hire from without; we always train from our inside staff.' That is a bunch of baloney!"

Sometimes, though, an executive will slice through the baloney to do what's right.

Joseph S. DiMartino, president of Dreyfus Corp., a New York mutual fund, stresses the importance of developing subordinates. "Hiring good quality people and encouraging and developing them is the most difficult part of the job. The minute I got into this position, I started working toward my obsolescence."

POOR CHEMISTRY

But, as every CEO knows, there are a myriad of job hazards that can bring about his *involuntary* obsolescence.

Bad chemistry, for one. Managers and acquisitions often precipitate an unstable situation. A company suddenly has two CEOs or two presidents when only one is needed. This is a chief reason why senior executives lose their jobs, Mr. MacKenna says.

Moreover, mergers and buyouts sometimes bring together top executives who are, simply, mismatched. The "chemistry" just isn't there. That's why James P. Thrasher, who had been chairman and CEO of Interway Corp., left the container-leasing company in 1981, two years after it had been acquired by Transamerica Corp. He didn't agree with Transamerica's plans for its new subsidiary—and also felt left out of the corporation's overall planning.

Mr. Thrasher wanted to streamline Transamerica, believing that the giant corporation should focus on financial services. "I'm pretty outspoken. I made my views known. I harassed them, asked questions, and wrote memos. I think I became very irritating to them.

"They let me know by subtle means that they wanted me to leave. So I did."

Does he have regrets? "I don't think the most important thing for a CEO is to keep his job," he says. "The most important thing is to be happy in what you're doing—and productive. You can have all kinds of character traits that go wrong or don't mix," adds Mr. Thrasher, now fifty-one and resolute that he will never again accept a job with a large corporation. "Chemistry and philosophy are the biggest things, particularly when one company buys another."

This is especially true when an entrepreneur sells his business to a large company, agrees Robert E. Levinson. His Stellcraft Mfg. Co., a Cincinnati manufacturer of metal doors, was purchased by American Standard Inc. in 1969. His private-company, entrepreneurial philosophy conflicted with that of the giant public corporation and—after "lasting" nine years as a group vice president—he was dismissed.

Mr. Levinson—who now owns hotels through his own company, REL Enterprises Inc., Boca Raton, Fla.—at first "conformed to everything" at American Standard. But eventually, he says, "they hired a guy between the president and me and he felt he should fire me because I was too much of a threat—not for his job, but for wanting to exercise my own philosophy."

Other things, too, can create the "wrong chemistry," Fuchs, Cuthrell's Mr. Prouty warns. "If you're chairman and the texture of the board changes, you may be in for trouble."

ISOLATION BOOTH

There may be big trouble looming as well for the executive who finds himself too lonely at the top.

Last spring, James F. Turner III, 49, left his post as president and CEO of a medium-sized East Coast manufacturer after he sank into a state of deep depression that rendered him fearful and unable to be effective at his job. Mr. Turner didn't recognize the depression, though, until it was too late. He still is unsure of its origin, but he now believes that executives are particularly vulnerable to this acute emotional state.

Making things worse, a CEO's need for "self-protection" means that he cannot unburden himself of his weakness with subordinates or peers. The chief executive is, he says, "the ultimate in emotional isolation."

"I sensed after a while that I wasn't doing my job," Mr. Turner says. "Things that used to be extremely easy to do became exceedingly difficult, like getting board meetings or management meetings together. I wasn't running on all eight cylinders, but who would tell me?"

Business was bad the last couple of years he was with the company, and Mr. Turner withdrew from associates and subordinates. He even stopped attending Presidents Association Roundtables, sponsored by the American Management Associations, where he customarily exchanged views with other leaders. That was wrong, he now knows. "You've got to take care of your mind as well as your body," he says.

Mr. Turner, who has since returned to his job, advises other top executives that depression can afflict anyone, and that a key warning signal is loss of the ability to have fun. "Things I normally would like to do, I wouldn't want to do," he reflects. The solution? "Do something, even if it's wrong."

Increasing reliance upon computers adds to the problem of isolated executives, says Dr. Paul H. Thompson, dean of the school of management at Brigham Young University. "People good at manipulating the computer bring massive amounts of data to the executive, and he begins to believe he can read these printouts and talk to a few people and he'll be all right. It's a very serious risk. A much more effective executive works very hard to stay in touch personally with what's going on out there."

Harbridge House's Ms. Cornwall suggests that isolation may also occur when subordinates are afraid to disagree with the boss. Ms. Cornwall observes that "many senior executives have the view that dissension is not good, that disagreement means conflict. But basically the only feedback they get are signals from their own people and, unfortunately, many subordinates spend a lot of effort trying to figure out what will make the boss happy, what does he want to hear? Yes men."

This is not planned "collusion," she stresses, pointing out that in most organizations feedback goes from top down, rarely from subordinate to boss. "Many senior executives have never learned ways of soliciting feedback," she says.

MORE TRAPS

Paradoxically, the list of executive pitfalls includes pluses that are really minuses in disguise.

Too Good: One self-made CEO of a major service company was "so right and so good that he created tremendous feeling of incompetence on the part of his subordinates," Ms. Cornwall says. "No matter what anyone did, he always had a way to do it better. He didn't realize that he was creating the opposite response [to what he intended]." As a result, his staff didn't accept his challenges but backed off instead, letting him do it.

Sometimes a CEO is so cocksure he's right that he doesn't bother soliciting other opinions—and his company pays. Richard L. Jandl of MacKenna, Jandl was once associated with a president who was on an acquisition kick. "He wouldn't bother to get the advice of his staff, but would just go out and make these acquisitions. We'd read about them in the paper and they would, one by one, turn out to be disasters. He was so sure these were good for the company that he just went out and did them; he wouldn't listen to his tax people or marketing specialists. He just had that gut feeling and he nearly destroyed a company."

Too Much Action: Boredom or lack of further challenge is cited by some analysts as a pitfall for executives, but Brigham Young's Dr. Thompson disagrees. "A more serious problem is that they get involved in too many activities," he says. "I find that a number of executives don't have time to sit back and think and really analyze. It's kind of an action trap—always on the move, doing things."

He believes executives and corporations should concentrate on the things they do best. "There's kind of an illusion in the U.S. that if you've got money and bright people, you can do anything. Some executives get into trouble because they try to do too many things. Companies get overextended and into difficulty." Bendix Corp. is, he says, a company "that tried to take on too much and got acquired instead."

CEO's face a variety of other occupational hazards too. Among them:

The Big Leap: Being promoted from chief operating officer to chief executive officer is a leap that causes some executives to stumble. "If you've been president and COO, you've been running the company on a day-to-day basis," says Lester B. Korn, chairman and CEO of Korn/Ferry International, a New York executive-search firm. "A CEO has to start thinking of strategic planning and policy and where the company's headed. It's quite a transition: some people make it and some don't."

Fear of Conflict: Reluctance to use power for the benefit of the organization is a pitfall that Dr. Thompson has observed in some chief executives. A case in point involved the managing partner of a large accounting firm. "He was a very good accountant and a good partner," says the Brigham Young dean. "But when he became managing partner he couldn't deal very well with conflict. He avoided it, he wouldn't confront."

As a result, the firm "came to a screeching halt" because he didn't address or resolve "a number of complex issues." After a year he was removed from office.

Burnout: Because of this occupational hazard, Dr. Thompson believes, more and more CEO's now serve only five years or so, and then retire. "It's hard to maintain excitement and new ideas much beyond five to seven years," he says.

However, premature burnout can be avoided, Dreyfus' Mr. DiMartino stresses. He believes that burnout occurs most often when the executive doesn't have a competent staff. "When you've got to do everything yourself, because you feel that's the only way it can be done right, you'll never get ahead in terms of what you *should do*—because you're doing *everything*," he says. Such frustration, with the resulting long hours spent attempting to do it all oneself, leads to early burnout.

Creator vs Manager: In start-ups and venture capital firms the founder or "idea man" establishes the company but, when it hits $10 million or so in sales, Mr. MacKenna says, "it becomes evident that the individual, no matter how brilliant he is, simply cannot be maintained as chief executive officer. He's often an expert specialist but, as the organization grows, it becomes necessary for him to be a generalist. In a sense, the 'Peter Principle' takes over."

Or, as Mr. Prouty puts it: "Many CEOs have no business being CEOs in the first place." Referring to the high-tech companies, he points to Apple Computer Inc.'s Steven Jobs as a pioneer who built a "dynamic, tremendous company" but had no training for—and was "not qualified" to be—a CEO. It's to his credit, Mr. Prouty says, that Mr. Jobs eventually lured marketing oriented John Sculley from PepsiCo Inc. to carry Apple to greater heights.

Mr. Thrasher, the former Interway CEO, observes that there are two types of CEOs—the entrepreneur and the runner. "There's a marked difference between them—one cannot do the other's job," he says. "There's no way the guy who worked up through the ranks and is running a General Motors-type company can ever be a successful entrepreneur, and vice versa. One is essentially an organization man, a manager of structure. The entrepreneur is the thinker-creator. He's creating structure, not operating it. They're completely different skills.

"I was more the entrepreneur type," Mr. Thrasher continues. "I enjoyed creating. I never enjoyed managing; that's when boredom came in. If a guy who likes creating is stopped [from] creating and just runs [a company], he's going to get bored."

The Numbers Men: Senior executives often find "a tremendous comfort in numbers," but these are "only as good as the assumptions behind them," Harbridge's Ms. Cornwall says. "There's a tendency to be heavily analytical and not sufficiently creative in running the business . . . a desire to prove everything, to minimize risks, to make big deals but be able to quantify everything so the big deal's safe.

"A tremendous amount of managerial time and effort is spent in generating numbers that are never used. The 'just-in-case-he-asks' numbers. A lot of senior executives would be shocked to find how much this is costing them."

The Detail Syndrome: The victim here rises in a corporation" simply by doing more," Ms. Cornwall says. By refusing to let go of details, he ultimately becomes a "tremendous bottleneck." And by expecting his immediate subordinates also to be involved in the nitty-gritty, "he ultimately sucks the entire management group into [too much concern with minutiae. As a result, not enough people pay attention to [long-term] strategic issues."

DISTRACTED

Even CEOs who manage to steer clear of these sundry difficulties may find themselves in jeopardy. Some chief executives weaken their companies because they spend too much time on outside activities—in community affairs, politics, or acquisition hunting. "They don't mind the store," observes Fuchs, Cuthrell's Mr. Prouty.

Many a CEO discovers too late that his talents no longer match the current needs of his company, a particularly painful problem for a top executive who cannot keep up when the company shifts direction.

And even when corporation and CEO are in harmony, not every CEO is able to convey to others the message and vision he so clearly perceives. Reaching the top introduces "a dimension of communication that many executives are not used to," Mr. Korn notes. "Whether a chief executive is extroverted or introverted, whether he's used to dealing with the press or shareholders or not, he becomes a spokesman for the industry." Some CEOs learn how to conduct themselves on television and in other public situations where they must project the image of a leader.

And some do not.

47.
HOW YOUR COMPANY CAN AVOID WEAK LEADERSHIP

Robert N. McMurry

Almost without exception, an enterprise that is free from manifestations of the Law of Diminishing Competence has executives who are strong and decisive.

The average life of American business is seven years. One reason many are so short-lived is that the people who run them are unaware of what I call the Law of Diminishing Competence and its potential for damage.

That fundamental of management works like this:

An insecure or indecisive straw boss, manager or chief executive officer views ambitious, assertive subordinates as threats and tries to replace them with subordinates even less secure than he. As a result the management structure becomes progressively weaker going down the line.

Middle and lower management levels, as well as some top positions reached by seniority, are filled with indecisive, frightened people. They may be competent in their own fields, but as decision makers, leaders and innovators, they are disasters.

Many symptoms of this disastrousness involve relationships with subordinates—failing to back them up even when they are right, intimidating them, praising them to their faces and criticizing them behind their backs, seeking scapegoats, playing favorites, discouraging creative thinking and constructive suggestions, and blocking their advancement. Other symptoms of executive weakness include operating without a plan, making promises that won't be kept, becoming disorganized in emergencies, being inconsistent in interpreting company policies and dealing obsequiously with superiors.

Few managers who prefer weak subordinates do so consciously. They are not aware of the nature and consequences of the Law of Diminishing Competence, nor do they know that their insecurities can set the law in motion at their companies. Since they are incapable of facing up to their own weakness, they do not look for evidence of it in their subordinates.

Weakness in those they select is often well masked. Their choices are frequently competent technically, even if not as decision makers; they are loyal hard working and of long service. In addition, they tend to be adept at concealing or rationalizing their failures. Also they may be selected in their superiors own images.

In many instances the chief determinants for advancement are, besides the candidate's technical expertise, his compatibility with his immediate superior—chemistry, the degree of congruence of their values—and his potential as a threat to the superior's security.

Therefore, the better the subordinate's qualifications, the less likely he is to be well regarded and to advance. Most companies depend on the superior's often biased judgement of the subordinate's competence. This can be costly to the well-qualified employee—and his employer.

Almost without exception, an enterprise that is free from manifestations of the Law of Diminishing Competence has executives who are strong and decisive. They are not reluctant to fight for what they believe is right and make decisions that can put their jobs at risk. As a corollary, they do not want indecisive, sycophantic mediocrities on their staffs but welcome upwardly mobile subordinates.

Though the CEO of such a company may not be familiar with the Law of Diminishing Competence by name, he is aware of its manifestations and is prepared to eliminate them. He also needs the support of his board of directors, if he has one. Ideally, the board has formed a special supervisory oversight committee to help identify problems and to take corrective action.

The action should include a program to ensure that everyone in middle management has at least minimal leadership qualifications.

First, the executive should assess each incumbent's operational unit as measured by:

- Operating costs, in relation to budgets and projections, and profit performance.
- Quality standards, customer complaints and product rejections.
- Creative contributions.
- Performance against deadlines.
- Degree of labor peace or unrest.
- Competence of employees whom the middle manager favors compared to that of those he deprecates.
- Rate of personnel turnover and the competence of those leaving.
- Absenteeism and tardiness.

Next, the CEO or outside consultants should interview and appraise each incumbent. And then employes throughout the company should anonymously fill out questionnaires that give them a chance to indicate their needs and problems without fear of reprisal. (Sears, Roebuck has conducted such polls for many years.) The questionnaires reveal, among other things, how subordinates regard their superiors and stress areas of strength and weakness.

To what extent are the superiors seen as secure, well-organized, knowledgeable and skilled? Believable and trustworthy? Concerned with their subordinates' welfare? Capable of making decisions without regard to job security? Willing to accept responsibility for their mistakes?

On the basis of all that, the CEO and the board's committee, if there is one, can decide what action to take in each superior's case. Each candidate for promotion is evaluated to fall into one of these categories:

- Well suited to line responsibilities; eligible to be promoted.
- Adequately suited to his job, should be retained where he is.
- Marginally qualified; should be moved into a staff, non-decision-making assignment.
- Unqualified.

Eliminating the effects of the Law of Diminishing Competence will not solve all of a company's management problems. A strong CEO must design and implement programs to improve methods of initial selection and training, ensure equitable compensation, provide clear channels of communication and offer outlets for employee grievances.

Do strong leadership and the other corrective steps improve employee morale? Two measures of morale are the rate of employee turnover and the degree to which employees are unionized. Chronic labor trouble is always a sign of weak management. Witness what happened at two companies where corrective action was taken. A manufacturer that has one-hundred-fifteen blue- and white-collar employes in its principal plant and does roughly $100 million per year in volume has no union despite several organizing drives. The company is in a community where employers average fifteen to twenty-five percent annual turnover but its turnover rate is three percent.

A savings and loan association with 300 employees—not unionized—has a turnover rate that has not exceeded seven percent for several years. Turnover at other savings and loans in its state average twenty-seven percent.

At both those organizations, the weak no longer lead the weaker.

Robert N. McMurry is a Chicago-based management expert.

BIBLIOGRAPHY

Adair, J. E. *The Skills of Leadership* (New York: Nichols Publishing Co., 1984).

Argyris, C. *Increasing Leadership Effectiveness* (New York: John Wiley, 1976).

Axelrod, N. *Executive Leadership* (Indianapolis, IN: Bobbs-Merrill, Inc., 1969).

Barber, C. J. *Nehemiah & the Dynamics of Effective Leadership* (Neptune, NJ: Loizeaux Brothers, 1976).

Basil, D. C. *Leadership Skills for Executive Action* (New York: American Management Association, 1971).

Bass, B. M. *Leadership & Performance Beyond Expectations* (New York: Free Press, a division of Macmillan, 1985).

Bass, B. M. *Leadership, Psychology, & Organizational Behavior* (Westport, CT: Greenwood Press, 1960).

Beal, G. M., et al. *Leadership & Dynamic Group Action* (Ames, IA: Iowa University Press, 1962).

Bennis, W. G. *Leaders: The Strategies for Taking Charge* (New York: Harper & Row, 1985).

Bennis, W. *The Unconscious Conspiracy: Why Leaders Can't Lead* (New York: American Management Association, 1976).

Bennis, W. G., et al. *Leadership & Motivation: Essays of Douglas McGregor* (Cambridge, MA: MIT Press, 1966).

Berman, L. M. *Supervision, Staff Development & Leadership* (Westerville, OH: Charles E. Merrill Publishing Co., 1971).

Betz, D. *Cultivating Leadership: An Approach* (Lanham, MD: University Press of America Inc., 1981).

Bittel, L. R. *Leadership, The Key to Management Success* (New York: Franklin Watts, 1984).

Blanchard, K. and Zigarmi, D. *Leadership and the One Minute Manager* (New York: William Morrow, 1985).

Bothwell, L. *The Art of Leadership* (Englewood Cliffs, NJ: Prentice-Hall, 1983).

Bradford, D. L. *Managing For Excellence* (New York: John Wiley, 1984).

Bradford, L. P. *Making Meetings Work: A Guide for Leaders & Group Members* (San Diego, CA: University Associates, 1976).

Brown, J. D. *The Human Nature of Organizations* (New York: American Management Association, 1973).

Burby, R.J. *Fundamentals of Leadership: A Guide for the Supervisor* (Reading, MA: Addison-Wesely Publishing Co., 1972).

Burns, J. M. *Leadership* (New York: Harper & Row, 1979).

Cleveland, H. *The Knowledge Executive: Leadership in an Information Society* (New York: E. P. Dutton, 1985).

Cuming, P. *The Power Handbook* (New York: Van Nostrand Reinhold, 1984).

Cunningham, L. L. *Leadership: The Science & the Art Today* (Itasca, IL: F. E. Peacock Publisher, Inc., 1973).

Daniels, M. M. *Realistic Leadership* (Englewood Cliffs, NJ: Prentice-Hall, 1983).

Doob, L. W. *Personality, Power, and Authority* (Westport, CT: Greenwood Press, 1983).

Dyer, F. C. and Dyer, J. M. *Bureaucracy vs Creativity: The Dilemma of Modern Leadership* (Miami, FL: University of Miami Press, 1965).

Fallon, W. K. *Leadership on the Job: Guides to Good Supervision* (New York: American Management Association, 1982).

Fiedler, F. *Theory of Leadership Effectiveness* (New York: McGraw-Hill, 1967).

Fiedler, F. E. *Improving Leadership Effectiveness: The Leader Match Concept* (New York: John Wiley, 1976).

Fiedler, F. E. *Leader Attitudes & Group Effectiveness* (Westport, CT: Greenwood Press, 1958).

Fiore, M. V. *How to Develop Dynamic Leadership: A Short Course for Professionals* (New York: John Wiley, 1977).

Gardner, J. W. *Excellence* (New York: Norton, 1984).

Glass, S. *Life Control: How to Assert Leadership in Any Situation* (New York: M. Evans, 1976).

Gordon, T. *Leadership Effectiveness Training* (New York: Harper & Row, 1978).

Gribbin, J. J. *Effective Managerial Leadership* (New York: American Management Association, 1978).

Gribbin, J. J. *Leadership: Strategies for Organizational Effectiveness* (New York: American Management Association, 1982).

Hart, L. B. *Moving Up: Women & Leadership* (New York: American Management Association, 1980).

Heller, T. *Women & Men as Leaders: Contemporary Images* (New York: Praeger Publishers, 1981).

Hersey. P. *The Situational Leader* (New York: Warner Books, 1985).

Hersey, P., and Stinson, J. E. *Perspectives In Leader Effectiveness* (Athens, OH: Ohio University Press, 1980).

Hodgkinson, C. *The Philosophy of Leadership* (New York: St. Martins, 1983).

Hollander, E. P. *Leadership Dynamics: A Practical Guide to Effective Relationships* (New York: Free Press, a division of Macmillan, 1978).

Hyde, D. *Dedication & Leadership* (Notre Dame, IN: University of Notre Dame Press, 1966).

Jentz, B. C., and Wofford, J. W. *Leadership & Learning: Personal Change in a Professional Setting* (New York: McGraw-Hill, 1979).

Knox, A. B. *Leadership Strategies for Meeting New Challenges* (San Francisco, CA: Jossey-Bass Inc., 1982).

Kokopeli, B., and Lakey, G. *Leadership for Change* (Philadelphia, PA: New Society Publishers, 1978).

Kottler, J. A. *Pragmatic Group Leadership* (Monterey, CA: Brooks/Cole Publishing, 1982).

Lawrie, J. *You Can Lead!* (New York: AMACOM, The American Management Association, 1985).

Lawson, L. G. *Lead On!* (San Luis Obispo, CA: Impact Publishers, Inc., 1982).

Lindgren, H. C. *Leadership, Authority and Managerial Powersharing* (Melbourne, FL: R. E. Krieger Publishing, 1982).

Loden, M. *Feminine Leadership* (New York: Times Books, 1985).

Losoncy, L. *The Motivating Leader* (Englewood Cliffs, NJ: Prentice-Hall, 1985).

Loye, D. *The Leadership Passion: A Psychology of Ideology* (San Francisco, CA: Jossey-Bass, Inc., 1977).

McCall, M. W., Jr. *Leadership: Where Else Can We Go?* (Durham, NC: Duke University Press, 1978).

Prior, P. J. *Leadership Is Not a Bowler Hat* (North Pomfret, VT: David & Charles, Inc., 1977).

Reed, H. W. *The Dynamics of Leadership* (Danville, IL: Interstate Printers and Publishers, Inc., 1982).

Sayles, L. R. *Leadership: What Effective Managers Really Do & How They Do It* (New York: McGraw-Hill, 1974).

Schein, E. *Organizational Culture and Leadership* (San Francisco, CA: Jossey-Bass Inc., 1985).

Stech, E. L. *Leadership Communication* (Chicago, IL: Nelson-Hall Publishers, 1983).

Stogdill, R. M. *Handbook of Leadership: A Survey of Theory and Research* (New York: Free Press, a division of Macmillan, 1974).

Tappen, R. *Leadership In Action* (Philadelphia, PA: F. A. Davis & Co., 1983).

Williamson, D. L. *Group Power* (Englewood Cliffs, NJ: Prentice-Hall, 1982).

Wilner, A. R. *The Spellbinders* (New Haven, CT: Yale University Press, 1984).

Wright, P. L. *Improving Leadership Performance* (Englewood Cliffs, NJ: Prentice-Hall International, 1984).

INDEX

Academy of Certified
Administrative Managers,
33-34
Acceptance Theory of
Authority, 210
Administrative Management
Society, 33
*The Administrative
Manager*, 37
Allied Corporation, 6
AMA. *See* American
Management Association
American Center for
the Quality of Work
Life, 335
American Management
Association (AMA), 28
American Productivity
Center, 335
American Standard Inc., 349
American Telephone &
Telegraph, 293, 314.
See also: Bell System
AMF Incorporated, 44
Andres, William A., 336
Anticipatory management,
341
Apple Computer Inc., 352
Aristotle, 208
Associated Baby Services,
Inc., 45
Atlantic Richfield Company,
335
Authority
granting of, 23-24

guidelines for
using, 64
line versus staff,
166
managerial, 72
power of, 61
Avis Inc., 44
Avon, 126

BankAmerica Corporation,
44, 126, 335
Barnard, Chester, 210
Bass brothers, 7
Behavior, 74, 264
change of, 273
classification of,
227
leadership, 108
phase of, 49
research, 227
theory of, 226, 235
Bell & Howell, 127
Bell System, 321, 327, 329
Bendix, 6, 351
Bennis, Walter, 179
Bennis, Warren, 98
Blake, F. T., Jr., 44
Blake, R., 114
Blanchard, Kenneth, 115,
166, 173
Bogardus, E. S., 227
Boiled frog phenomenon,
295
Boren, Charles, 10, 15, 17
Boston Globe, 27